Hayate the combat butler

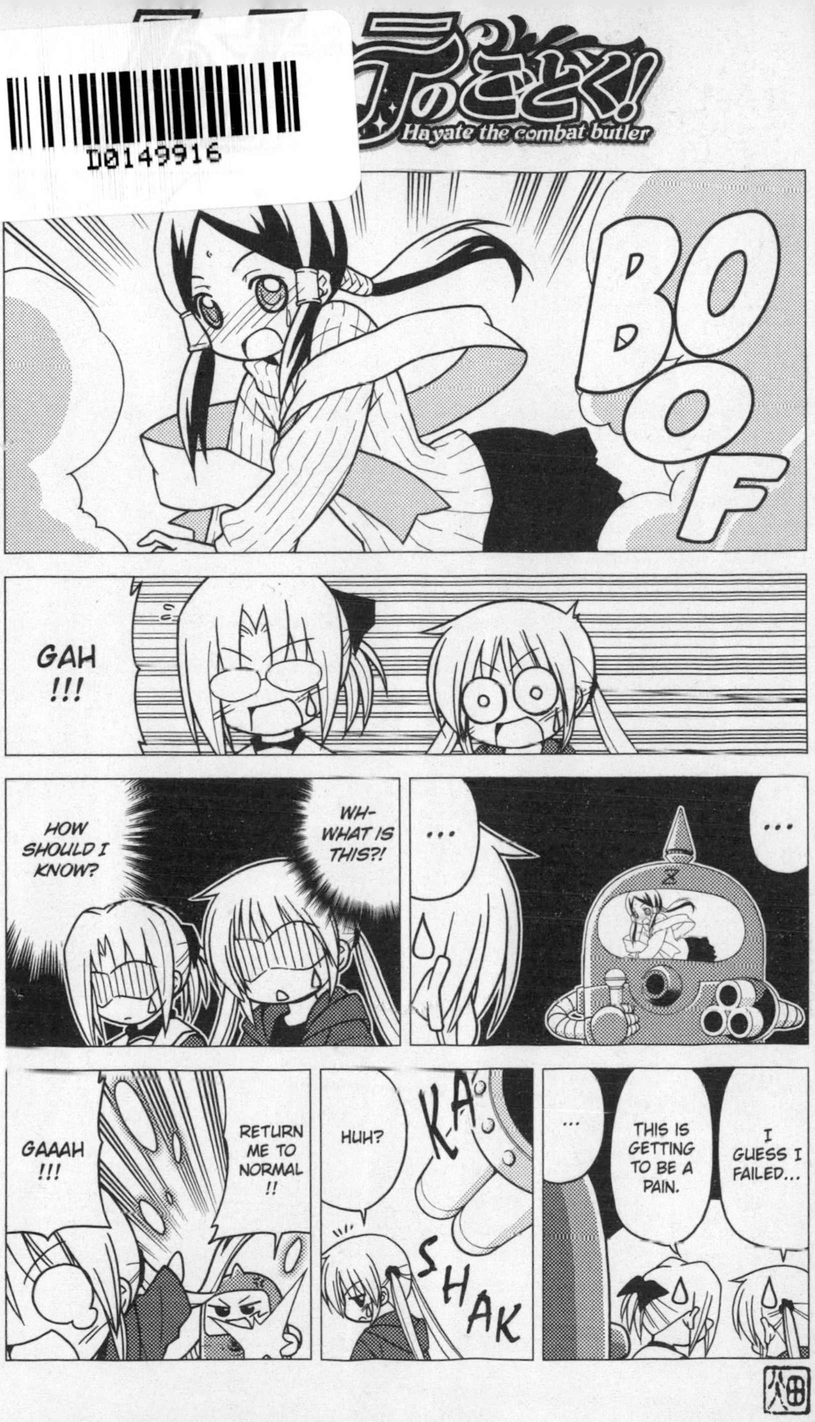
BOOF
GAH !!!
...
...
WH- WHAT IS THIS?!
HOW SHOULD I KNOW?
I GUESS I FAILED...
THIS IS GETTING TO BE A PAIN.
...
KA SHAK
HUH?
RETURN ME TO NORMAL !!
GAAAH !!!

HAYATE THE COMBAT BUTLER
VOL. 24
Shonen Sunday Edition

STORY AND ART BY
KENJIRO HATA

HAYATE NO GOTOKU! Vol. 24
by Kenjiro HATA
© 2005 Kenjiro HATA
All rights reserved.
Original Japanese edition published by SHOGAKUKAN.
English translation rights in the United States of America, Canada, the United Kingdom and
Ireland arranged with SHOGAKUKAN.

Translation/John Werry
Touch-up Art & Lettering/John Hunt
Design/Yukiko Whitley
Editor/Shaenon K. Garrity

Printed in Canada

Published by VIZ Media, LLC
P.O. Box 77010
San Francisco, CA 94107

10 9 8 7 6 5 4 3 2 1
First printing, September 2014

Hayate
the Combat Butler
24

KENJIRO HATA

*The stars spell out "Table of Contents."

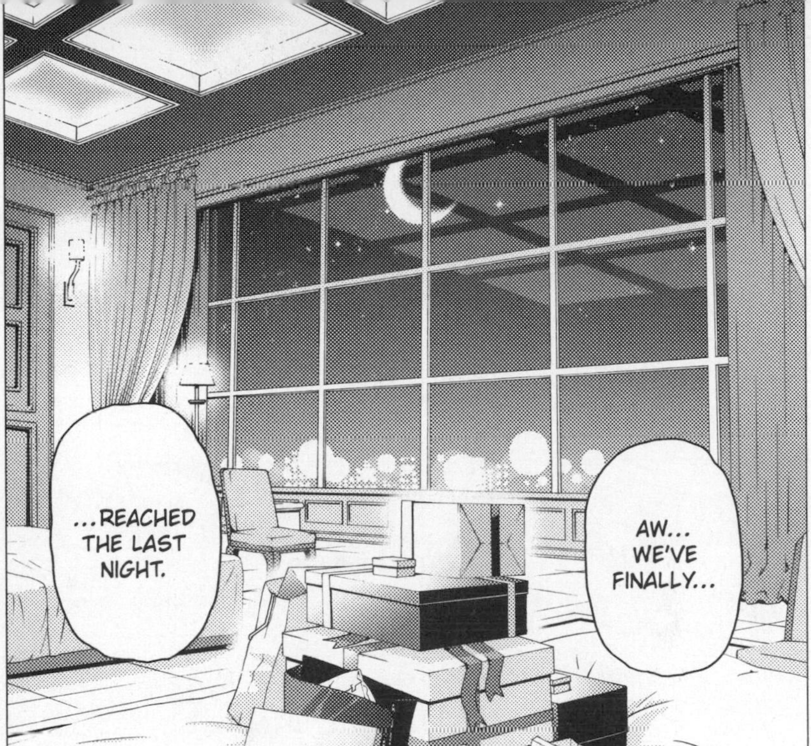
AW... WE'VE FINALLY...
...REACHED THE LAST NIGHT.
Episode 1:
"Shining at Night"

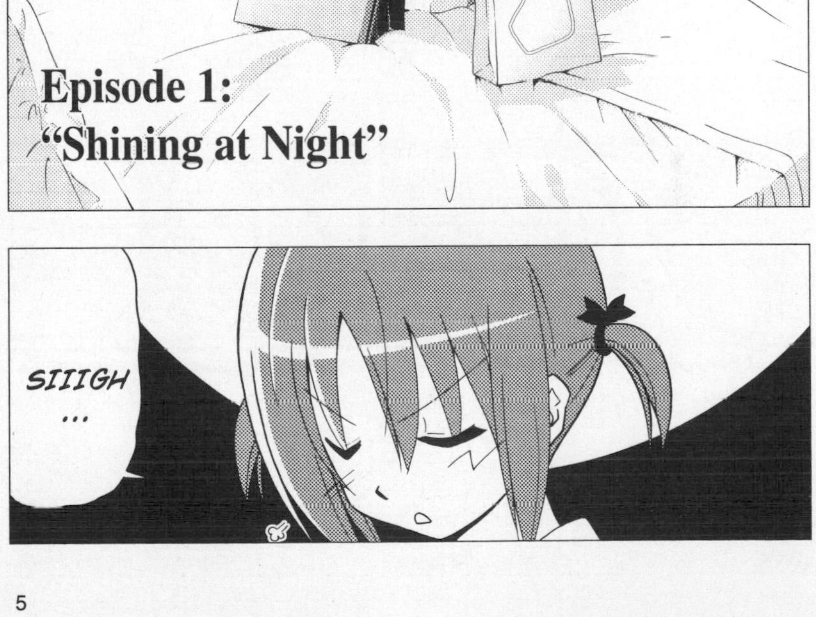
SIIIGH
...

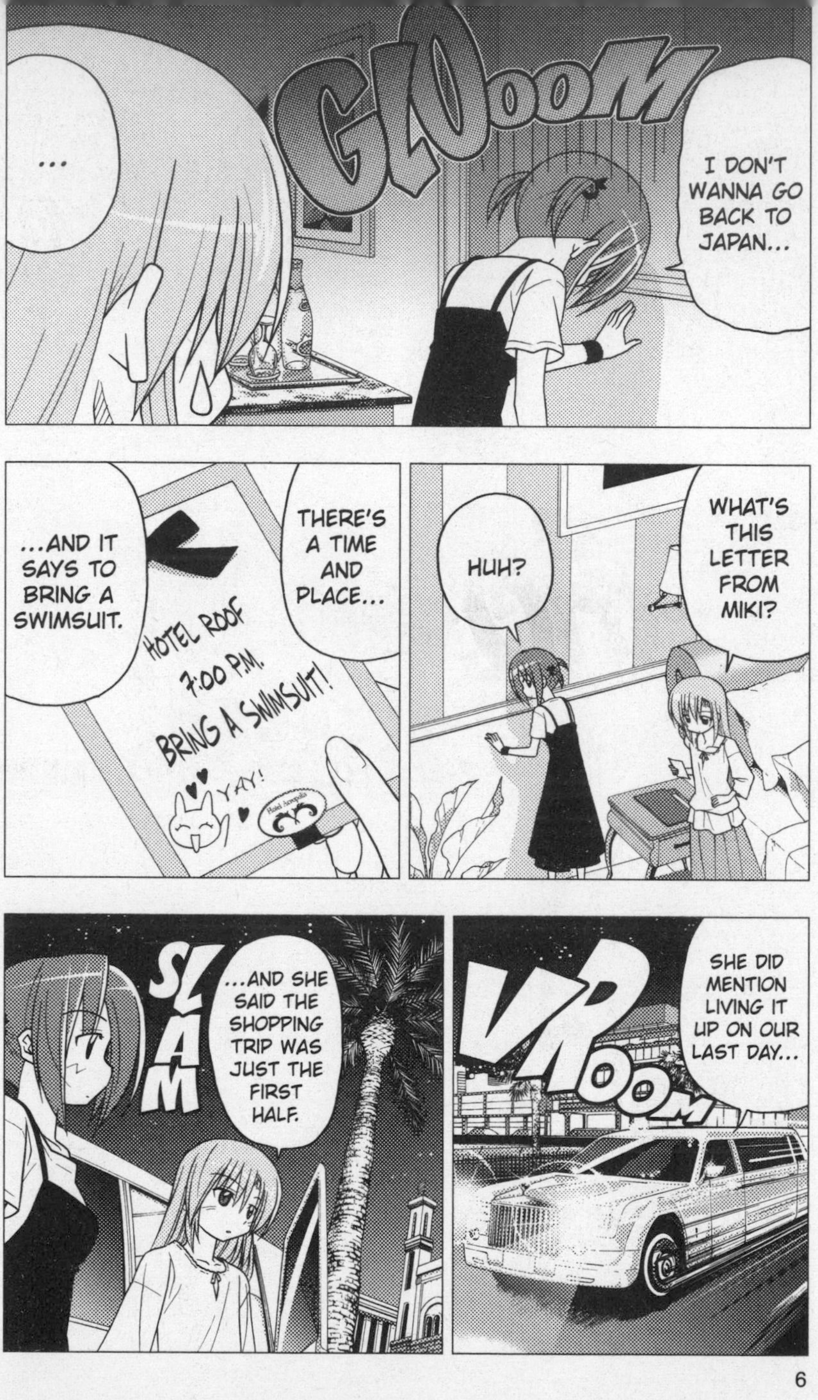
I DON'T WANNA GO BACK TO JAPAN...
GLOOOOM
...
WHAT'S THIS LETTER FROM MIKI?
HUH?
THERE'S A TIME AND PLACE...
...AND IT SAYS TO BRING A SWIMSUIT.
HOTEL ROOF
7:00 P.M.
BRING A SWIMSUIT!
YAY!
SHE DID MENTION LIVING IT UP ON OUR LAST DAY...
VROOOM
SLAM
...AND SHE SAID THE SHOPPING TRIP WAS JUST THE FIRST HALF.

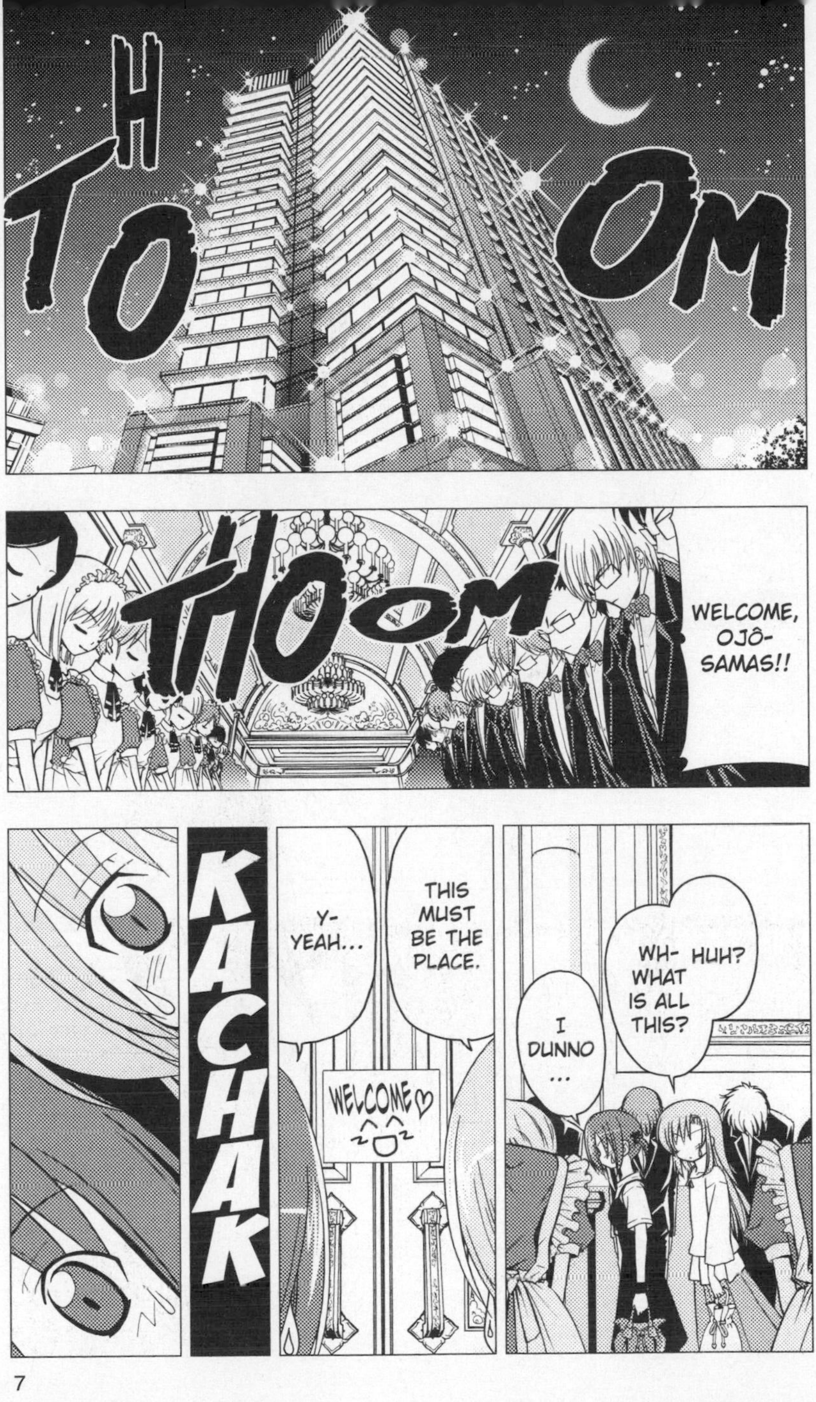
THOOM
WELCOME, OJÔ-SAMAS!!
THOOM
HUH? WH- WHAT IS ALL THIS?
I DUNNO...
THIS MUST BE THE PLACE.
Y-YEAH...
WELCOME
KACHAK

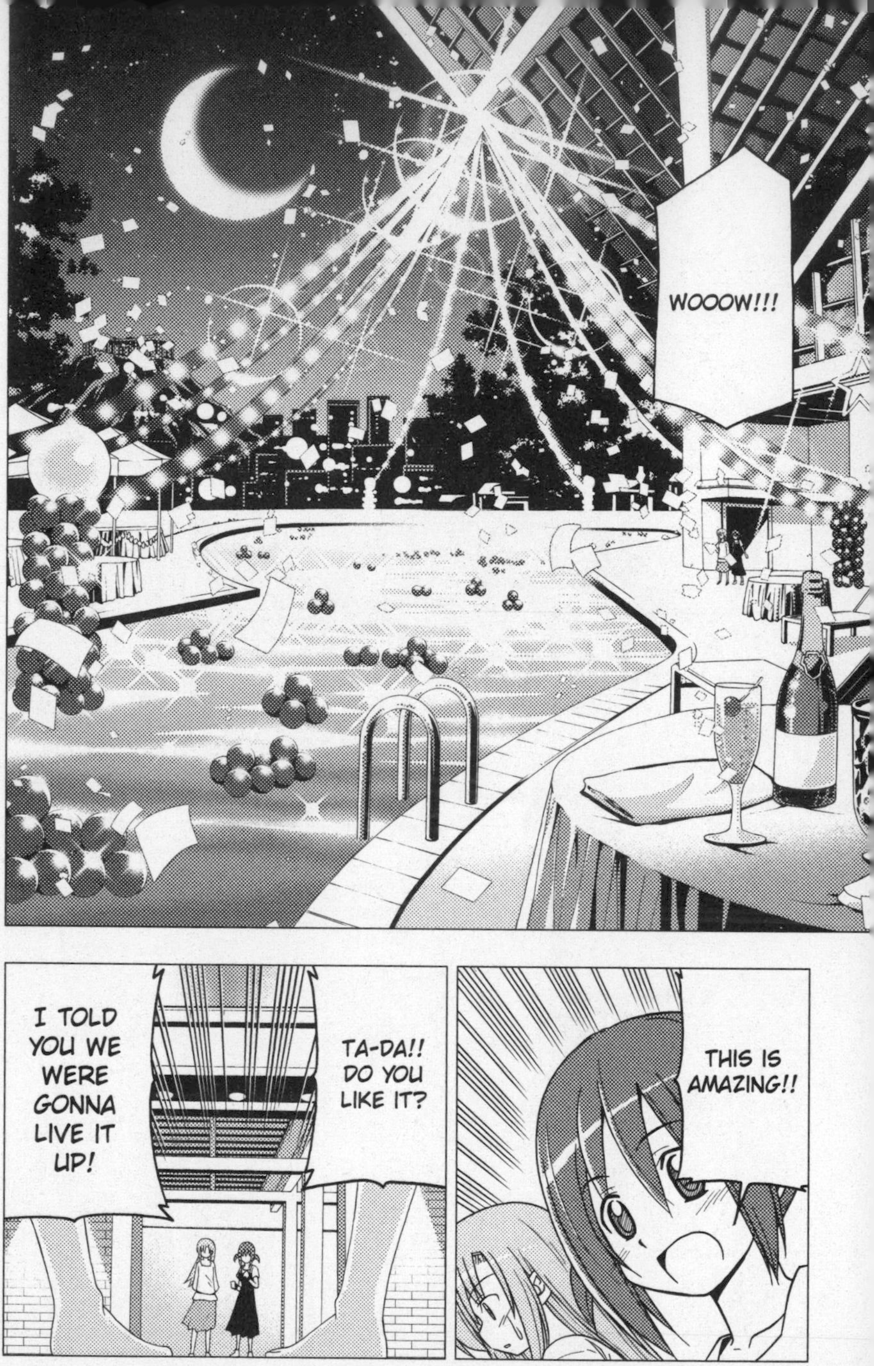
WOOOW!!!
THIS IS AMAZING!!
TA-DA!! DO YOU LIKE IT?
I TOLD YOU WE WERE GONNA LIVE IT UP!

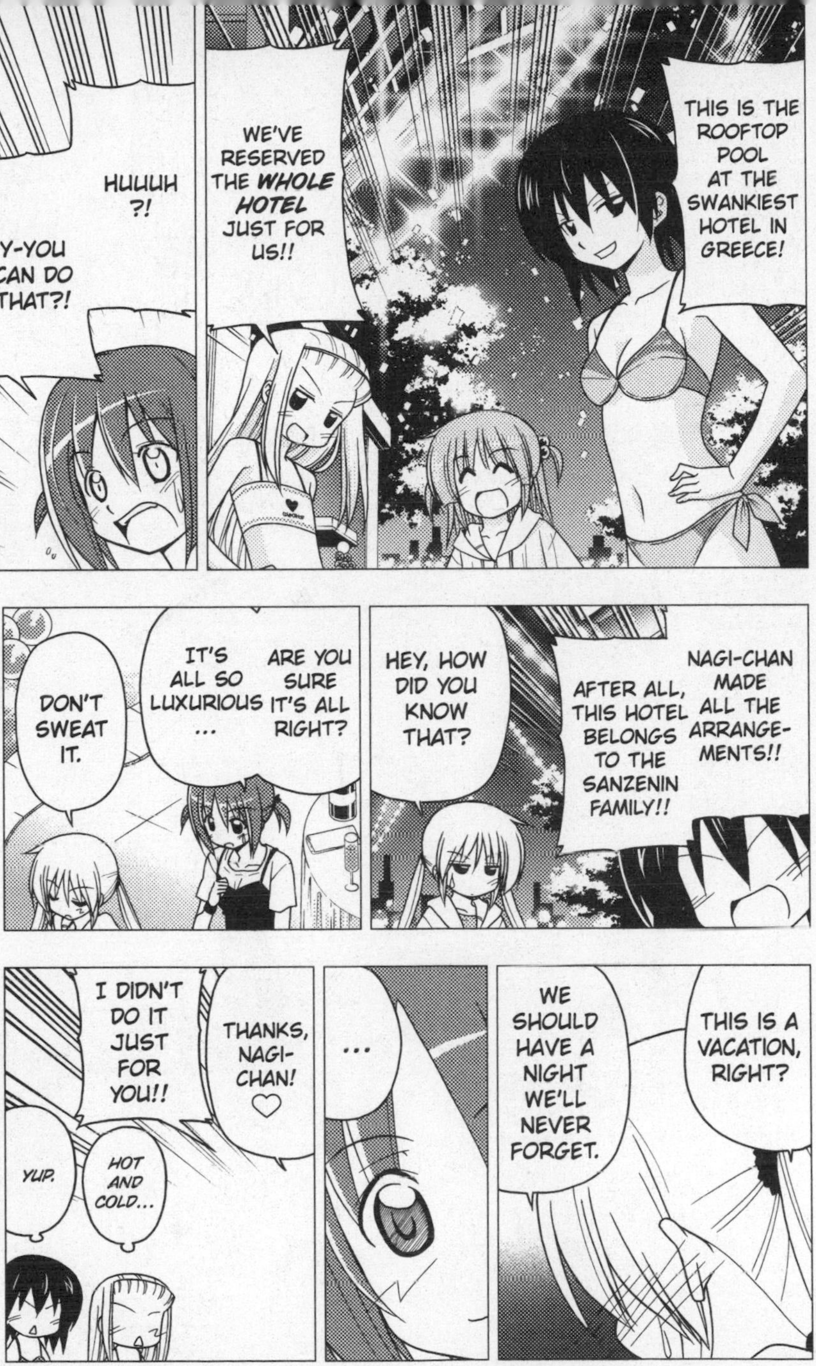
THIS IS THE ROOFTOP POOL AT THE SWANKIEST HOTEL IN GREECE!
WE'VE RESERVED THE ***WHOLE HOTEL*** JUST FOR US!!
HUUUH ?!
Y-YOU CAN DO THAT?!
NAGI-CHAN MADE ALL THE ARRANGE-MENTS!!
AFTER ALL, THIS HOTEL BELONGS TO THE SANZENIN FAMILY!!
HEY, HOW DID YOU KNOW THAT?
ARE YOU SURE IT'S ALL RIGHT?
IT'S ALL SO LUXURIOUS ...
DON'T SWEAT IT.
THIS IS A VACATION, RIGHT?
WE SHOULD HAVE A NIGHT WE'LL NEVER FORGET.
...
THANKS, NAGI-CHAN! ♡
I DIDN'T DO IT JUST FOR YOU!!
HOT AND COLD...
YUP.

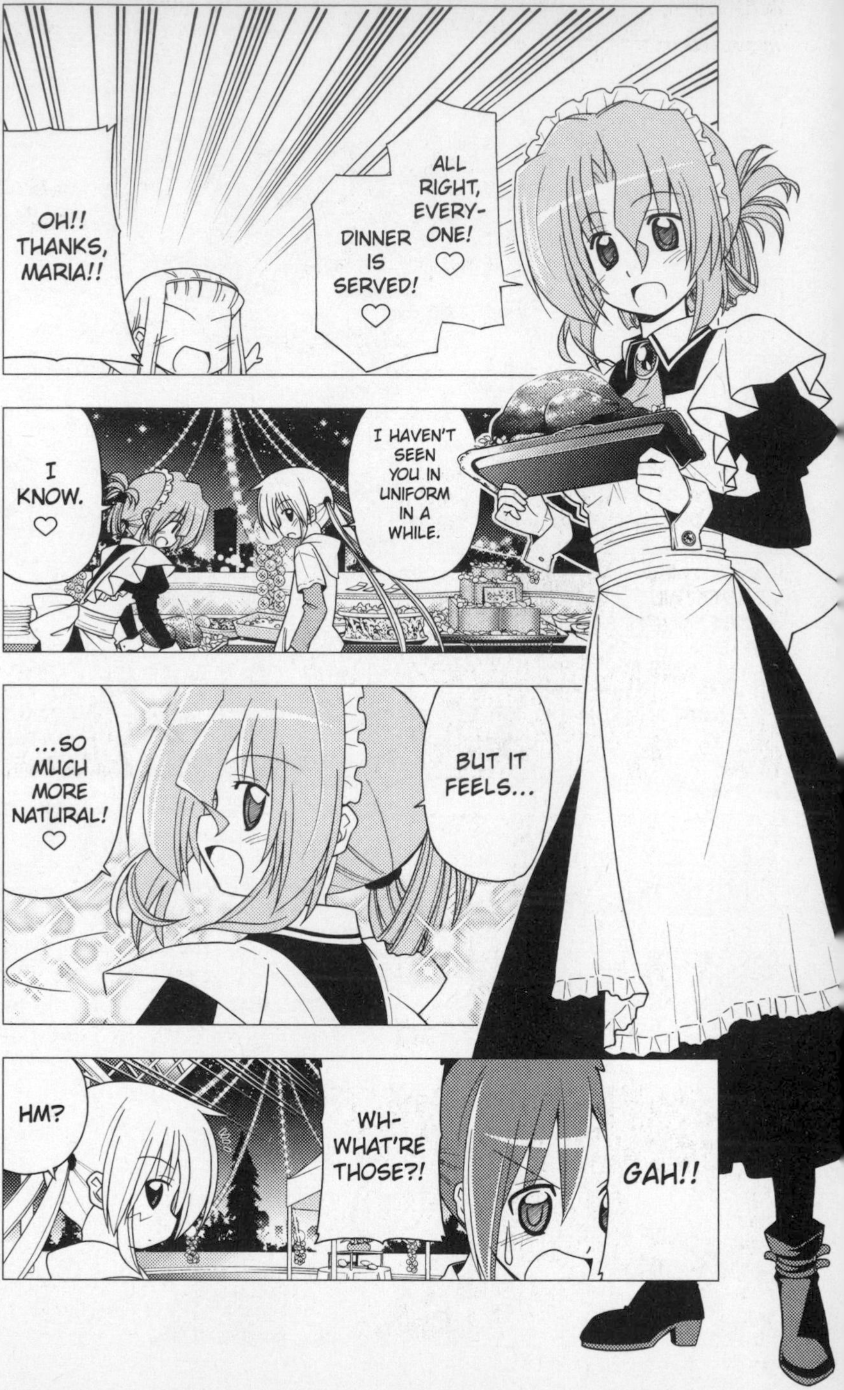
ALL RIGHT, EVERY-ONE! ♡
DINNER IS SERVED! ♡
OH!! THANKS, MARIA!!
I HAVEN'T SEEN YOU IN UNIFORM IN A WHILE.
I KNOW. ♡
BUT IT FEELS...
...SO MUCH MORE NATURAL! ♡
GAH!!
WH-WHAT'RE THOSE?!
HM?

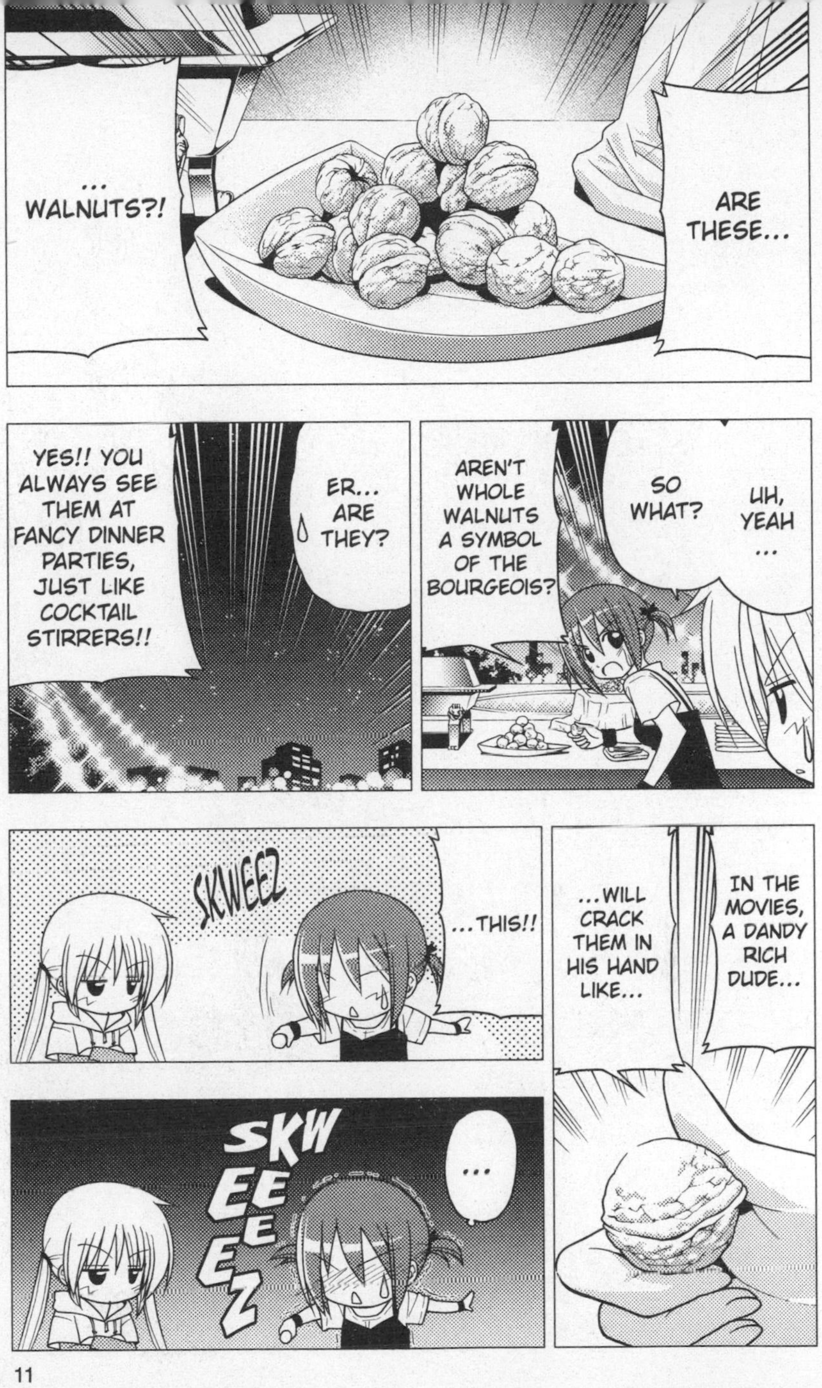
ARE THESE...
...WALNUTS?!
UH, YEAH ...
SO WHAT?
AREN'T WHOLE WALNUTS A SYMBOL OF THE BOURGEOIS?
ER... ARE THEY?
YES!! YOU ALWAYS SEE THEM AT FANCY DINNER PARTIES, JUST LIKE COCKTAIL STIRRERS!!
IN THE MOVIES, A DANDY RICH DUDE...
...WILL CRACK THEM IN HIS HAND LIKE...
...THIS!!
SKWEEZ
...
SKWEEEEZ

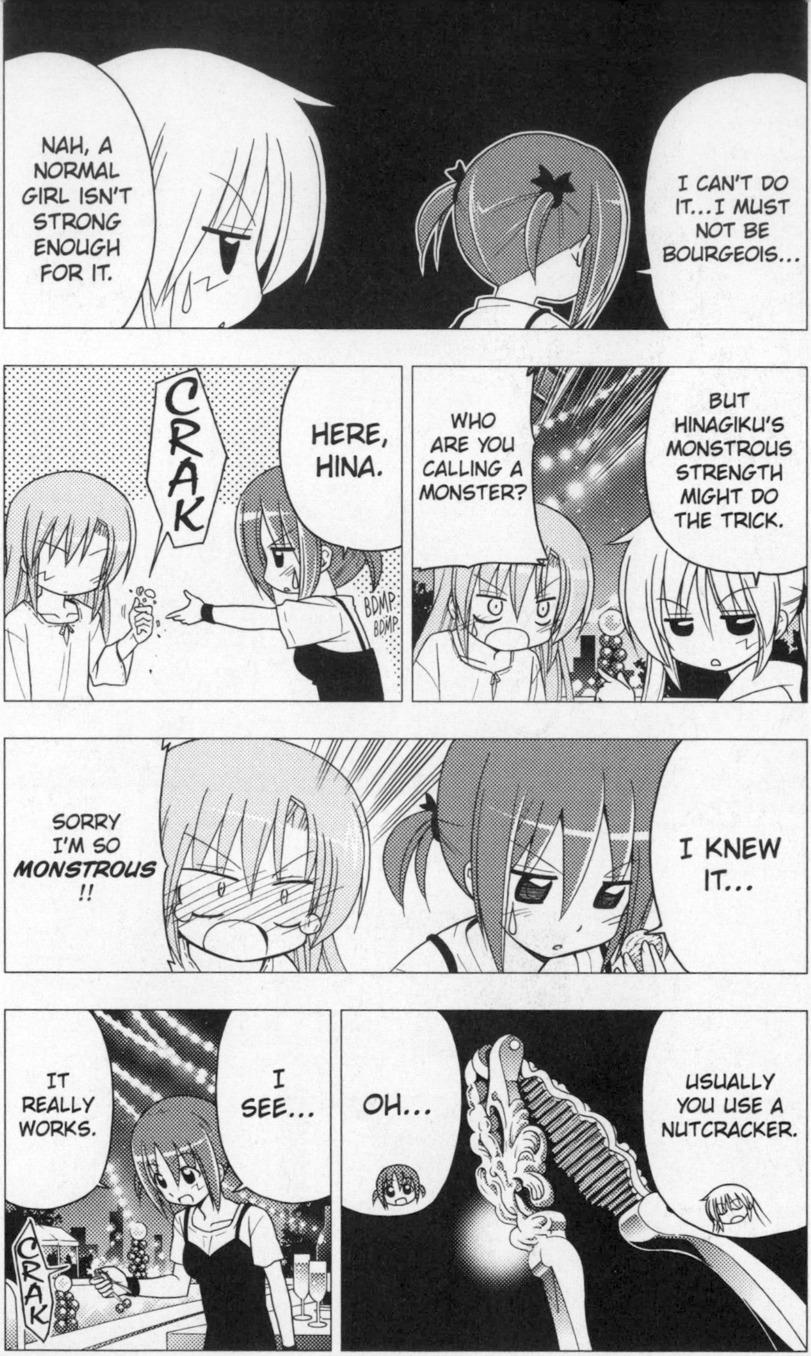
I CAN'T DO IT...I MUST NOT BE BOURGEOIS...
NAH, A NORMAL GIRL ISN'T STRONG ENOUGH FOR IT.
BUT HINAGIKU'S MONSTROUS STRENGTH MIGHT DO THE TRICK.
WHO ARE YOU CALLING A MONSTER?
HERE, HINA.
CRAK
BDMP BDMP
I KNEW IT...
SORRY I'M SO *MONSTROUS*!!
USUALLY YOU USE A NUTCRACKER.
OH...
I SEE...
IT REALLY WORKS.
CRAK

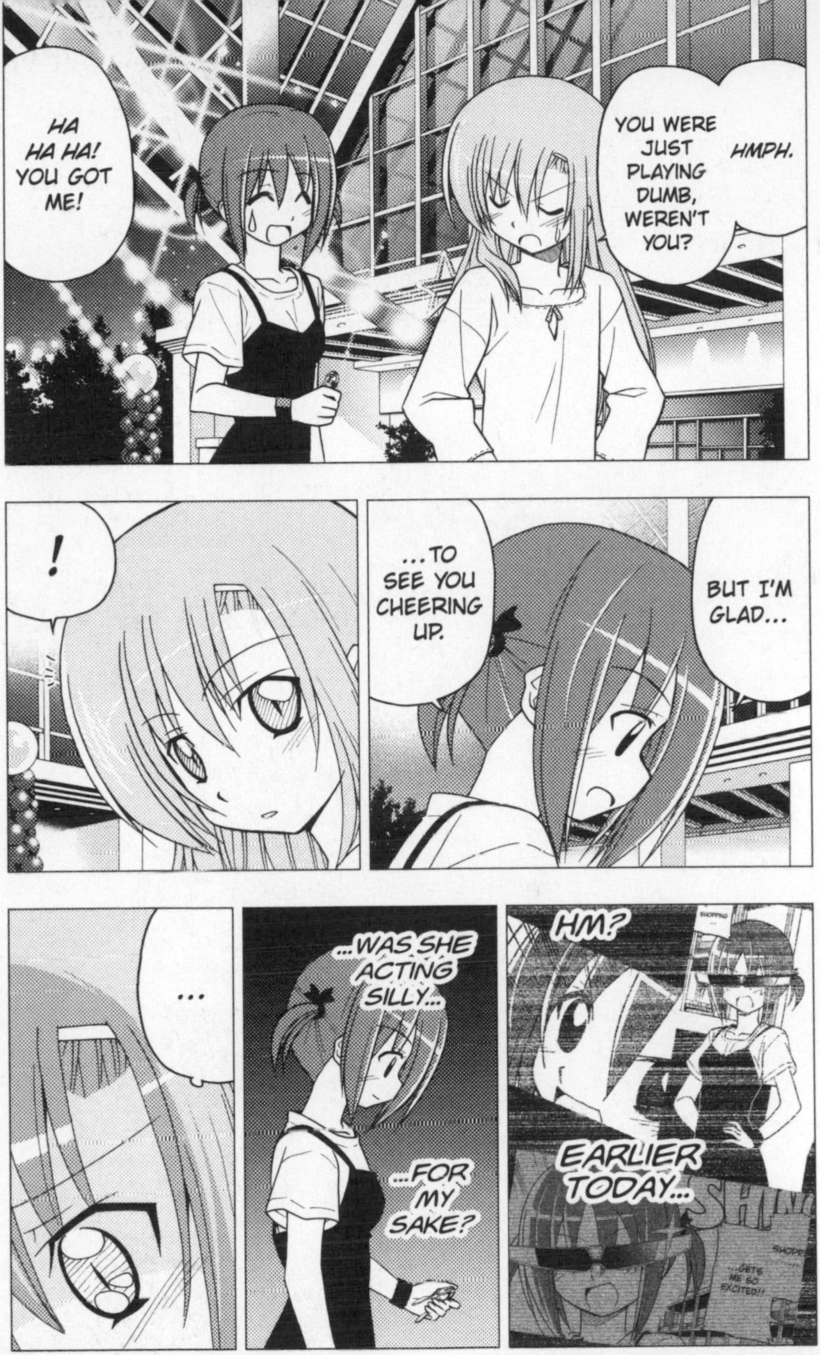
YOU WERE JUST PLAYING DUMB, WEREN'T YOU? HMPH.
HA HA HA! YOU GOT ME!
BUT I'M GLAD...
...TO SEE YOU CHEERING UP.
!
HM?
SHOPPING ...
EARLIER TODAY...
...GETS ME SO EXCITED!!
...WAS SHE ACTING SILLY...
...FOR MY SAKE?
...

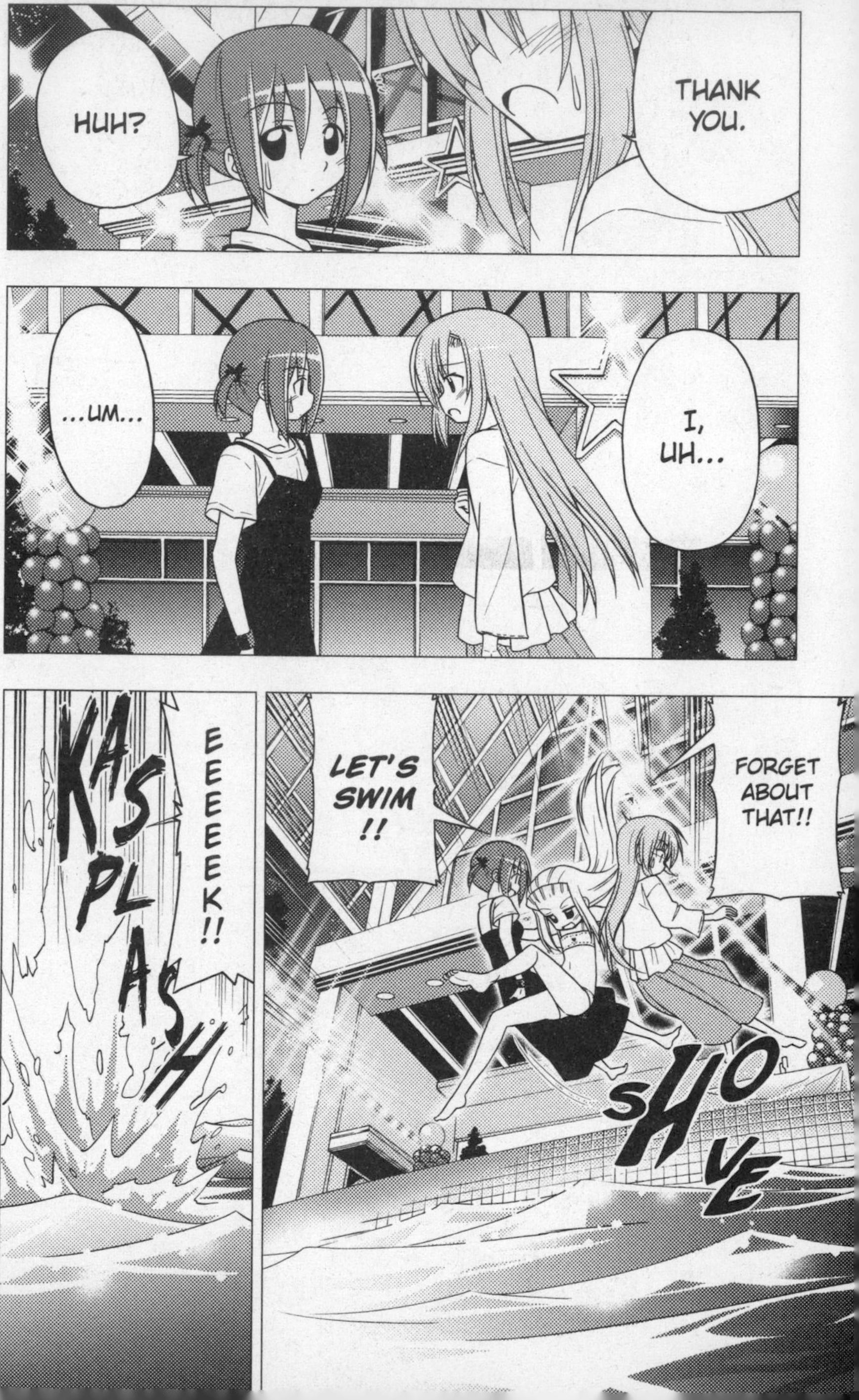
THANK YOU.
HUH?
I, UH...
...UM...
FORGET ABOUT THAT!!
LET'S SWIM!!
SHOVE
EEEEEEK!!
KASPLASH

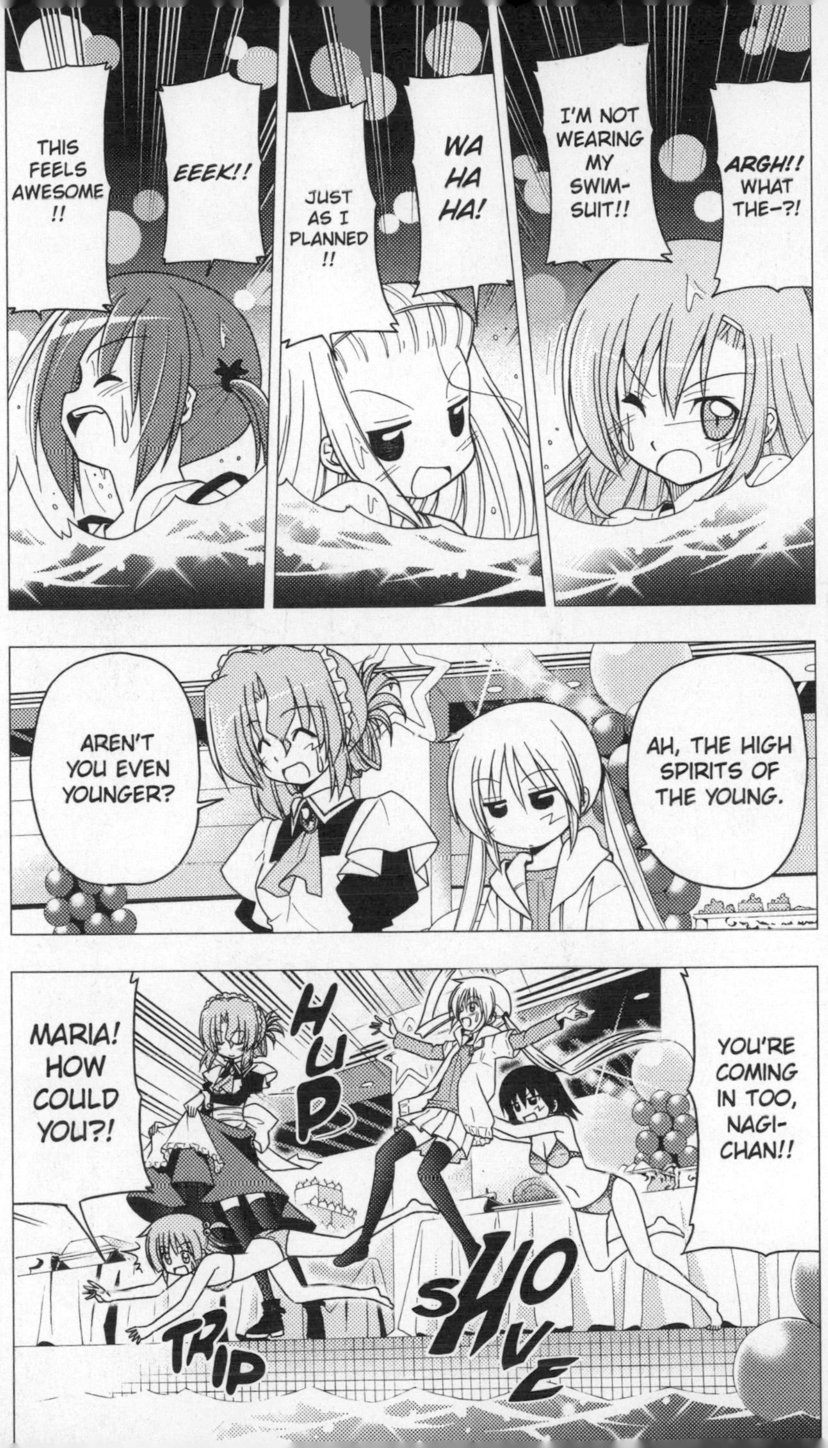
ARGH!! WHAT THE-?!
I'M NOT WEARING MY SWIM-SUIT!!
WA HA HA!
JUST AS I PLANNED!!
EEEK!!
THIS FEELS AWESOME!!
AH, THE HIGH SPIRITS OF THE YOUNG.
AREN'T YOU EVEN YOUNGER?
YOU'RE COMING IN TOO, NAGI-CHAN!!
HUP
MARIA! HOW COULD YOU?!
SHOVE
TRIP

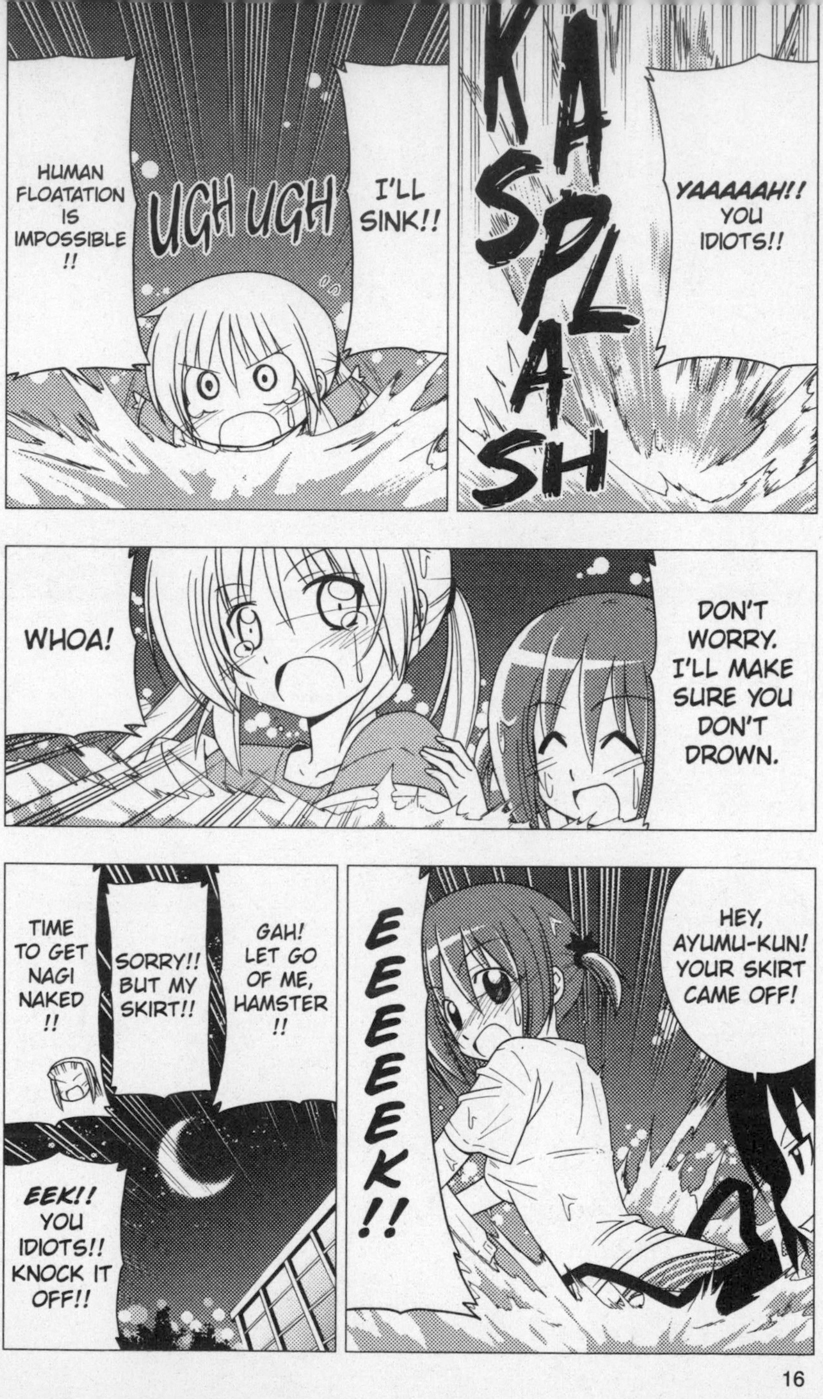
KASPLASH
YAAAAAH!! YOU IDIOTS!!
I'LL SINK!!
UGH UGH
HUMAN FLOATATION IS IMPOSSIBLE!!
DON'T WORRY. I'LL MAKE SURE YOU DON'T DROWN.
WHOA!
HEY, AYUMU-KUN! YOUR SKIRT CAME OFF!
EEEEEEK!!
GAH! LET GO OF ME, HAMSTER!!
SORRY!! BUT MY SKIRT!!
TIME TO GET NAGI NAKED!!
EEK!! YOU IDIOTS!! KNOCK IT OFF!!

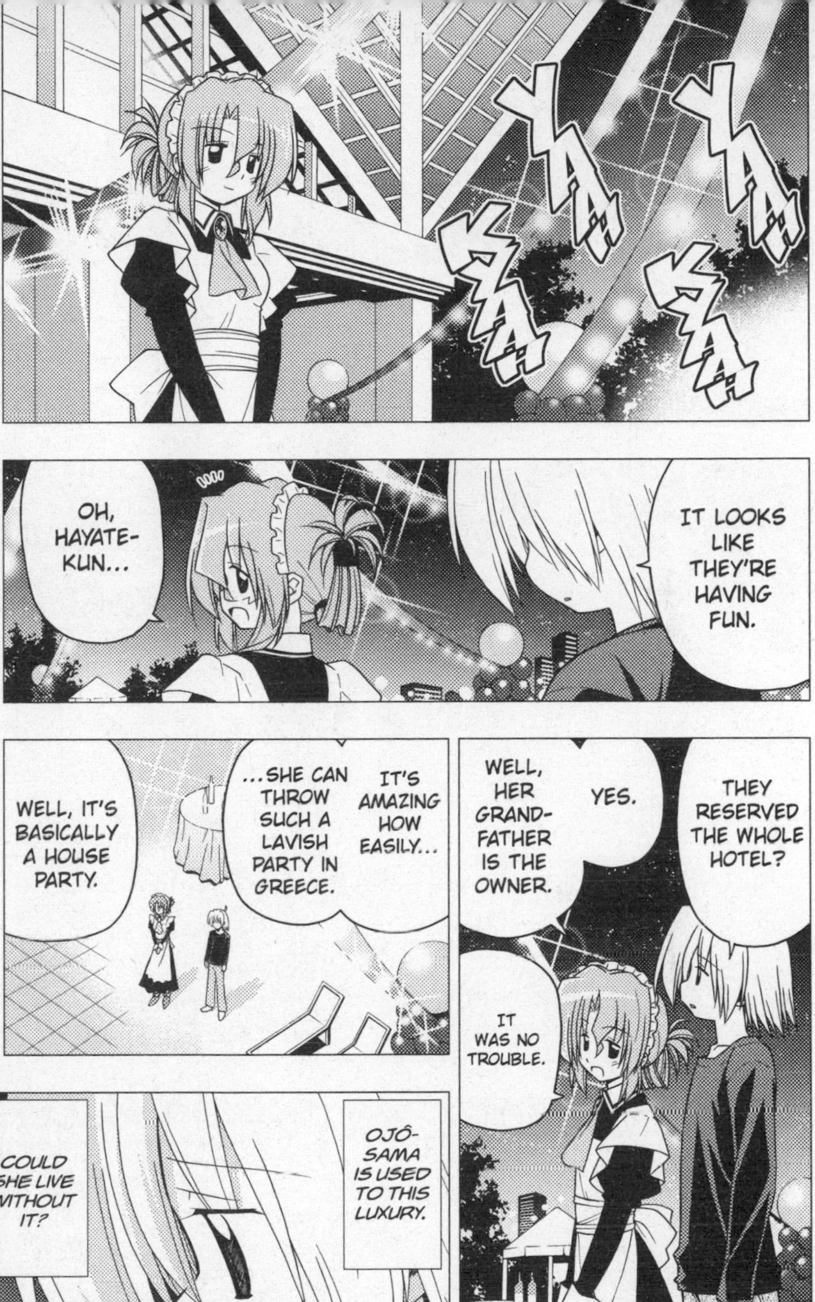
IT LOOKS LIKE THEY'RE HAVING FUN.
OH, HAYATE-KUN...
THEY RESERVED THE WHOLE HOTEL?
YES.
WELL, HER GRANDFATHER IS THE OWNER.
IT WAS NO TROUBLE.
IT'S AMAZING HOW EASILY...
...SHE CAN THROW SUCH A LAVISH PARTY IN GREECE.
WELL, IT'S BASICALLY A HOUSE PARTY.
OJÔ-SAMA IS USED TO THIS LUXURY.
COULD SHE LIVE WITHOUT IT?

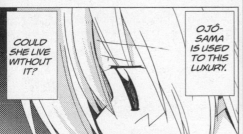

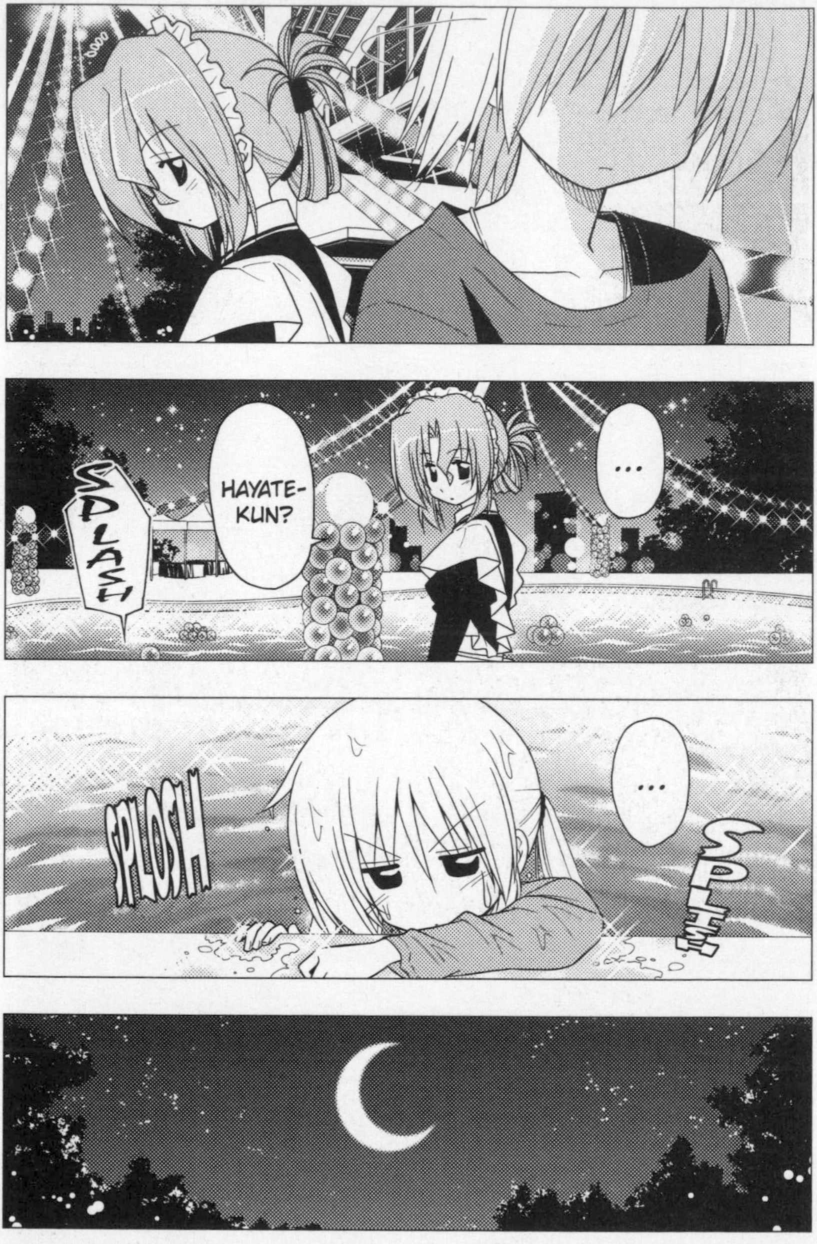
...
HAYATE-KUN?
SPLASH
...
SPLOSH

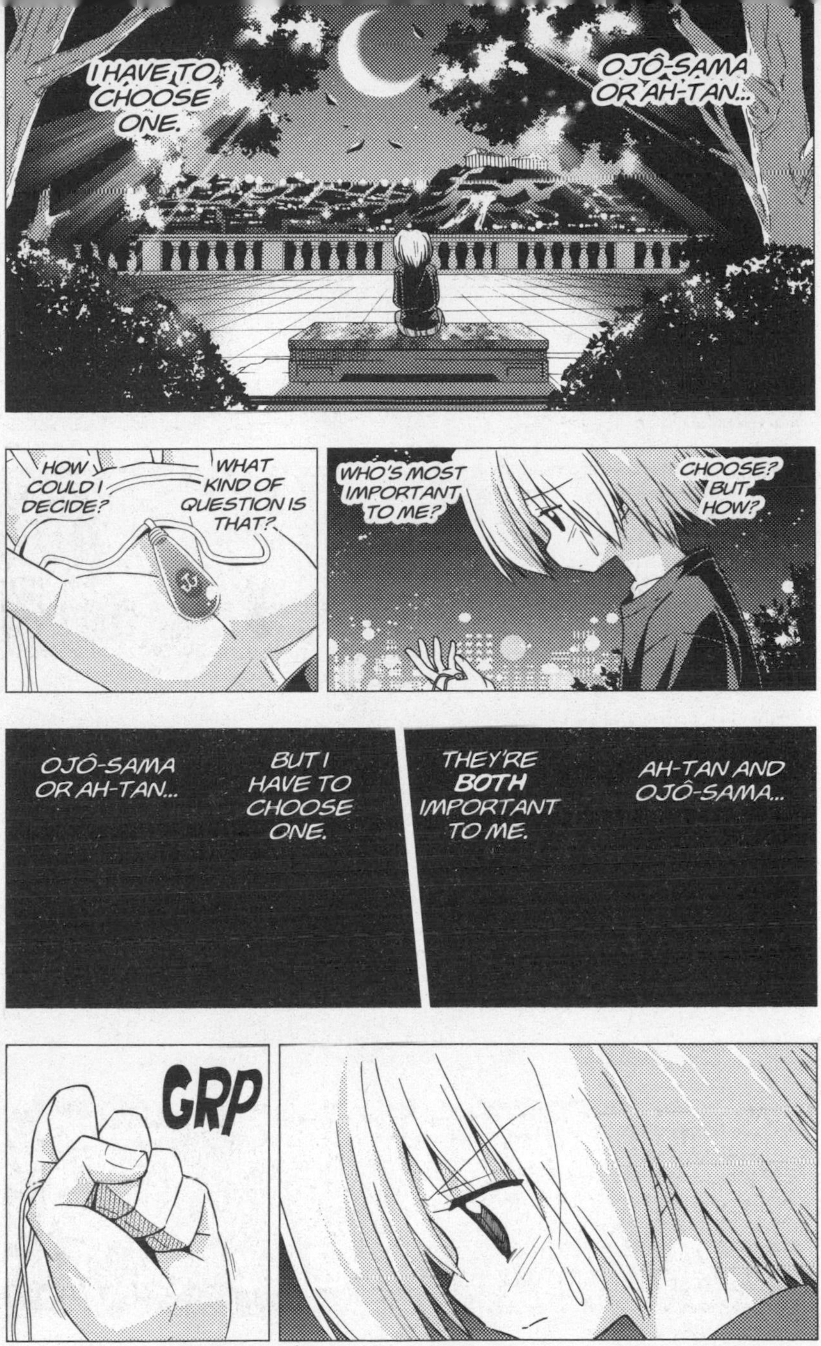
OJÔ-SAMA OR AH-TAN...
I HAVE TO CHOOSE ONE.
CHOOSE? BUT HOW?
WHO'S MOST IMPORTANT TO ME?
WHAT KIND OF QUESTION IS THAT?
HOW COULD I DECIDE?
AH-TAN AND OJÔ-SAMA...
THEY'RE BOTH IMPORTANT TO ME.
BUT I HAVE TO CHOOSE ONE.
OJÔ-SAMA OR AH-TAN...
GRP

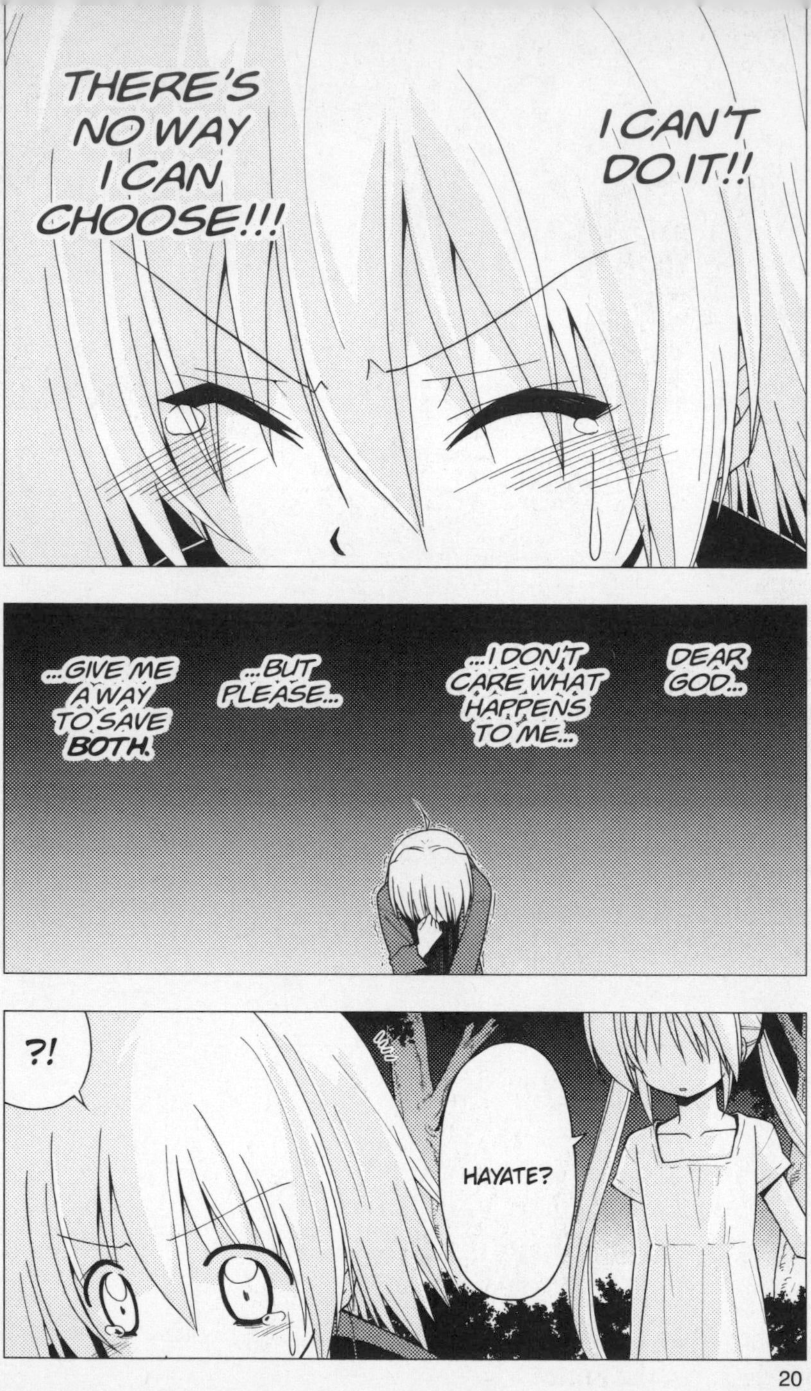
I CAN'T DO IT!!
THERE'S NO WAY I CAN CHOOSE!!!
DEAR GOD...
...I DON'T CARE WHAT HAPPENS TO ME...
...BUT PLEASE...
...GIVE ME A WAY TO SAVE BOTH.
HAYATE?
?!

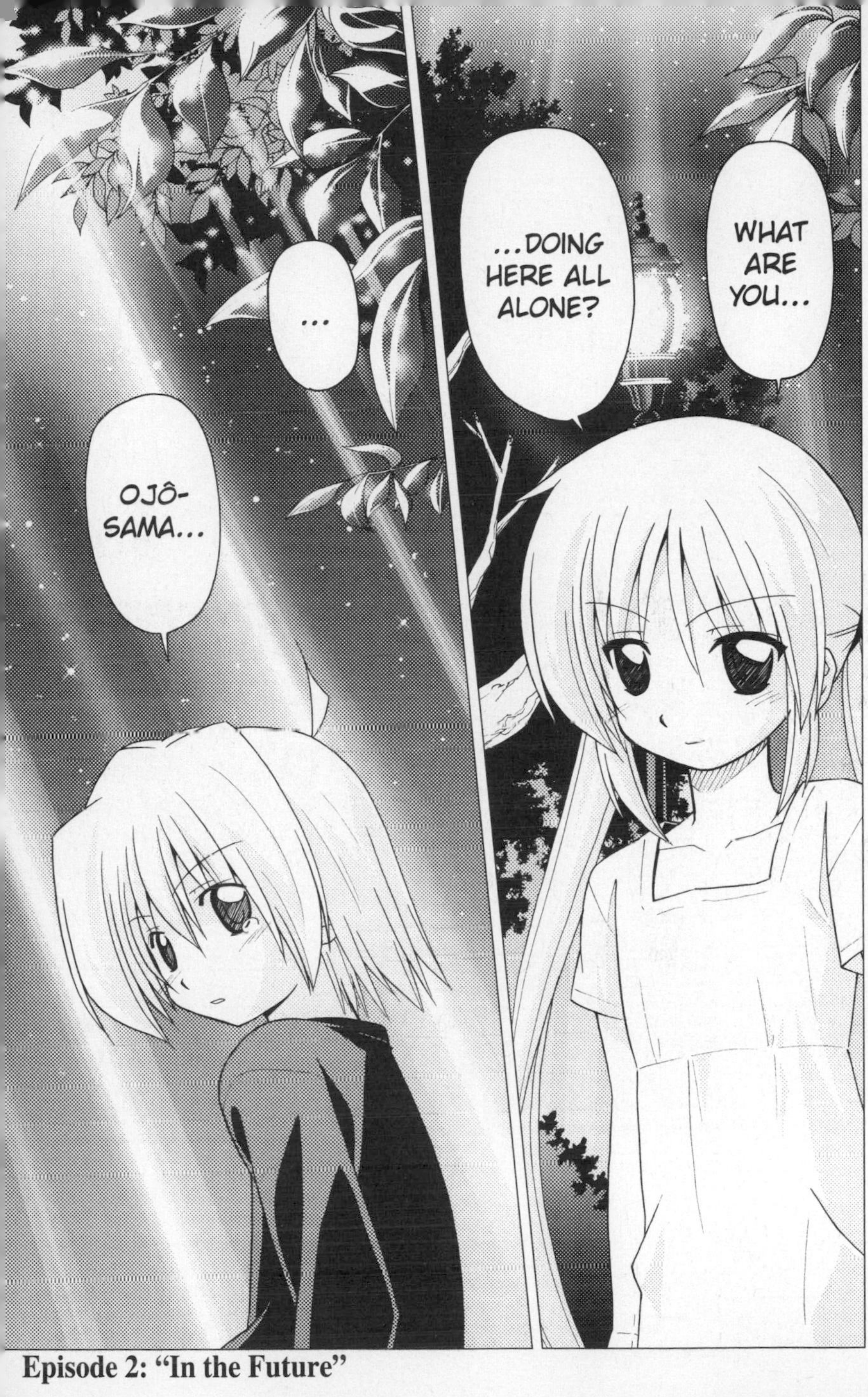
WHAT ARE YOU...
...DOING HERE ALL ALONE?
...
OJÔ-SAMA...

Episode 2: "In the Future"

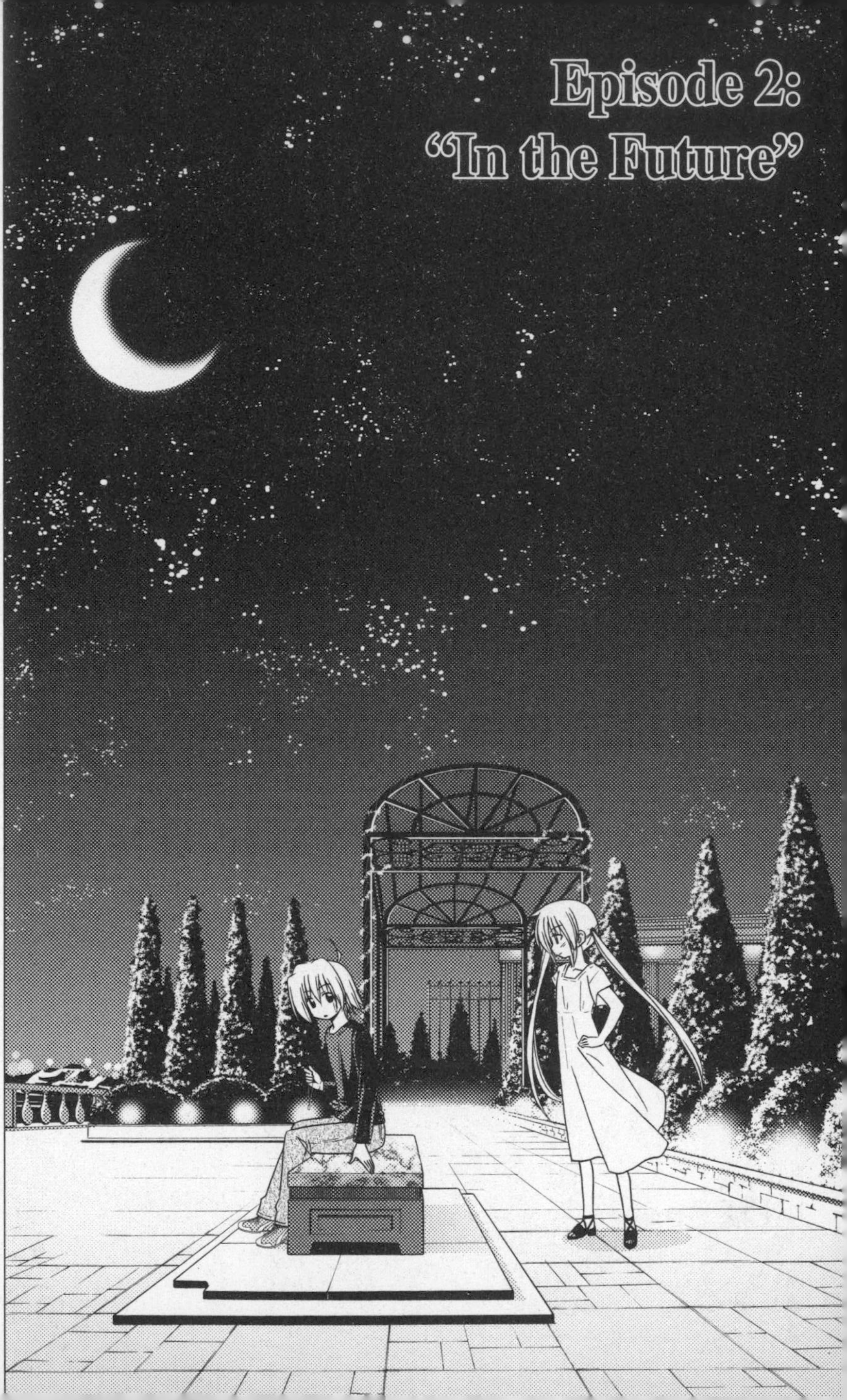
Episode 2:
"In the Future"

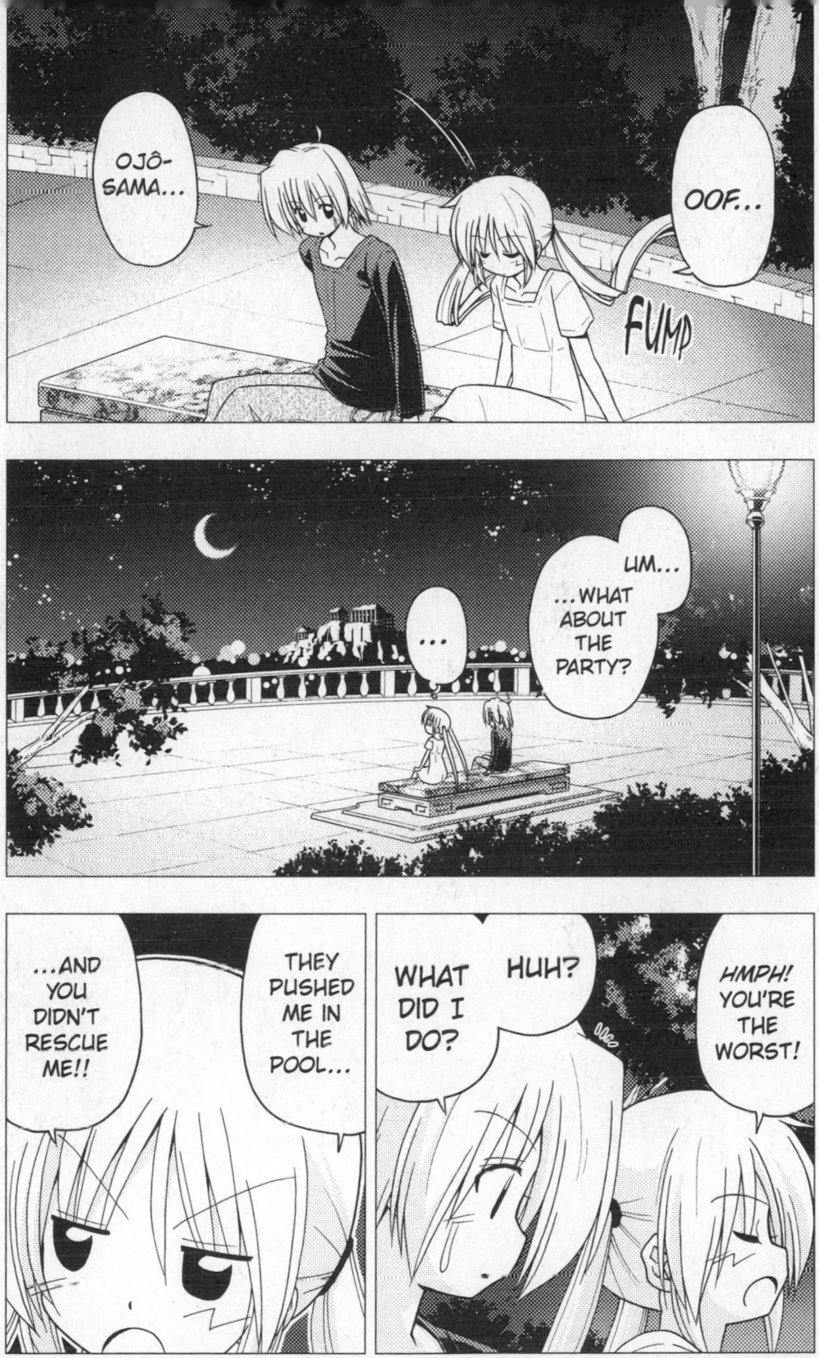
OOF...
FUMP
OJÔ-SAMA...
UM... ...WHAT ABOUT THE PARTY?
...
HMPH! YOU'RE THE WORST!
HUH? WHAT DID I DO?
THEY PUSHED ME IN THE POOL...
...AND YOU DIDN'T RESCUE ME!!

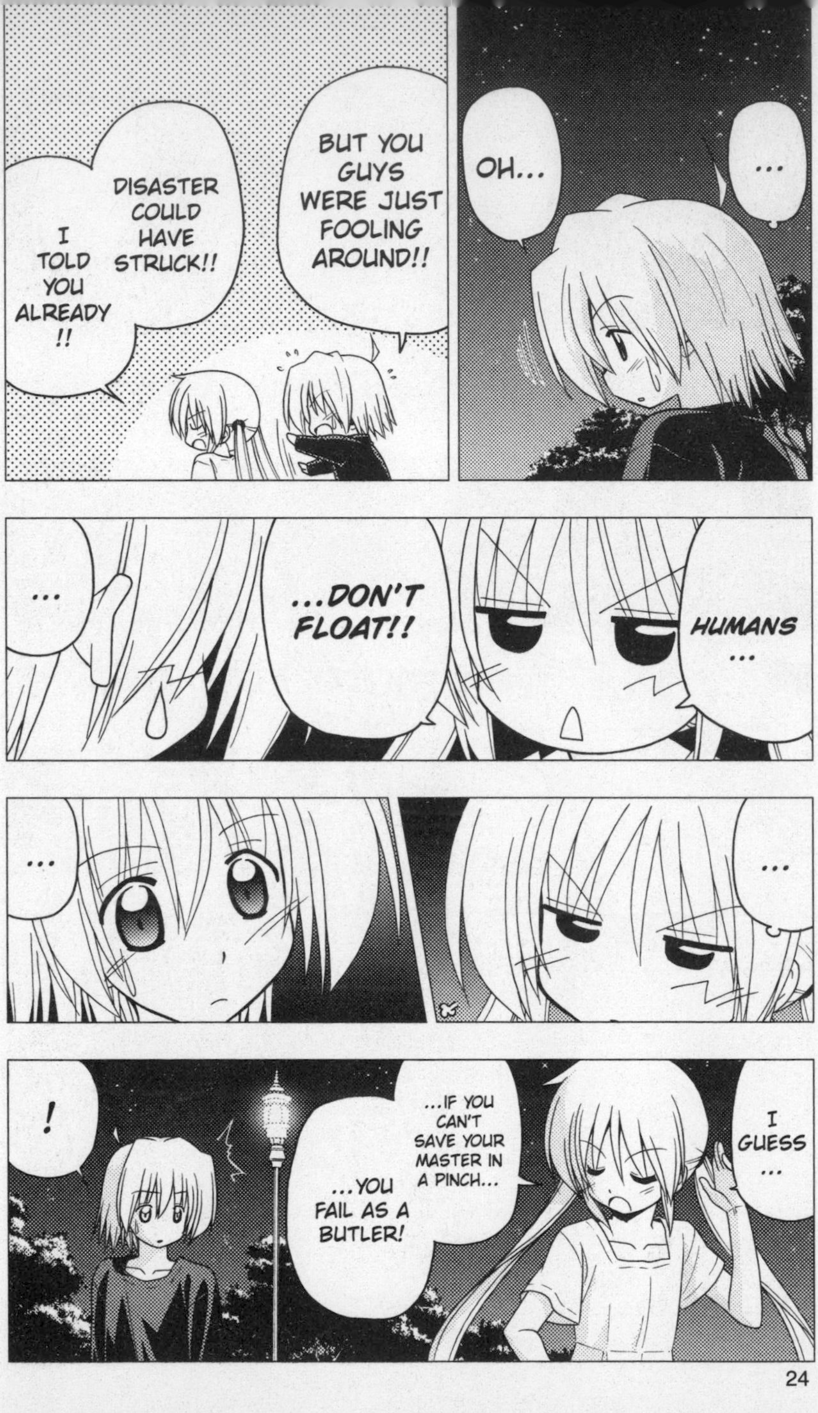
...
OH...
BUT YOU GUYS WERE JUST FOOLING AROUND!!
DISASTER COULD HAVE STRUCK!!
I TOLD YOU ALREADY!!
HUMANS...
...DON'T FLOAT!!
...
...
...
I GUESS...
...IF YOU CAN'T SAVE YOUR MASTER IN A PINCH...
...YOU FAIL AS A BUTLER!
!

...I'M SORRY.

OKAY...

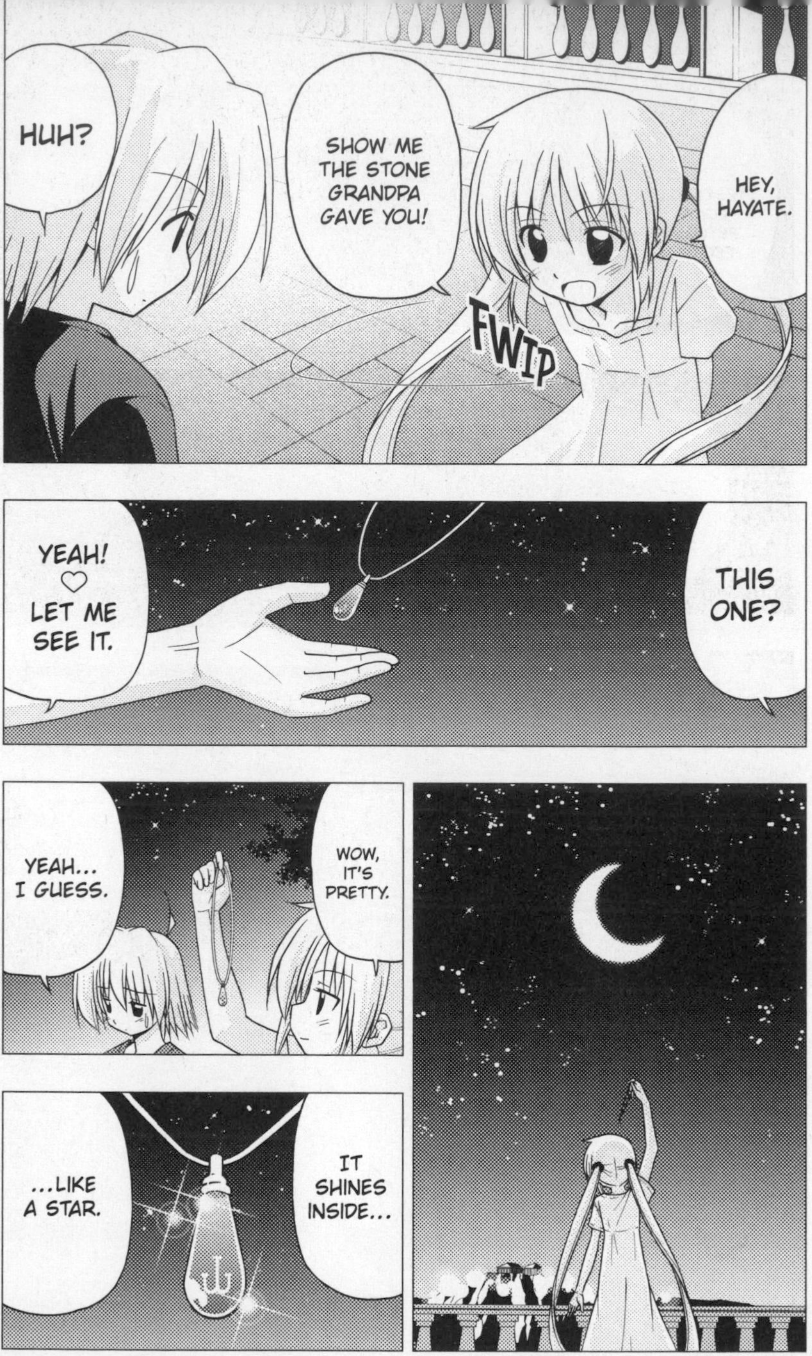
HEY, HAYATE.
SHOW ME THE STONE GRANDPA GAVE YOU!
FWIP
HUH?
THIS ONE?
YEAH! ♡ LET ME SEE IT.
WOW, IT'S PRETTY.
YEAH... I GUESS.
IT SHINES INSIDE...
...LIKE A STAR.

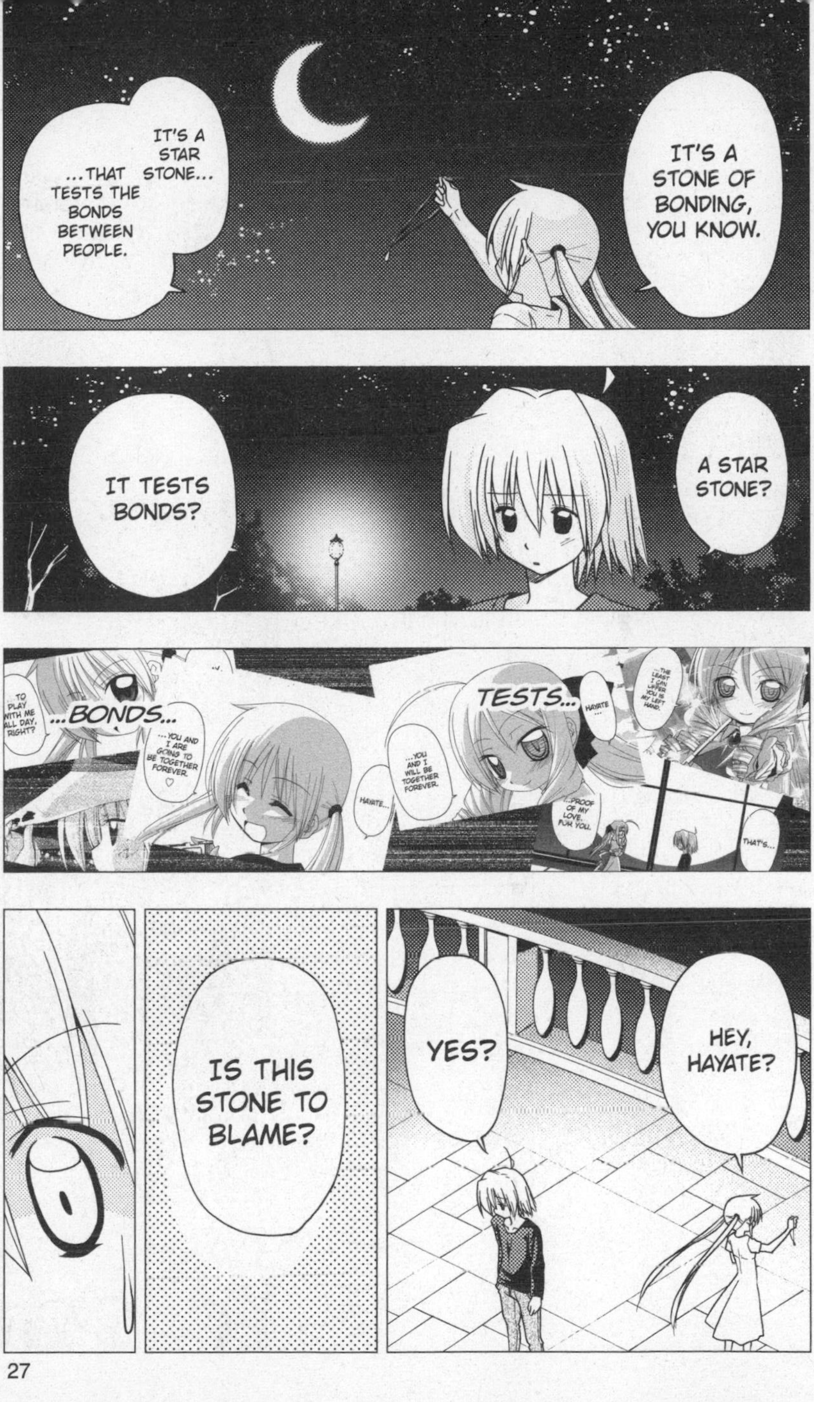
IT'S A STONE OF BONDING, YOU KNOW.
IT'S A STAR STONE... ...THAT TESTS THE BONDS BETWEEN PEOPLE.
A STAR STONE?
IT TESTS BONDS?
THAT'S...
...THE LEAST I CAN OFFER YOU IS MY LEFT HAND.
...PROOF OF MY LOVE... FOR YOU.
HAYATE...
TESTS...
...YOU AND I WILL BE TOGETHER FOREVER.
HAYATE...
...YOU AND I ARE GOING TO BE TOGETHER FOREVER. ♡
...BONDS...
...TO PLAY WITH ME ALL DAY, RIGHT?
HEY, HAYATE?
YES?
IS THIS STONE TO BLAME?

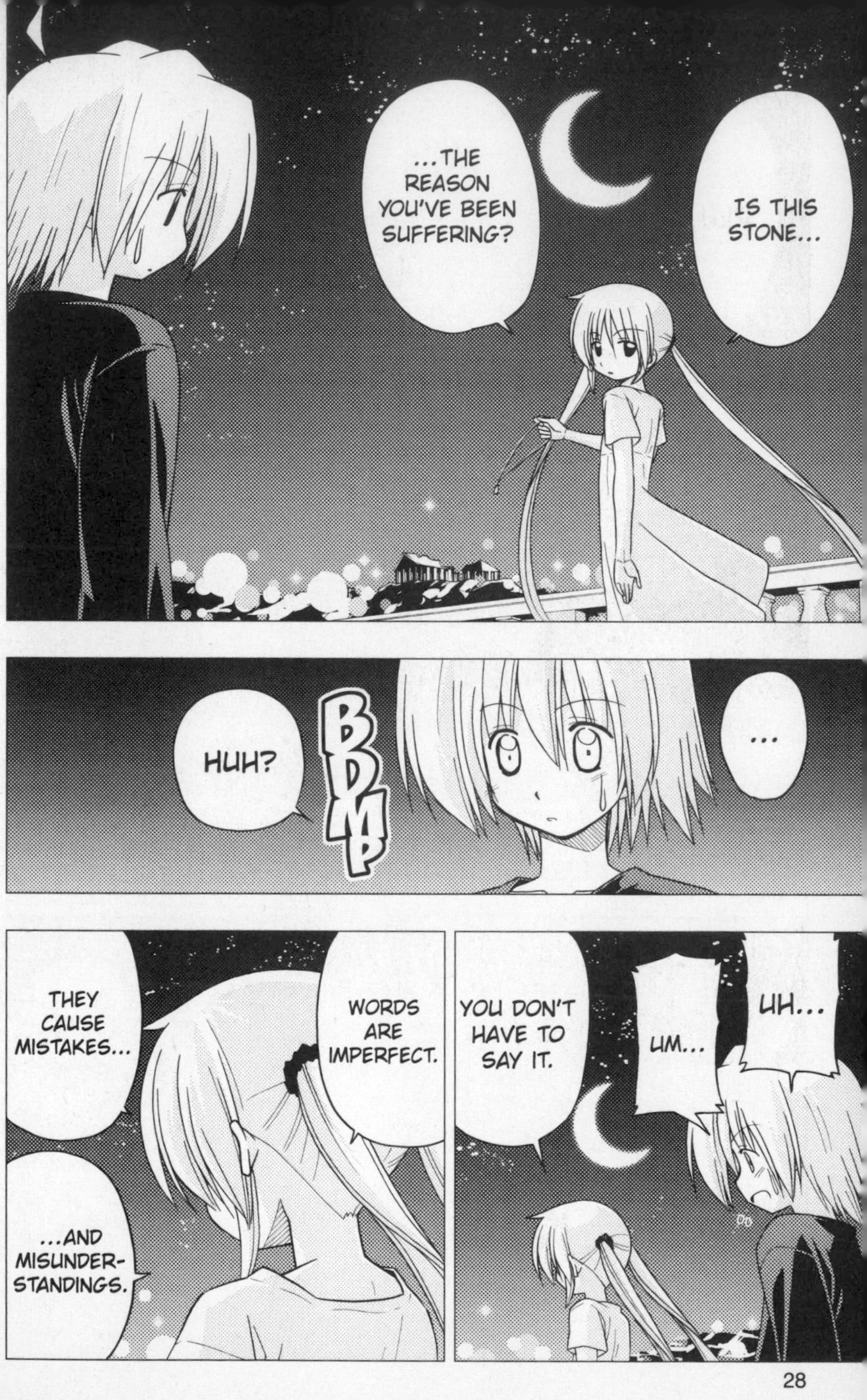
IS THIS STONE...
...THE REASON YOU'VE BEEN SUFFERING?
...
BDMP
HUH?
UH...
UM...
YOU DON'T HAVE TO SAY IT.
WORDS ARE IMPERFECT.
THEY CAUSE MISTAKES...
...AND MISUNDER-STANDINGS.

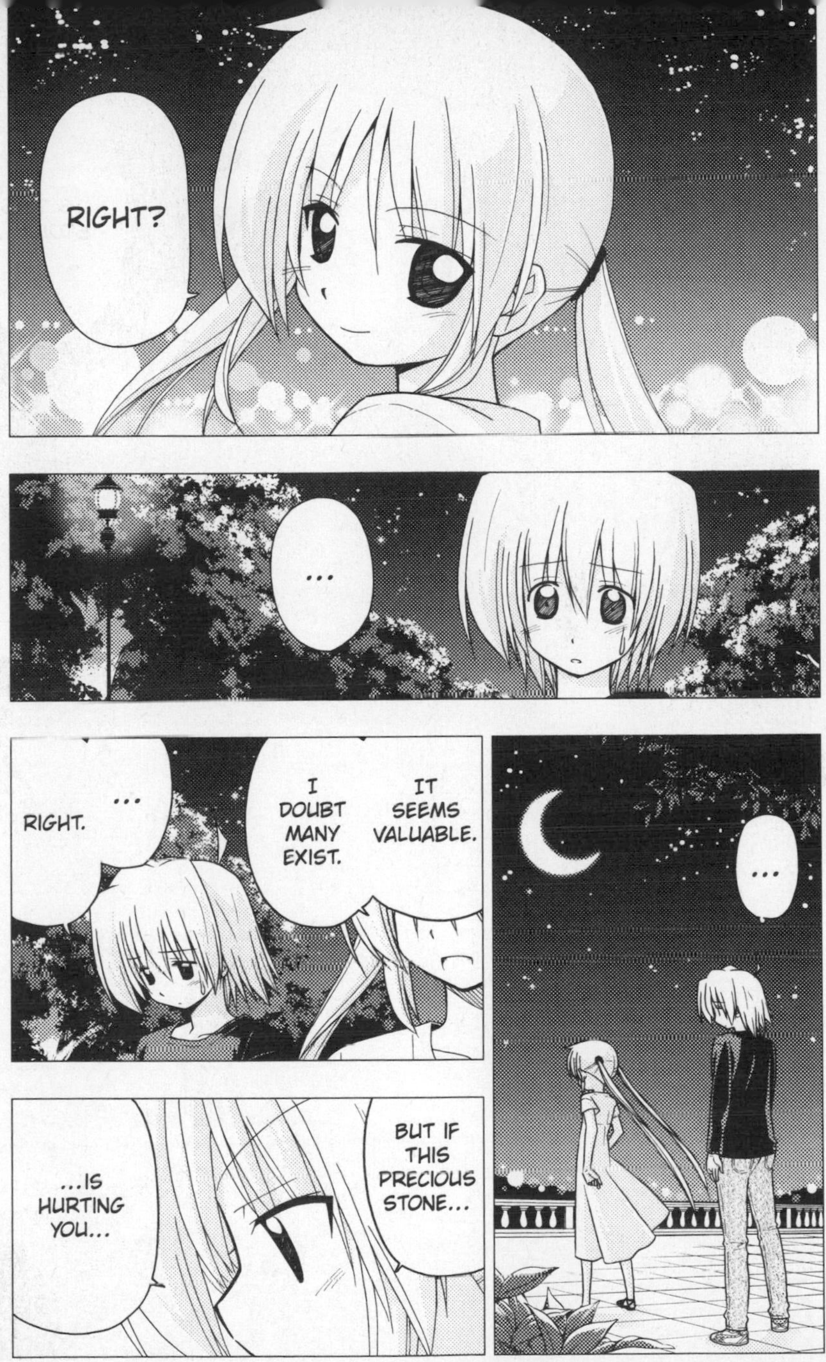
RIGHT?
...
...
IT SEEMS VALUABLE.
I DOUBT MANY EXIST.
...
RIGHT.
BUT IF THIS PRECIOUS STONE...
...IS HURTING YOU...

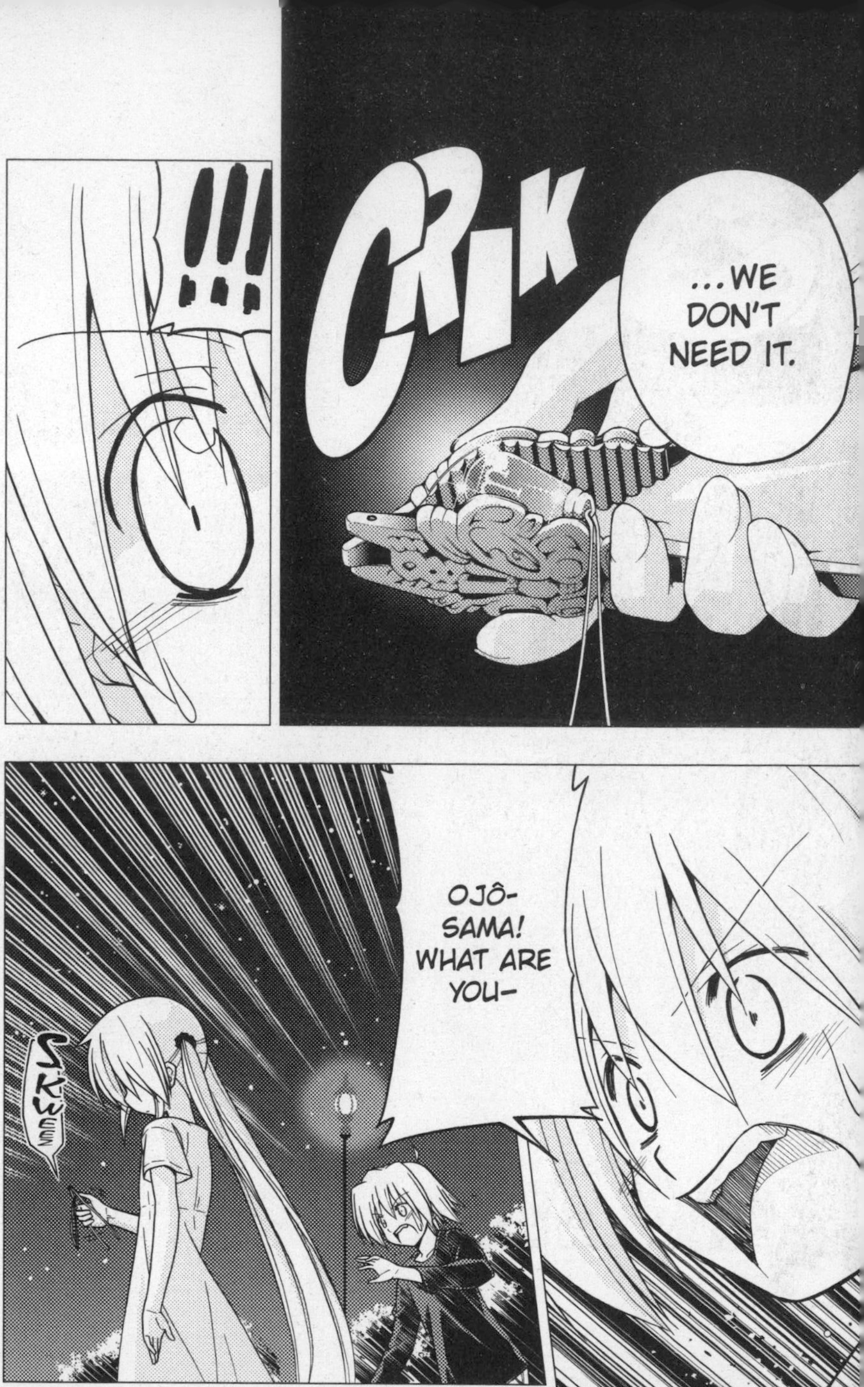
...WE DON'T NEED IT.
CRIK
!!!
OJÔ-SAMA! WHAT ARE YOU-
SKWEE

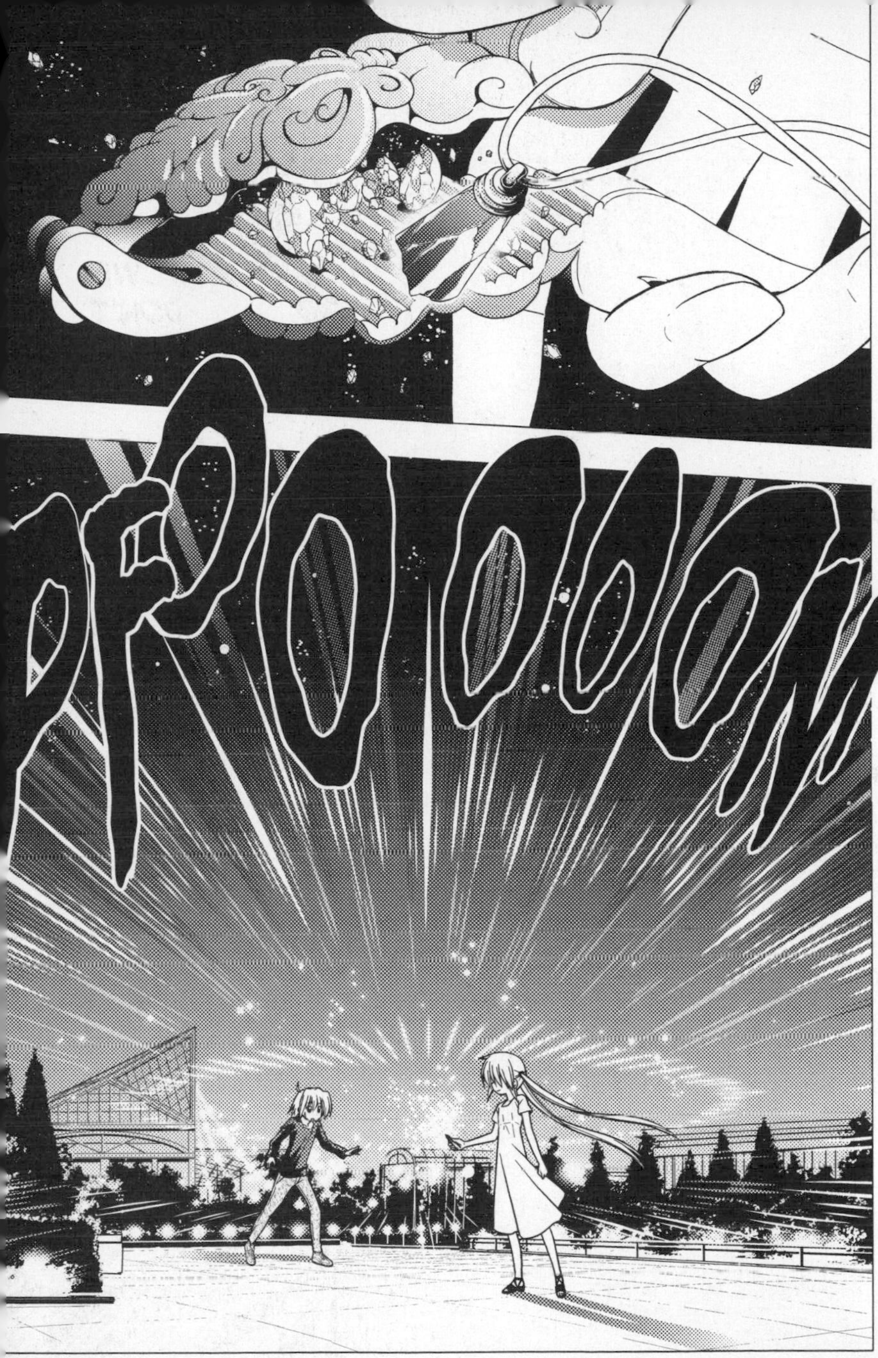

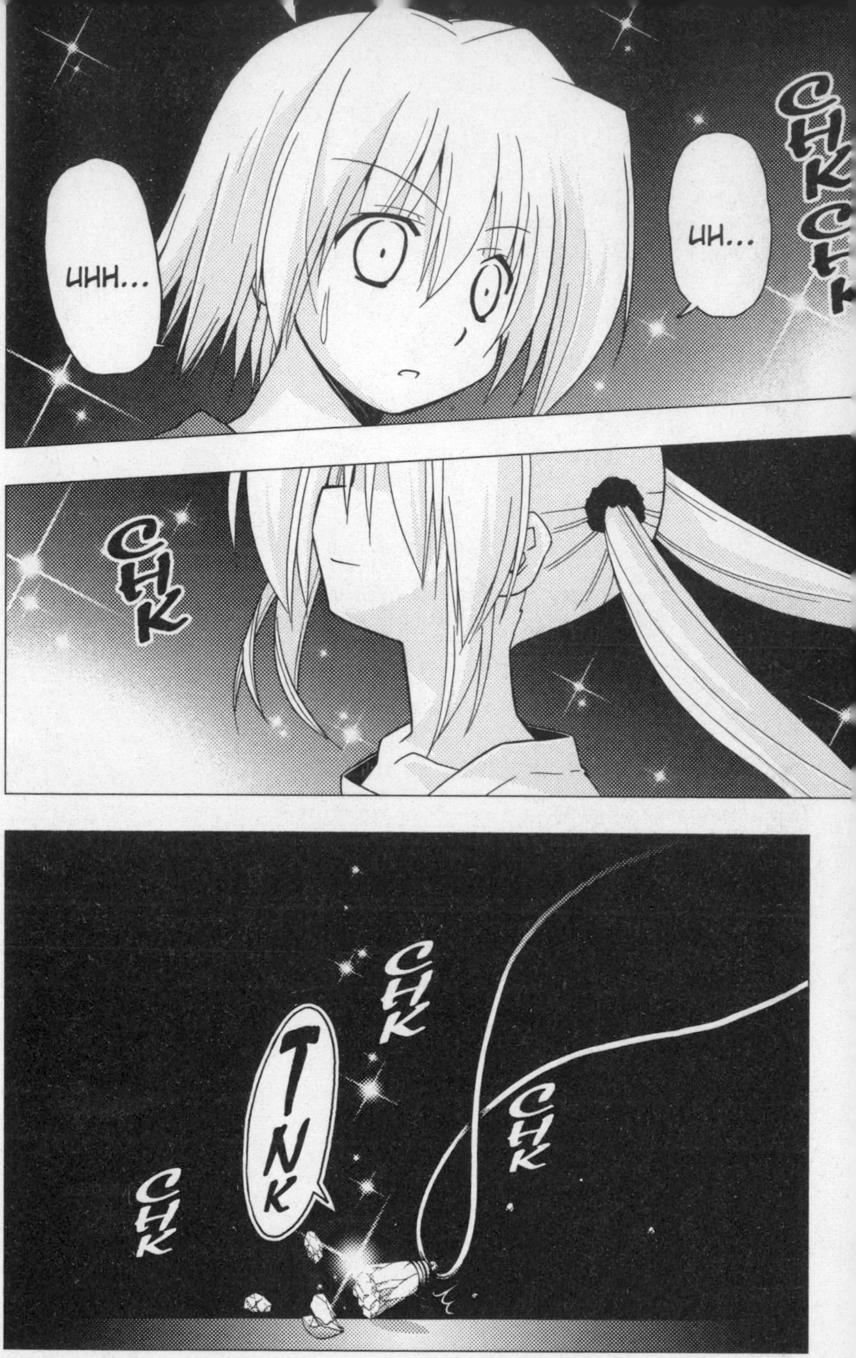
CHK CHK
UH...
UHH...
CHK
CHK
CHK
TNK
CHK

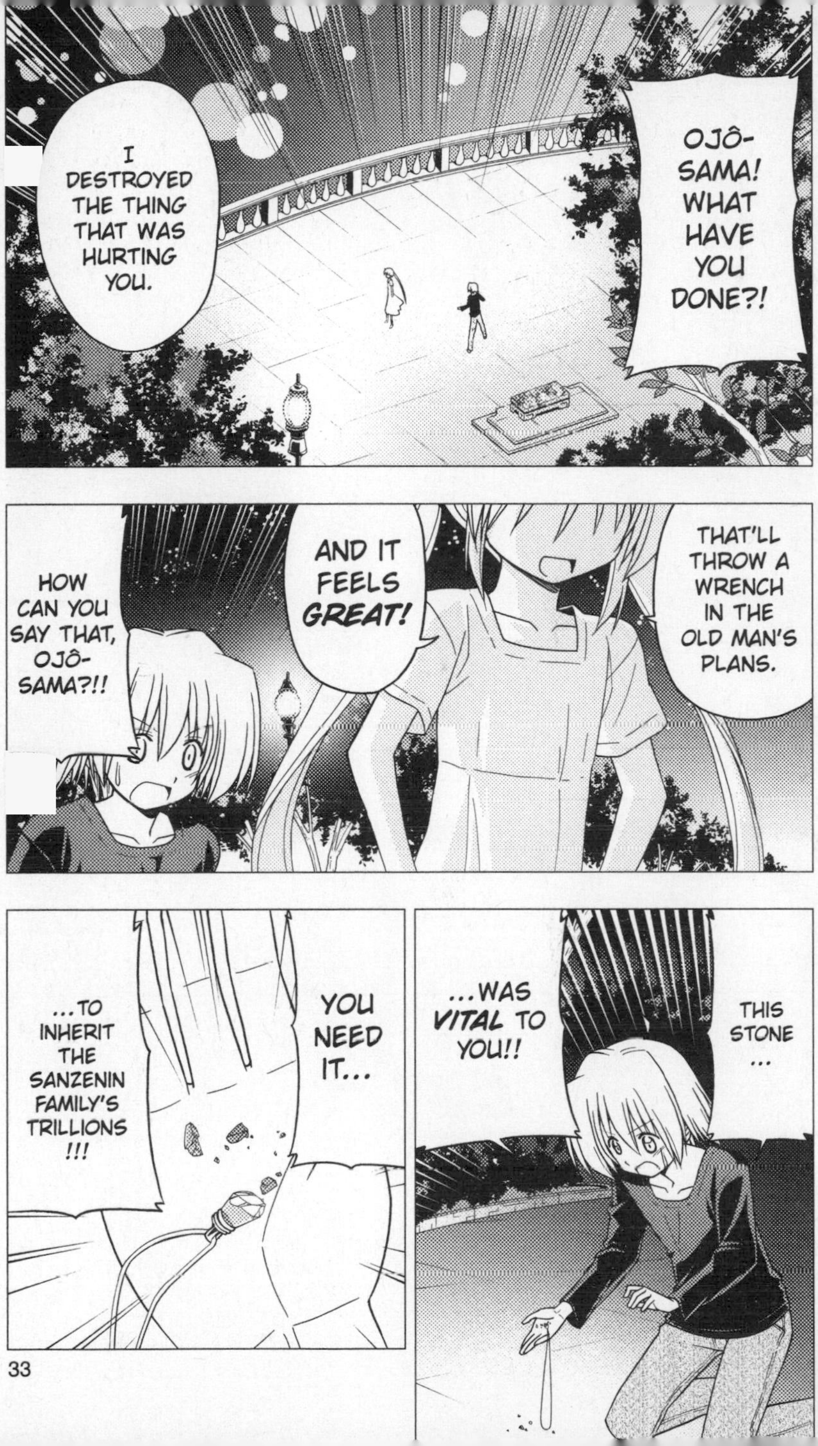
OJÔ-SAMA! WHAT HAVE YOU DONE?!
I DESTROYED THE THING THAT WAS HURTING YOU.
THAT'LL THROW A WRENCH IN THE OLD MAN'S PLANS.
AND IT FEELS *GREAT!*
HOW CAN YOU SAY THAT, OJÔ-SAMA?!!
THIS STONE...
...WAS *VITAL* TO YOU!!
YOU NEED IT...
...TO INHERIT THE SANZENIN FAMILY'S TRILLIONS!!!

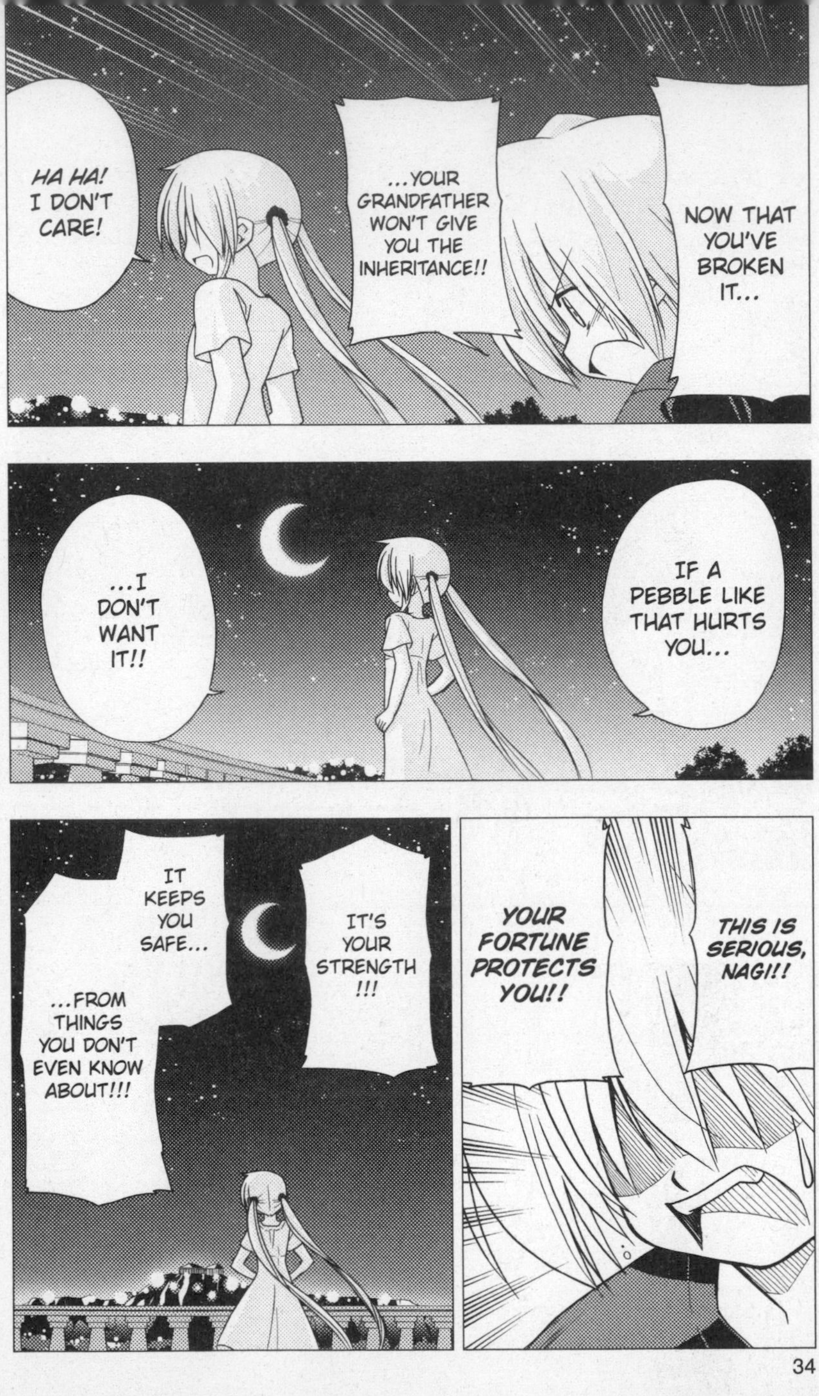
NOW THAT YOU'VE BROKEN IT...
...YOUR GRANDFATHER WON'T GIVE YOU THE INHERITANCE!!
HA HA! I DON'T CARE!
IF A PEBBLE LIKE THAT HURTS YOU...
...I DON'T WANT IT!!
THIS IS SERIOUS, NAGI!!
YOUR FORTUNE PROTECTS YOU!!
IT'S YOUR STRENGTH!!!
IT KEEPS YOU SAFE...
...FROM THINGS YOU DON'T EVEN KNOW ABOUT!!!

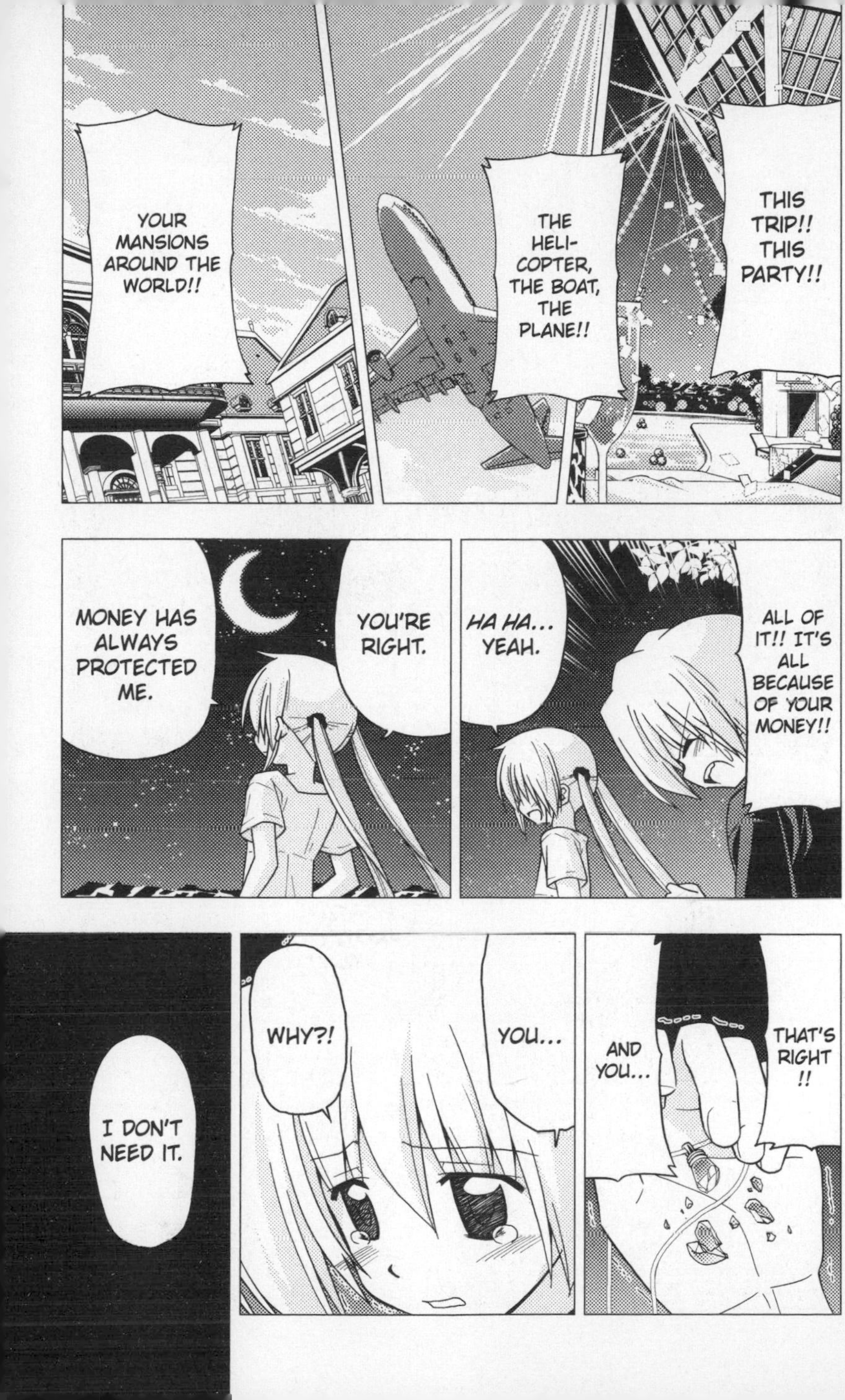
THIS TRIP!! THIS PARTY!!
THE HELI-COPTER, THE BOAT, THE PLANE!!
YOUR MANSIONS AROUND THE WORLD!!
ALL OF IT!! IT'S ALL BECAUSE OF YOUR MONEY!!
HA HA... YEAH.
YOU'RE RIGHT.
MONEY HAS ALWAYS PROTECTED ME.
THAT'S RIGHT !!
AND YOU...
YOU...
WHY?!
I DON'T NEED IT.

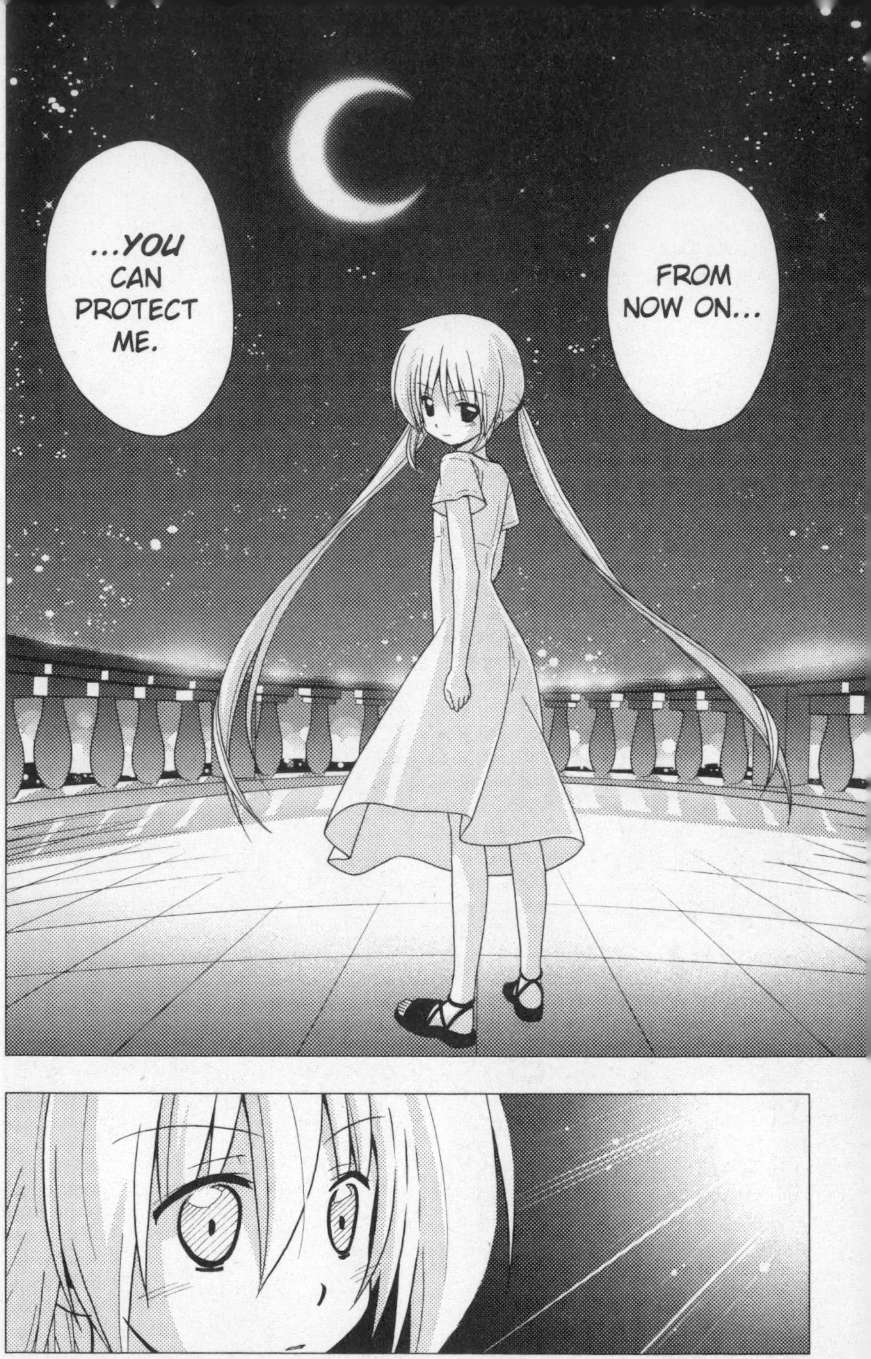
FROM NOW ON...
...YOU CAN PROTECT ME.

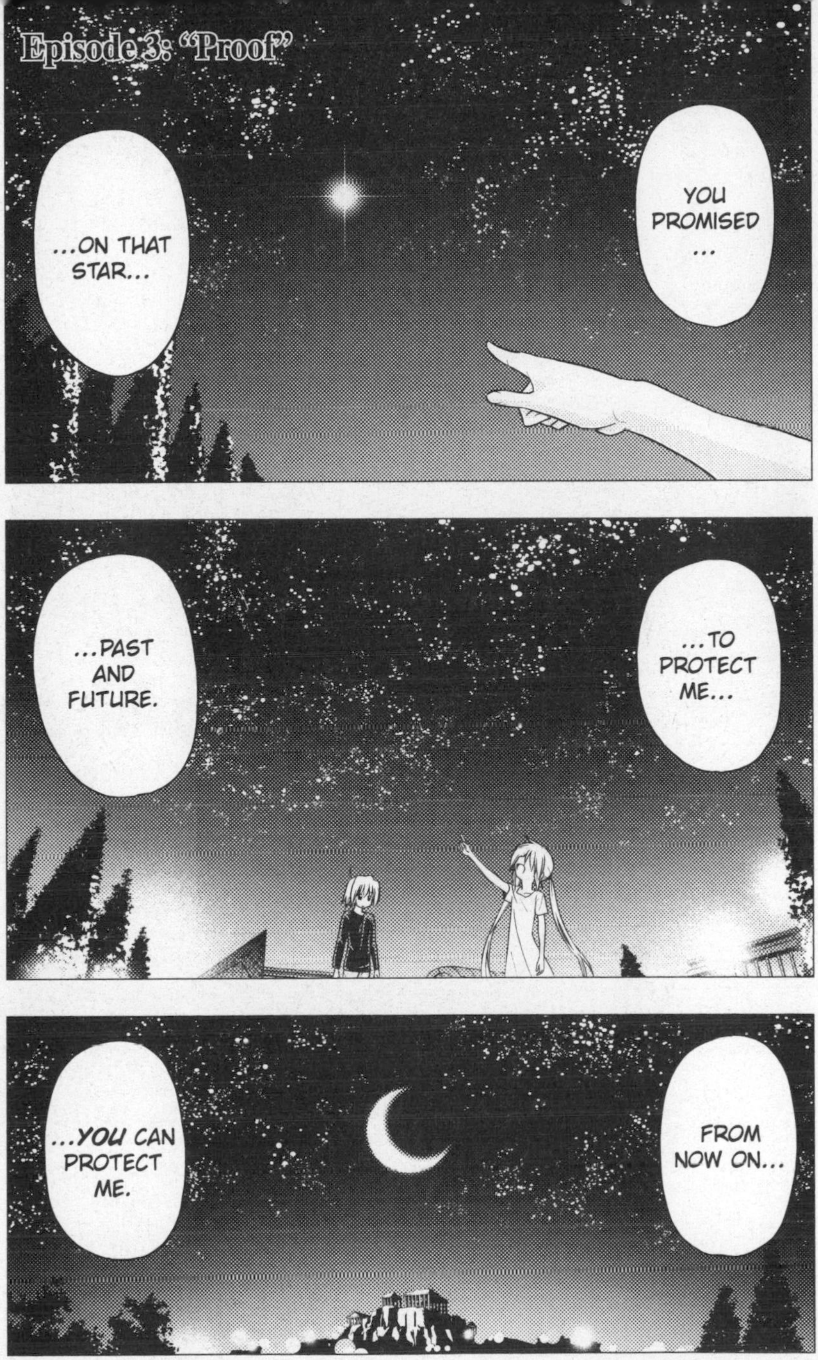
Episode 3: "Proof"
YOU PROMISED ...
...ON THAT STAR...
...TO PROTECT ME...
...PAST AND FUTURE.
FROM NOW ON...
...YOU CAN PROTECT ME.

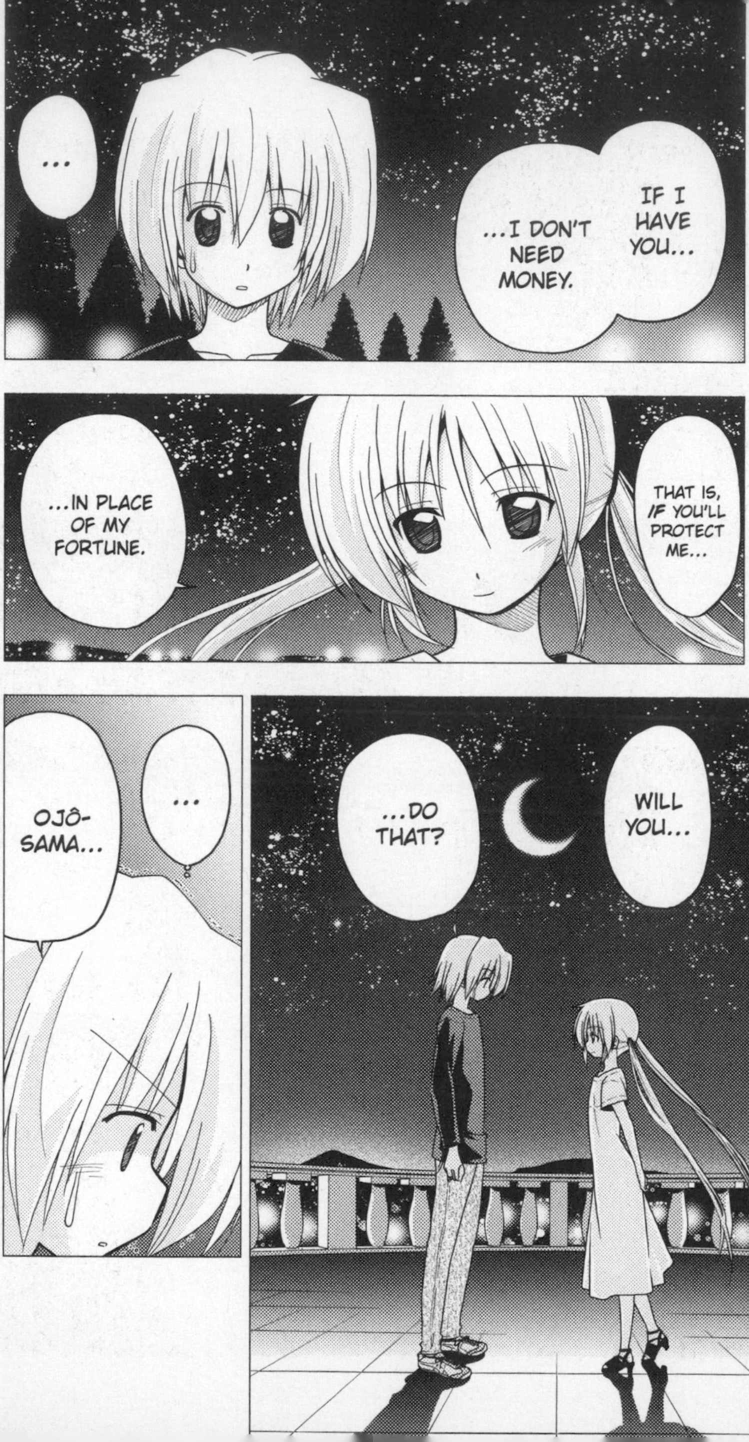
IF I HAVE YOU...
...I DON'T NEED MONEY.
...
THAT IS, IF YOU'LL PROTECT ME...
...IN PLACE OF MY FORTUNE.
WILL YOU...
...DO THAT?
...
OJÔ-SAMA...

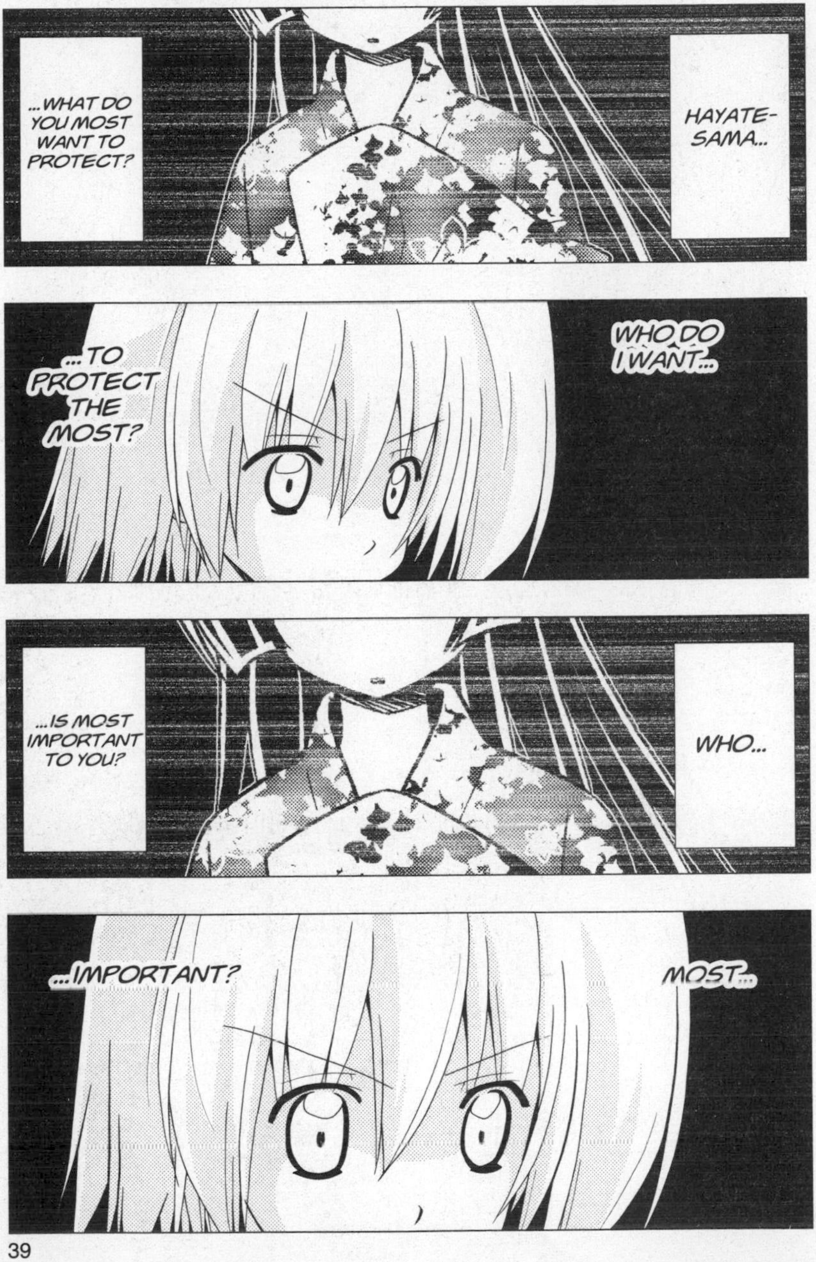
HAYATE-SAMA...
...WHAT DO YOU MOST WANT TO PROTECT?
WHO DO I WANT...
...TO PROTECT THE MOST?
WHO...
...IS MOST IMPORTANT TO YOU?
MOST...
...IMPORTANT?

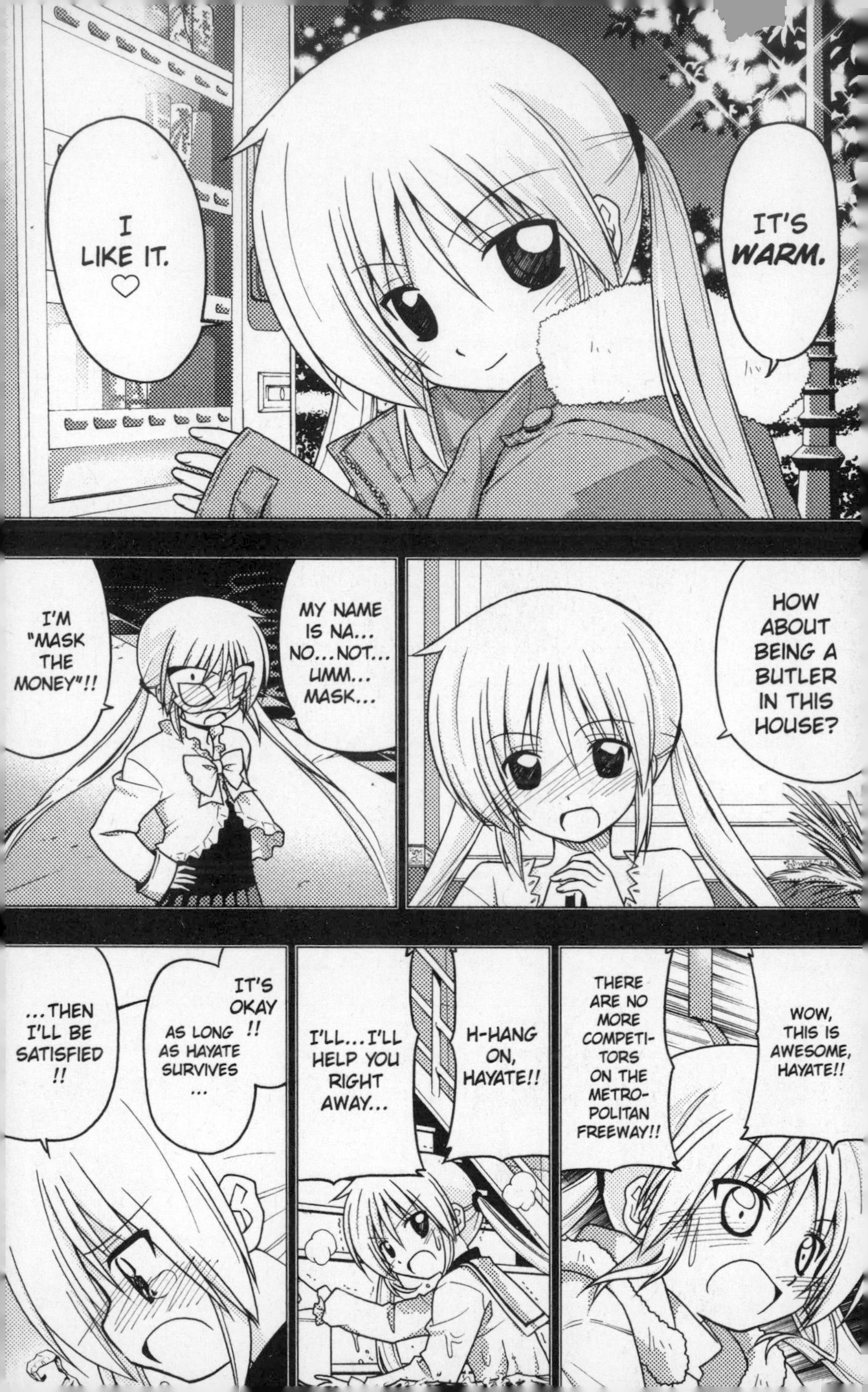
IT'S WARM.
I LIKE IT. ♡
HOW ABOUT BEING A BUTLER IN THIS HOUSE?
MY NAME IS NA... NO...NOT... UMM... MASK...
I'M "MASK THE MONEY"!!
WOW, THIS IS AWESOME, HAYATE!!
THERE ARE NO MORE COMPETITORS ON THE METROPOLITAN FREEWAY!!
H-HANG ON, HAYATE!!
I'LL...I'LL HELP YOU RIGHT AWAY...
IT'S OKAY!! AS LONG AS HAYATE SURVIVES...
...THEN I'LL BE SATISFIED!!

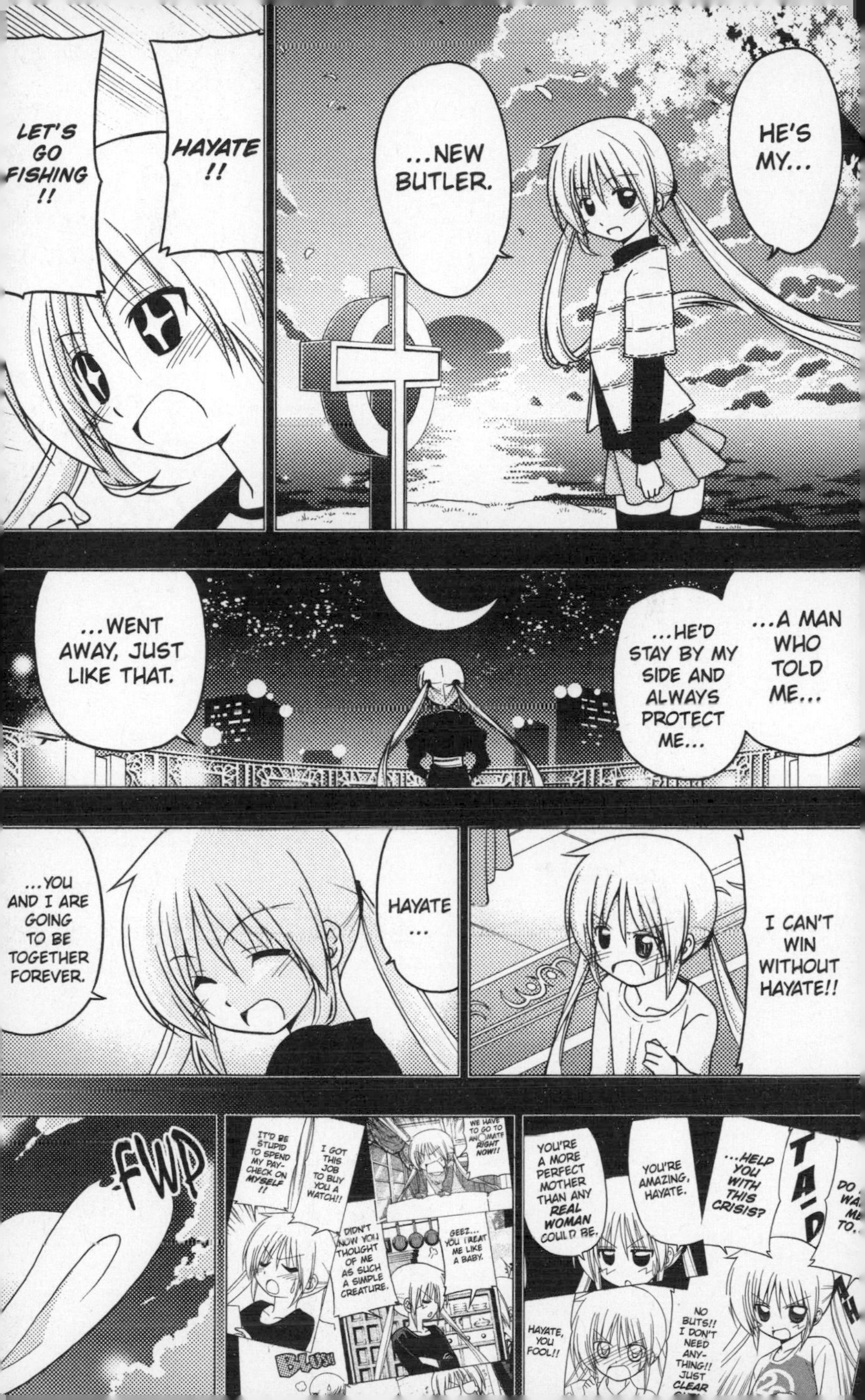
HE'S MY...
...NEW BUTLER.
HAYATE!!
LET'S GO FISHING!!
...A MAN WHO TOLD ME...
...HE'D STAY BY MY SIDE AND ALWAYS PROTECT ME...
...WENT AWAY, JUST LIKE THAT.
I CAN'T WIN WITHOUT HAYATE!!
HAYATE...
...YOU AND I ARE GOING TO BE TOGETHER FOREVER.
TA-D
...HELP YOU WITH THIS CRISIS?
YOU'RE AMAZING, HAYATE.
YOU'RE A MORE PERFECT MOTHER THAN ANY REAL WOMAN COULD BE.
NO BUTS!! I DON'T NEED ANYTHING!! JUST CLEAR
HAYATE, YOU FOOL!!
WE HAVE TO GO TO ANIMATE RIGHT NOW!!
I GOT THIS JOB TO BUY YOU A WATCH!!
IT'D BE STUPID TO SPEND MY PAYCHECK ON MYSELF!!
GEEZ... YOU TREAT ME LIKE A BABY.
DIDN'T KNOW YOU THOUGHT OF ME AS SUCH A SIMPLE CREATURE.
BLUSH
FWP

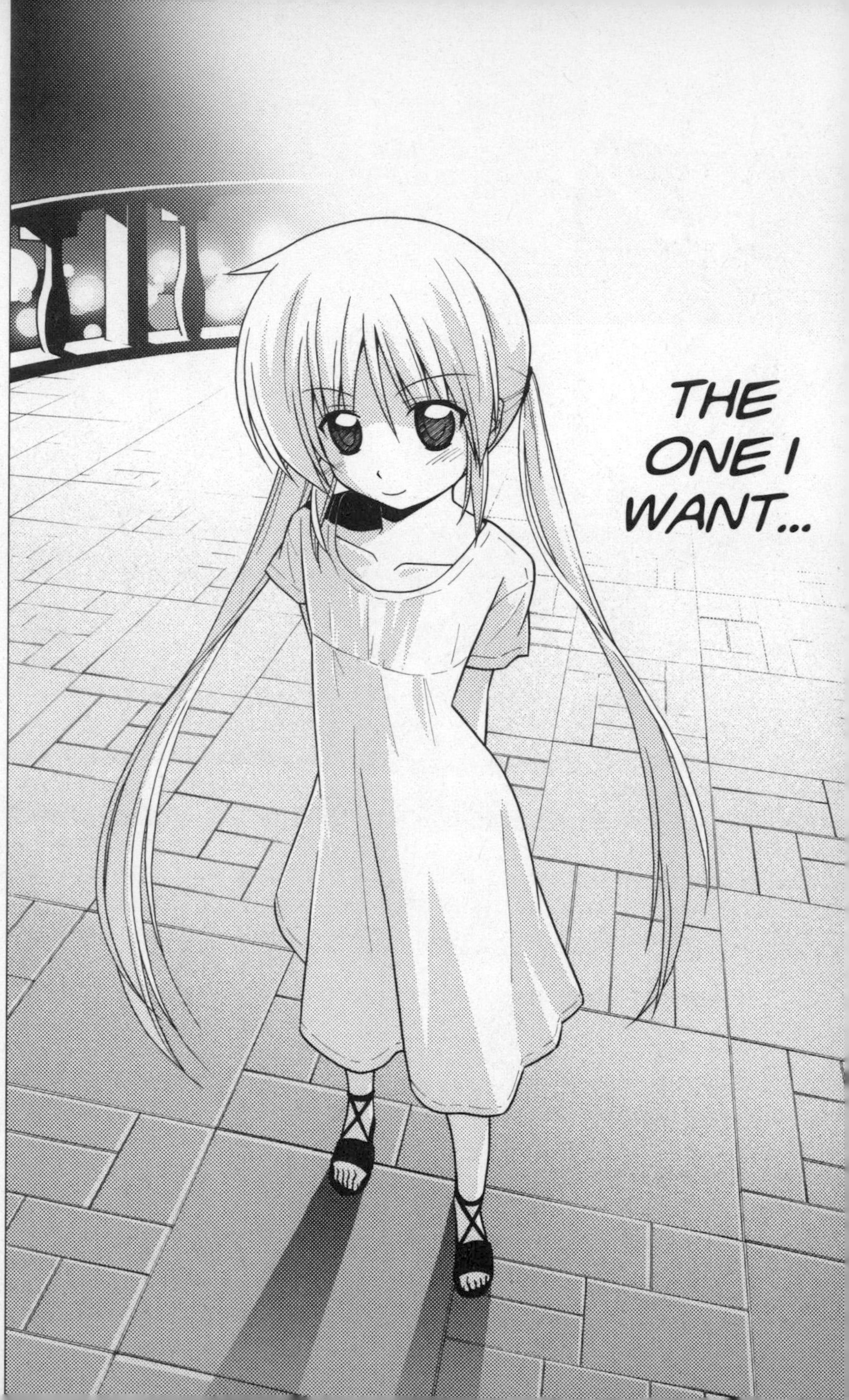
THE ONE I WANT...

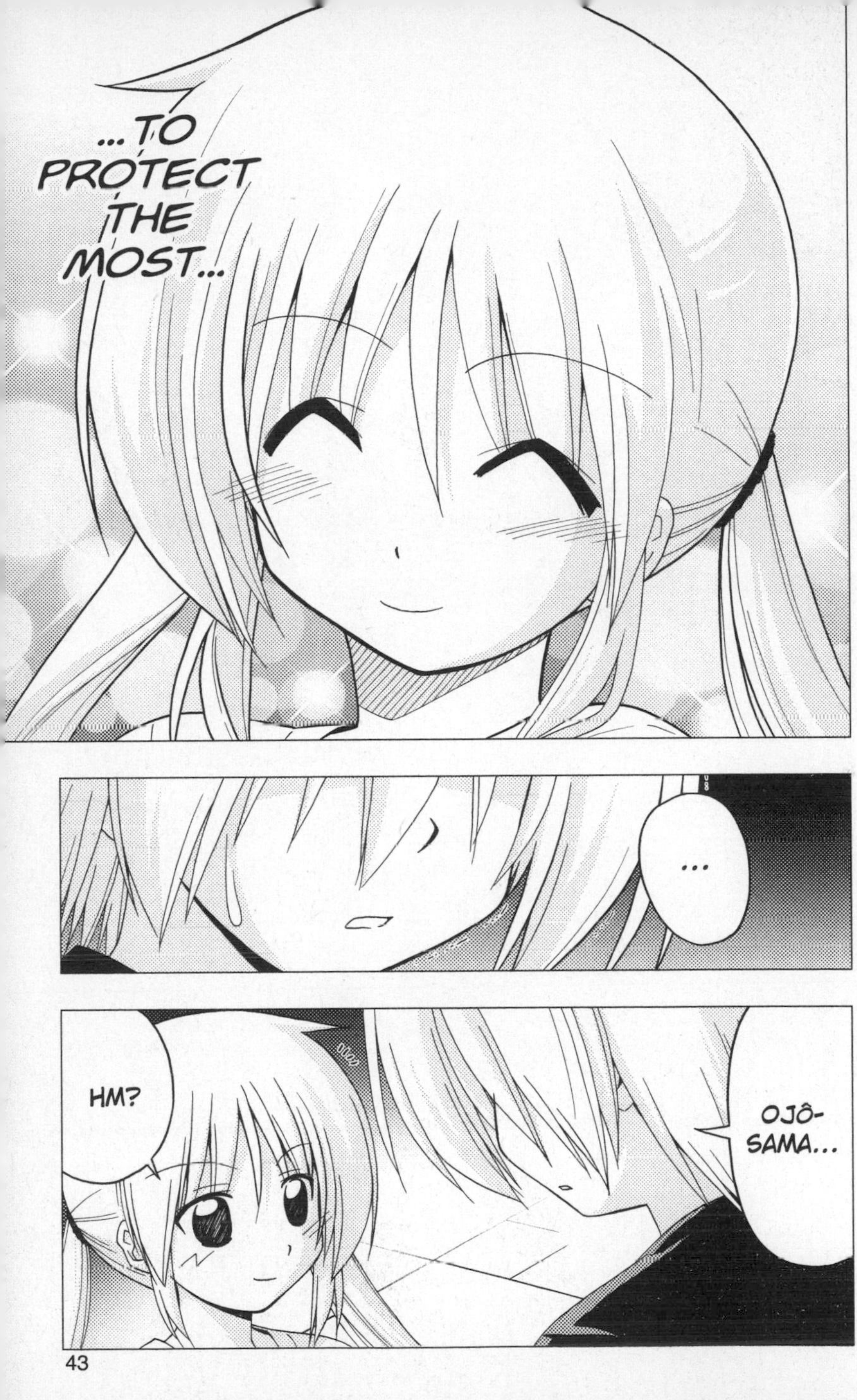
...TO PROTECT THE MOST...
...
OJÔ-SAMA...
HM?

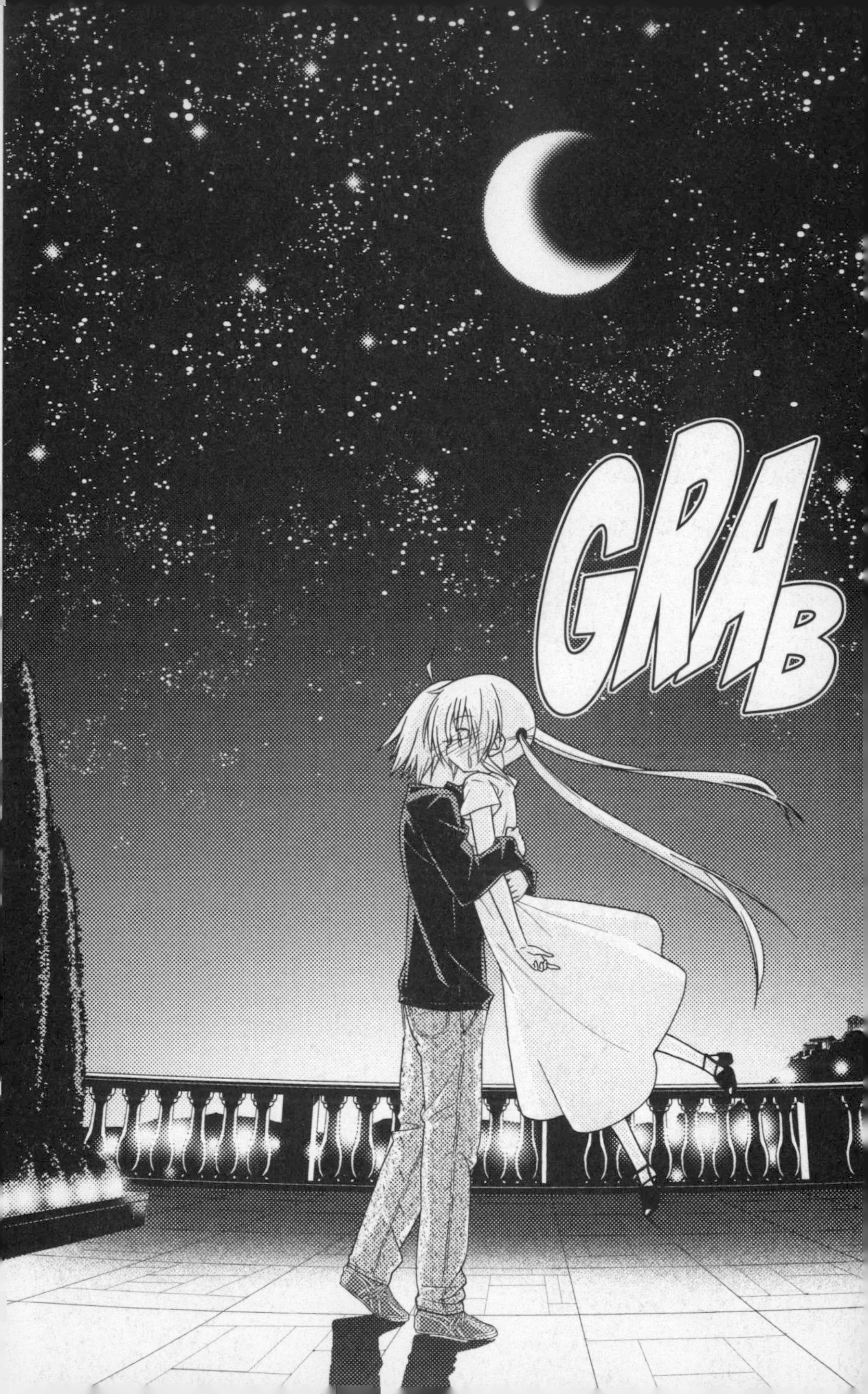
GRAB

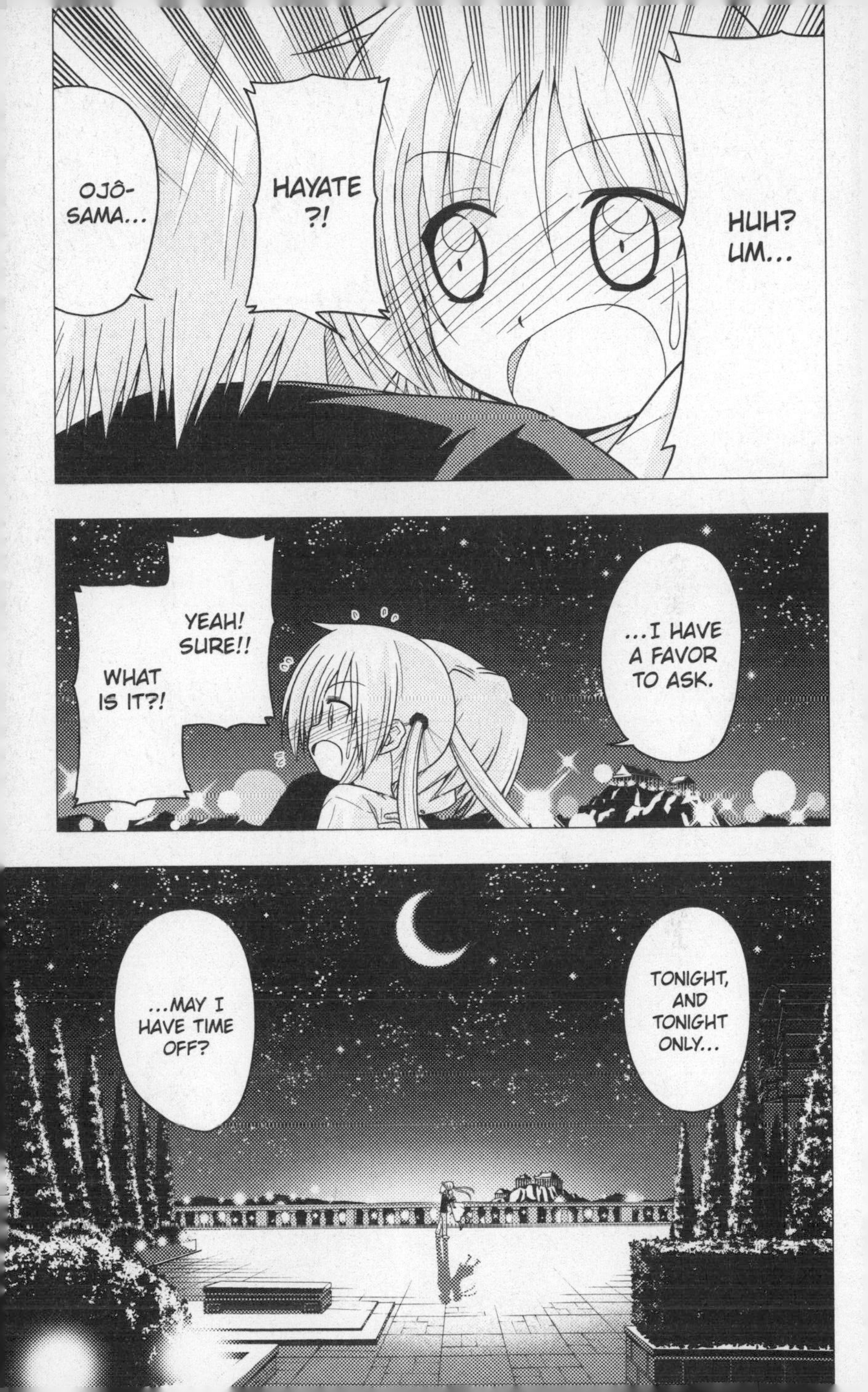
HUH? UM...
HAYATE ?!
OJÔ-SAMA...
...I HAVE A FAVOR TO ASK.
YEAH! SURE!!
WHAT IS IT?!
TONIGHT, AND TONIGHT ONLY...
...MAY I HAVE TIME OFF?

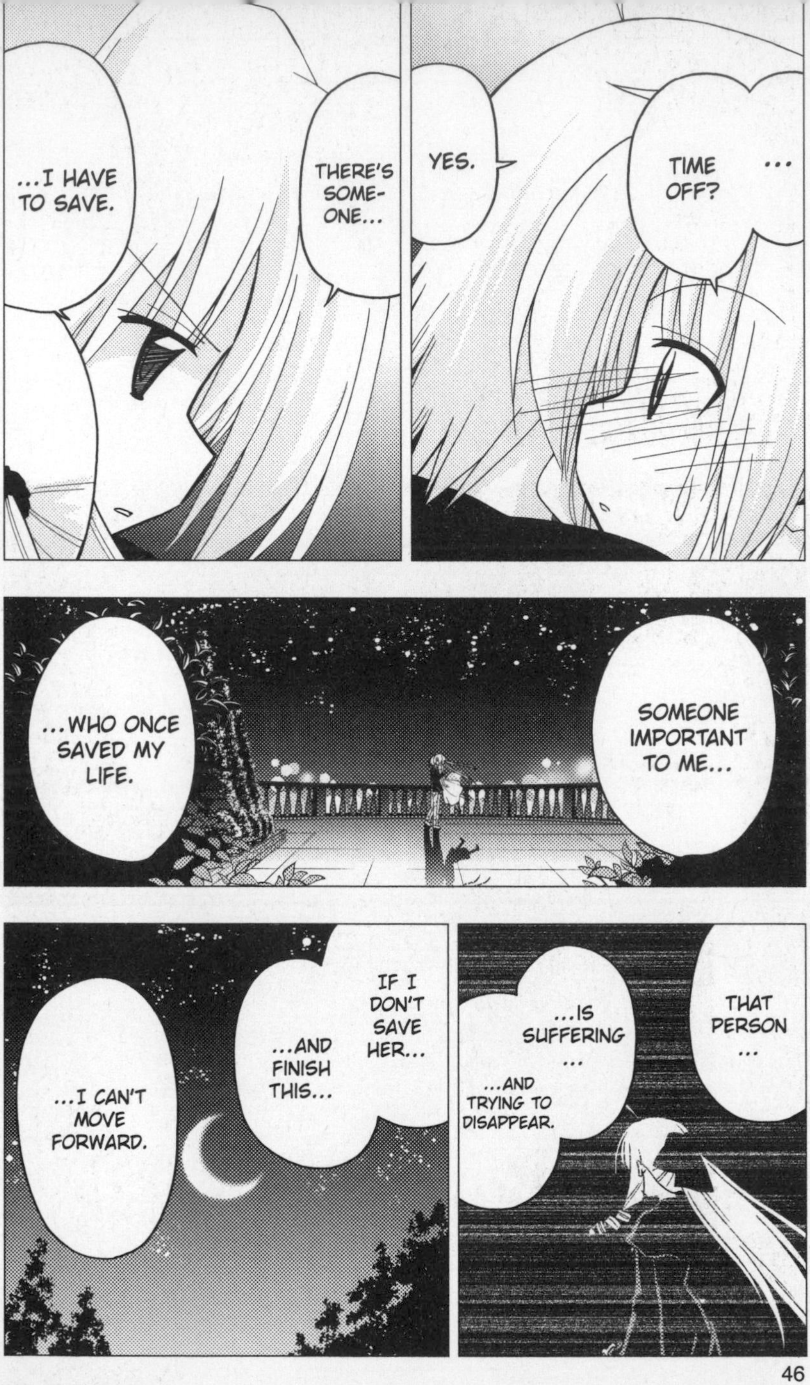
...
TIME OFF?
YES.
THERE'S SOME-ONE...
...I HAVE TO SAVE.
SOMEONE IMPORTANT TO ME...
...WHO ONCE SAVED MY LIFE.
THAT PERSON ...
...IS SUFFERING ...
...AND TRYING TO DISAPPEAR.
IF I DON'T SAVE HER...
...AND FINISH THIS...
...I CAN'T MOVE FORWARD.

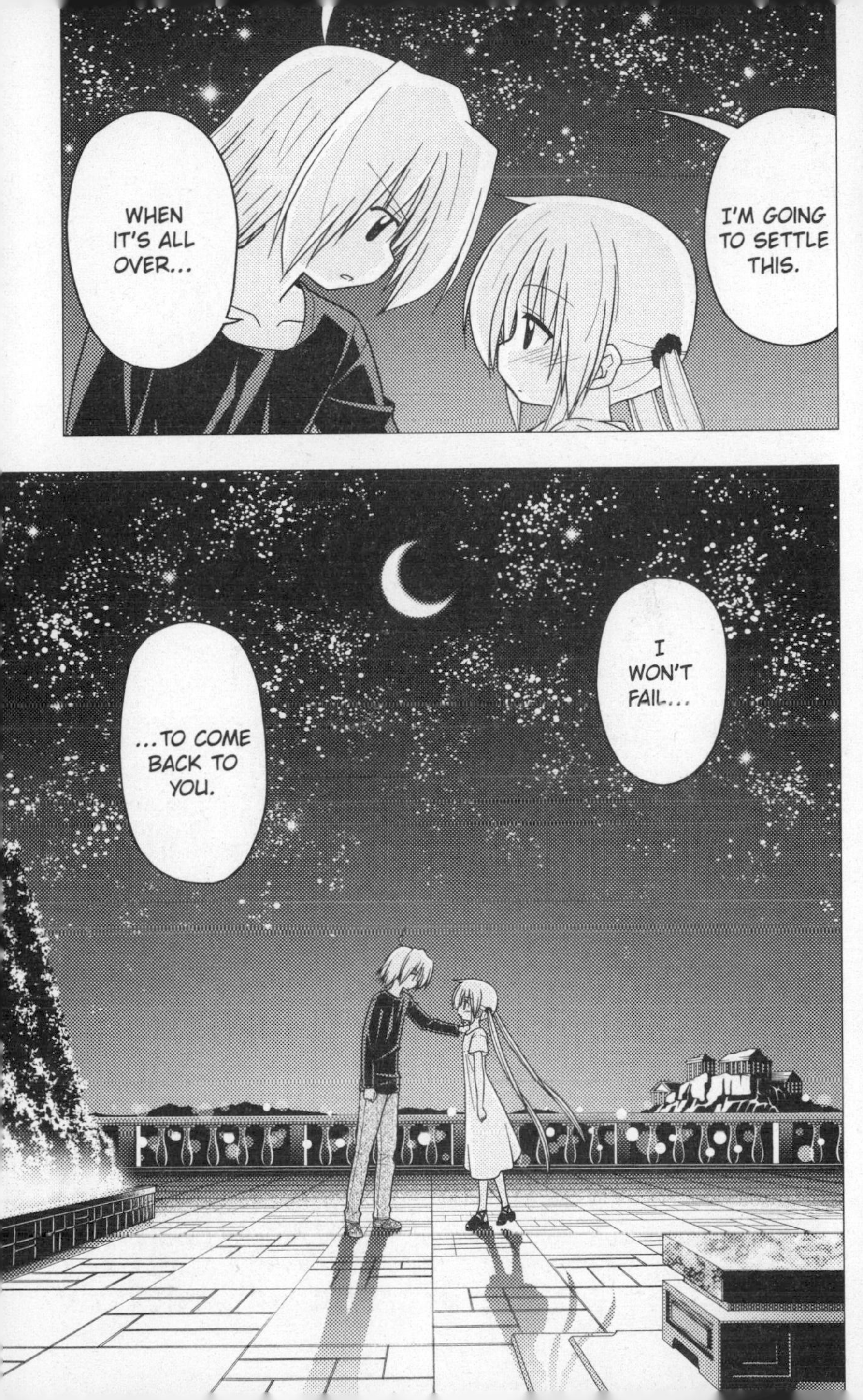
I'M GOING TO SETTLE THIS.
WHEN IT'S ALL OVER...
I WON'T FAIL...
...TO COME BACK TO YOU.

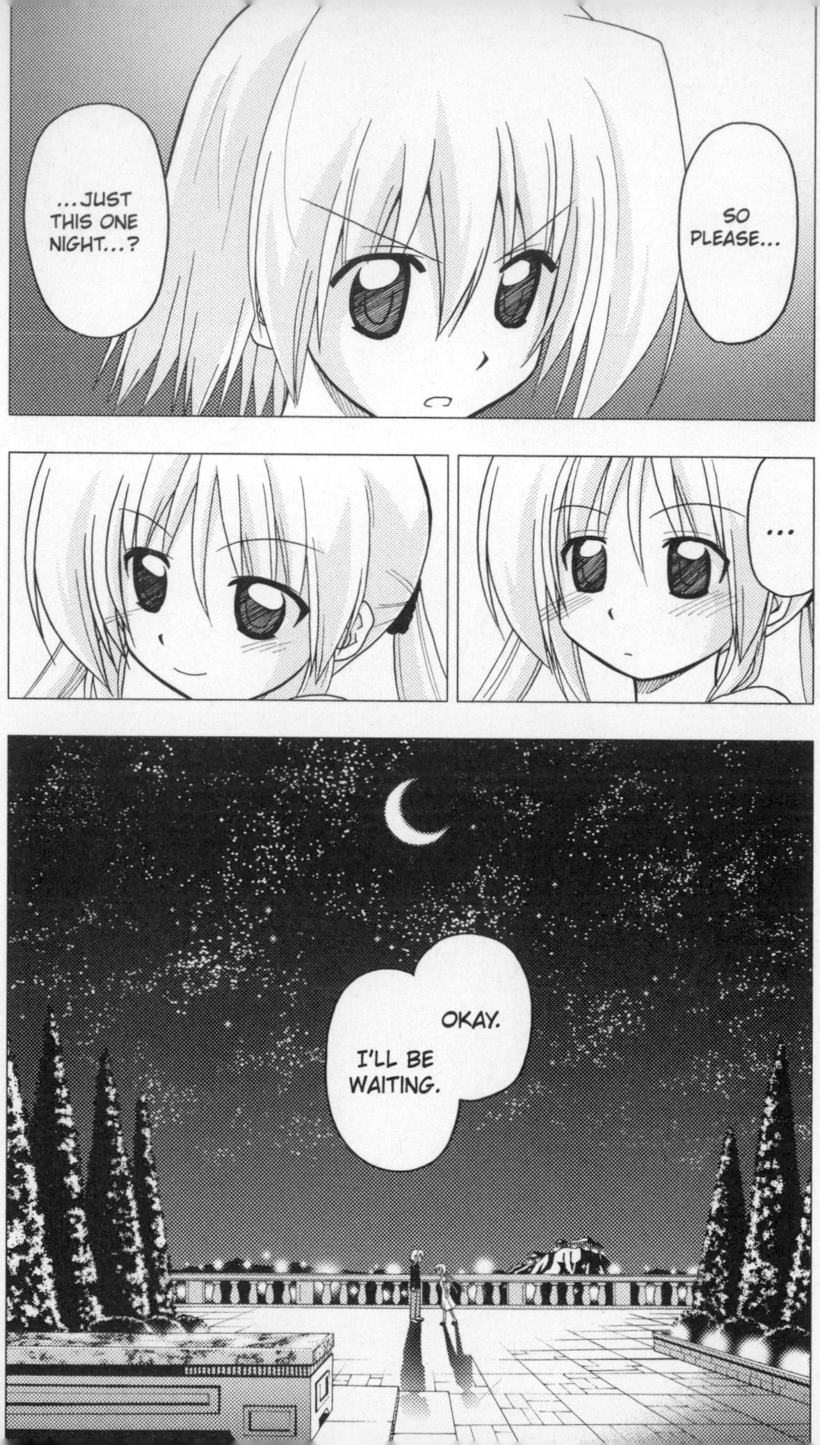
SO PLEASE...
...JUST THIS ONE NIGHT...?
...
OKAY. I'LL BE WAITING.

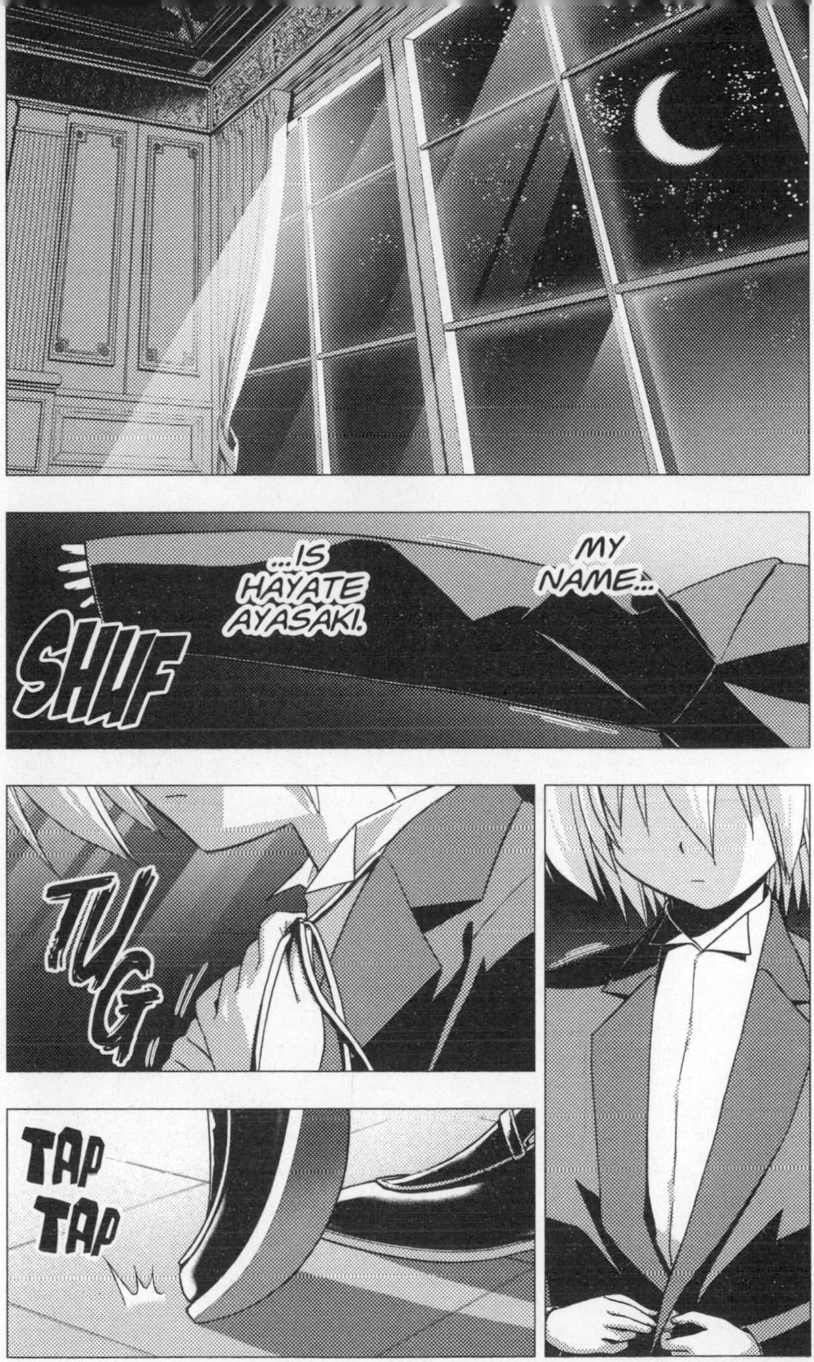
MY NAME...
...IS HAYATE AYASAKI.
SHUF
TUG
TAP TAP

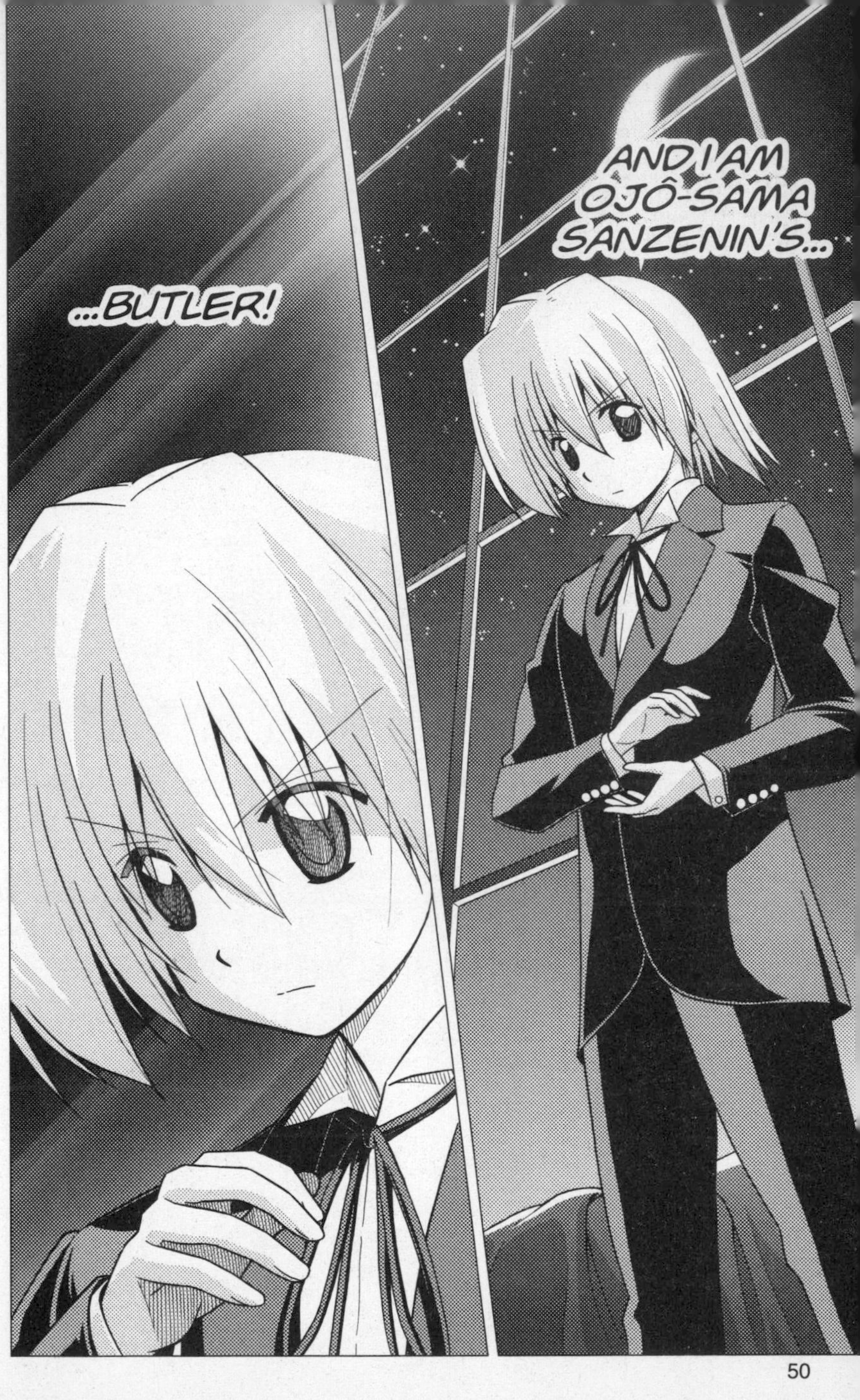
AND I AM OJÔ-SAMA SANZENIN'S...
...BUTLER!

...A
CONCLUSION?

HAVE YOU
REACHED...

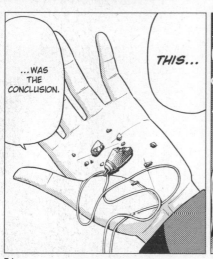

...WAS
THE
CONCLUSION.

THIS...

SW
IP

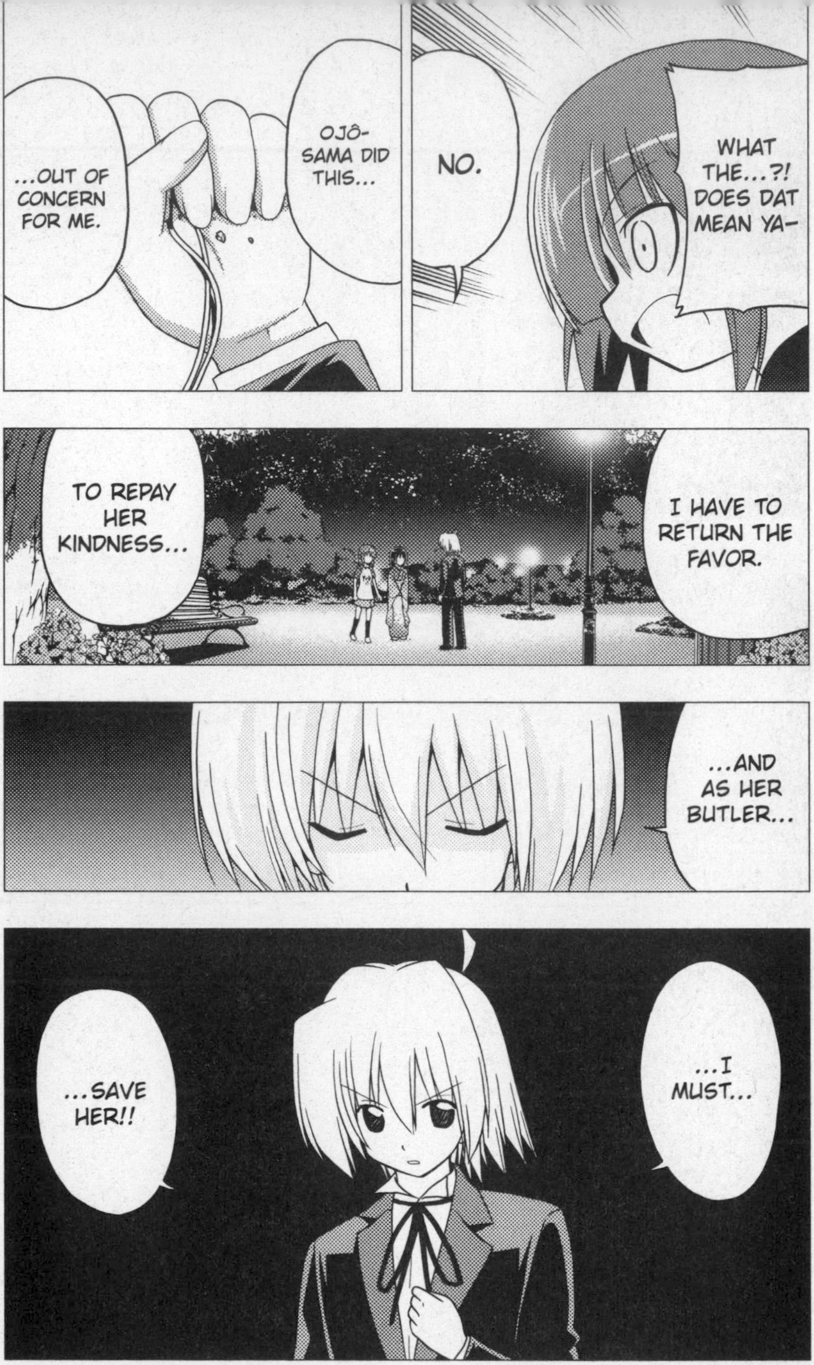
WHAT THE...?! DOES DAT MEAN YA-
NO.
OJÔ-SAMA DID THIS...
...OUT OF CONCERN FOR ME.
I HAVE TO RETURN THE FAVOR.
TO REPAY HER KINDNESS...
...AND AS HER BUTLER...
...I MUST...
...SAVE HER!!

Episode 4:
"The Final Battle"

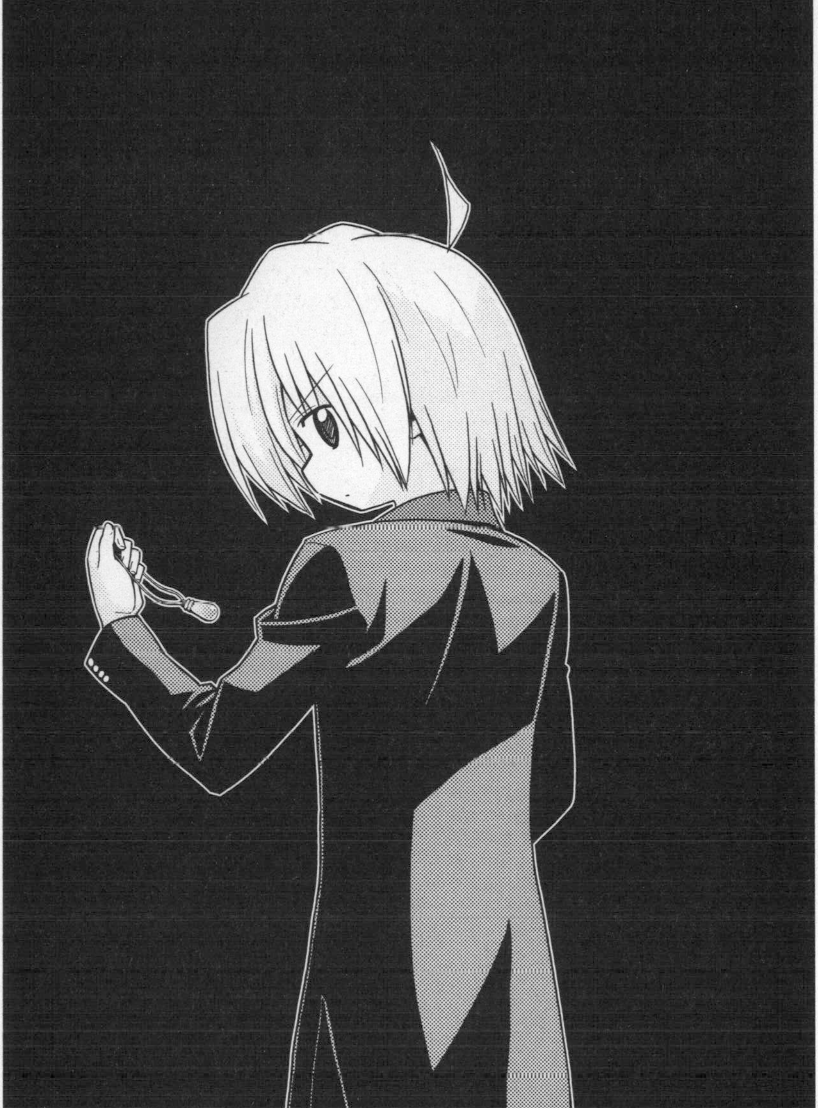

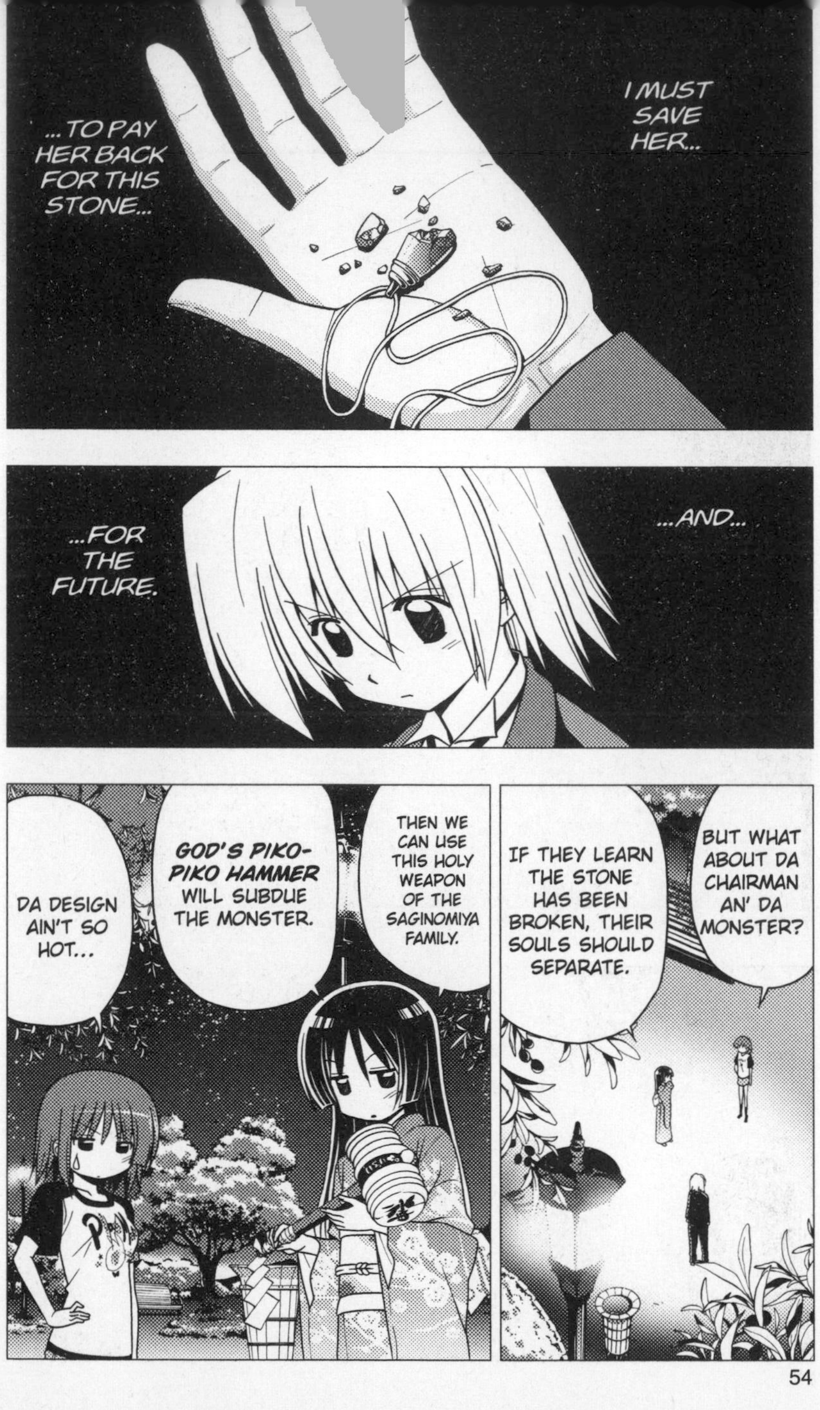
I MUST SAVE HER...
...TO PAY HER BACK FOR THIS STONE...
...AND...
...FOR THE FUTURE.
BUT WHAT ABOUT DA CHAIRMAN AN' DA MONSTER?
IF THEY LEARN THE STONE HAS BEEN BROKEN, THEIR SOULS SHOULD SEPARATE.
THEN WE CAN USE THIS HOLY WEAPON OF THE SAGINOMIYA FAMILY.
GOD'S PIKO-PIKO HAMMER WILL SUBDUE THE MONSTER.
DA DESIGN AIN'T SO HOT...

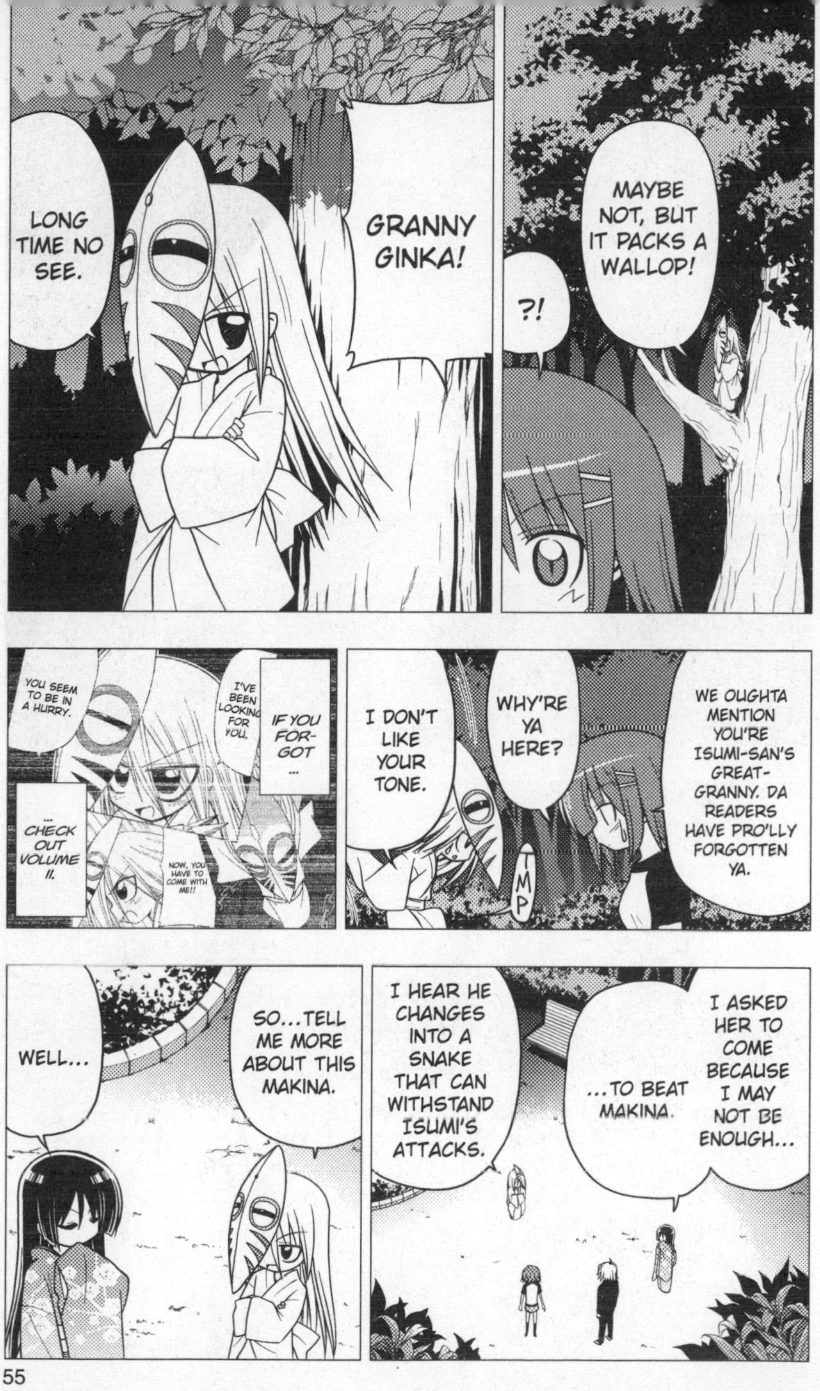
MAYBE NOT, BUT IT PACKS A WALLOP!
?!
GRANNY GINKA!
LONG TIME NO SEE.
WE OUGHTA MENTION YOU'RE ISUMI-SAN'S GREAT-GRANNY. DA READERS HAVE PRO'LLY FORGOTTEN YA.
WHY'RE YA HERE?
TMP
I DON'T LIKE YOUR TONE.
IF YOU FOR-GOT ...
I'VE BEEN LOOKING FOR YOU.
YOU SEEM TO BE IN A HURRY.
NOW, YOU HAVE TO COME WITH ME!!
... CHECK OUT VOLUME 11.
I ASKED HER TO COME BECAUSE I MAY NOT BE ENOUGH...
...TO BEAT MAKINA.
I HEAR HE CHANGES INTO A SNAKE THAT CAN WITHSTAND ISUMI'S ATTACKS.
SO...TELL ME MORE ABOUT THIS MAKINA.
WELL...

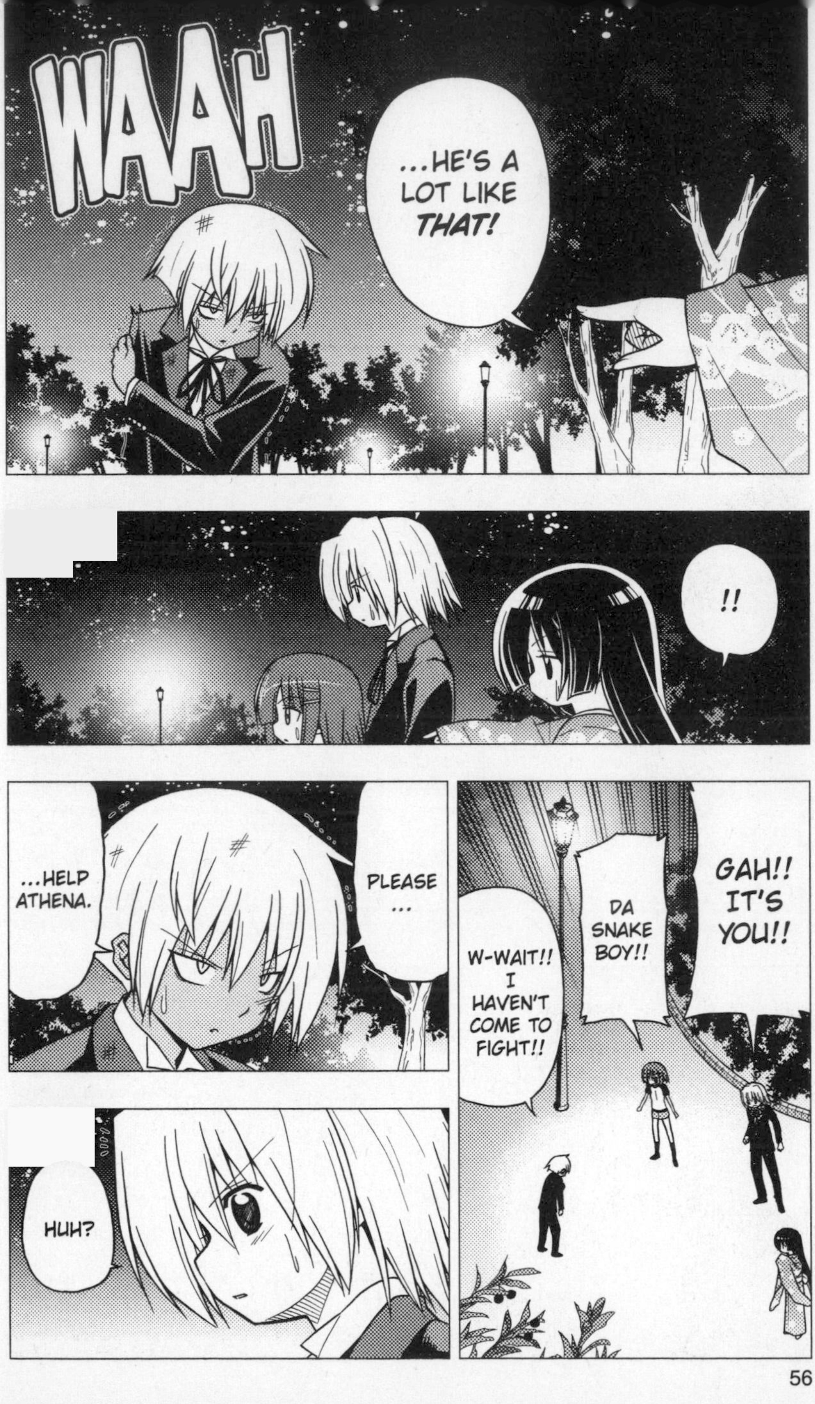
...HE'S A LOT LIKE THAT!
WAAH
!!
GAH!! IT'S YOU!!
DA SNAKE BOY!!
W-WAIT!! I HAVEN'T COME TO FIGHT!!
PLEASE ...
...HELP ATHENA.
HUH?

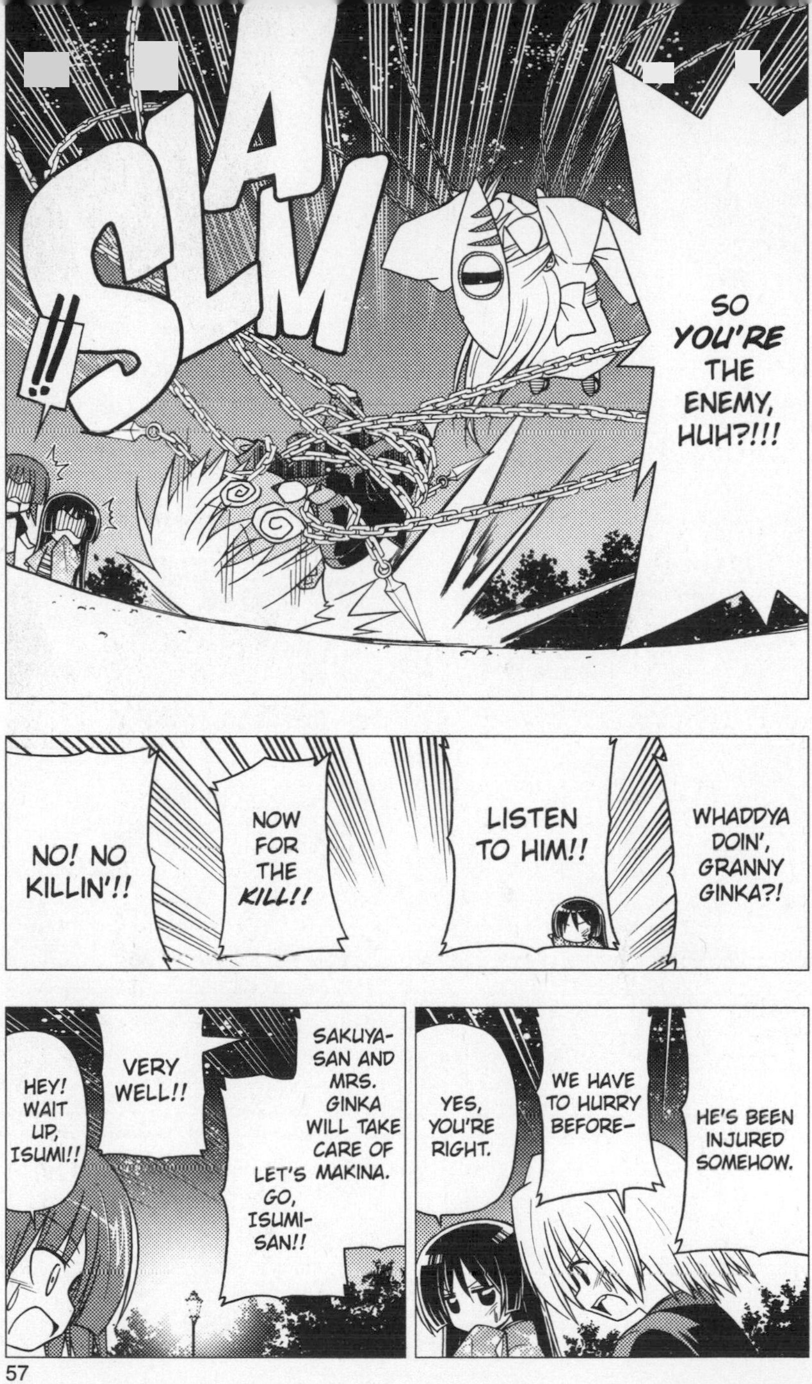
SO YOU'RE THE ENEMY, HUH?!!!
SLAM!!
WHADDYA DOIN', GRANNY GINKA?!
LISTEN TO HIM!!
NOW FOR THE KILL!!
NO! NO KILLIN'!!
HE'S BEEN INJURED SOMEHOW.
WE HAVE TO HURRY BEFORE-
YES, YOU'RE RIGHT.
SAKUYA-SAN AND MRS. GINKA WILL TAKE CARE OF MAKINA.
LET'S GO, ISUMI-SAN!!
VERY WELL!!
HEY! WAIT UP, ISUMI!!

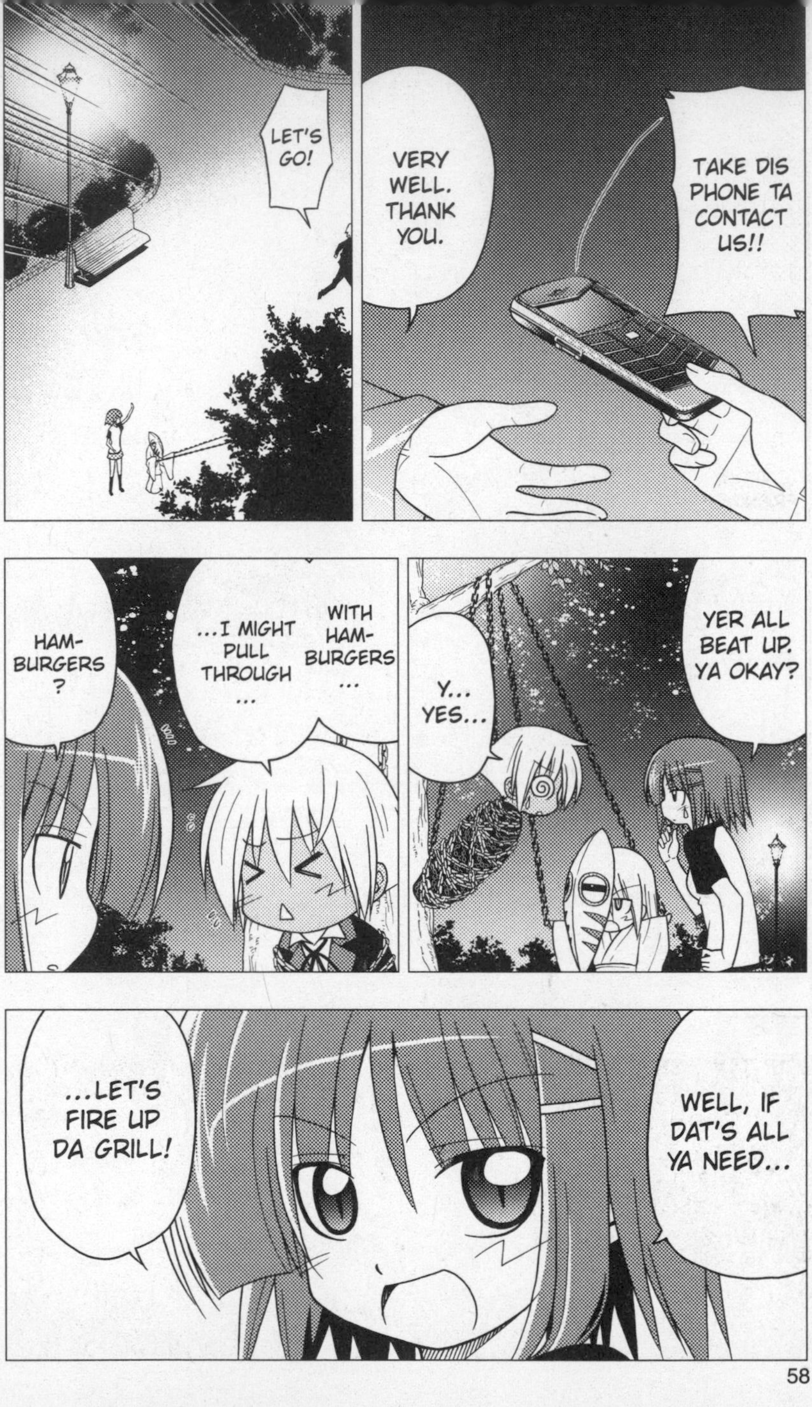
TAKE DIS PHONE TA CONTACT US!!
VERY WELL. THANK YOU.
LET'S GO!
YER ALL BEAT UP. YA OKAY?
Y... YES...
WITH HAM-BURGERS ...
...I MIGHT PULL THROUGH ...
HAM-BURGERS ?
WELL, IF DAT'S ALL YA NEED...
...LET'S FIRE UP DA GRILL!

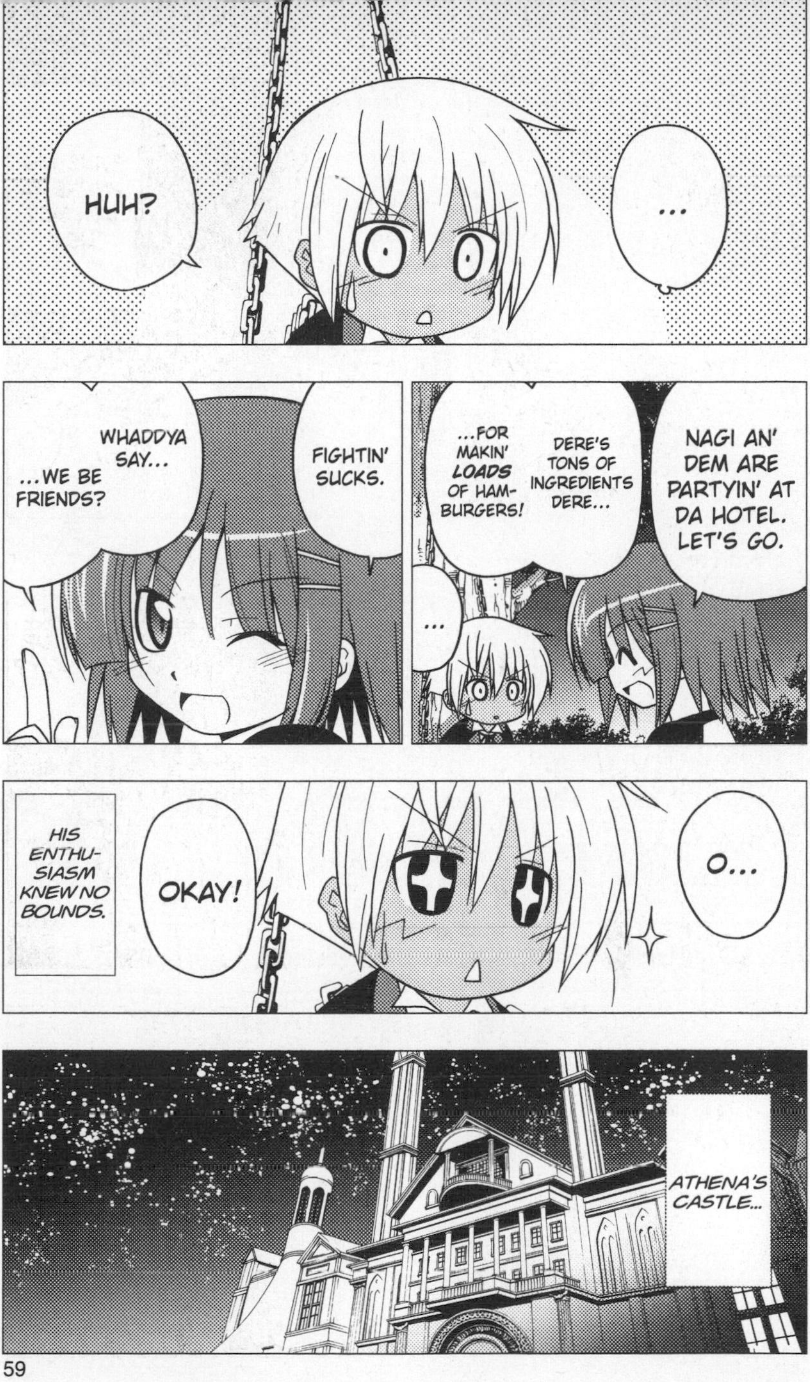
...
HUH?
NAGI AN' DEM ARE PARTYIN' AT DA HOTEL. LET'S GO.
DERE'S TONS OF INGREDIENTS DERE...
...FOR MAKIN' *LOADS* OF HAM-BURGERS!
...
FIGHTIN' SUCKS.
WHADDYA SAY...
...WE BE FRIENDS?
O...
OKAY!
HIS ENTHU-SIASM KNEW NO BOUNDS.
ATHENA'S CASTLE...

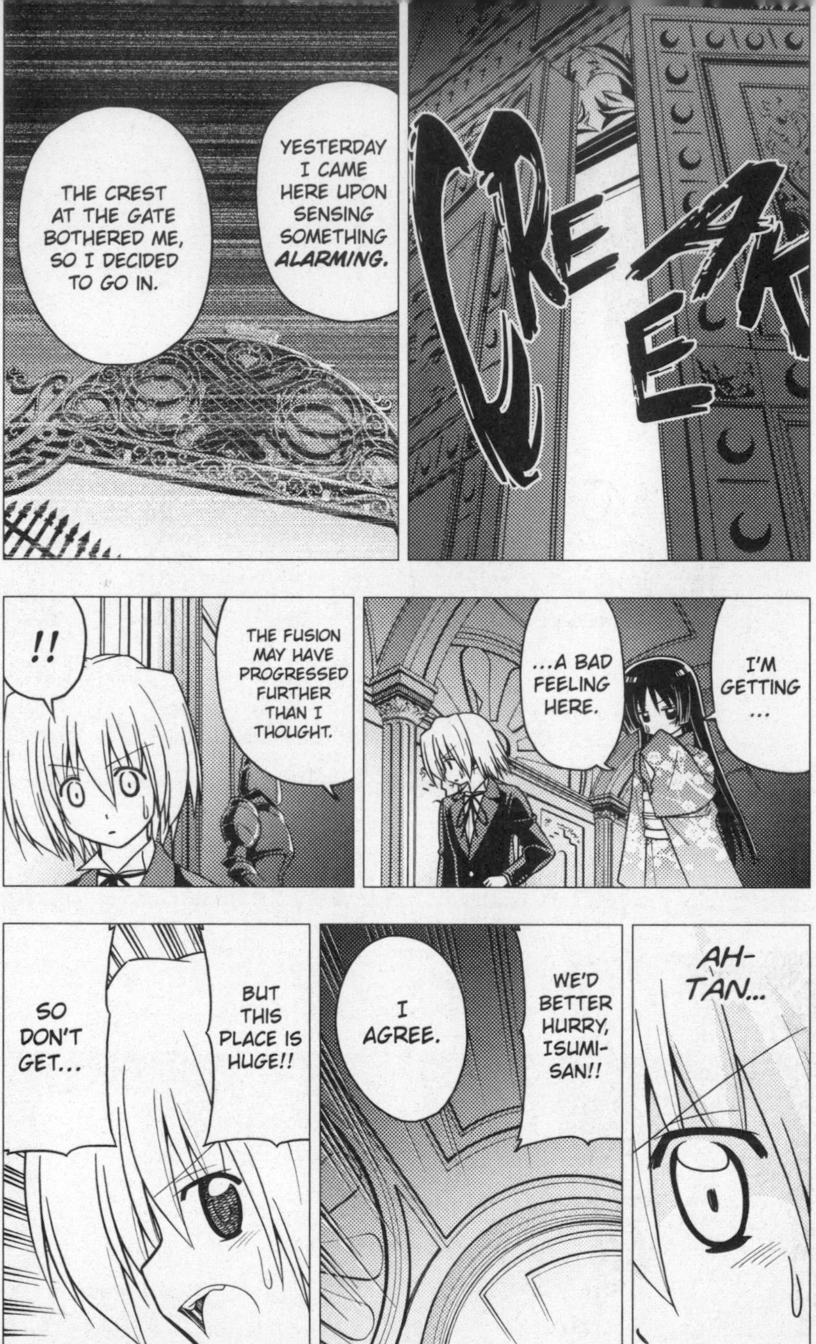
CREEAK
YESTERDAY I CAME HERE UPON SENSING SOMETHING ***ALARMING.***
THE CREST AT THE GATE BOTHERED ME, SO I DECIDED TO GO IN.
I'M GETTING...
...A BAD FEELING HERE.
THE FUSION MAY HAVE PROGRESSED FURTHER THAN I THOUGHT.
!!
AH-TAN...
WE'D BETTER HURRY, ISUMI-SAN!!
I AGREE.
BUT THIS PLACE IS HUGE!!
SO DON'T GET...

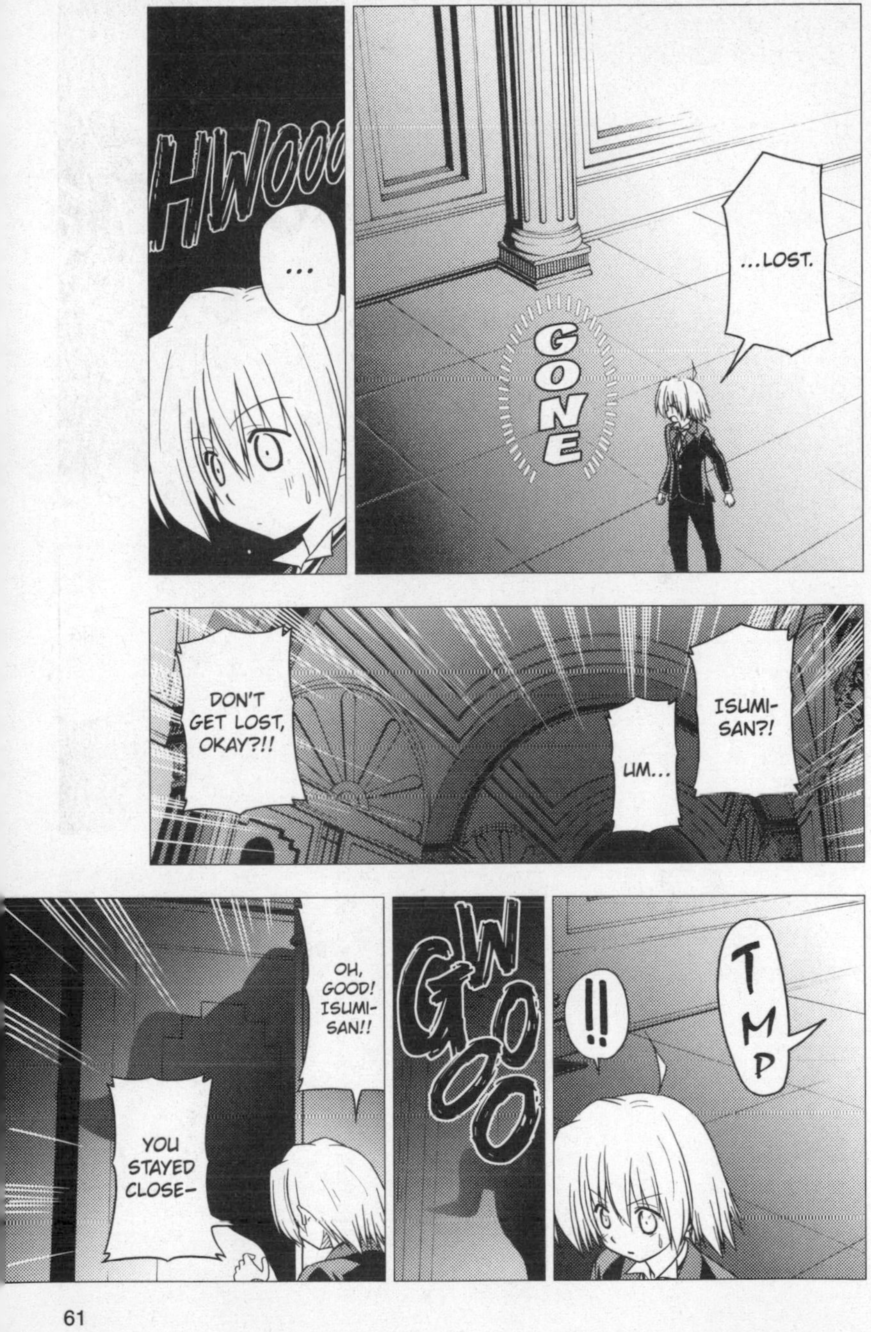
...LOST.
GONE
HWOOO
...
ISUMI-SAN?!
UM...
DON'T GET LOST, OKAY?!!
TMP
!!
GWOOOO
OH, GOOD! ISUMI-SAN!!
YOU STAYED CLOSE-

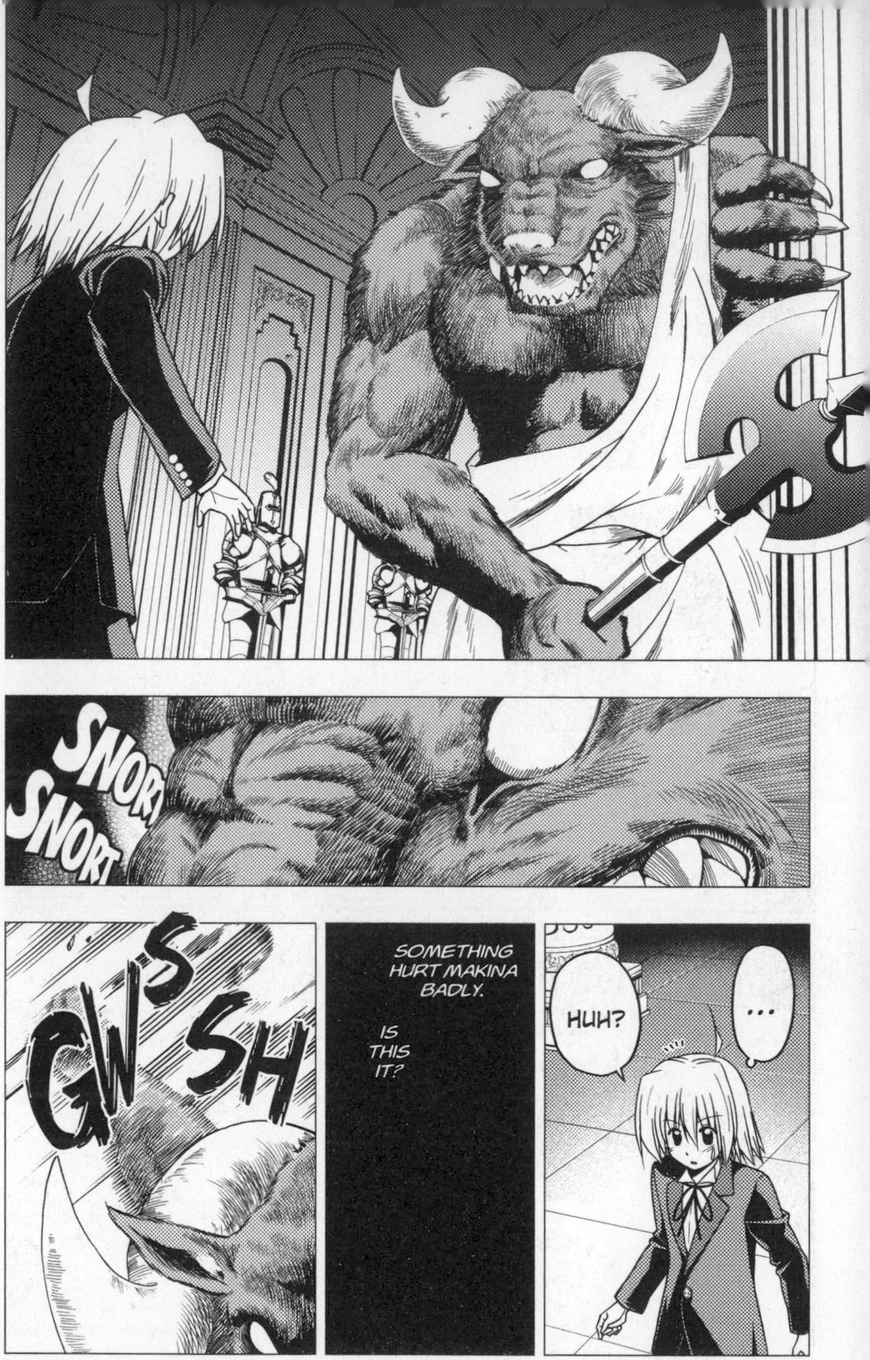
SNORT
SNORT
...
HUH?
SOMETHING HURT MAKINA BADLY.
IS THIS IT?
GWSSH

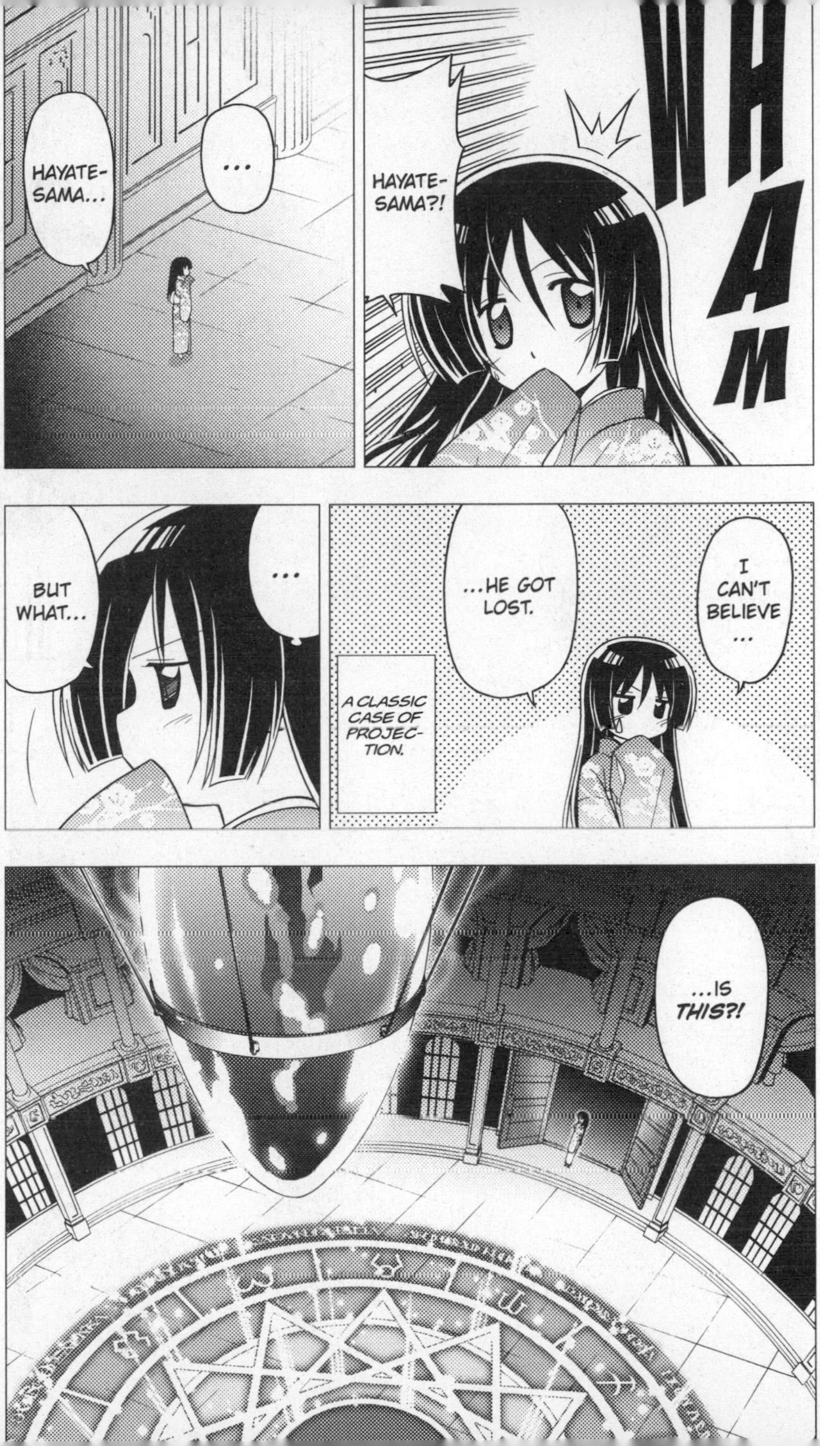
WHAM
HAYATE-SAMA?!
...
HAYATE-SAMA...
I CAN'T BELIEVE ...
...HE GOT LOST.
A CLASSIC CASE OF PROJECTION.
...
BUT WHAT...
...IS THIS?!

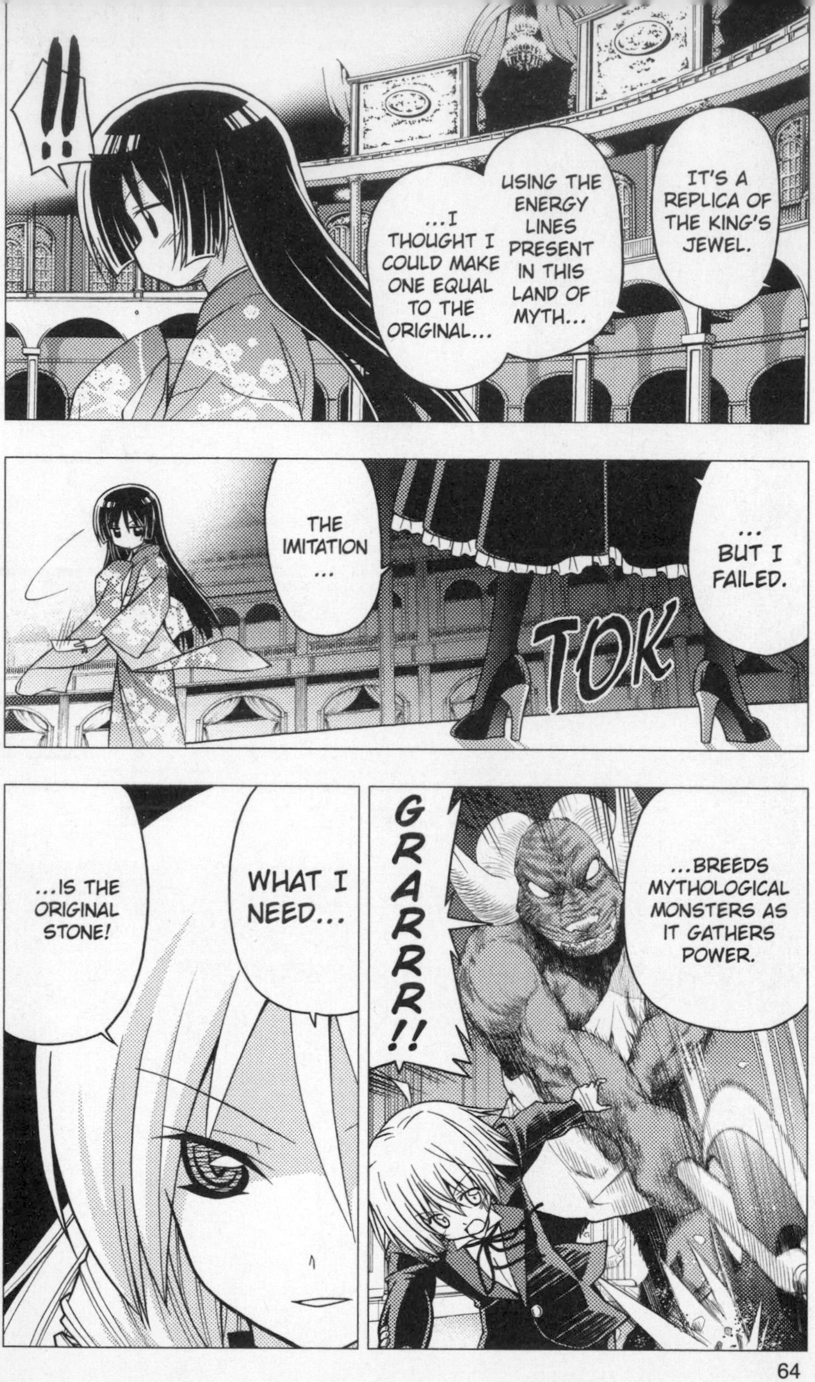
IT'S A REPLICA OF THE KING'S JEWEL.
USING THE ENERGY LINES PRESENT IN THIS LAND OF MYTH...
...I THOUGHT I COULD MAKE ONE EQUAL TO THE ORIGINAL...
!!
... BUT I FAILED.
TOK
THE IMITATION ...
...BREEDS MYTHOLOGICAL MONSTERS AS IT GATHERS POWER.
GRARRR!!
WHAT I NEED...
...IS THE ORIGINAL STONE!

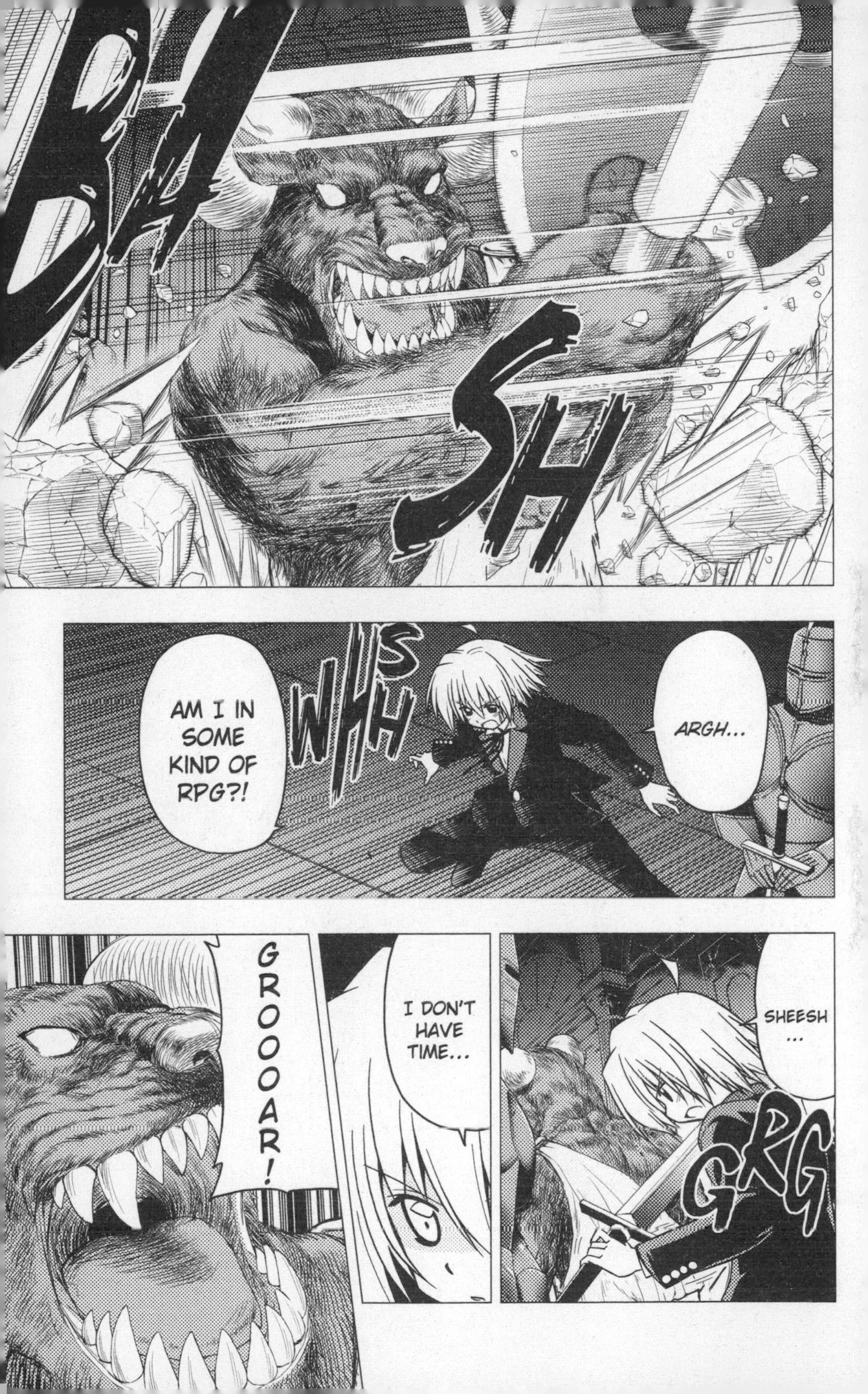
BSH
SH
ARGH...
WHSH
AM I IN SOME KIND OF RPG?!
SHEESH...
GRG
I DON'T HAVE TIME...
GROOOOAR!

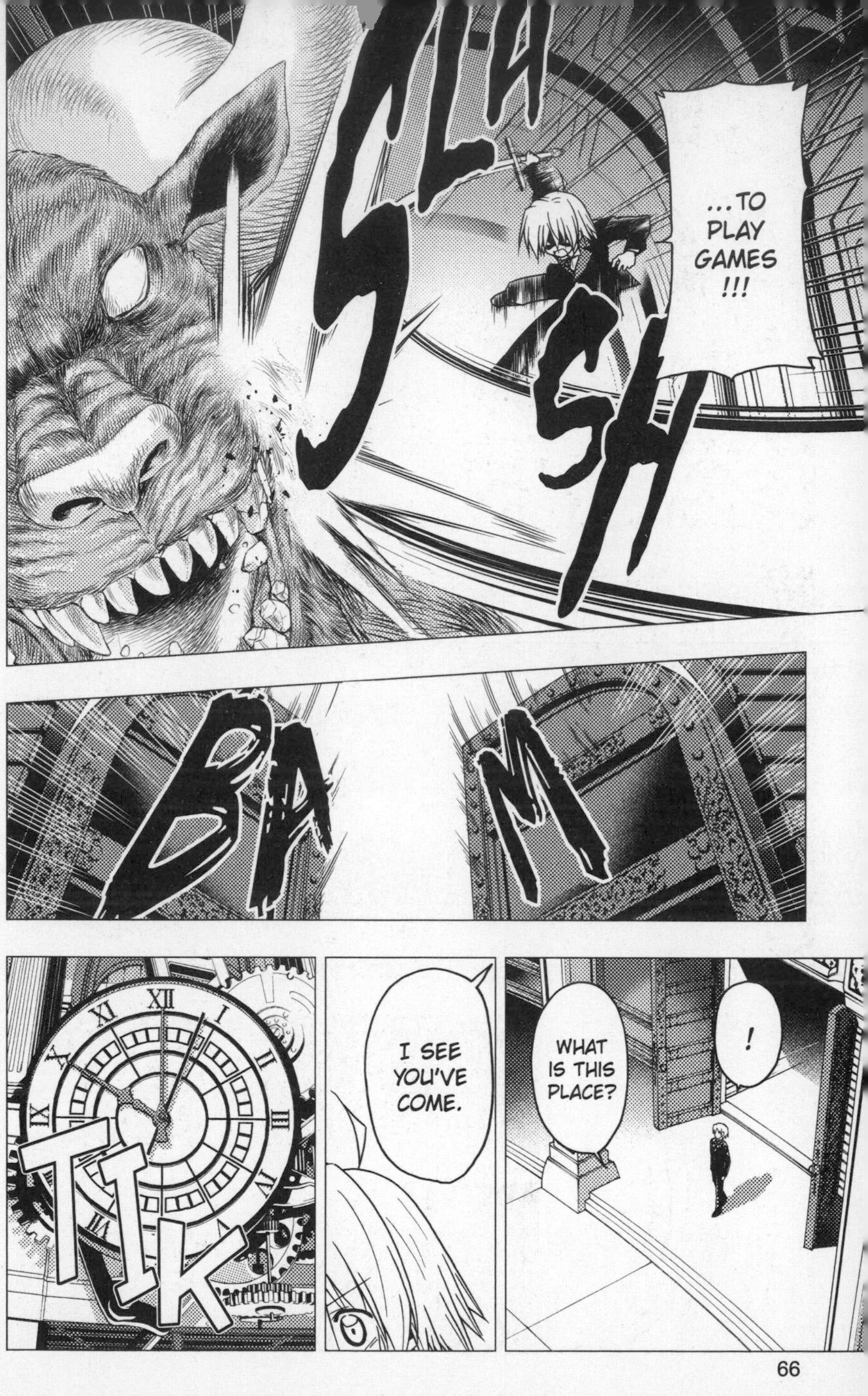
...TO PLAY GAMES !!!
SLASH
BAM
!
WHAT IS THIS PLACE?
I SEE YOU'VE COME.
TIK

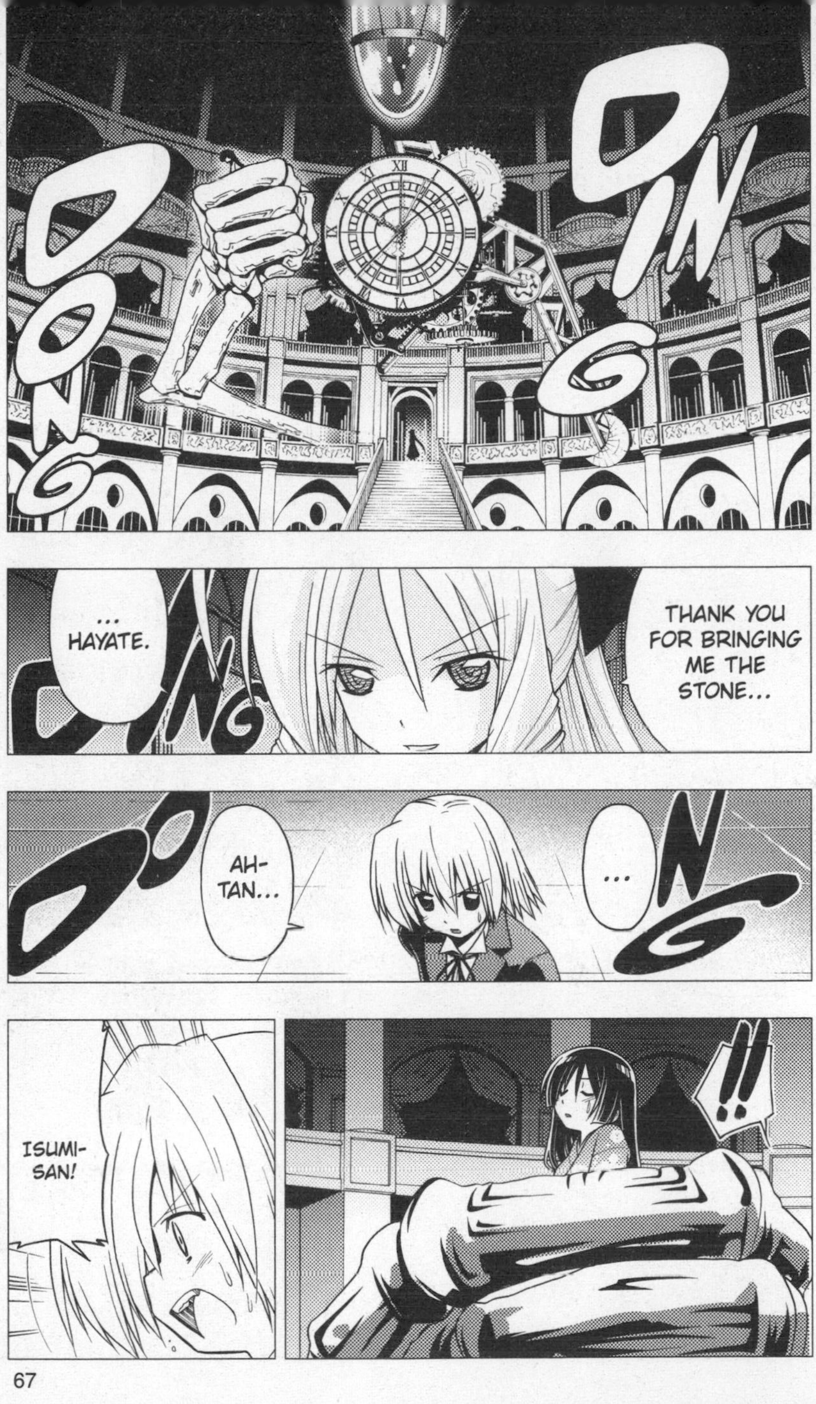
DING
DONG
THANK YOU FOR BRINGING ME THE STONE...
...HAYATE.
...
AH-TAN...
DONG
!!
ISUMI-SAN!

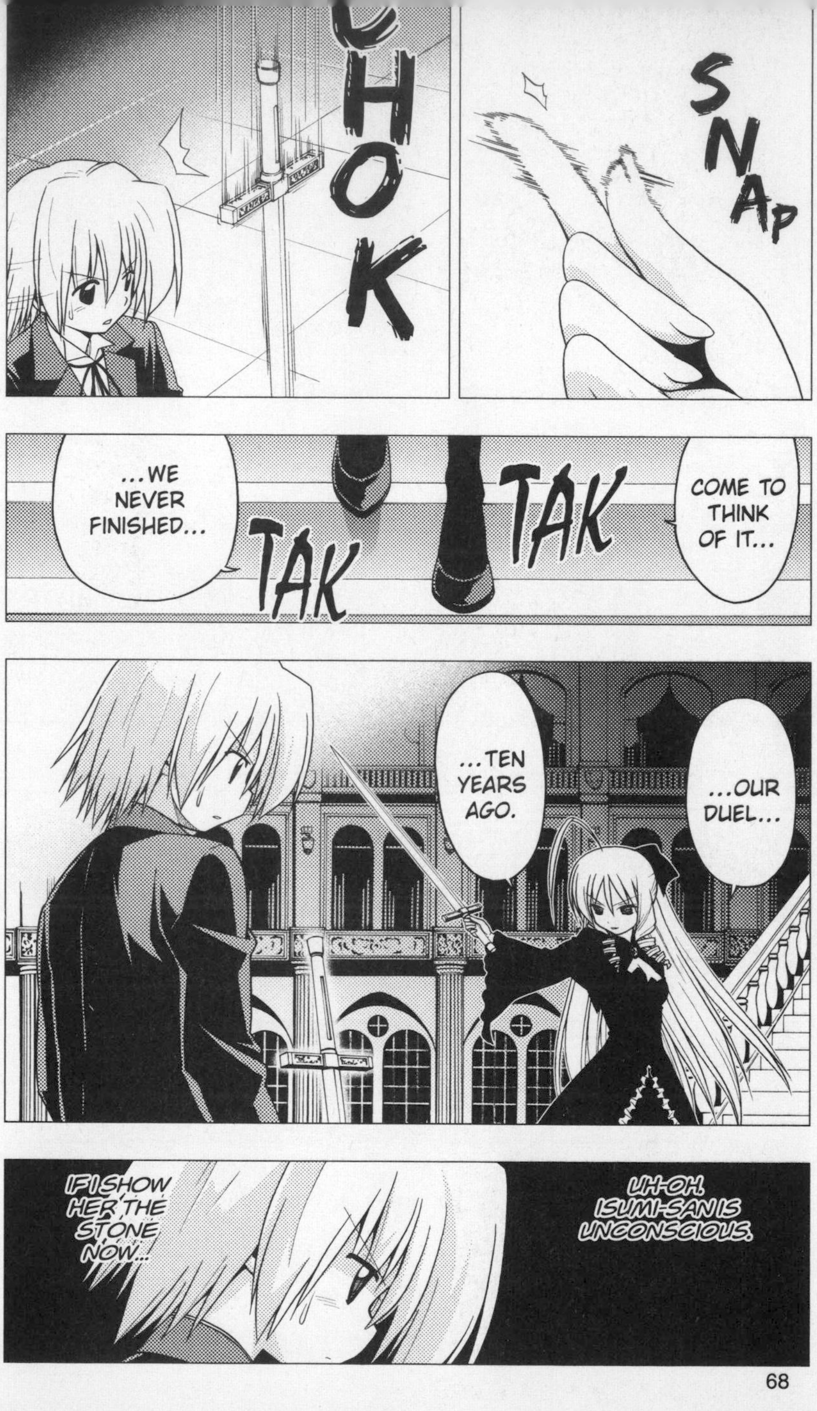
SNAP
CHOK
COME TO THINK OF IT...
TAK
TAK
...WE NEVER FINISHED...
...OUR DUEL...
...TEN YEARS AGO.
UH-OH. ISUMI-SAN IS UNCONSCIOUS.
IF I SHOW HER THE STONE NOW...

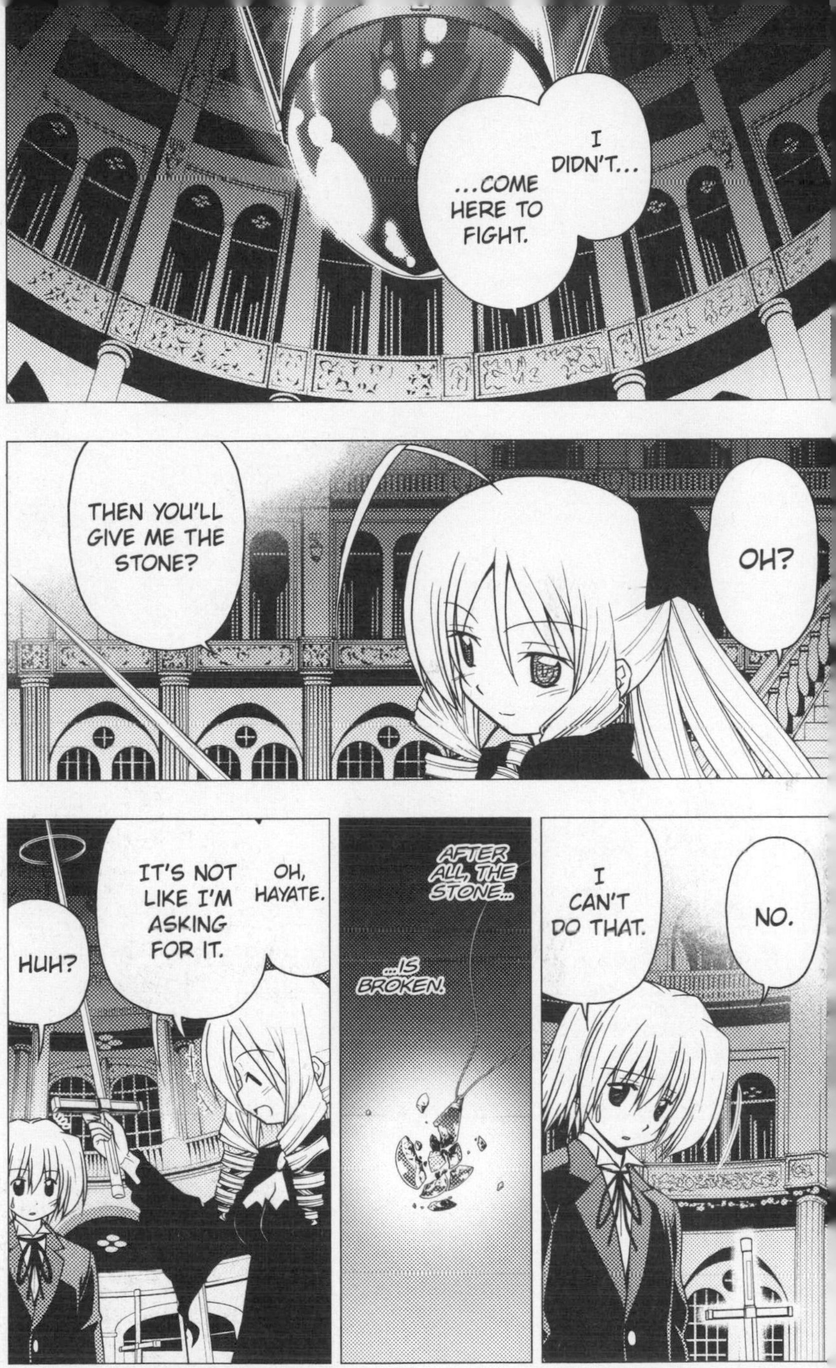
I DIDN'T...
...COME HERE TO FIGHT.
OH?
THEN YOU'LL GIVE ME THE STONE?
NO.
I CAN'T DO THAT.
AFTER ALL, THE STONE...
...IS BROKEN.
OH, HAYATE.
IT'S NOT LIKE I'M ASKING FOR IT.
HUH?

Episode 5: "The First Word"

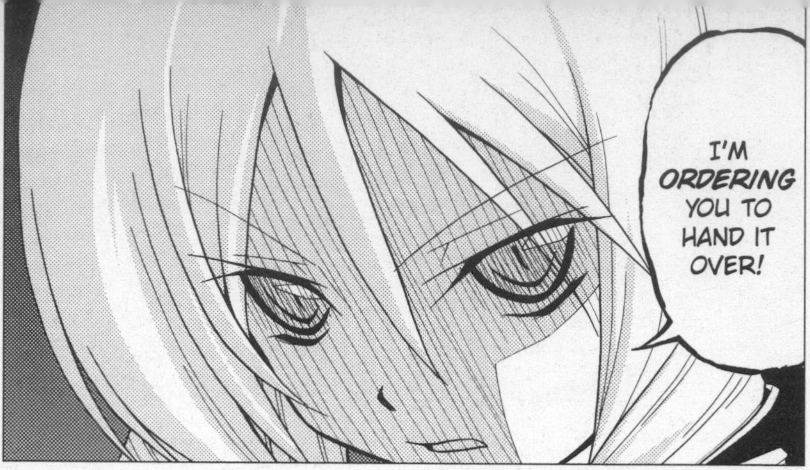
I'M ORDERING YOU TO HAND IT OVER!

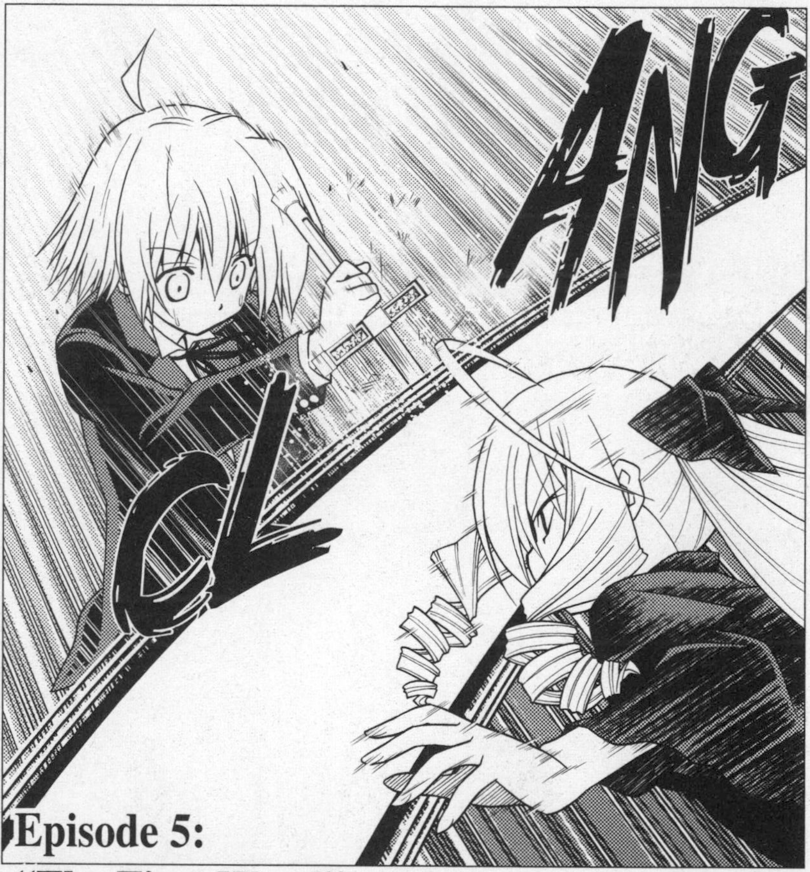
CLANG

Episode 5: "The First Word"

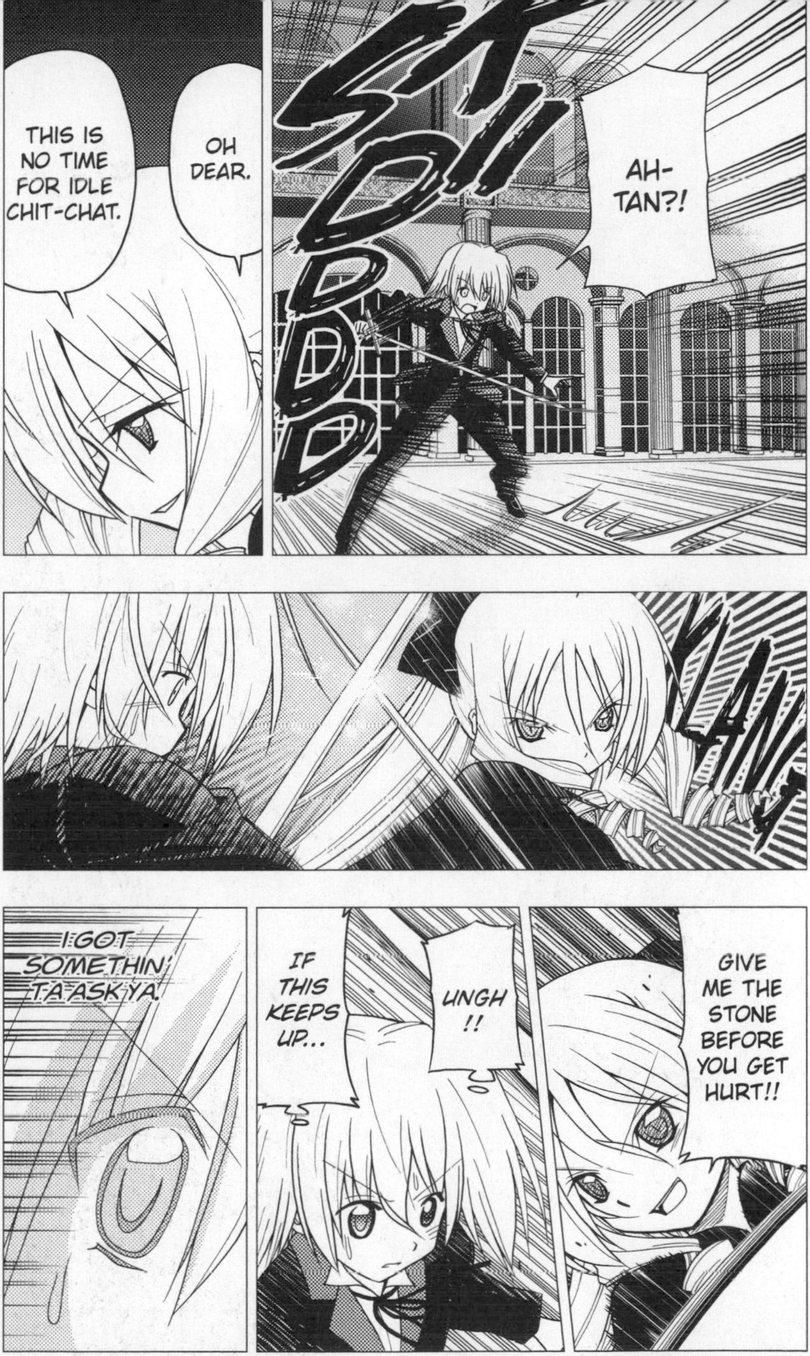
AH-TAN?!
OH DEAR.
THIS IS NO TIME FOR IDLE CHIT-CHAT.
GIVE ME THE STONE BEFORE YOU GET HURT!!
UNGH !!
IF THIS KEEPS UP...
I GOT SOMETHIN' TA ASK YA.

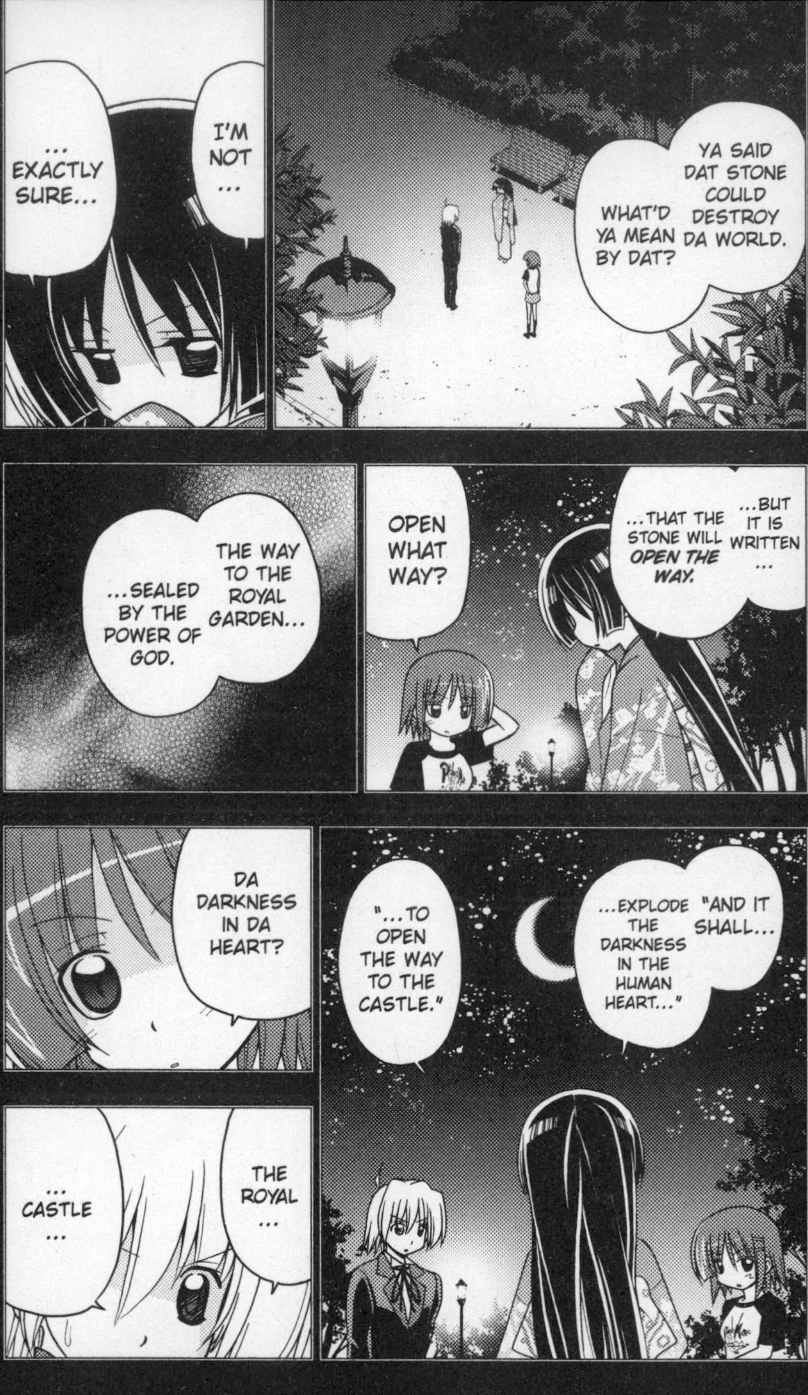
YA SAID DAT STONE COULD DESTROY DA WORLD.
WHAT'D YA MEAN BY DAT?
I'M NOT ...
... EXACTLY SURE...
...BUT IT IS WRITTEN ...
...THAT THE STONE WILL *OPEN THE WAY.*
OPEN WHAT WAY?
THE WAY TO THE ROYAL GARDEN...
...SEALED BY THE POWER OF GOD.
"AND IT SHALL...
...EXPLODE THE DARKNESS IN THE HUMAN HEART..."
"...TO OPEN THE WAY TO THE CASTLE."
DA DARKNESS IN DA HEART?
THE ROYAL ...
... CASTLE ...

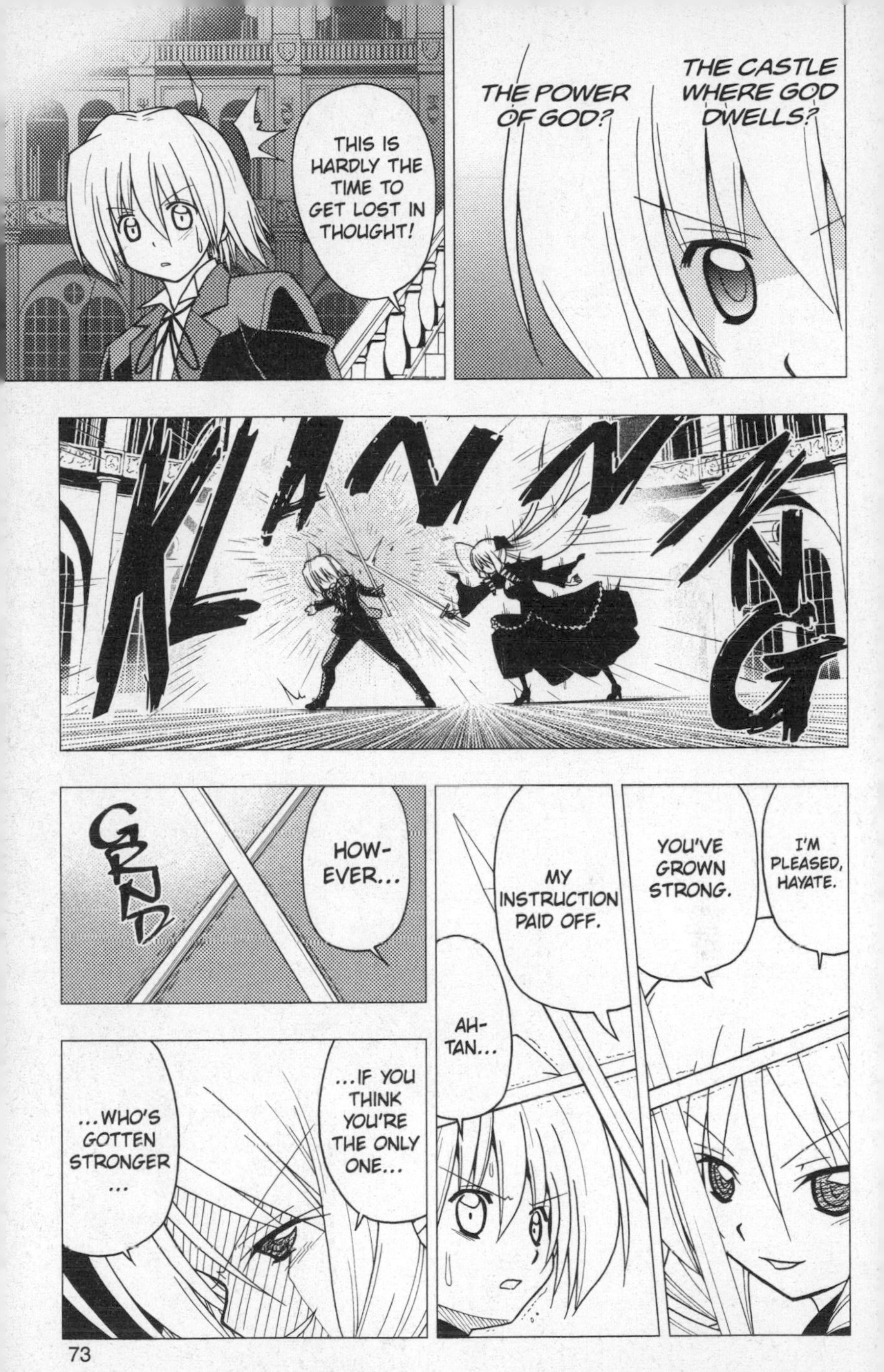
THE CASTLE WHERE GOD DWELLS?
THE POWER OF GOD?
THIS IS HARDLY THE TIME TO GET LOST IN THOUGHT!
KLANNNG
I'M PLEASED, HAYATE.
YOU'VE GROWN STRONG.
MY INSTRUCTION PAID OFF.
AH-TAN...
HOW-EVER...
GRRD
...IF YOU THINK YOU'RE THE ONLY ONE...
...WHO'S GOTTEN STRONGER ...

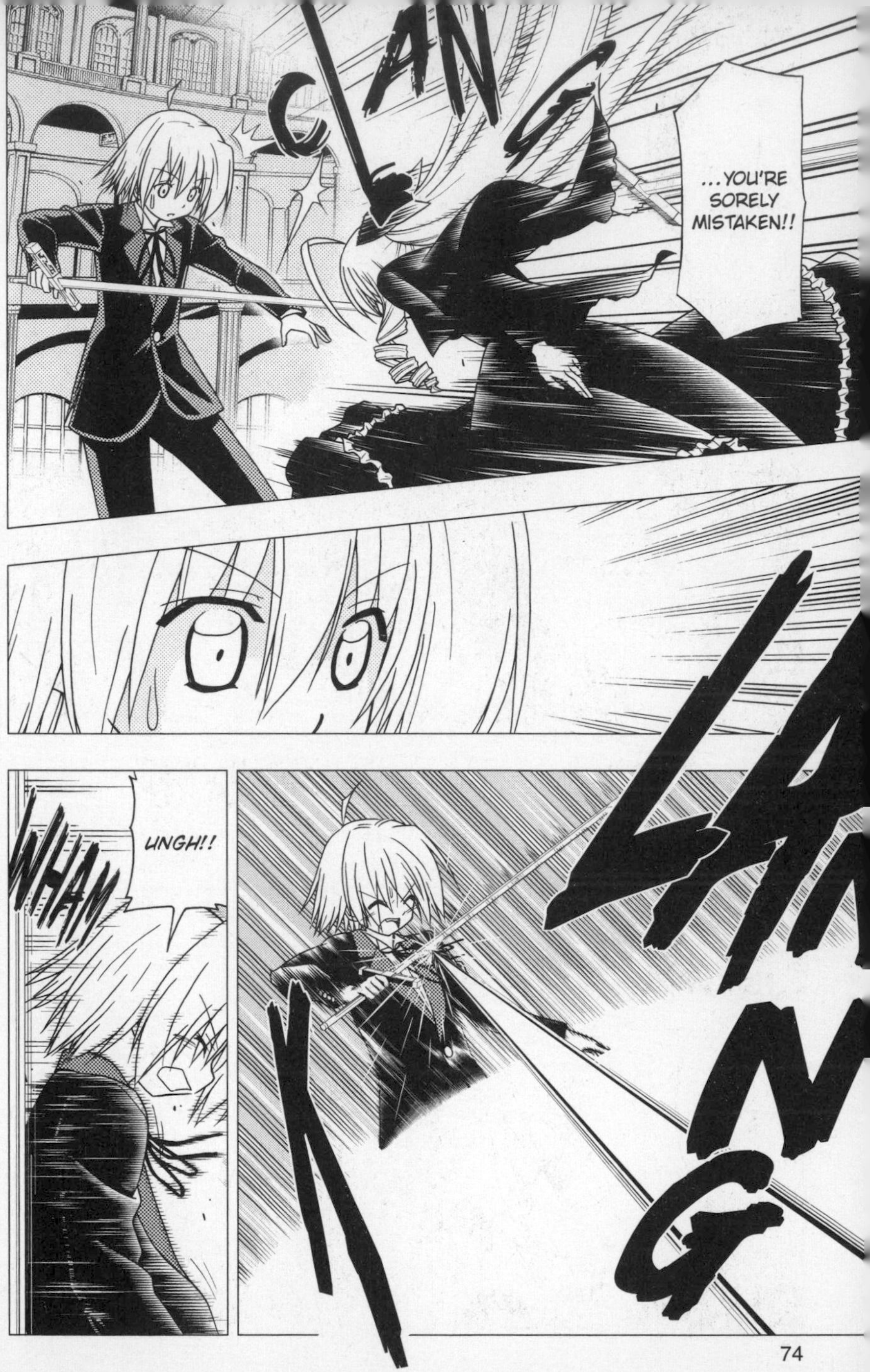
CLANG
...YOU'RE SORELY MISTAKEN!!
UNGH!!
WHAM

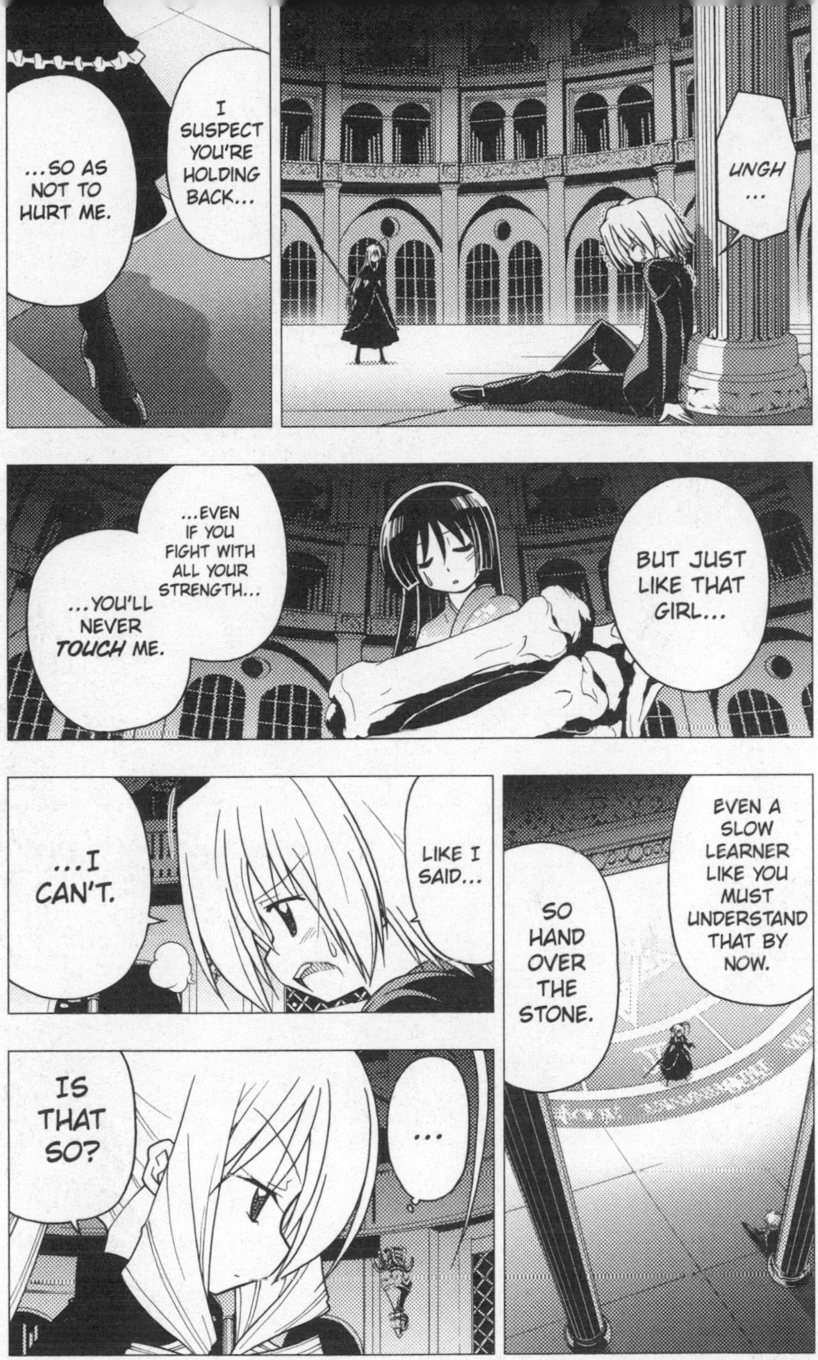
UNGH ...
I SUSPECT YOU'RE HOLDING BACK...
...SO AS NOT TO HURT ME.
BUT JUST LIKE THAT GIRL...
...EVEN IF YOU FIGHT WITH ALL YOUR STRENGTH...
...YOU'LL NEVER *TOUCH* ME.
EVEN A SLOW LEARNER LIKE YOU MUST UNDERSTAND THAT BY NOW.
SO HAND OVER THE STONE.
LIKE I SAID...
...I CAN'T.
...
IS THAT SO?

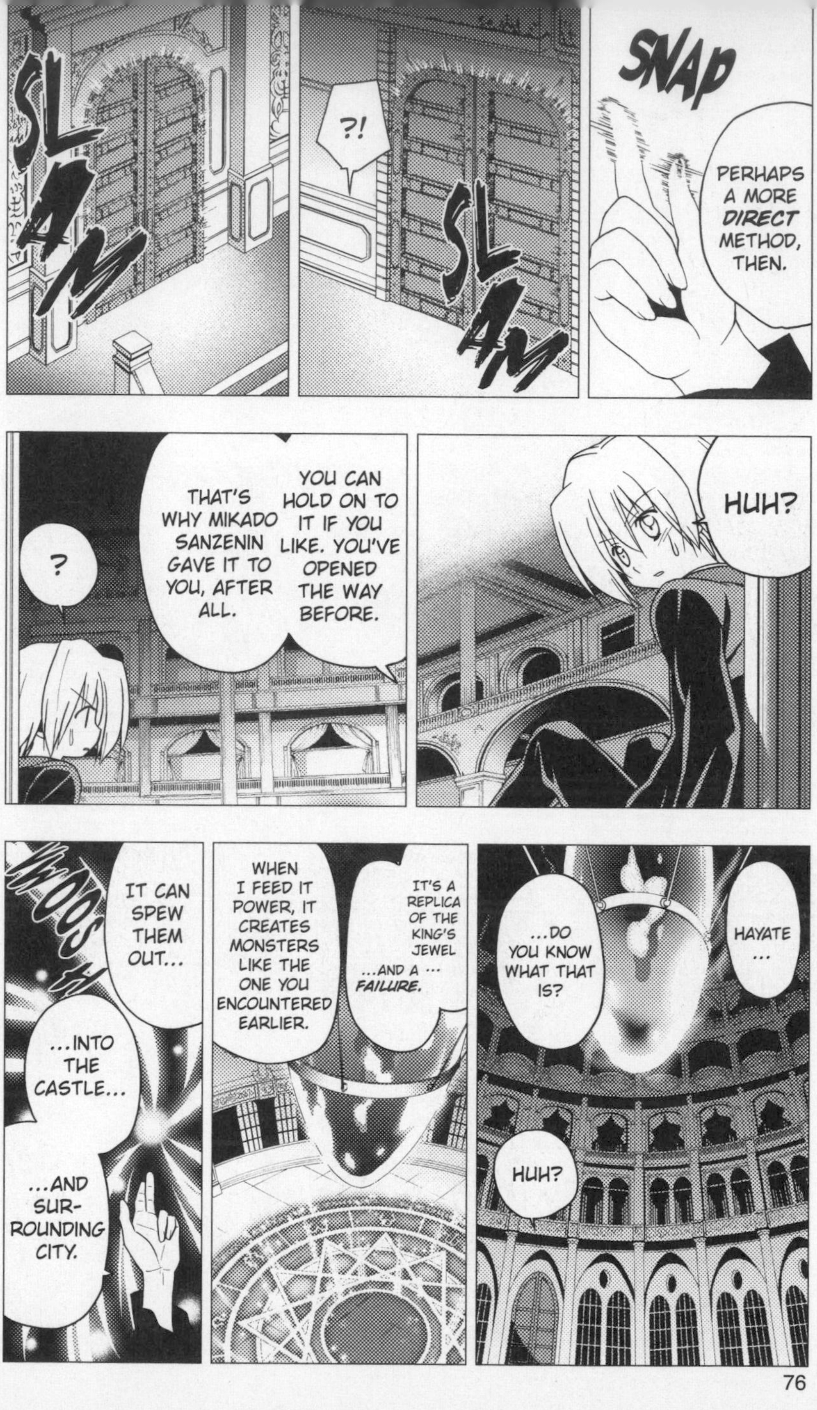
SNAP
PERHAPS A MORE *DIRECT* METHOD, THEN.
?!
SLAM
SLAM
HUH?
YOU CAN HOLD ON TO IT IF YOU LIKE. YOU'VE OPENED THE WAY BEFORE.
THAT'S WHY MIKADO SANZENIN GAVE IT TO YOU, AFTER ALL.
?
HAYATE...
...DO YOU KNOW WHAT THAT IS?
HUH?
IT'S A REPLICA OF THE KING'S JEWEL
...AND A ... *FAILURE.*
WHEN I FEED IT POWER, IT CREATES MONSTERS LIKE THE ONE YOU ENCOUNTERED EARLIER.
IT CAN SPEW THEM OUT...
...INTO THE CASTLE...
...AND SUR-ROUNDING CITY.

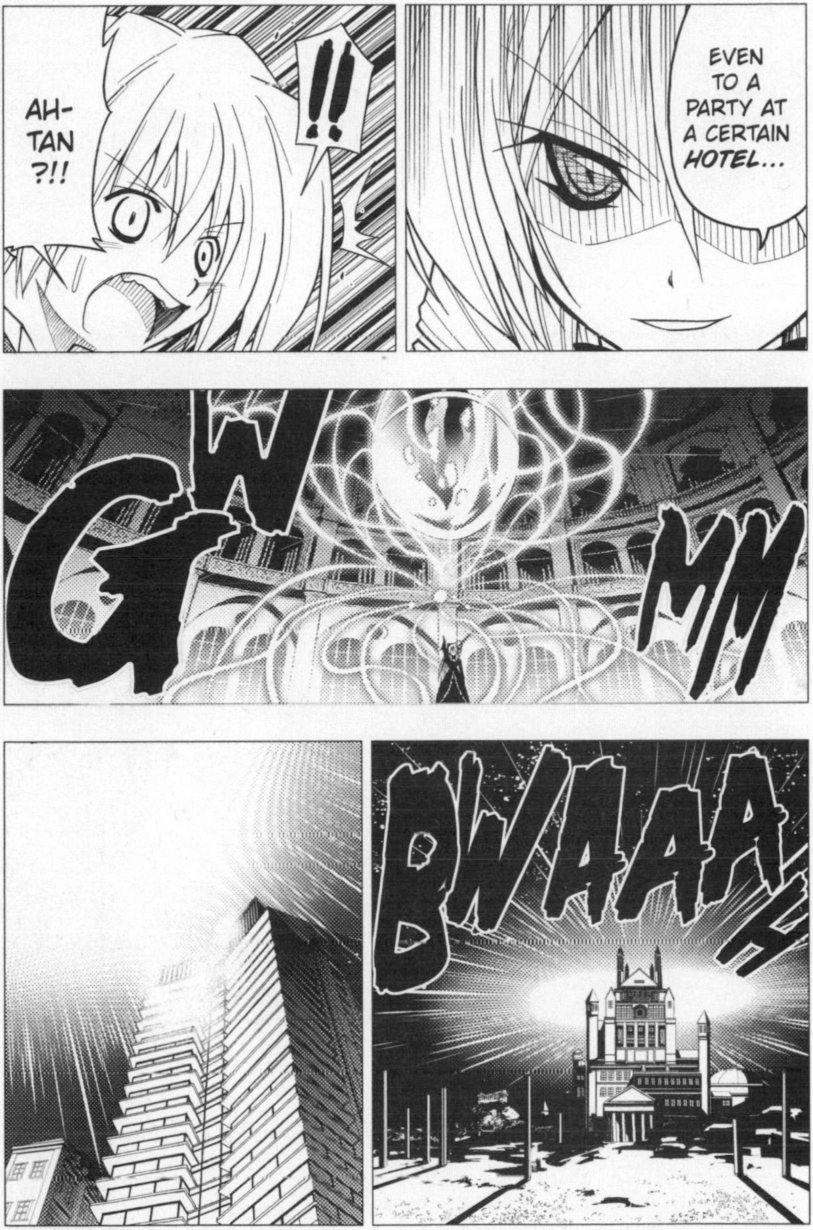
EVEN TO A PARTY AT A CERTAIN HOTEL...
!!
AH-TAN ?!!
GWMM
BWAAA

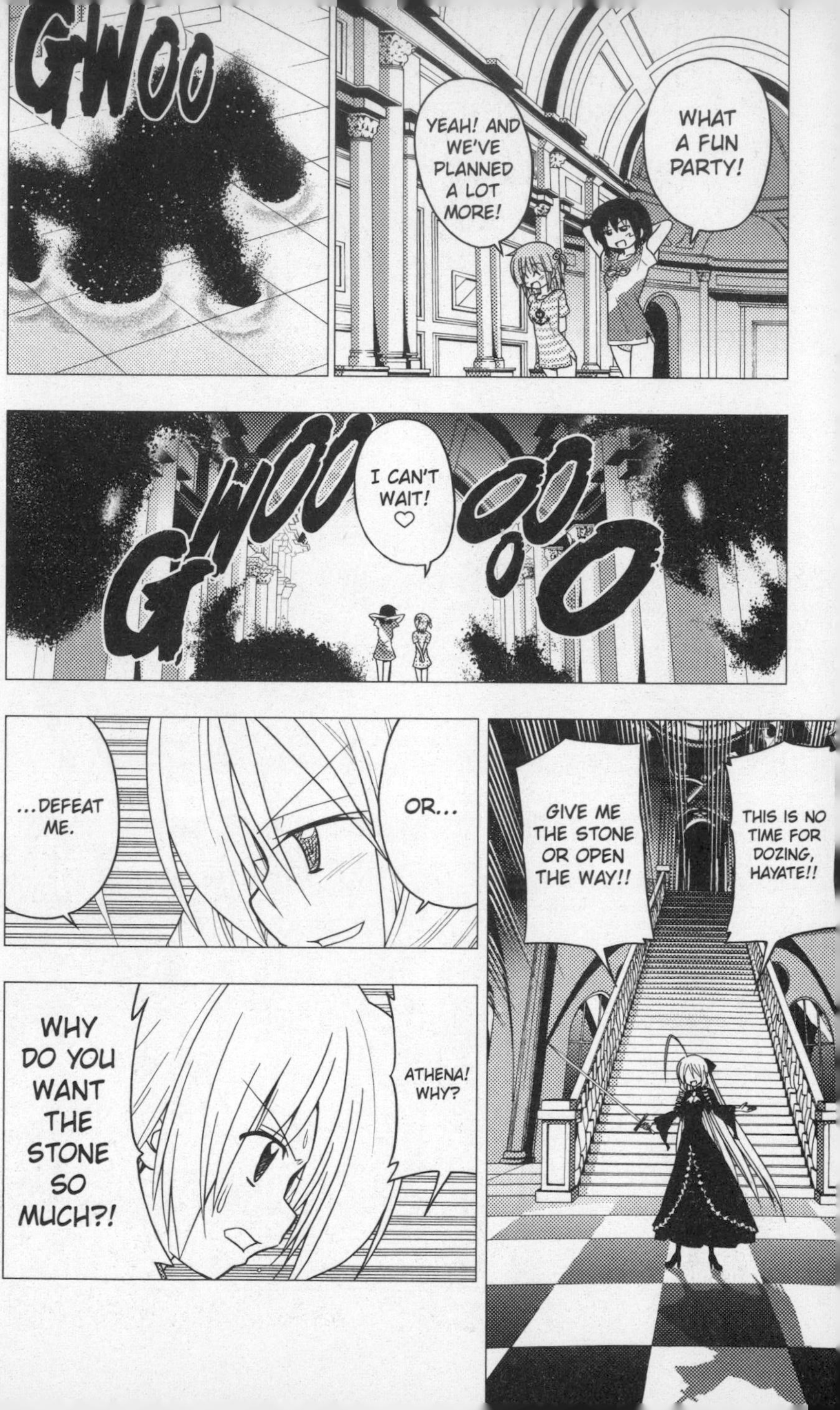
WHAT A FUN PARTY!
YEAH! AND WE'VE PLANNED A LOT MORE!
GWOO
I CAN'T WAIT! ♥
GWOOOOOOO
THIS IS NO TIME FOR DOZING, HAYATE!!
GIVE ME THE STONE OR OPEN THE WAY!!
OR...
...DEFEAT ME.
ATHENA! WHY?
WHY DO YOU WANT THE STONE SO MUCH?!

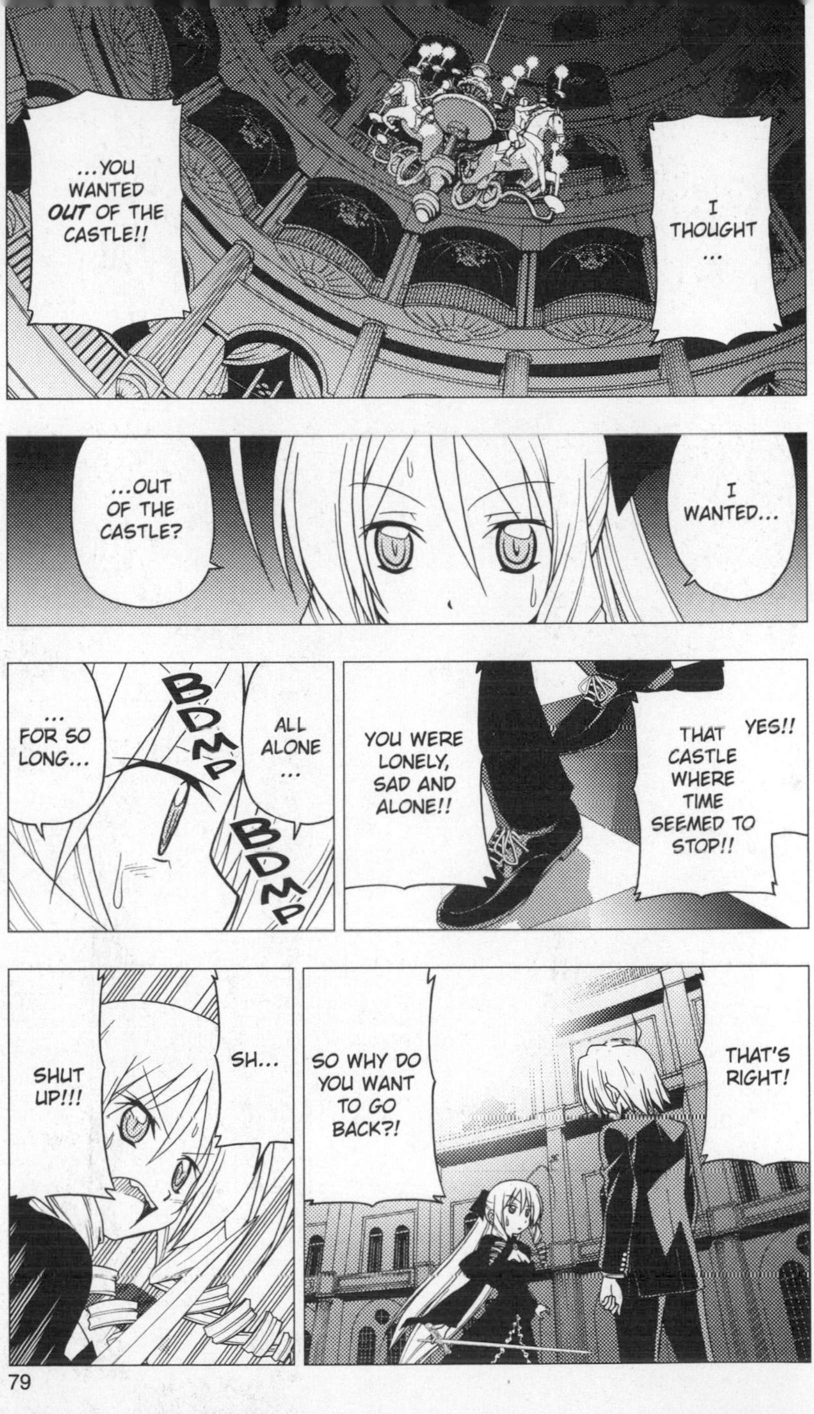
I THOUGHT ...
...YOU WANTED OUT OF THE CASTLE!!
I WANTED...
...OUT OF THE CASTLE?
YES!!
THAT CASTLE WHERE TIME SEEMED TO STOP!!
YOU WERE LONELY, SAD AND ALONE!!
ALL ALONE ...
BDMP
BDMP
... FOR SO LONG...
THAT'S RIGHT!
SO WHY DO YOU WANT TO GO BACK?!
SH...
SHUT UP!!!

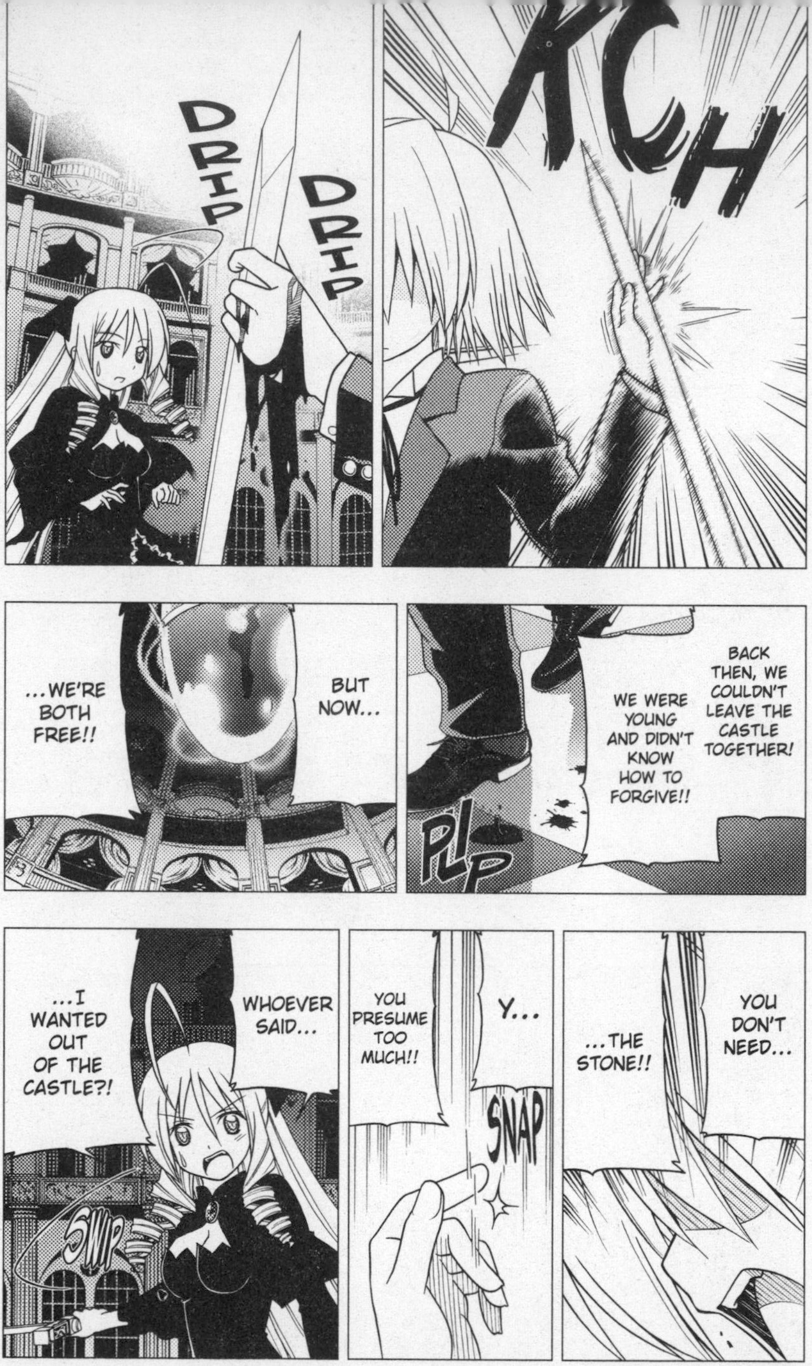
KCH
DRIP
DRIP
BACK THEN, WE COULDN'T LEAVE THE CASTLE TOGETHER!
WE WERE YOUNG AND DIDN'T KNOW HOW TO FORGIVE!!
PLIP
BUT NOW...
...WE'RE BOTH FREE!!
YOU DON'T NEED...
...THE STONE!!
Y...
YOU PRESUME TOO MUCH!!
SNAP
WHOEVER SAID...
...I WANTED OUT OF THE CASTLE?!
SWIP

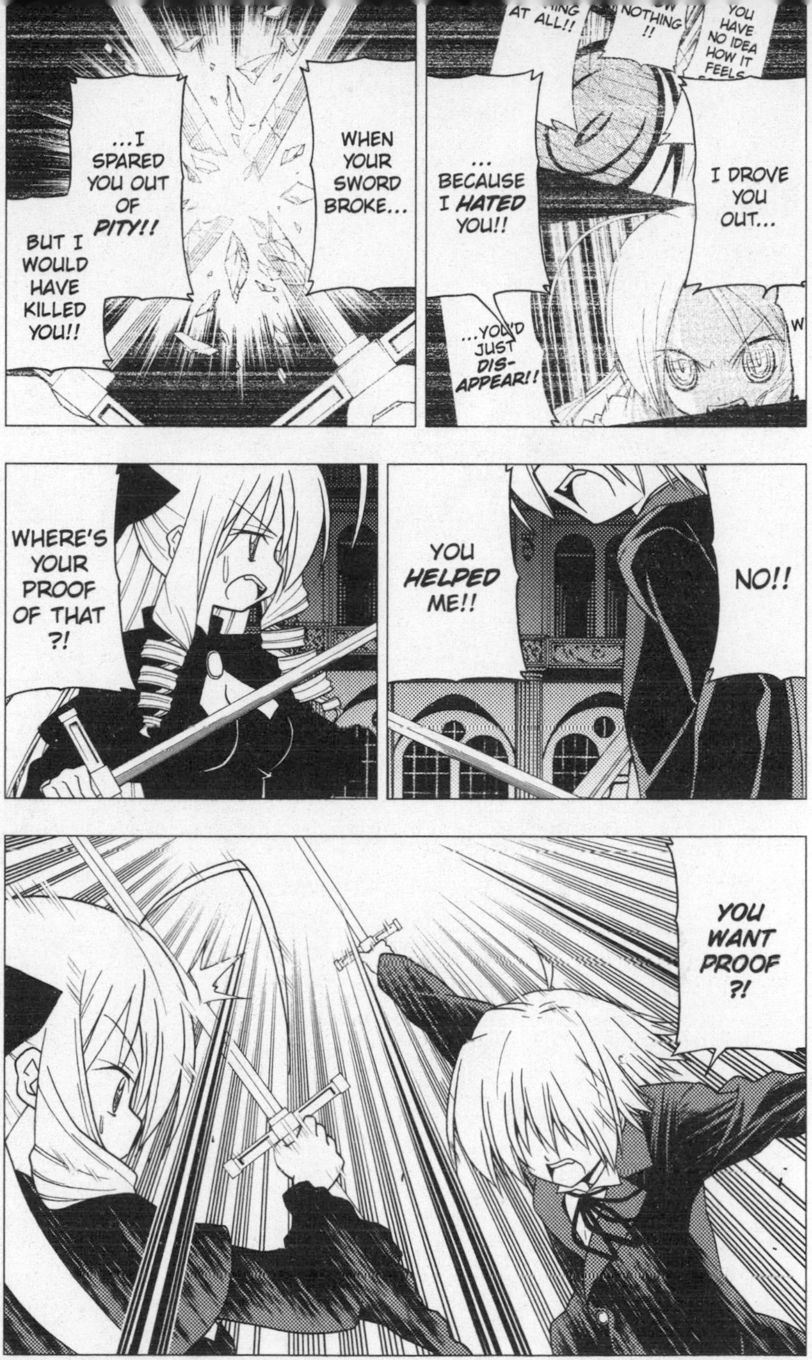
YOU HAVE NO IDEA HOW IT FEELS
NOTHING !!
AT ALL!!
I DROVE YOU OUT...
...BECAUSE I *HATED* YOU!!
...YOU'D JUST *DIS-APPEAR!!*
WHEN YOUR SWORD BROKE...
...I SPARED YOU OUT OF *PITY!!*
BUT I WOULD HAVE KILLED YOU!!
NO!!
YOU *HELPED* ME!!
WHERE'S YOUR PROOF OF THAT ?!
YOU WANT PROOF ?!

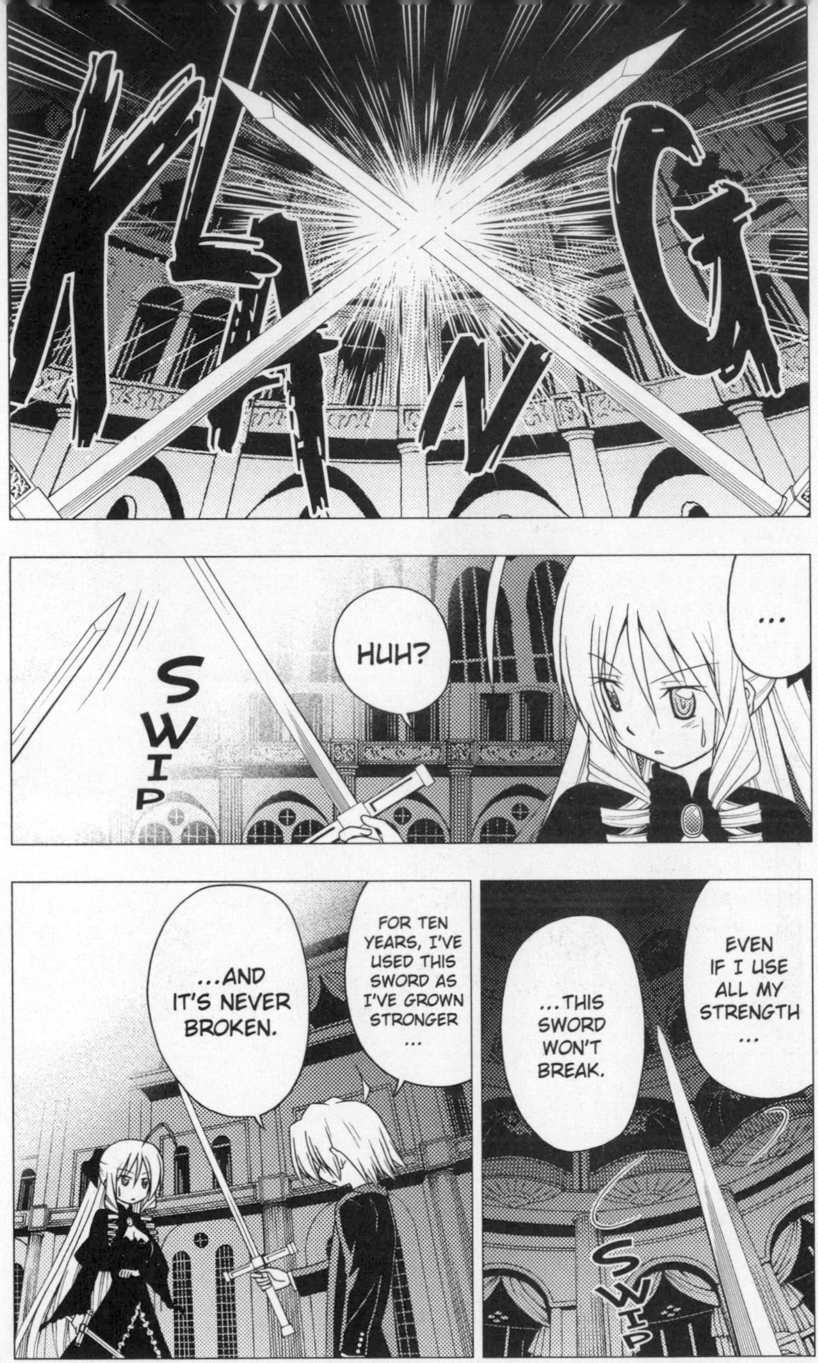
KLANG
...
HUH?
SWIP
EVEN IF I USE ALL MY STRENGTH ...
...THIS SWORD WON'T BREAK.
SWIP
FOR TEN YEARS, I'VE USED THIS SWORD AS I'VE GROWN STRONGER ...
...AND IT'S NEVER BROKEN.

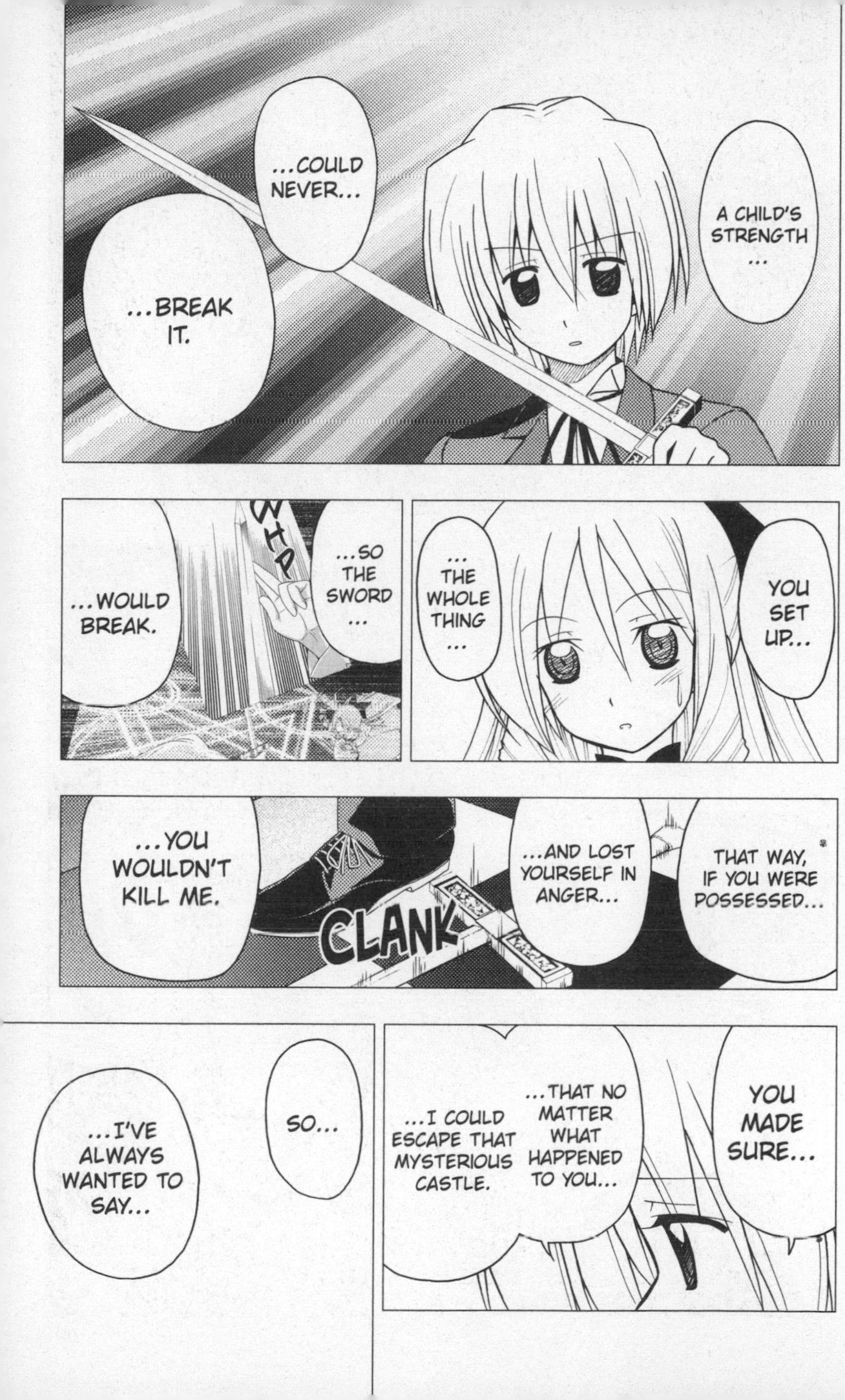
A CHILD'S STRENGTH ...
...COULD NEVER...
...BREAK IT.
YOU SET UP...
... THE WHOLE THING ...
...SO THE SWORD ...
WHIP
...WOULD BREAK.
THAT WAY, IF YOU WERE POSSESSED...
...AND LOST YOURSELF IN ANGER...
CLANK
...YOU WOULDN'T KILL ME.
YOU MADE SURE...
...THAT NO MATTER WHAT HAPPENED TO YOU...
...I COULD ESCAPE THAT MYSTERIOUS CASTLE.
SO...
...I'VE ALWAYS WANTED TO SAY...

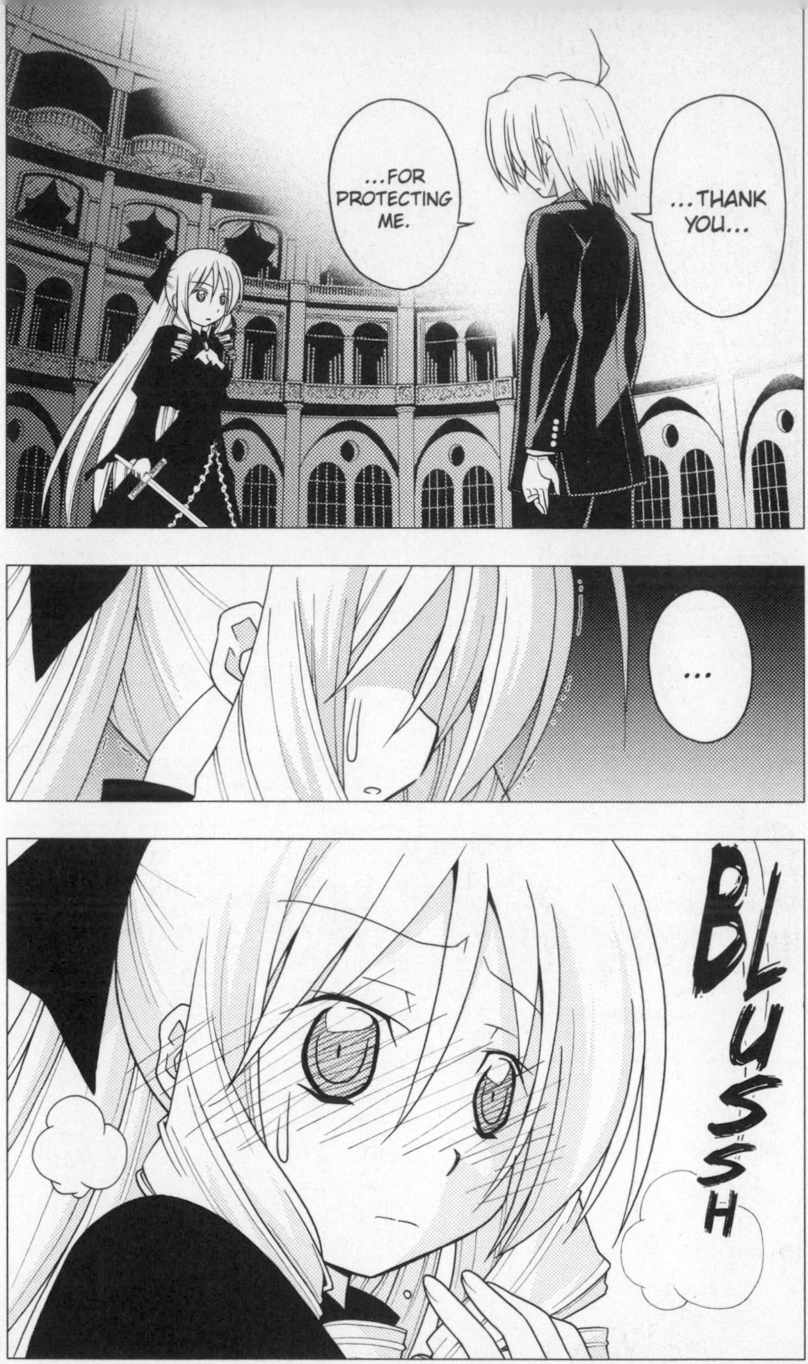
...THANK YOU...
...FOR PROTECTING ME.
...
BLUSSH

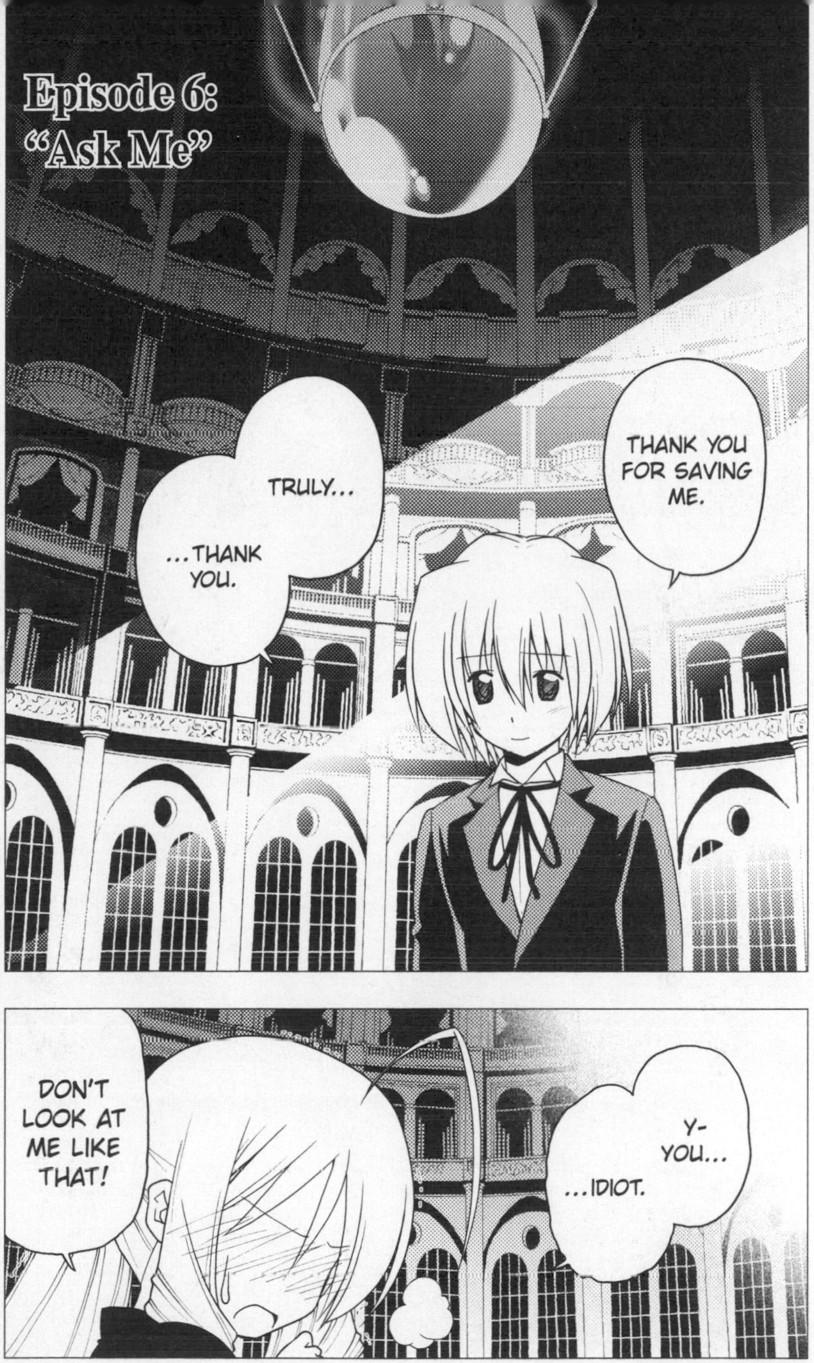
Episode 6: "Ask Me"
THANK YOU FOR SAVING ME.
TRULY... ...THANK YOU.
Y- YOU... ...IDIOT.
DON'T LOOK AT ME LIKE THAT!

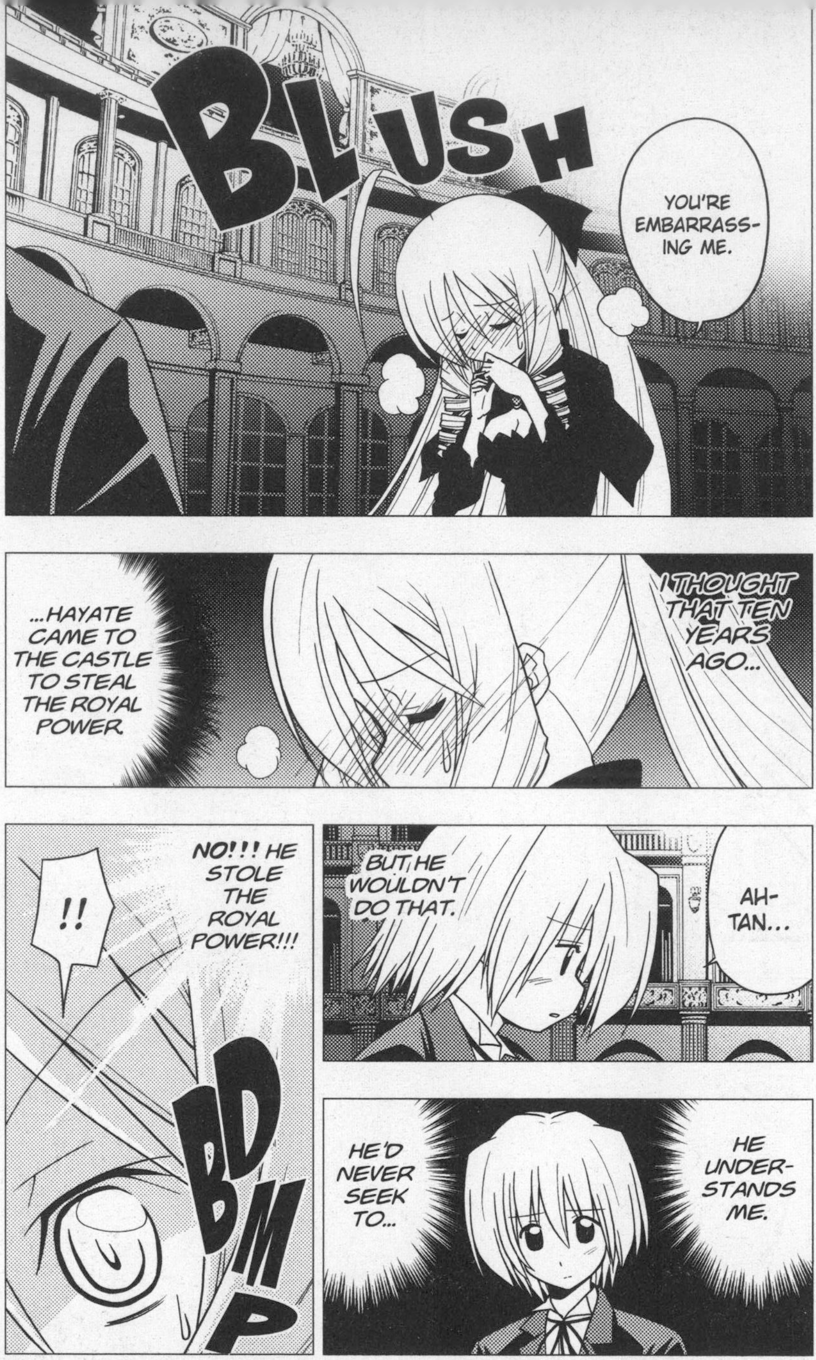
BLUSH
YOU'RE EMBARRASS-ING ME.
I THOUGHT THAT TEN YEARS AGO...
...HAYATE CAME TO THE CASTLE TO STEAL THE ROYAL POWER.
AH-TAN...
BUT HE WOULDN'T DO THAT.
HE UNDER-STANDS ME.
HE'D NEVER SEEK TO...
NO!!! HE STOLE THE ROYAL POWER!!!
!!
BDMP

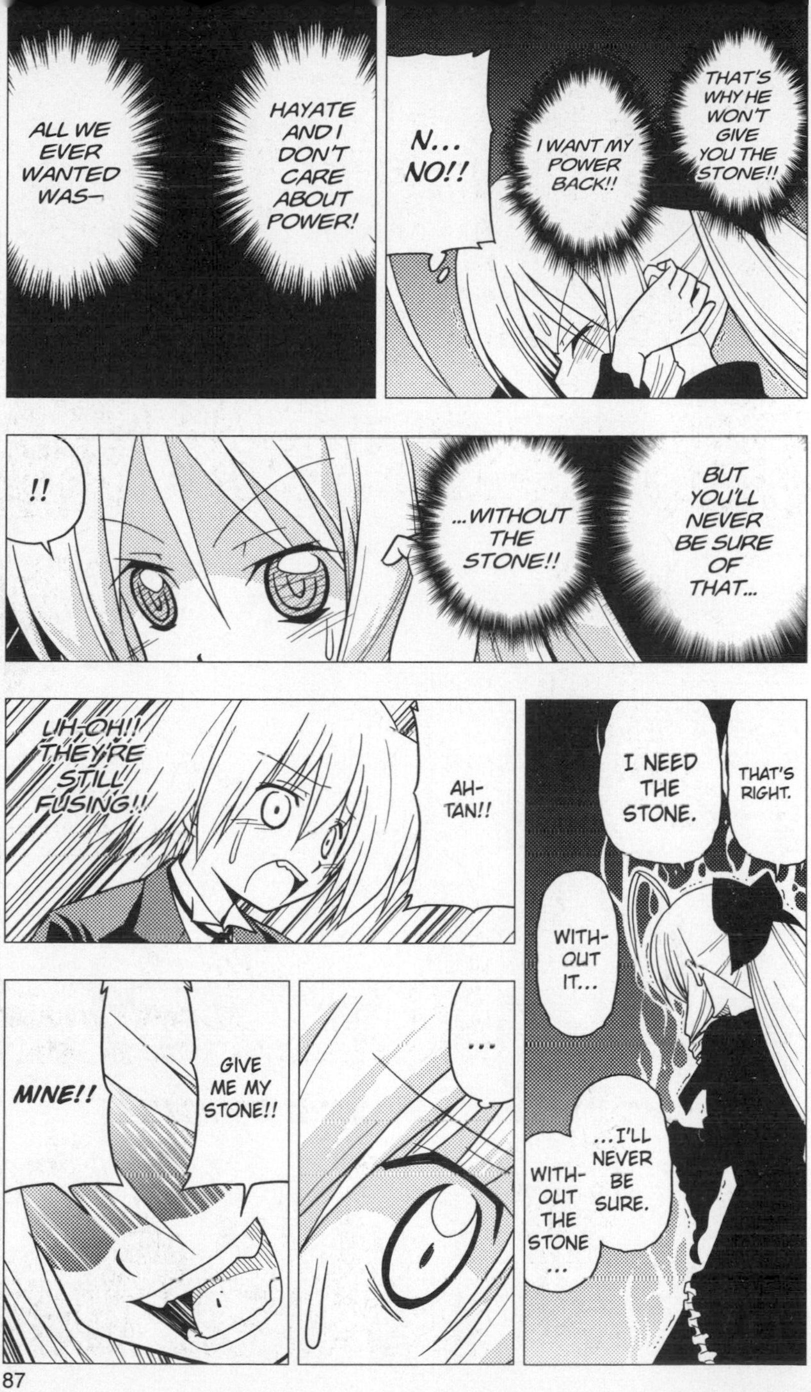
THAT'S WHY HE WON'T GIVE YOU THE STONE!!
I WANT MY POWER BACK!!
N... NO!!
HAYATE AND I DON'T CARE ABOUT POWER!
ALL WE EVER WANTED WAS—
BUT YOU'LL NEVER BE SURE OF THAT...
...WITHOUT THE STONE!!
!!
THAT'S RIGHT.
I NEED THE STONE.
WITHOUT IT...
...I'LL NEVER BE SURE.
WITHOUT THE STONE...
AH-TAN!!
UH-OH!! THEY'RE STILL FUSING!!
...
GIVE ME MY STONE!!
MINE!!

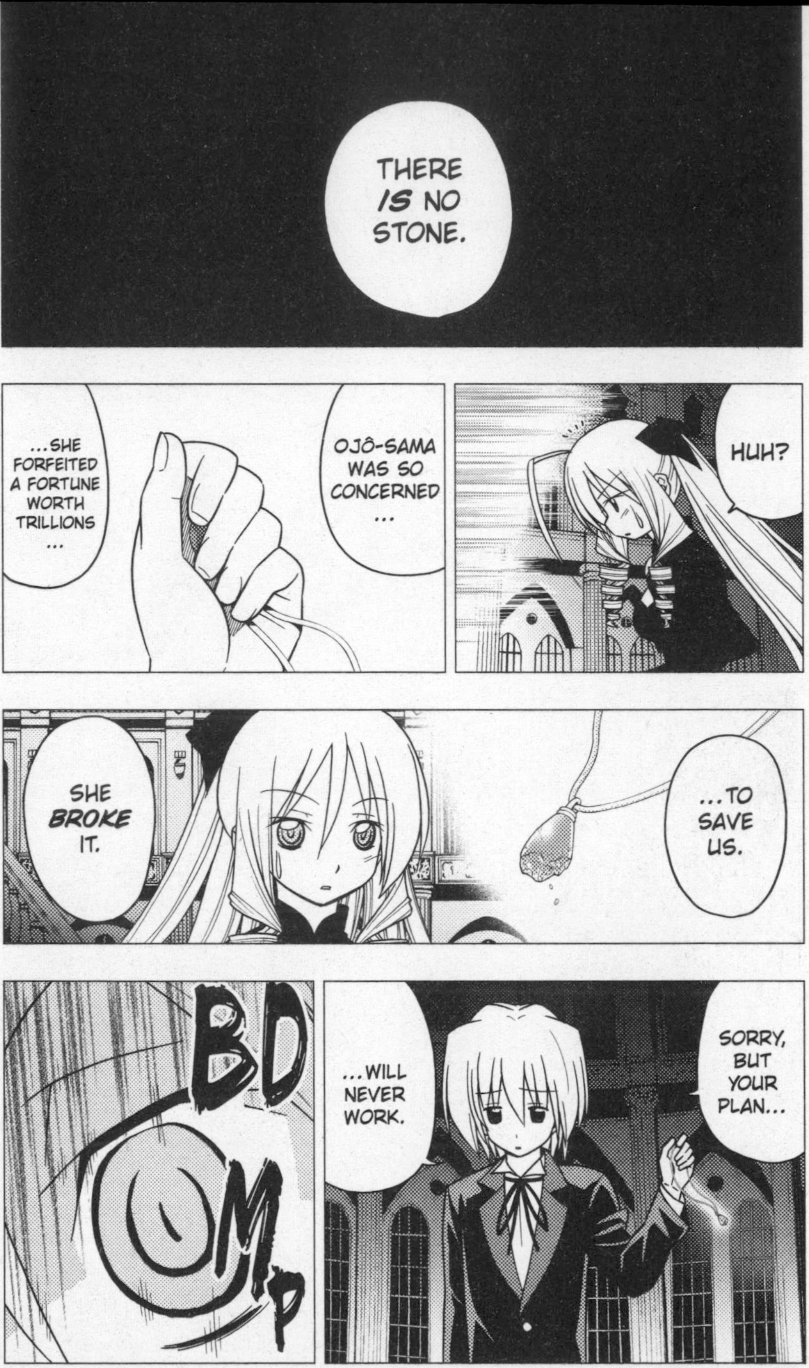
THERE *IS* NO STONE.
HUH?
OJÔ-SAMA WAS SO CONCERNED...
...SHE FORFEITED A FORTUNE WORTH TRILLIONS...
...TO SAVE US.
SHE *BROKE* IT.
SORRY, BUT YOUR PLAN...
...WILL NEVER WORK.
BDOMP

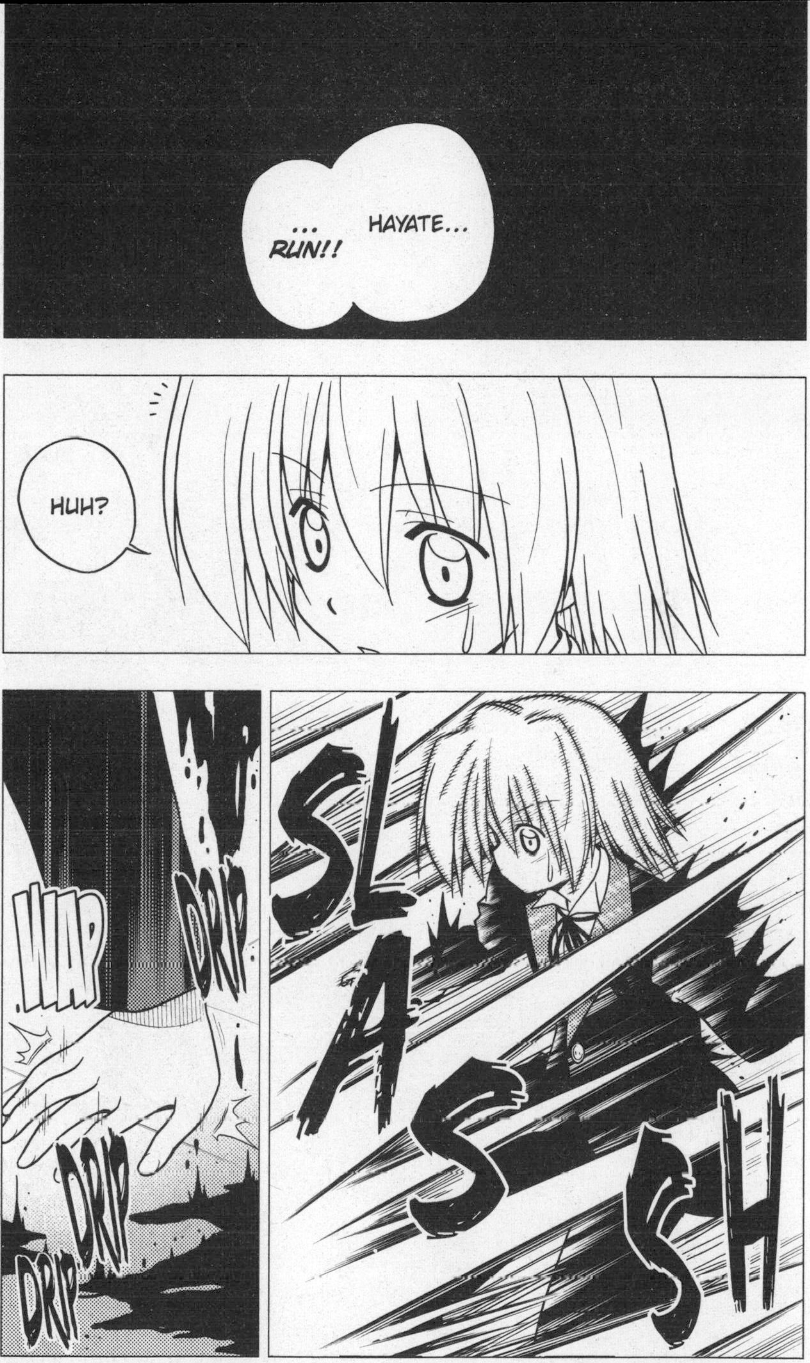
HAYATE...
...RUN!!
HUH?
SLASH
WAP
DRIP
DRIP
DRIP

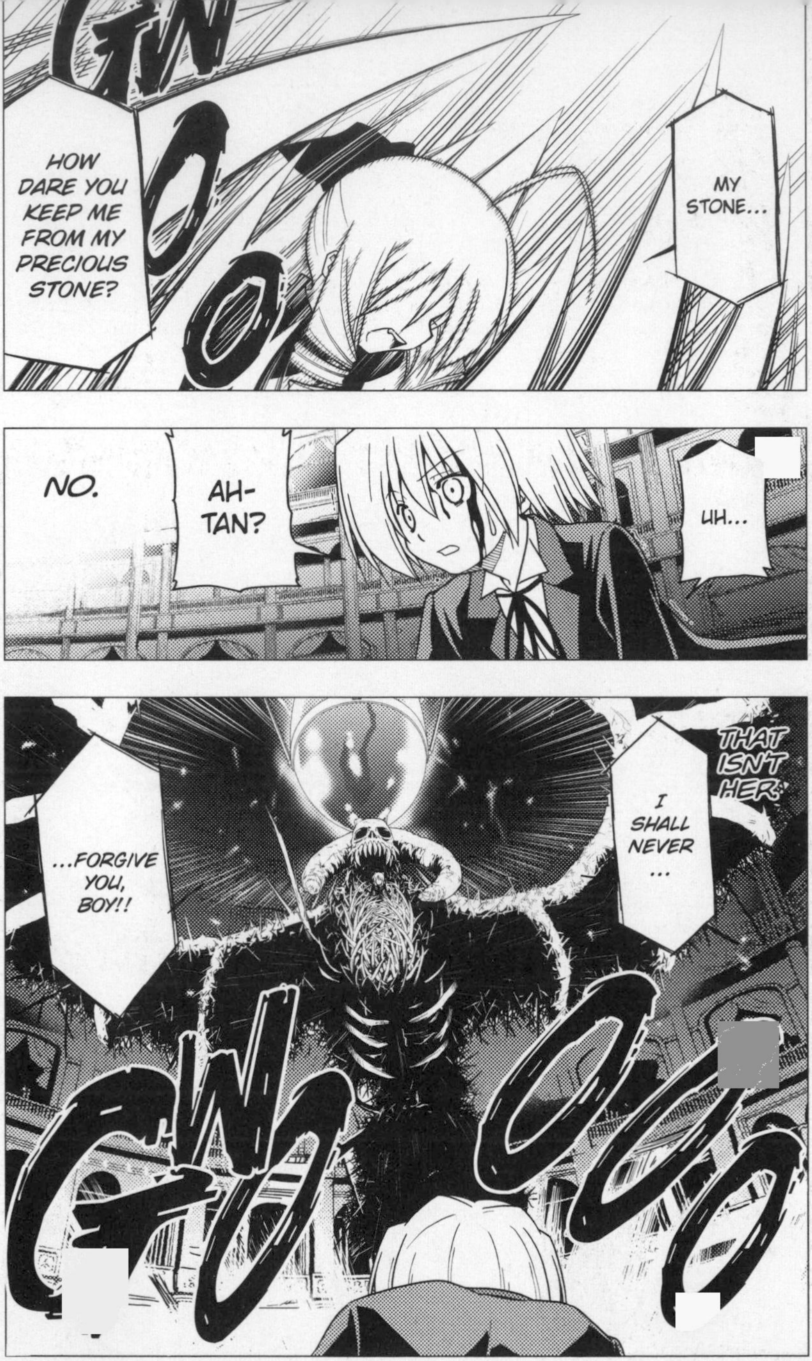
MY STONE...
HOW DARE YOU KEEP ME FROM MY PRECIOUS STONE?
UH...
AH-TAN?
NO.
THAT ISN'T HER.
I SHALL NEVER ...
...FORGIVE YOU, BOY!!

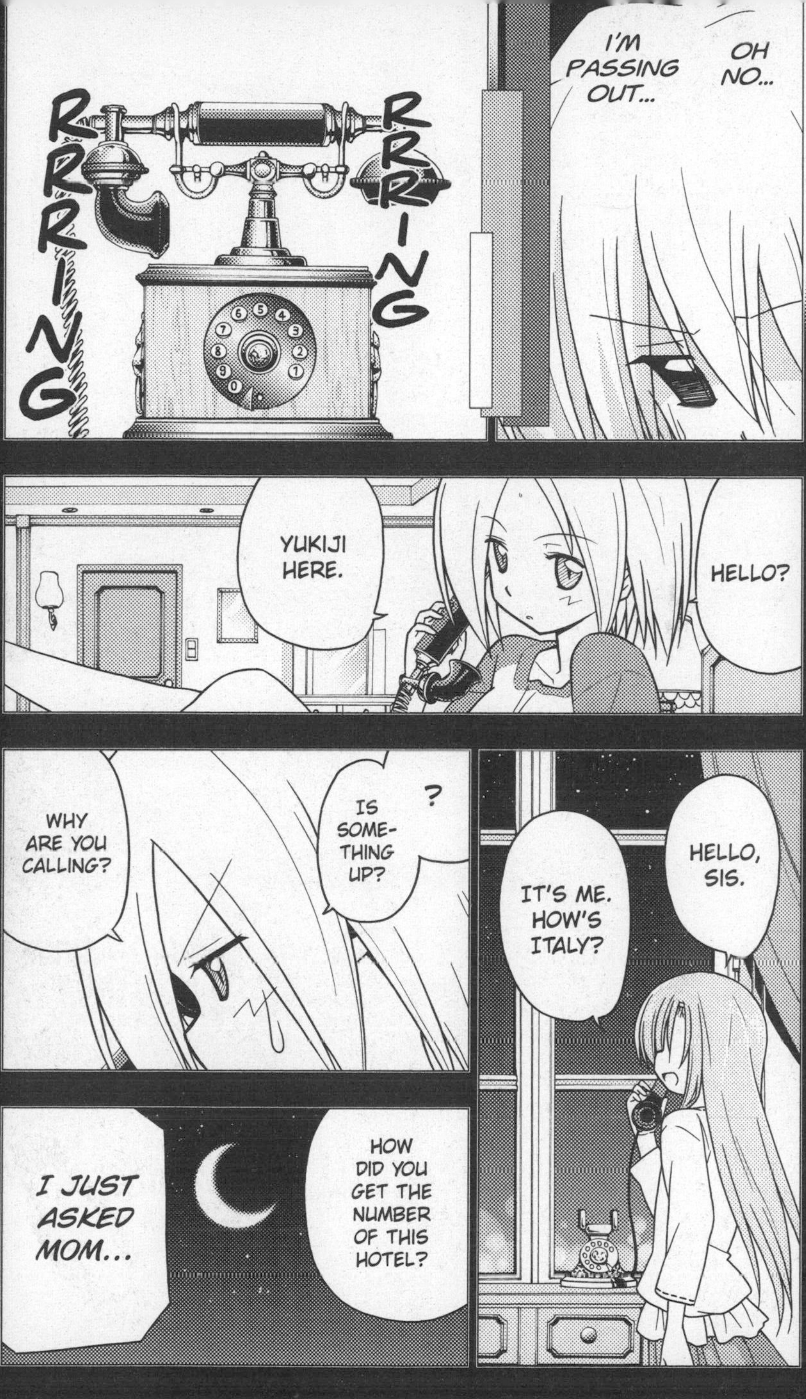
OH NO...
I'M PASSING OUT...
RRRING
RRRING
HELLO?
YUKIJI HERE.
HELLO, SIS.
IT'S ME. HOW'S ITALY?
?
IS SOMETHING UP?
WHY ARE YOU CALLING?
HOW DID YOU GET THE NUMBER OF THIS HOTEL?
I JUST ASKED MOM...

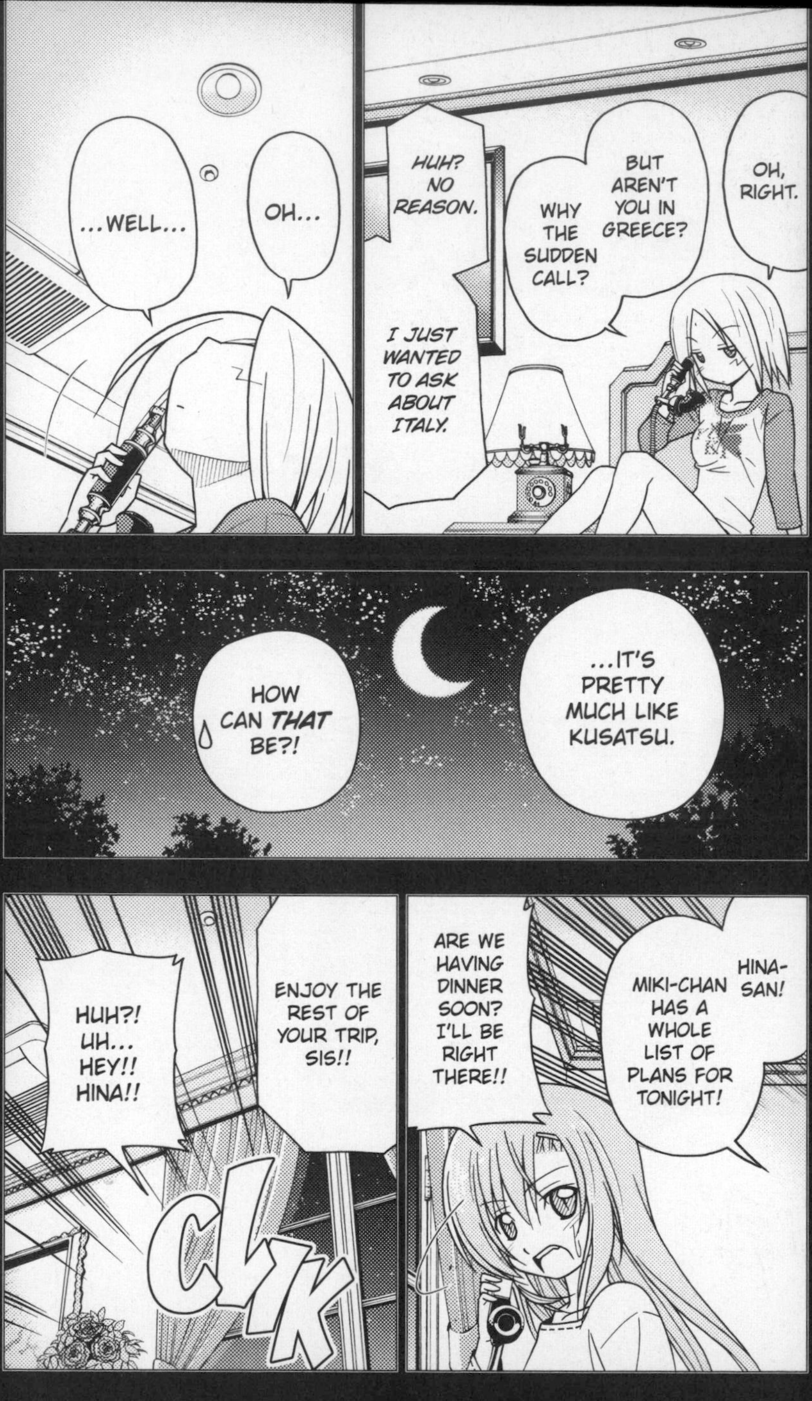
OH, RIGHT.
BUT AREN'T YOU IN GREECE?
WHY THE SUDDEN CALL?
HUH? NO REASON.
I JUST WANTED TO ASK ABOUT ITALY.
OH...
...WELL...
...IT'S PRETTY MUCH LIKE KUSATSU.
HOW CAN *THAT* BE?!
HINA-SAN!
MIKI-CHAN HAS A WHOLE LIST OF PLANS FOR TONIGHT!
ARE WE HAVING DINNER SOON? I'LL BE RIGHT THERE!!
ENJOY THE REST OF YOUR TRIP, SIS!!
HUH?! UH... HEY!! HINA!!
CLIK

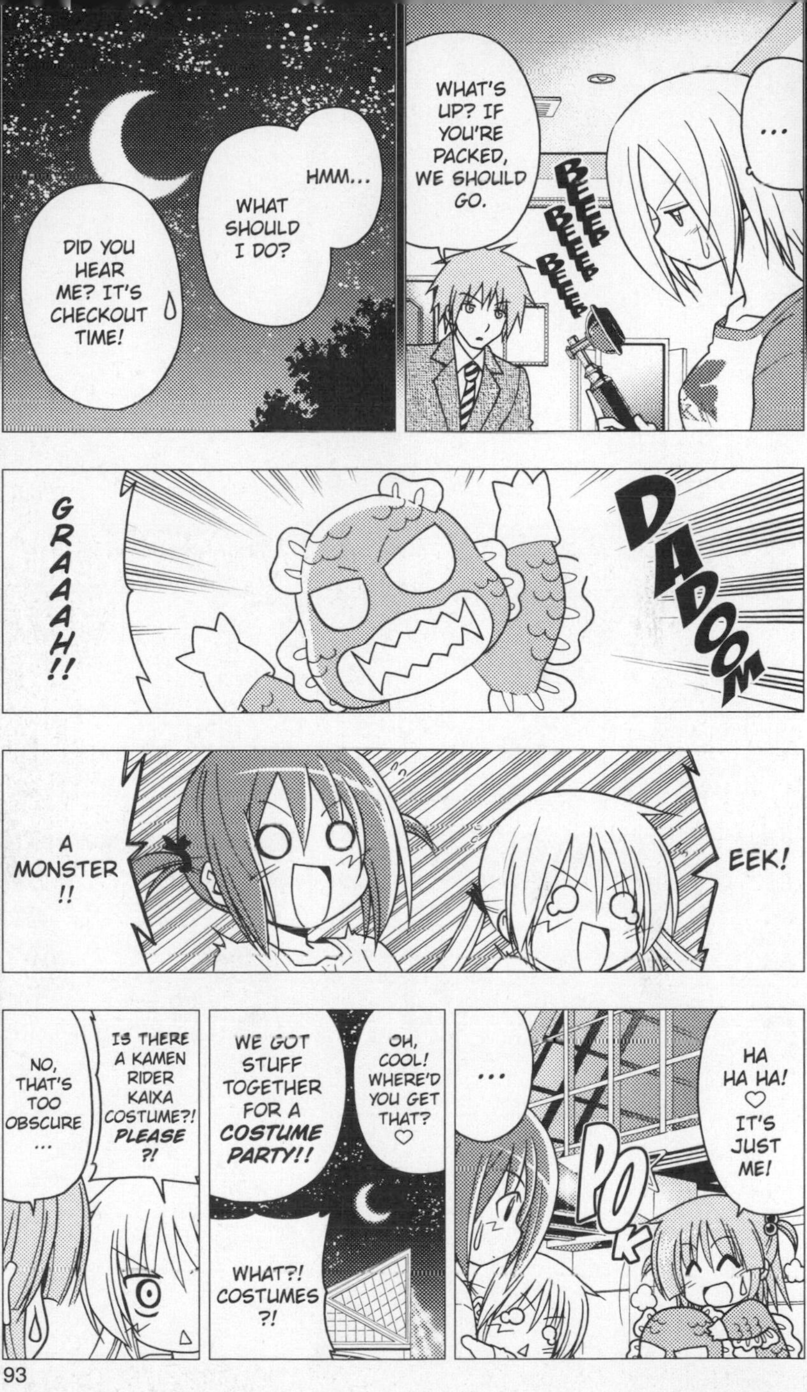
...
WHAT'S UP? IF YOU'RE PACKED, WE SHOULD GO.
BEEEP BEEEP BEEEP
HMM...
WHAT SHOULD I DO?
DID YOU HEAR ME? IT'S CHECKOUT TIME!
DADOOM
GRAAAAH!!
EEK!
A MONSTER!!
HA HA HA! ♡ IT'S JUST ME!
...
POK
OH, COOL! WHERE'D YOU GET THAT? ♡
WE GOT STUFF TOGETHER FOR A COSTUME PARTY!!
WHAT?! COSTUMES?!
IS THERE A KAMEN RIDER KAIXA COSTUME?! PLEASE?!
NO, THAT'S TOO OBSCURE...

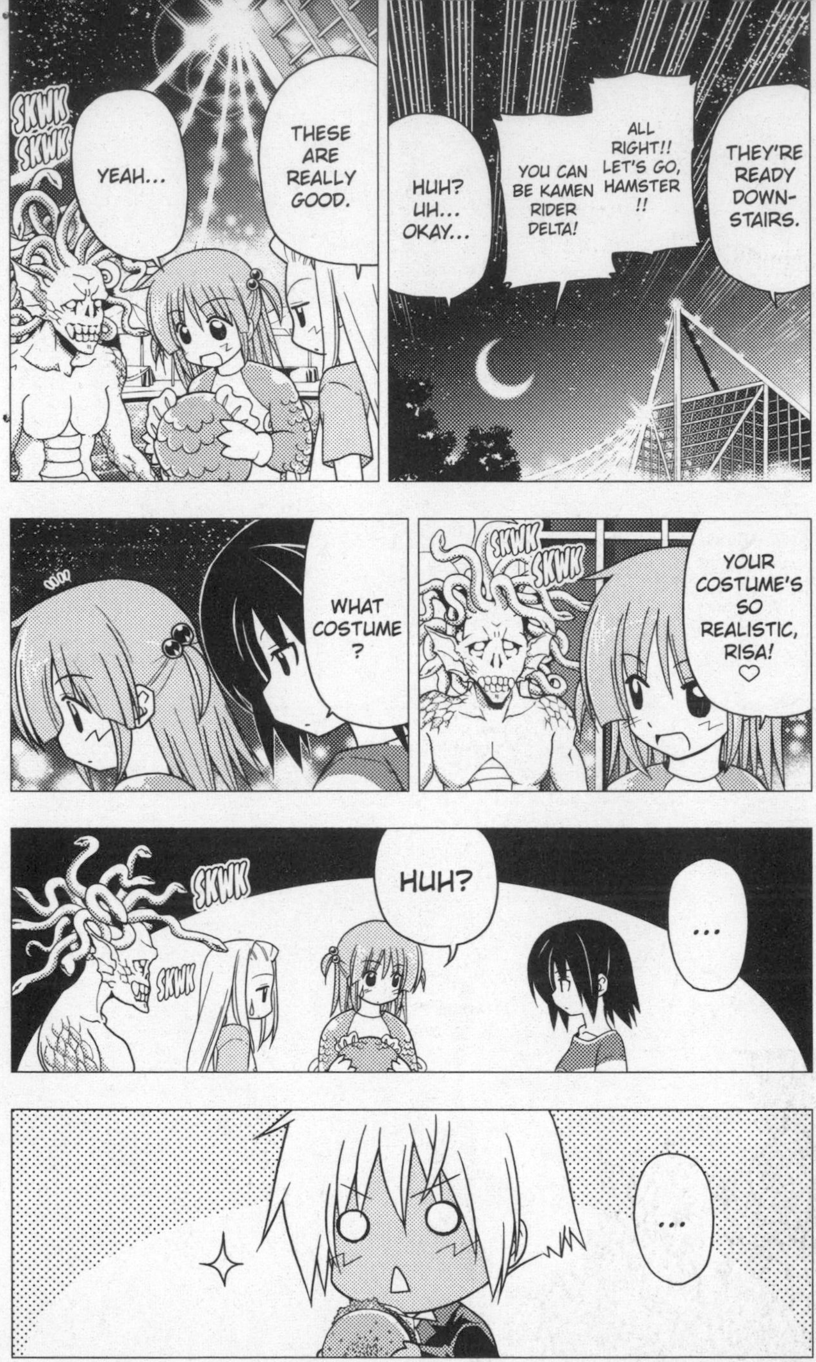
THEY'RE READY DOWNSTAIRS.
ALL RIGHT!! LET'S GO, HAMSTER!!
YOU CAN BE KAMEN RIDER DELTA!
HUH? UH... OKAY...
THESE ARE REALLY GOOD.
YEAH...
SKWK SKWK
YOUR COSTUME'S SO REALISTIC, RISA! ♡
SKWK SKWK
WHAT COSTUME?
...
HUH?
SKWK
SKWK
...

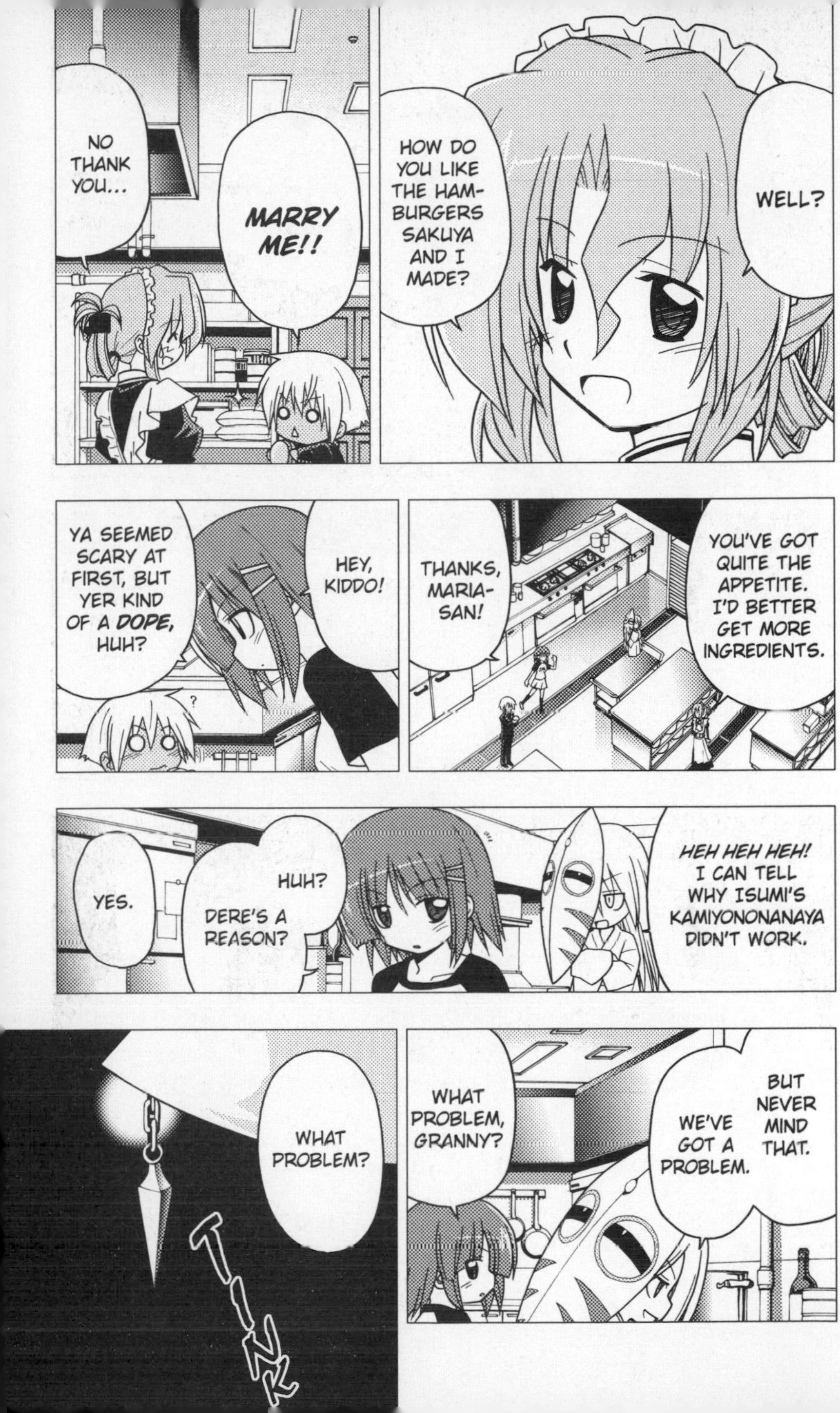
WELL?
HOW DO YOU LIKE THE HAM-BURGERS SAKUYA AND I MADE?
MARRY ME!!
NO THANK YOU...
YOU'VE GOT QUITE THE APPETITE. I'D BETTER GET MORE INGREDIENTS.
THANKS, MARIA-SAN!
HEY, KIDDO!
YA SEEMED SCARY AT FIRST, BUT YER KIND OF A DOPE, HUH?
?
HEH HEH HEH! I CAN TELL WHY ISUMI'S KAMIYONONANAYA DIDN'T WORK.
HUH?
DERE'S A REASON?
YES.
BUT NEVER MIND THAT.
WE'VE GOT A PROBLEM.
WHAT PROBLEM, GRANNY?
WHAT PROBLEM?
TINK

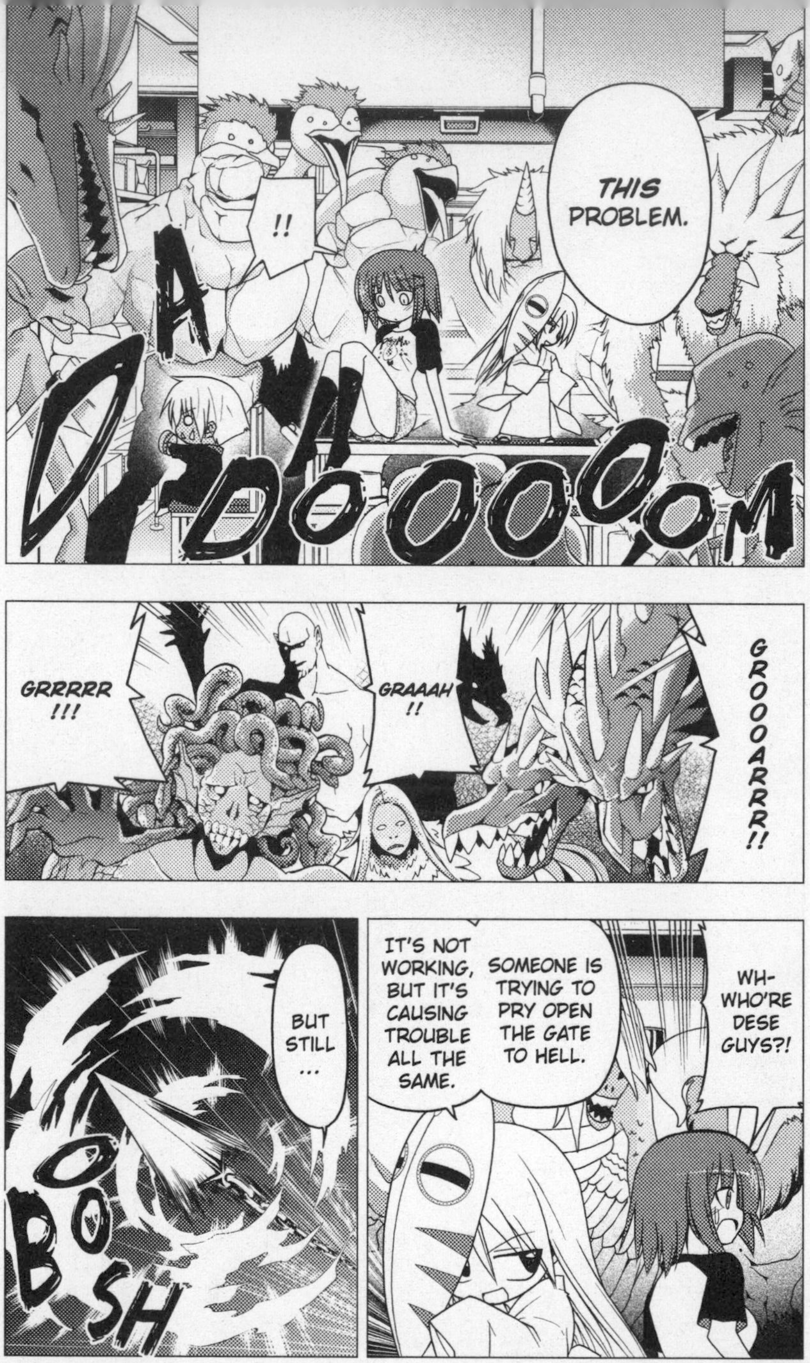
THIS PROBLEM.
!!
DADOOOOOM
GROOOARRR!!
GRAAAH!!
GRRRRR!!!
WH- WHO'RE DESE GUYS?!
SOMEONE IS TRYING TO PRY OPEN THE GATE TO HELL.
IT'S NOT WORKING, BUT IT'S CAUSING TROUBLE ALL THE SAME.
BUT STILL...
BOOSH

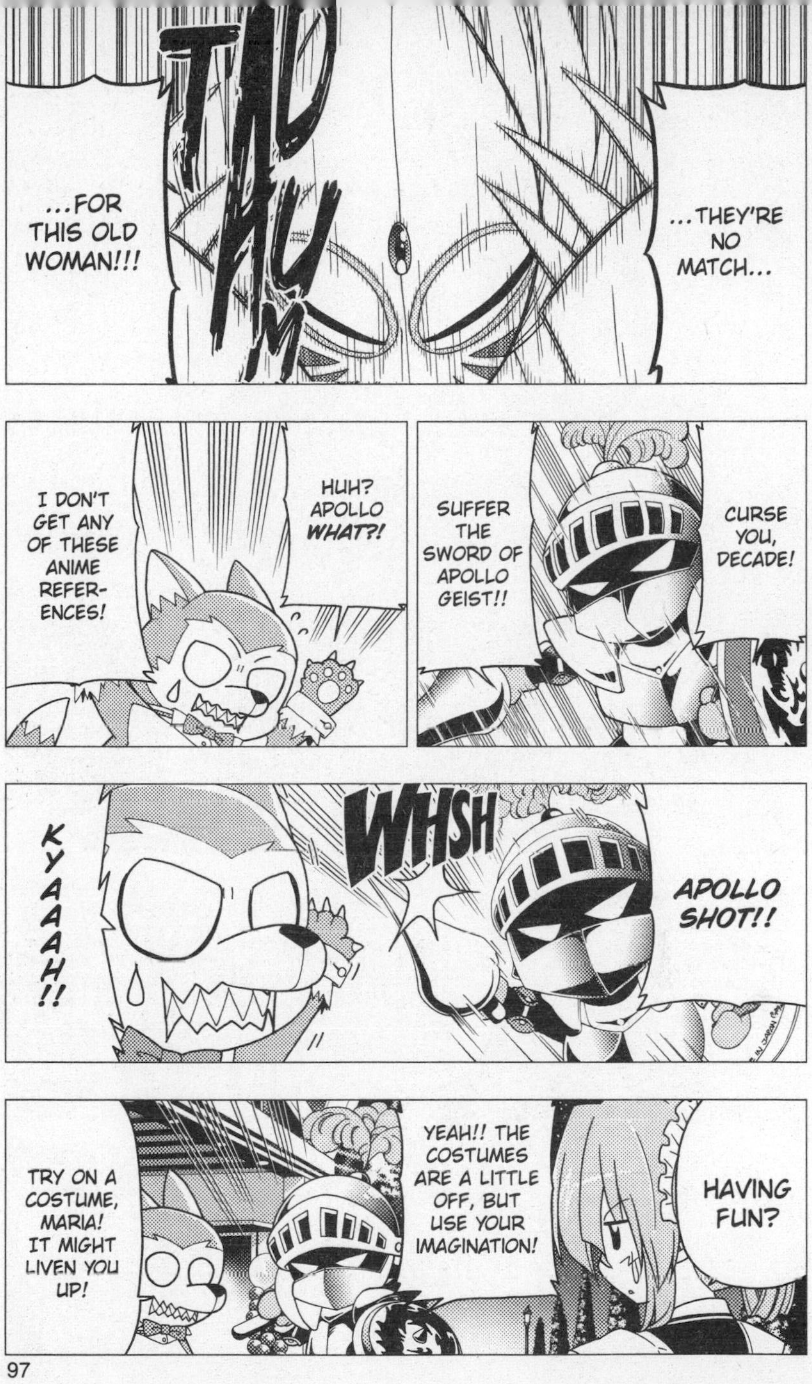
...THEY'RE NO MATCH...
...FOR THIS OLD WOMAN!!!
CURSE YOU, DECADE!
SUFFER THE SWORD OF APOLLO GEIST!!
HUH? APOLLO WHAT?!
I DON'T GET ANY OF THESE ANIME REFER-ENCES!
APOLLO SHOT!!
WHSH
KYAAAAH!!
HAVING FUN?
YEAH!! THE COSTUMES ARE A LITTLE OFF, BUT USE YOUR IMAGINATION!
TRY ON A COSTUME, MARIA! IT MIGHT LIVEN YOU UP!

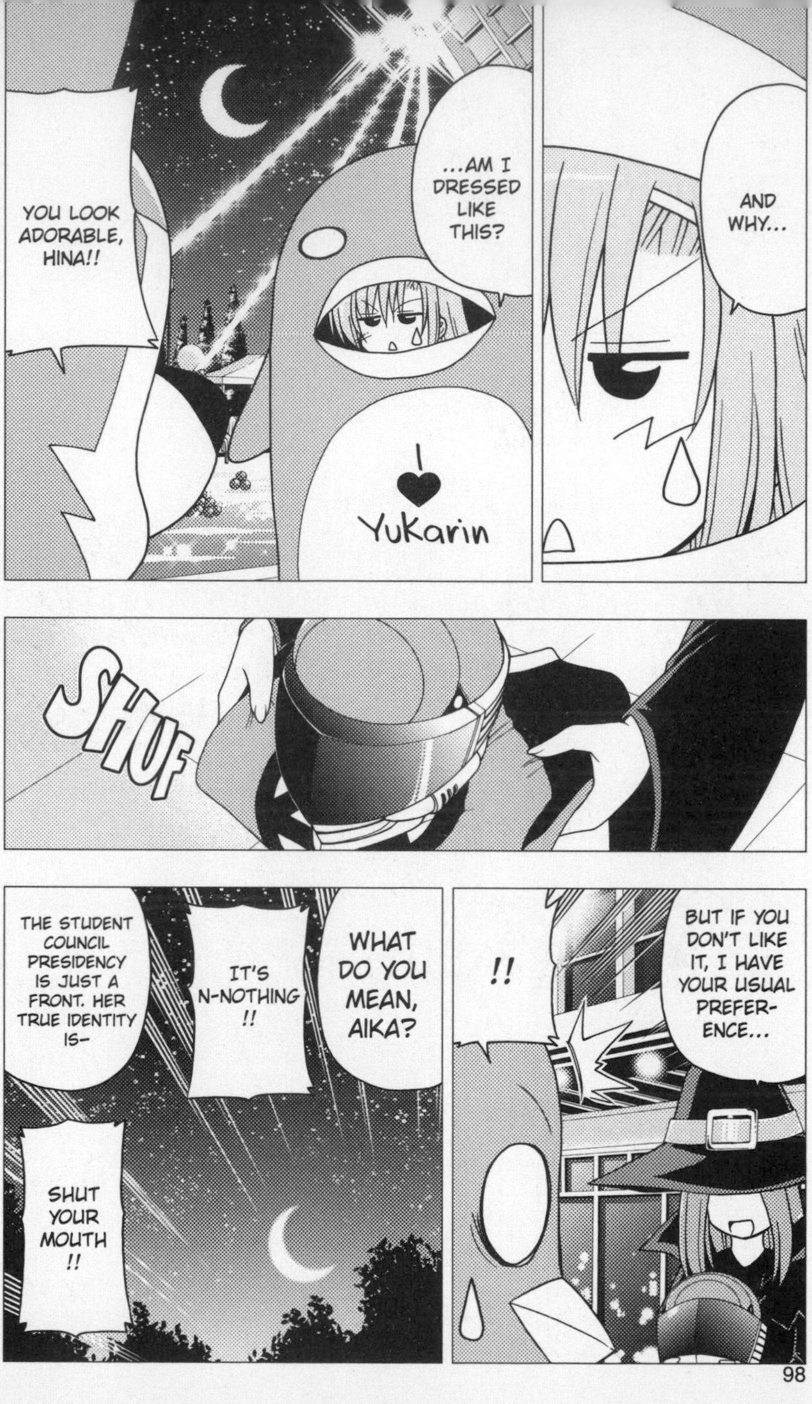
AND WHY...
...AM I DRESSED LIKE THIS?
I ♥ YuKarin
YOU LOOK ADORABLE, HINA!!
SHUF
BUT IF YOU DON'T LIKE IT, I HAVE YOUR USUAL PREFER-ENCE...
!!
WHAT DO YOU MEAN, AIKA?
IT'S N-NOTHING !!
THE STUDENT COUNCIL PRESIDENCY IS JUST A FRONT. HER TRUE IDENTITY IS–
SHUT YOUR MOUTH !!

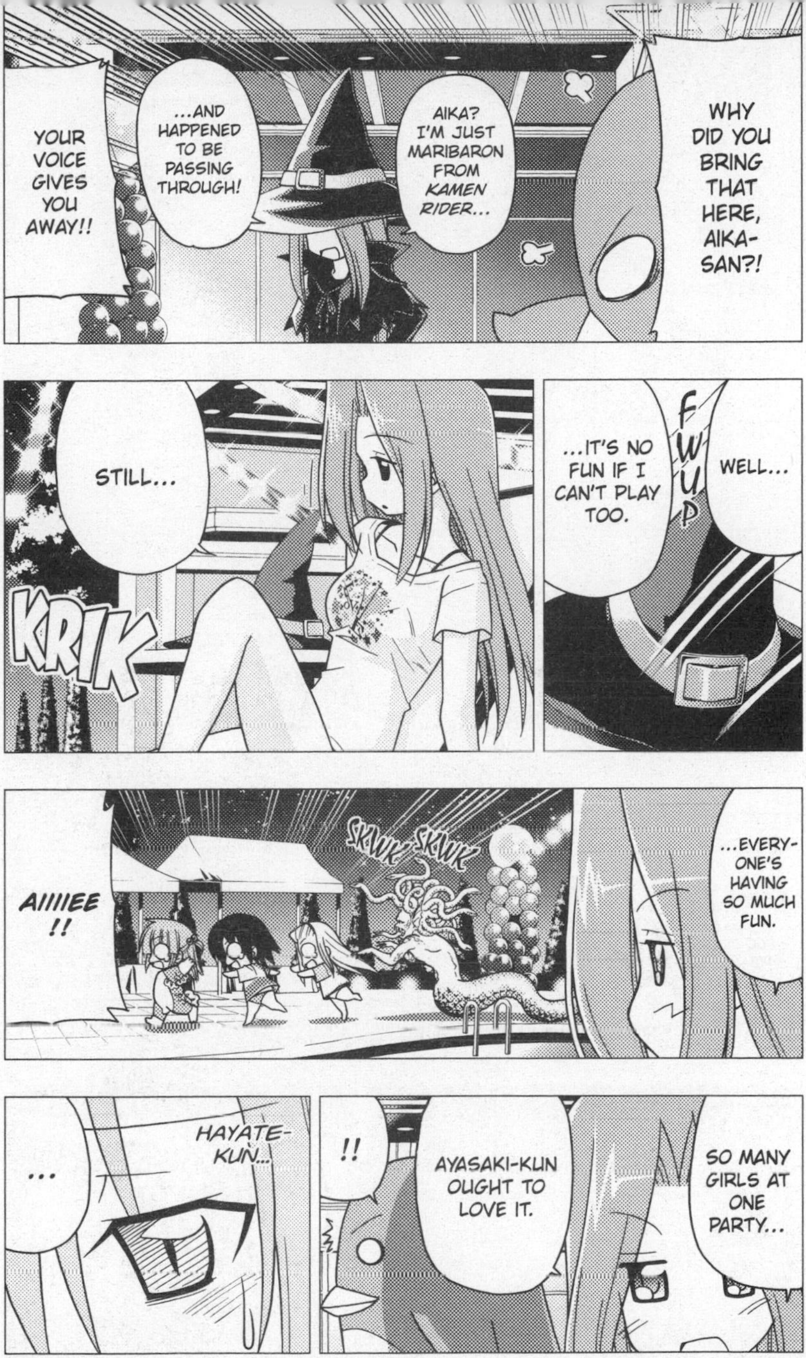
WHY DID YOU BRING THAT HERE, AIKA-SAN?!
AIKA? I'M JUST MARIBARON FROM KAMEN RIDER...
...AND HAPPENED TO BE PASSING THROUGH!
YOUR VOICE GIVES YOU AWAY!!
WELL...
FWUP
...IT'S NO FUN IF I CAN'T PLAY TOO.
STILL...
KRIK
...EVERY-ONE'S HAVING SO MUCH FUN.
SKWK SKWK
AIIIIEE !!
SO MANY GIRLS AT ONE PARTY...
AYASAKI-KUN OUGHT TO LOVE IT.
!!
HAYATE-KUN...
...

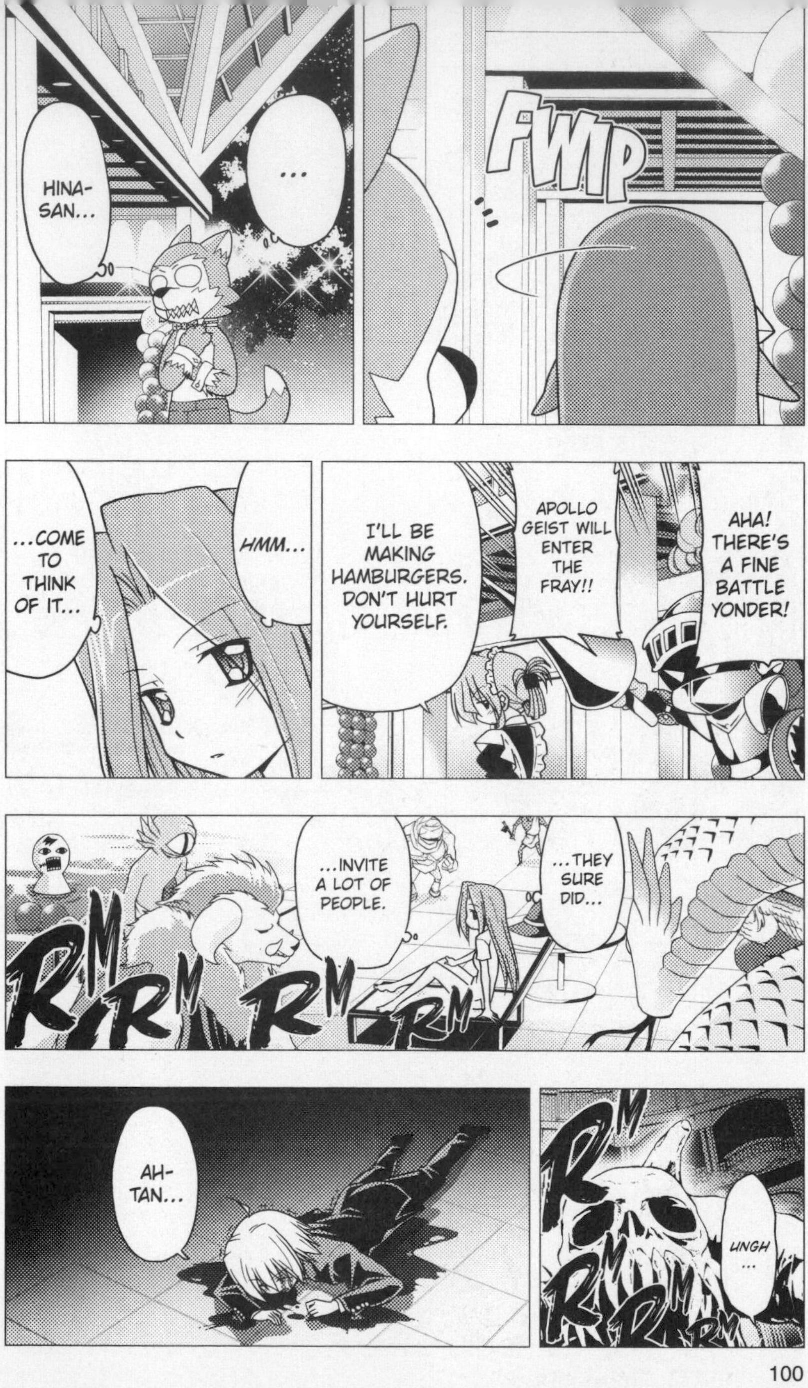
FWIP
...
HINA-SAN...
AHA! THERE'S A FINE BATTLE YONDER!
APOLLO GEIST WILL ENTER THE FRAY!!
I'LL BE MAKING HAMBURGERS. DON'T HURT YOURSELF.
HMM...
...COME TO THINK OF IT...
...THEY SURE DID...
...INVITE A LOT OF PEOPLE.
RMM RMM RMM RMM
UNGH...
RMM RMM
AH-TAN...

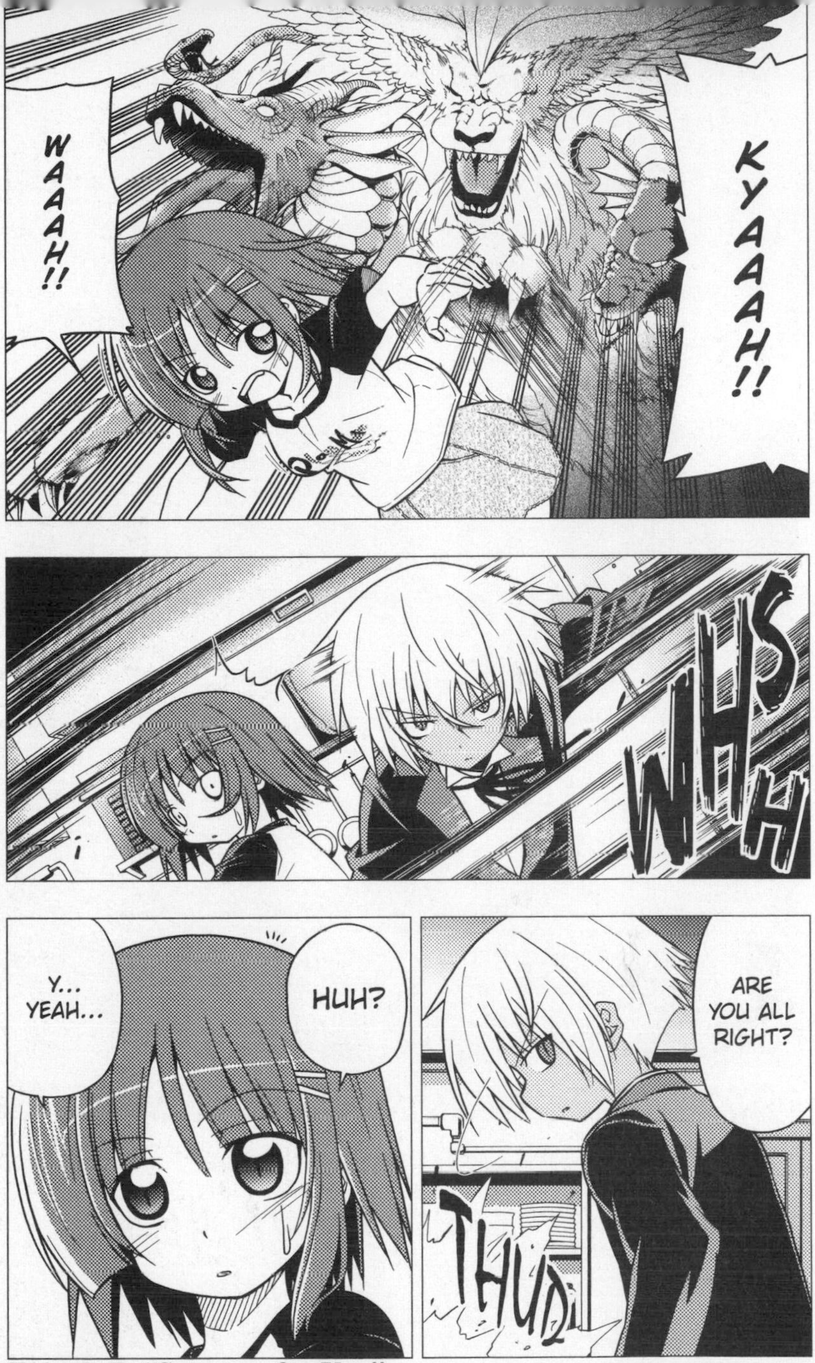
KYAAAAH!!
WAAAAH!!
WHSH
ARE YOU ALL RIGHT?
THUD
HUH?
Y... YEAH...

Episode 7: "Someone for You"

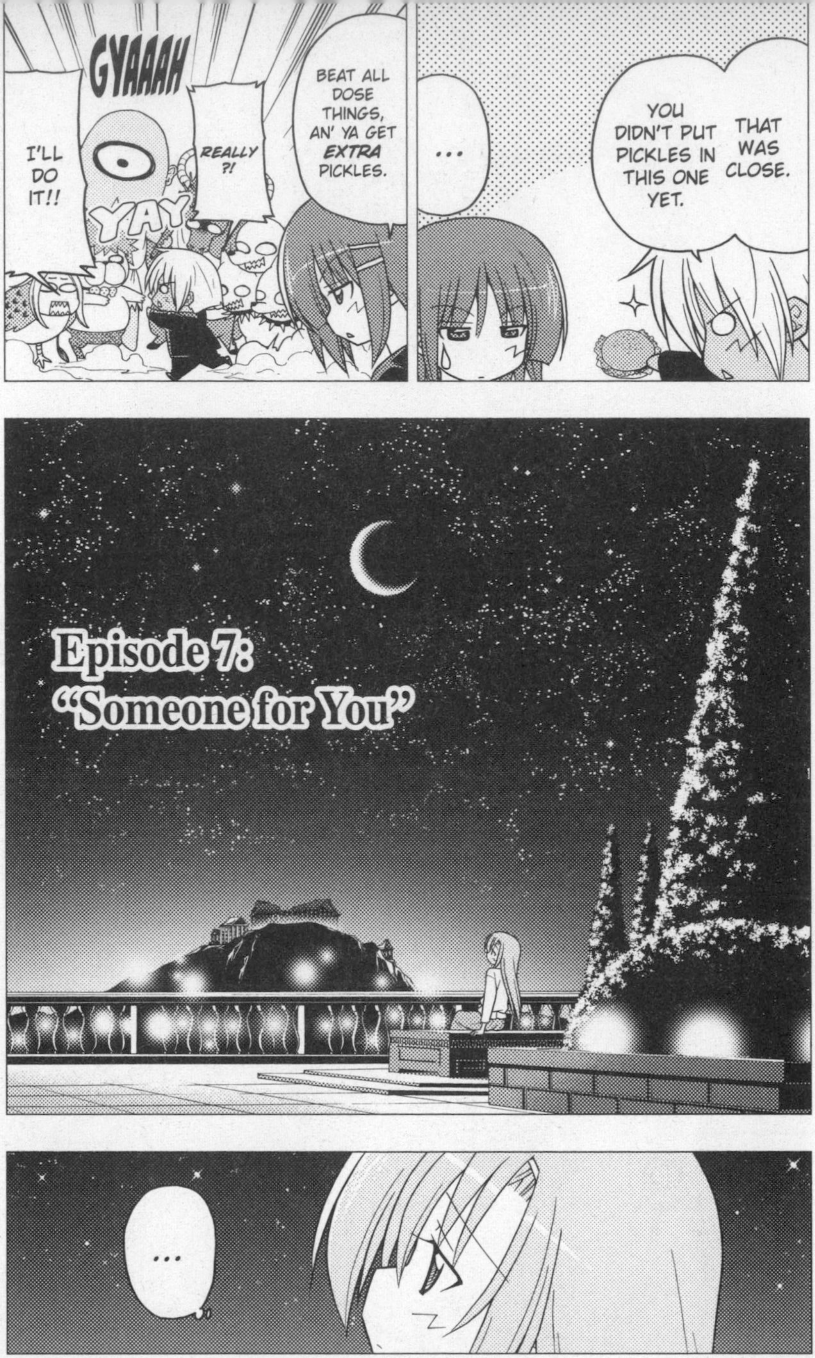
THAT WAS CLOSE.
YOU DIDN'T PUT PICKLES IN THIS ONE YET.
...
BEAT ALL DOSE THINGS, AN' YA GET EXTRA PICKLES.
REALLY?!
GYAAAH
I'LL DO IT!!
YAY
Episode 7: "Someone for You"
...

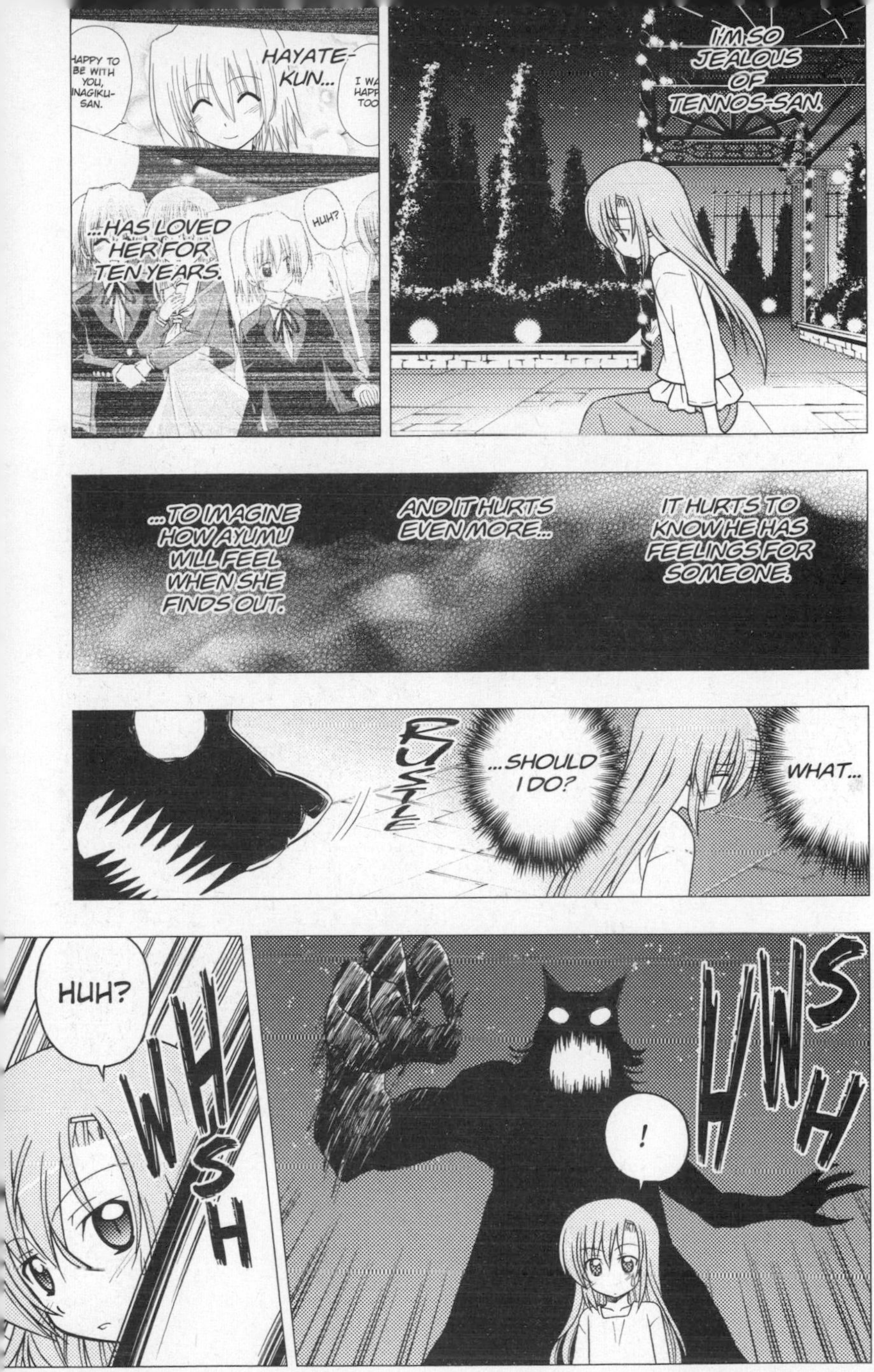
I'M SO JEALOUS OF TENNOS-SAN.
HAYATE-KUN...
HAPPY TO BE WITH YOU, INAGIKU-SAN.
HUH?
...HAS LOVED HER FOR TEN YEARS.
IT HURTS TO KNOW HE HAS FEELINGS FOR SOMEONE.
AND IT HURTS EVEN MORE...
...TO IMAGINE HOW AYUMU WILL FEEL WHEN SHE FINDS OUT.
WHAT...
...SHOULD I DO?
RUSTLE
WHSH
!
HUH?
WHSH

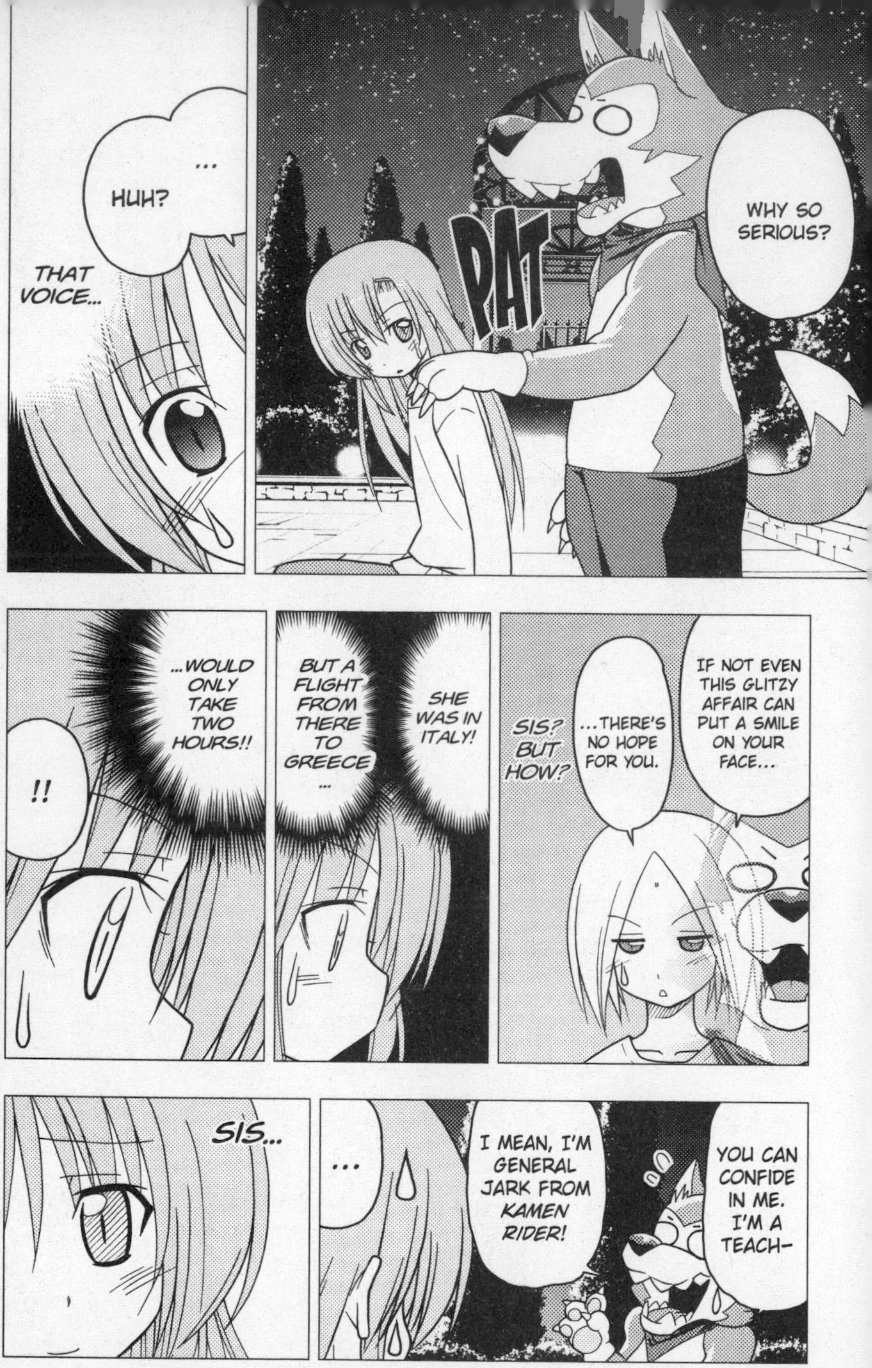
WHY SO SERIOUS?
PAT
...
HUH?
THAT VOICE...
IF NOT EVEN THIS GLITZY AFFAIR CAN PUT A SMILE ON YOUR FACE...
...THERE'S NO HOPE FOR YOU.
SIS? BUT HOW?
SHE WAS IN ITALY!
BUT A FLIGHT FROM THERE TO GREECE ...
...WOULD ONLY TAKE TWO HOURS!!
!!
YOU CAN CONFIDE IN ME. I'M A TEACH—
I MEAN, I'M GENERAL JARK FROM KAMEN RIDER!
...
SIS...

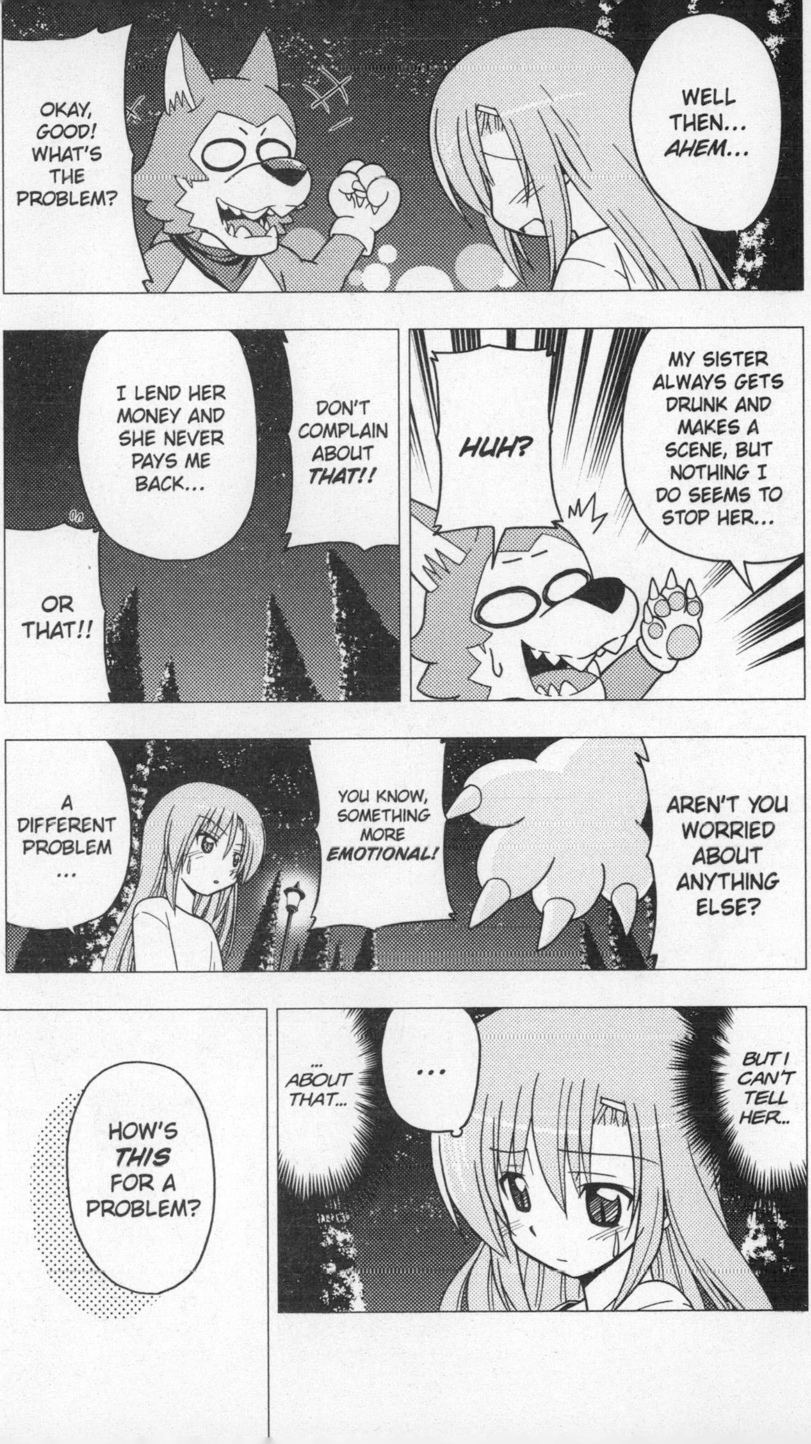
WELL THEN... *AHEM*...
OKAY, GOOD! WHAT'S THE PROBLEM?
MY SISTER ALWAYS GETS DRUNK AND MAKES A SCENE, BUT NOTHING I DO SEEMS TO STOP HER...
HUH?
DON'T COMPLAIN ABOUT *THAT!!*
I LEND HER MONEY AND SHE NEVER PAYS ME BACK...
OR THAT!!
AREN'T YOU WORRIED ABOUT ANYTHING ELSE?
YOU KNOW, SOMETHING MORE *EMOTIONAL!*
A DIFFERENT PROBLEM ...
BUT I CAN'T TELL HER..
...
... ABOUT THAT...
HOW'S *THIS* FOR A PROBLEM?

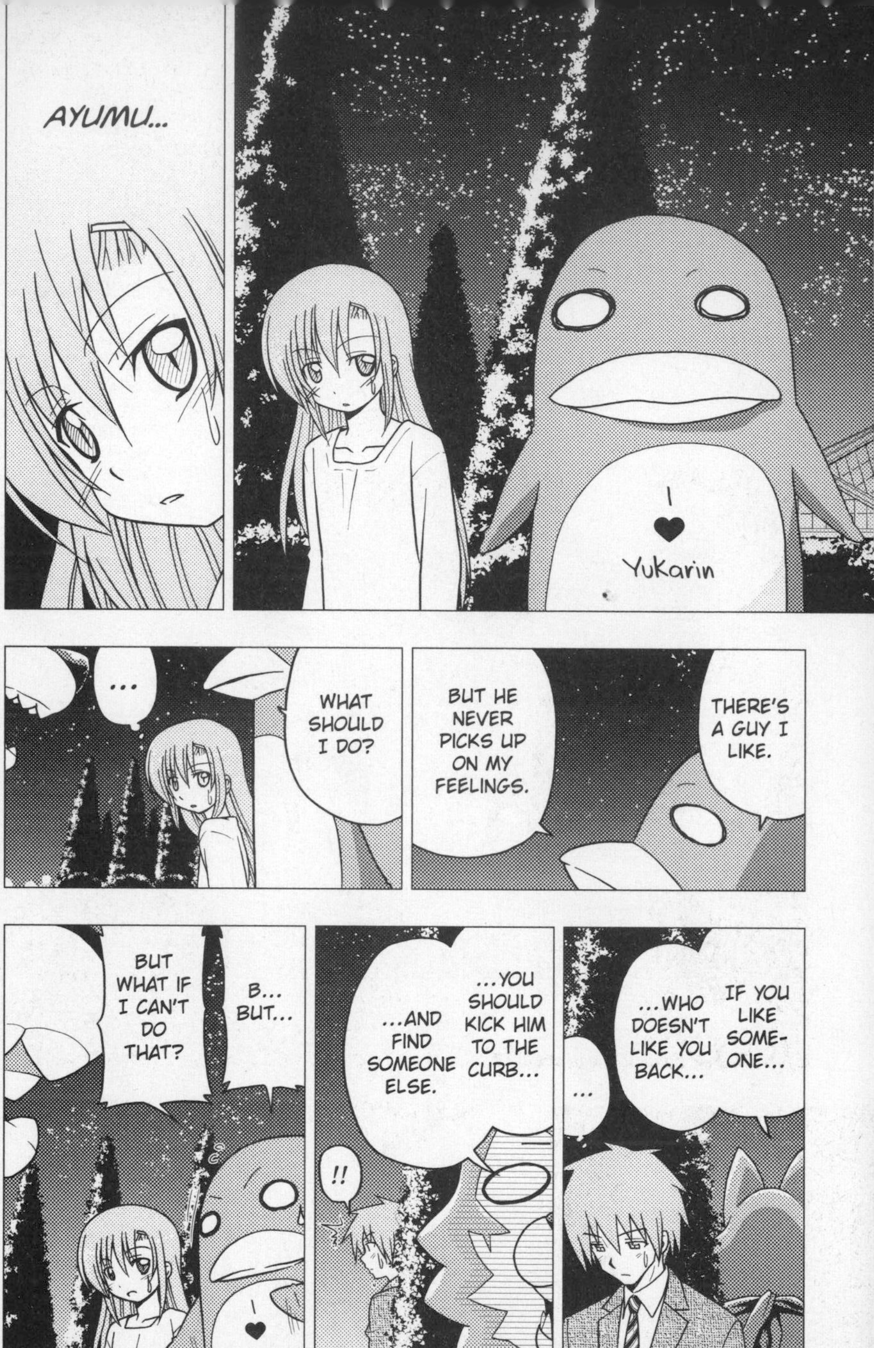
I ♥ YuKarin
AYUMU...
THERE'S A GUY I LIKE.
BUT HE NEVER PICKS UP ON MY FEELINGS.
WHAT SHOULD I DO?
...
IF YOU LIKE SOME-ONE...
...WHO DOESN'T LIKE YOU BACK...
...
...YOU SHOULD KICK HIM TO THE CURB...
...AND FIND SOMEONE ELSE.
!!
B... BUT...
BUT WHAT IF I CAN'T DO THAT?

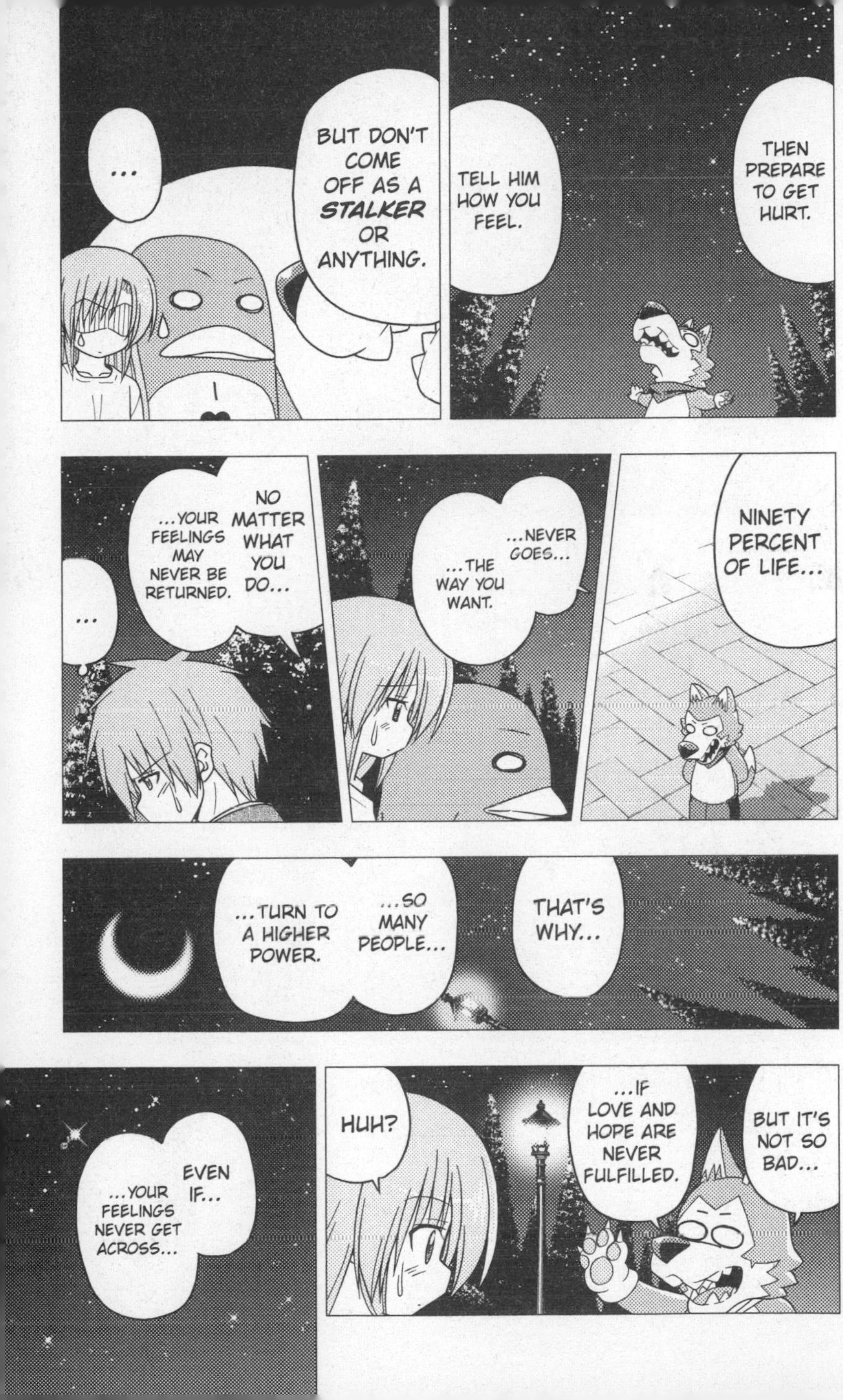
THEN PREPARE TO GET HURT.
TELL HIM HOW YOU FEEL.
BUT DON'T COME OFF AS A *STALKER* OR ANYTHING.
...
NINETY PERCENT OF LIFE...
...NEVER GOES...
...THE WAY YOU WANT.
NO MATTER WHAT YOU DO...
...YOUR FEELINGS MAY NEVER BE RETURNED.
...
THAT'S WHY...
...SO MANY PEOPLE...
...TURN TO A HIGHER POWER.
BUT IT'S NOT SO BAD...
...IF LOVE AND HOPE ARE NEVER FULFILLED.
HUH?
EVEN IF...
...YOUR FEELINGS NEVER GET ACROSS...

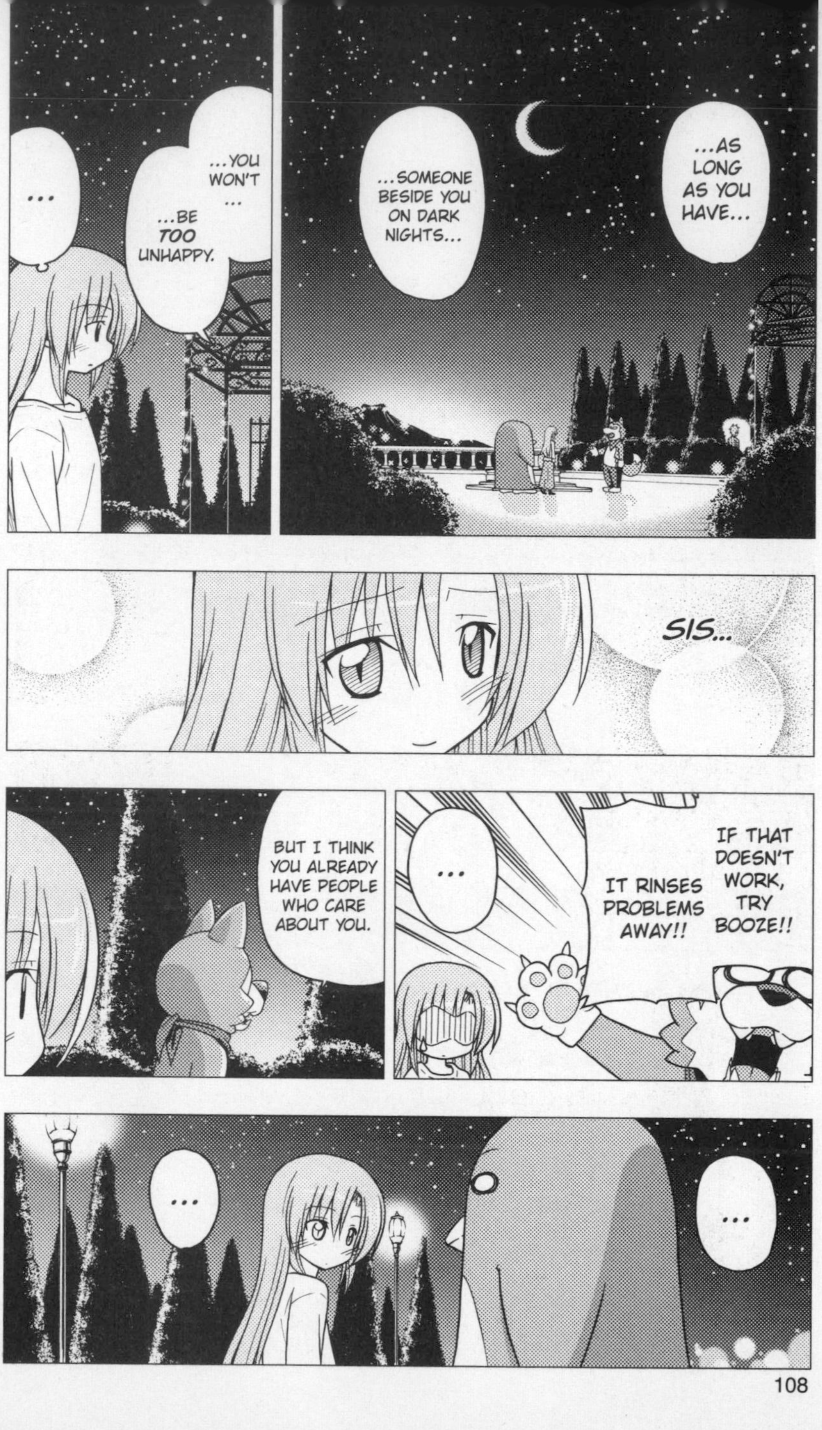
...AS LONG AS YOU HAVE...
...SOMEONE BESIDE YOU ON DARK NIGHTS...
...YOU WON'T ...
...BE *TOO* UNHAPPY.
...
SIS...
IF THAT DOESN'T WORK, TRY BOOZE!!
IT RINSES PROBLEMS AWAY!!
...
BUT I THINK YOU ALREADY HAVE PEOPLE WHO CARE ABOUT YOU.
...
...

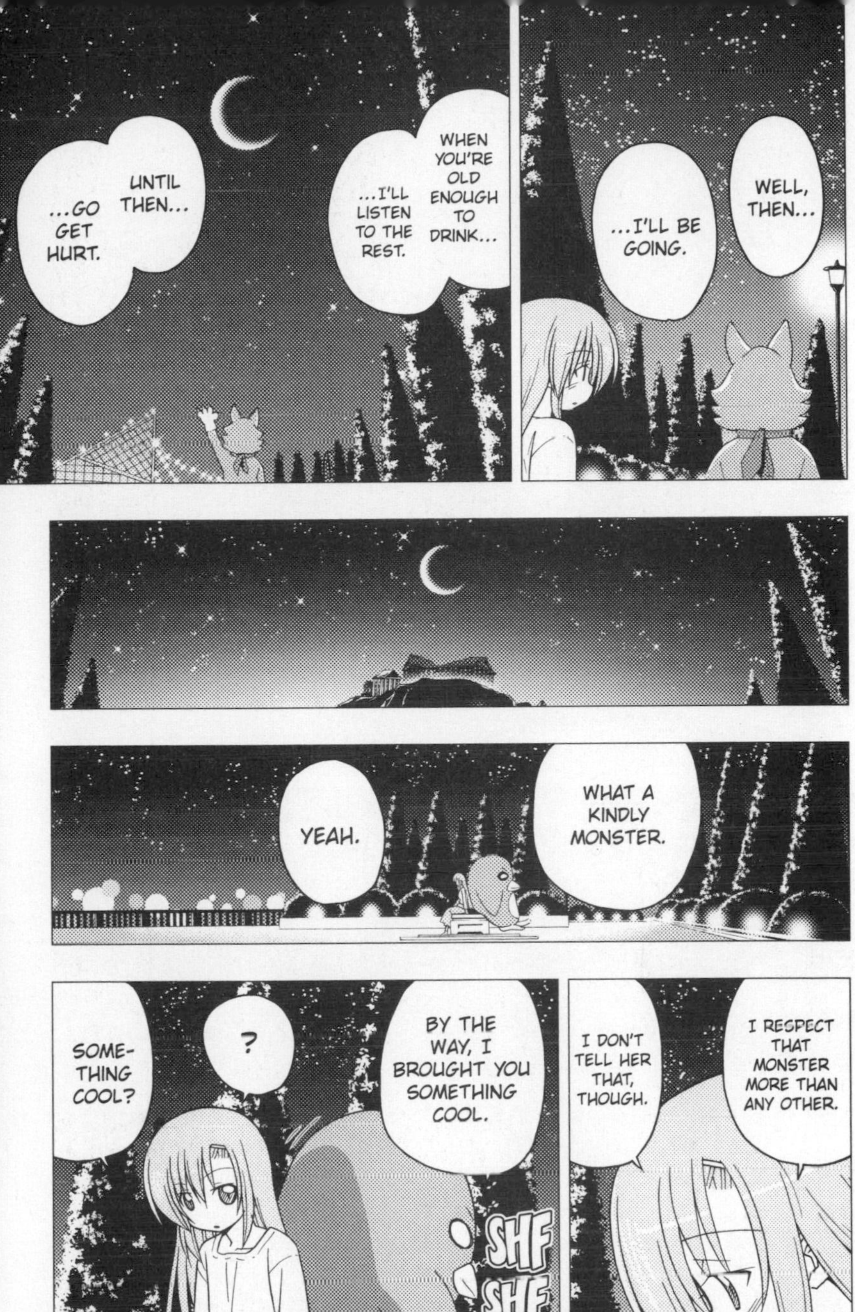
WELL, THEN...
...I'LL BE GOING.
WHEN YOU'RE OLD ENOUGH TO DRINK...
...I'LL LISTEN TO THE REST.
UNTIL THEN...
...GO GET HURT.
WHAT A KINDLY MONSTER.
YEAH.
I RESPECT THAT MONSTER MORE THAN ANY OTHER.
I DON'T TELL HER THAT, THOUGH.
BY THE WAY, I BROUGHT YOU SOMETHING COOL.
?
SOME-THING COOL?
SHF SHF

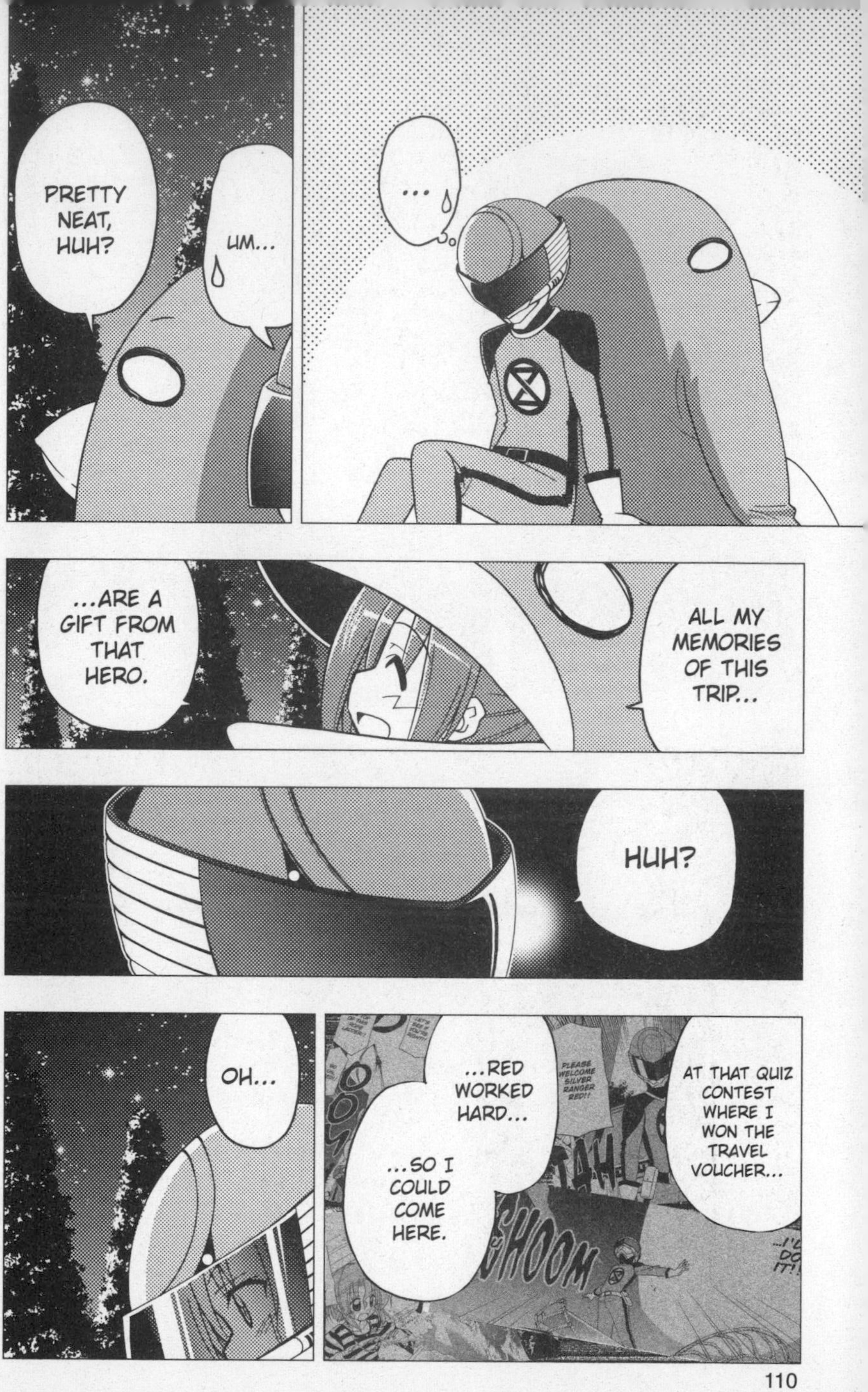
...
PRETTY NEAT, HUH?
UM...
ALL MY MEMORIES OF THIS TRIP...
...ARE A GIFT FROM THAT HERO.
HUH?
AT THAT QUIZ CONTEST WHERE I WON THE TRAVEL VOUCHER...
PLEASE WELCOME SILVER RANGER RED!!
...RED WORKED HARD...
...SO I COULD COME HERE.
OH...

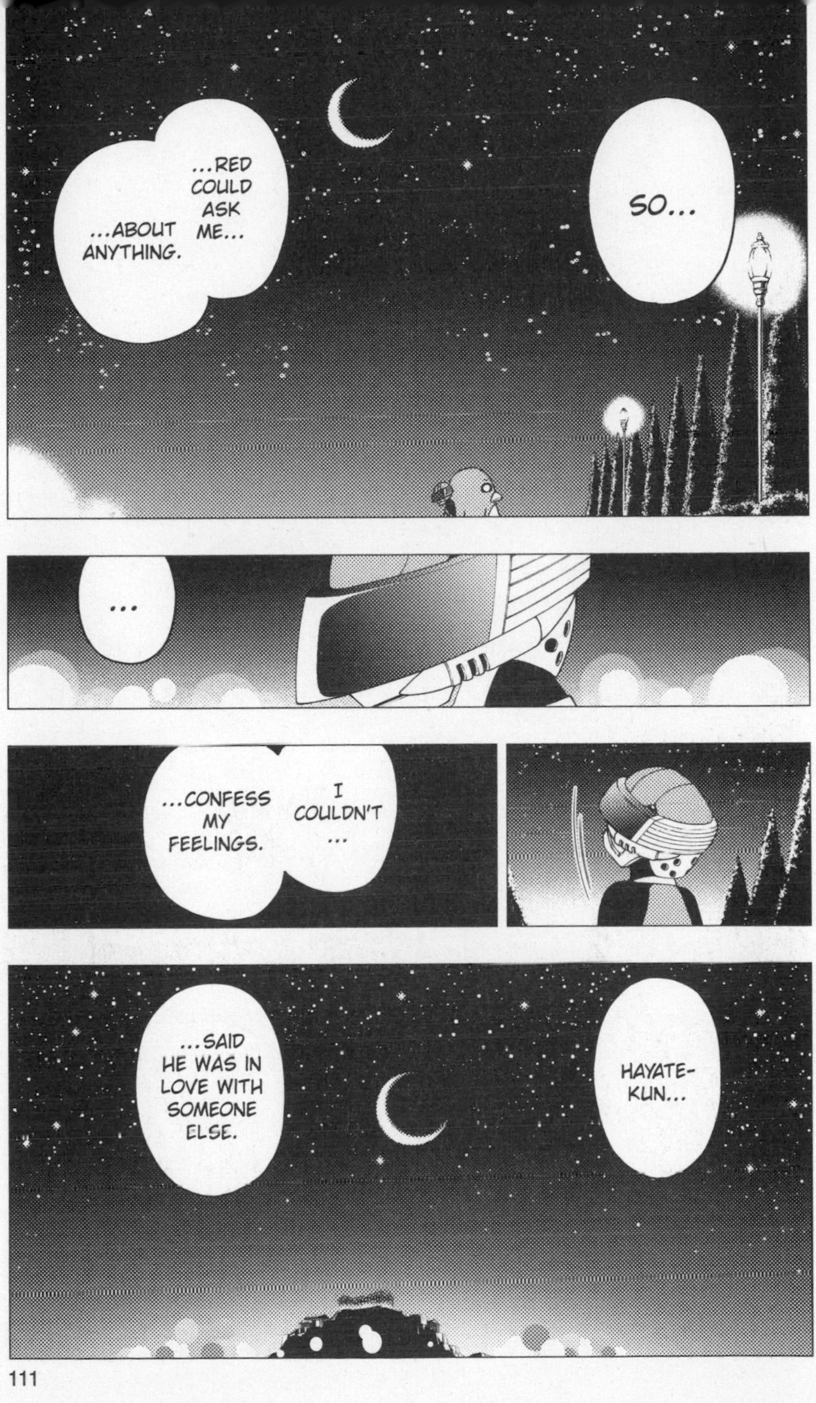
SO...
...RED COULD ASK ME...
...ABOUT ANYTHING.
...
I COULDN'T ...
...CONFESS MY FEELINGS.
HAYATE-KUN...
...SAID HE WAS IN LOVE WITH SOMEONE ELSE.

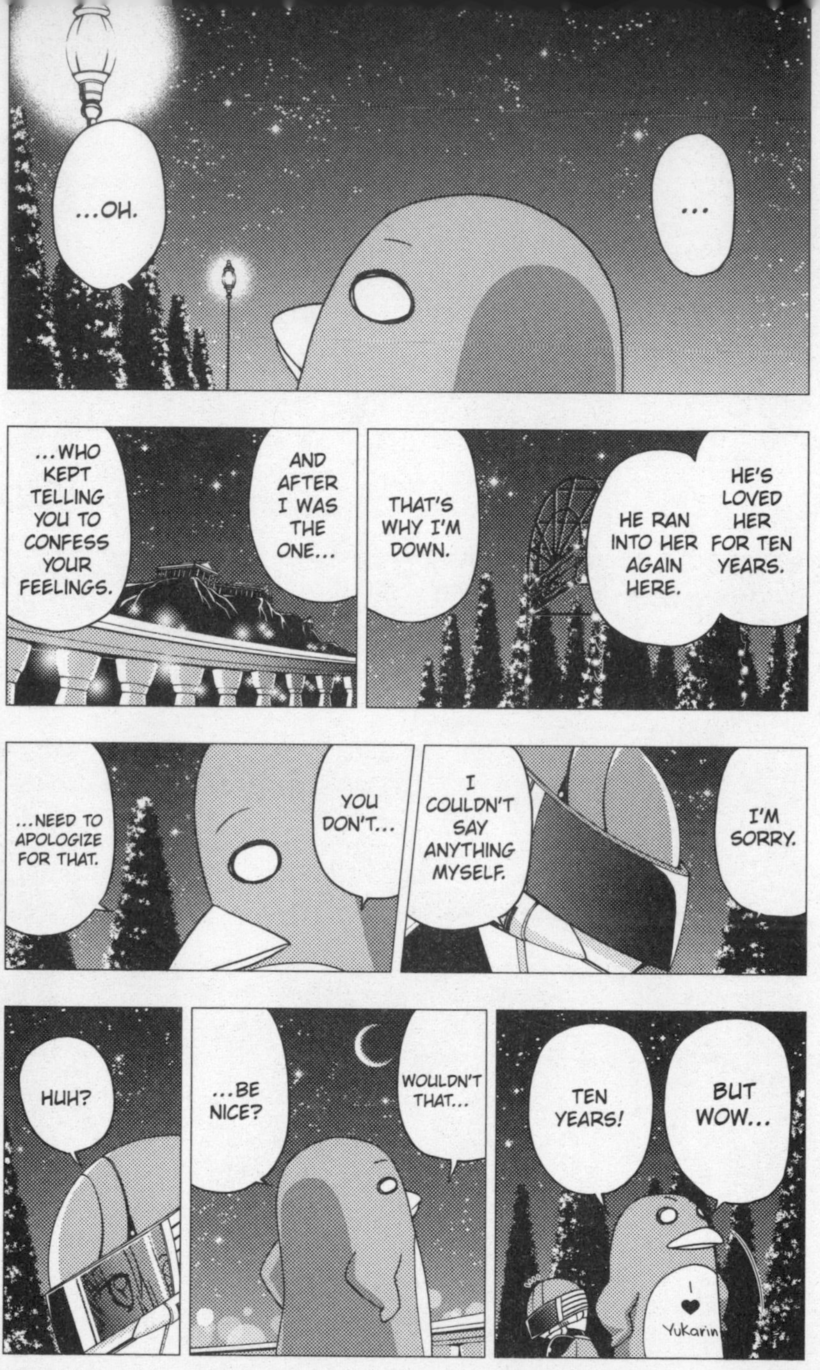
...
...OH.
HE'S LOVED HER FOR TEN YEARS.
HE RAN INTO HER AGAIN HERE.
THAT'S WHY I'M DOWN.
AND AFTER I WAS THE ONE...
...WHO KEPT TELLING YOU TO CONFESS YOUR FEELINGS.
I'M SORRY.
I COULDN'T SAY ANYTHING MYSELF.
YOU DON'T...
...NEED TO APOLOGIZE FOR THAT.
BUT WOW...
TEN YEARS!
I ♥ Yukarin
WOULDN'T THAT...
...BE NICE?
HUH?

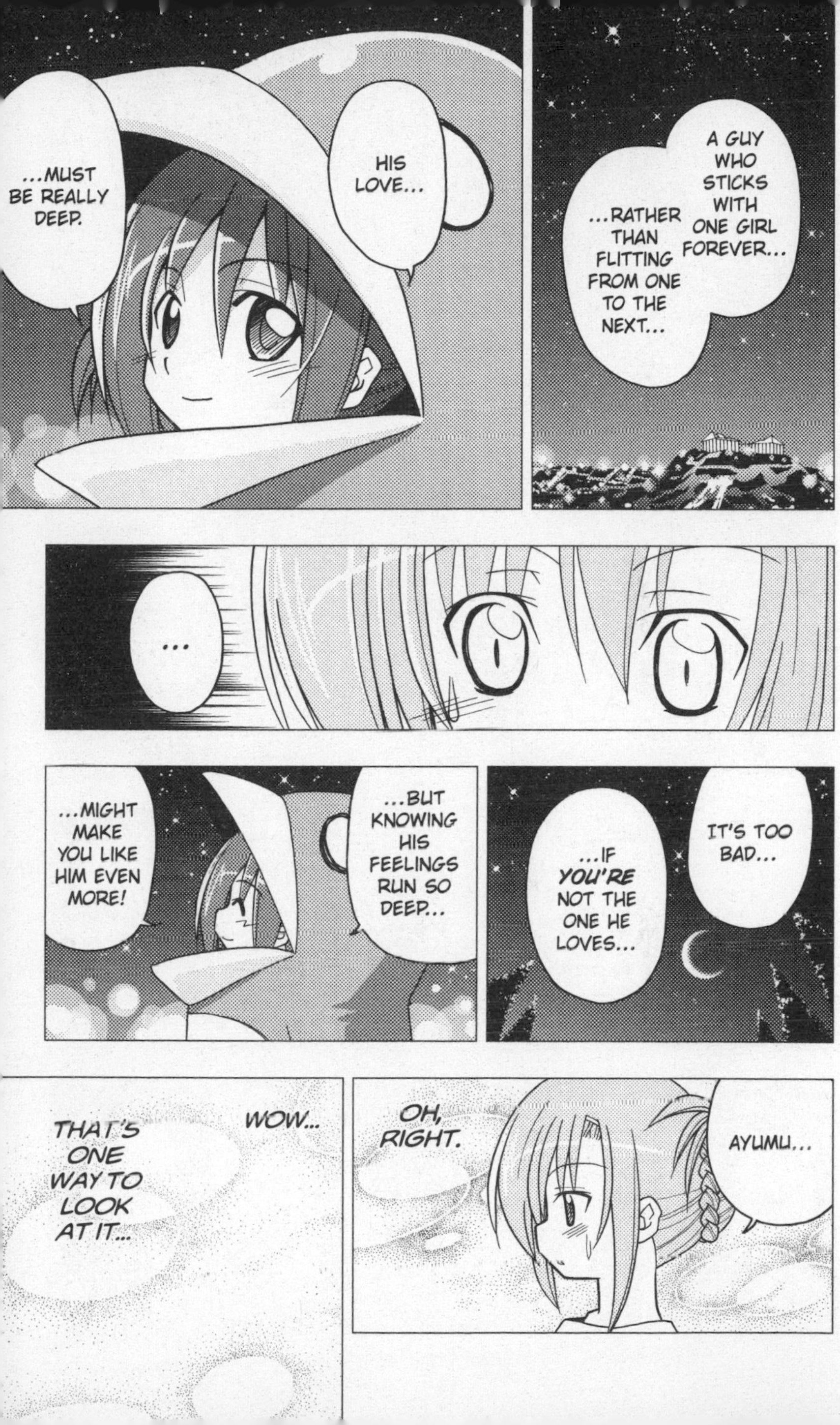
A GUY WHO STICKS WITH ONE GIRL FOREVER...
...RATHER THAN FLITTING FROM ONE TO THE NEXT...
HIS LOVE...
...MUST BE REALLY DEEP.
...
IT'S TOO BAD...
...IF *YOU'RE* NOT THE ONE HE LOVES...
...BUT KNOWING HIS FEELINGS RUN SO DEEP...
...MIGHT MAKE YOU LIKE HIM EVEN MORE!
AYUMU...
OH, RIGHT.
WOW...
THAT'S ONE WAY TO LOOK AT IT...

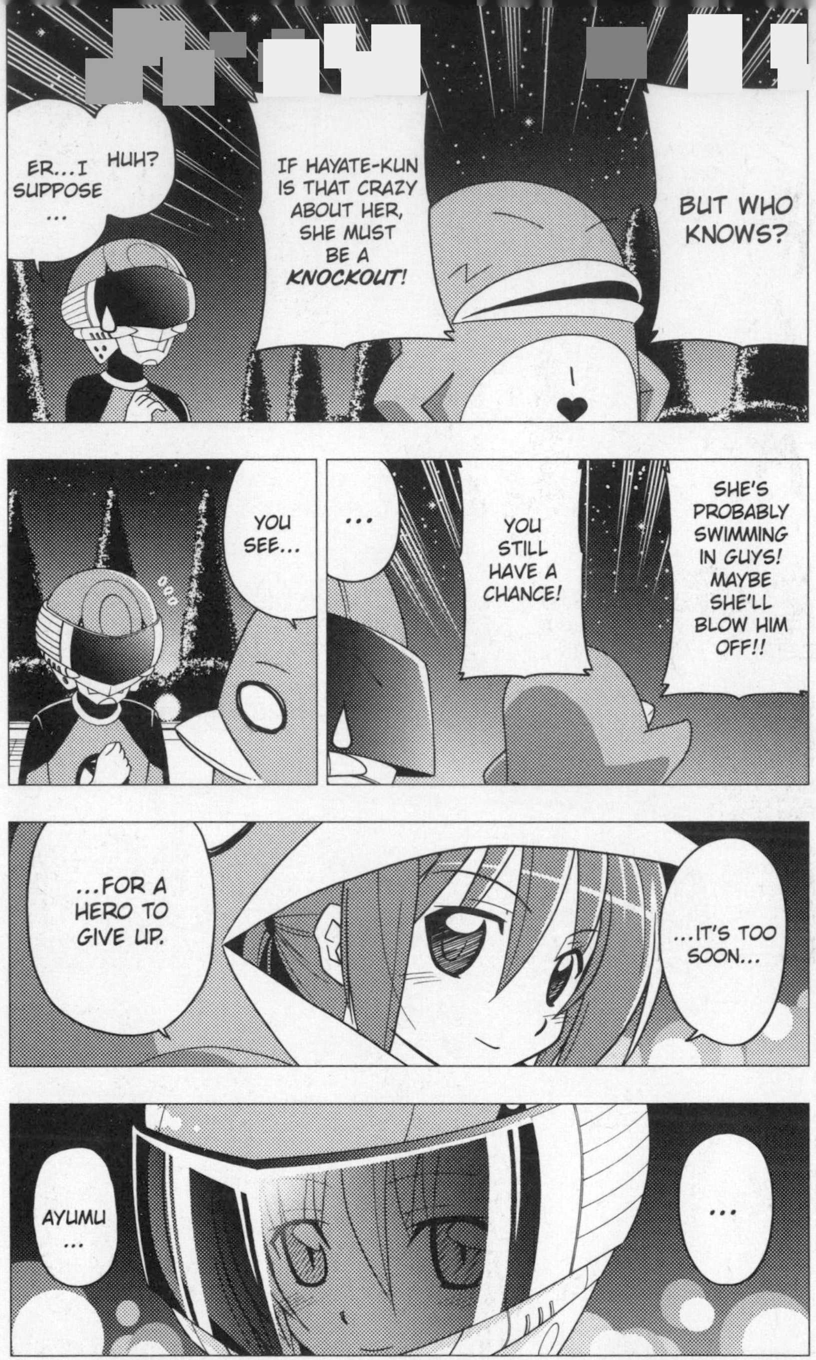
BUT WHO KNOWS?
IF HAYATE-KUN IS THAT CRAZY ABOUT HER, SHE MUST BE A *KNOCKOUT*!
HUH?
ER...I SUPPOSE ...
SHE'S PROBABLY SWIMMING IN GUYS! MAYBE SHE'LL BLOW HIM OFF!!
YOU STILL HAVE A CHANCE!
...
YOU SEE...
...IT'S TOO SOON...
...FOR A HERO TO GIVE UP.
...
AYUMU ...

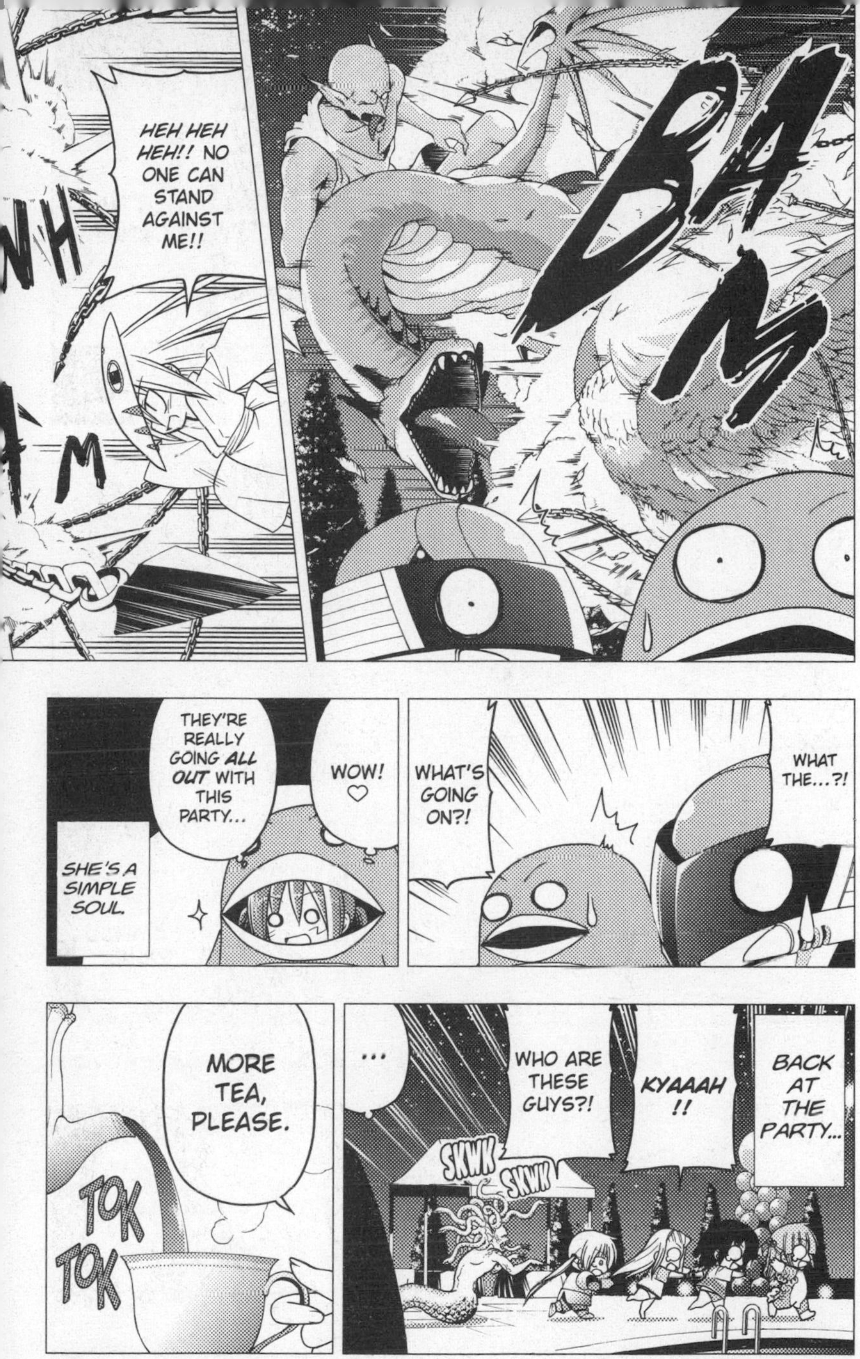
BAM
HEH HEH HEH!! NO ONE CAN STAND AGAINST ME!!
WHAT THE...?!
WHAT'S GOING ON?!
WOW! ♡
THEY'RE REALLY GOING ALL OUT WITH THIS PARTY...
SHE'S A SIMPLE SOUL.
BACK AT THE PARTY...
KYAAAH !!
WHO ARE THESE GUYS?!
SKWK
SKWK
...
MORE TEA, PLEASE.
TOK TOK

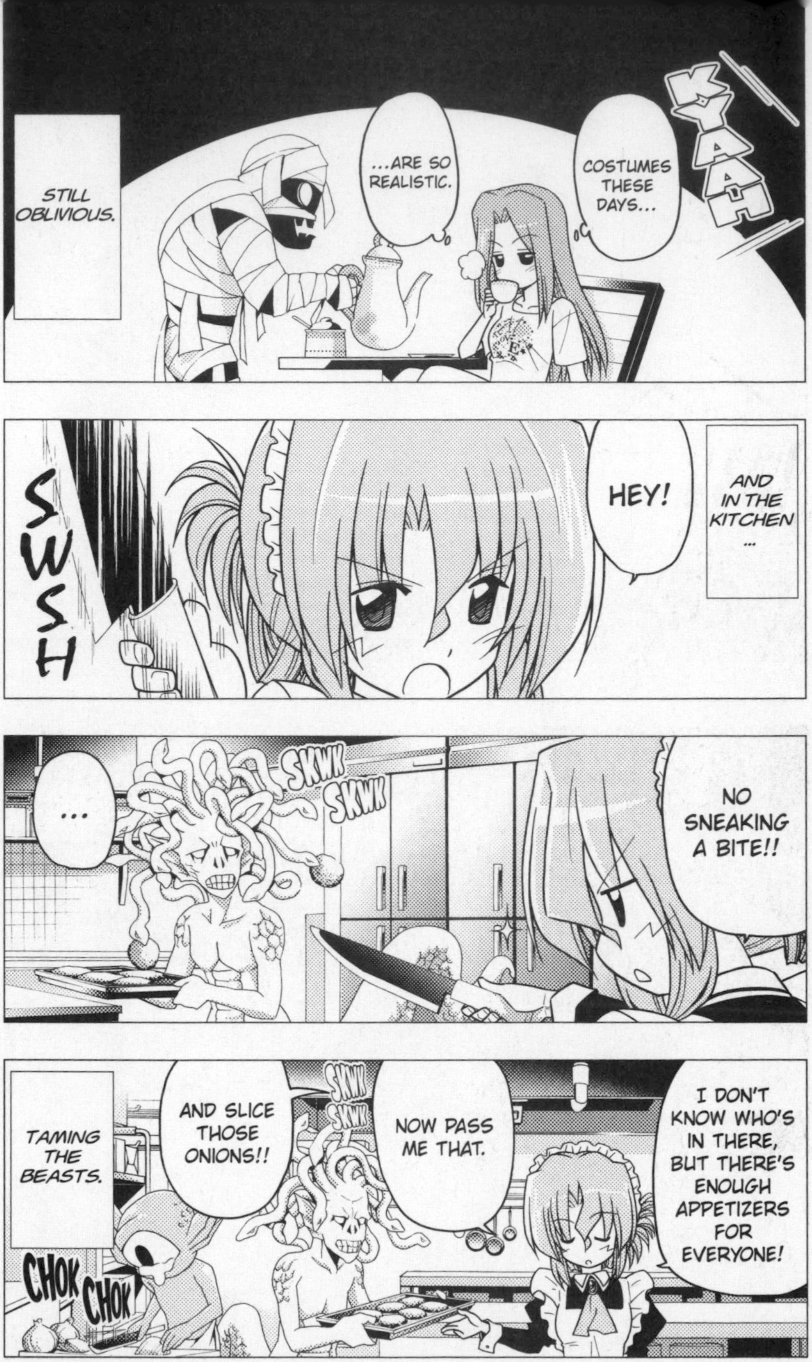
KYAAAH
COSTUMES THESE DAYS...
...ARE SO REALISTIC.
STILL OBLIVIOUS.
AND IN THE KITCHEN ...
HEY!
SWSH
NO SNEAKING A BITE!!
SKWK SKWK
...
I DON'T KNOW WHO'S IN THERE, BUT THERE'S ENOUGH APPETIZERS FOR EVERYONE!
NOW PASS ME THAT.
SKWK SKWK
AND SLICE THOSE ONIONS!!
TAMING THE BEASTS.
CHOK CHOK

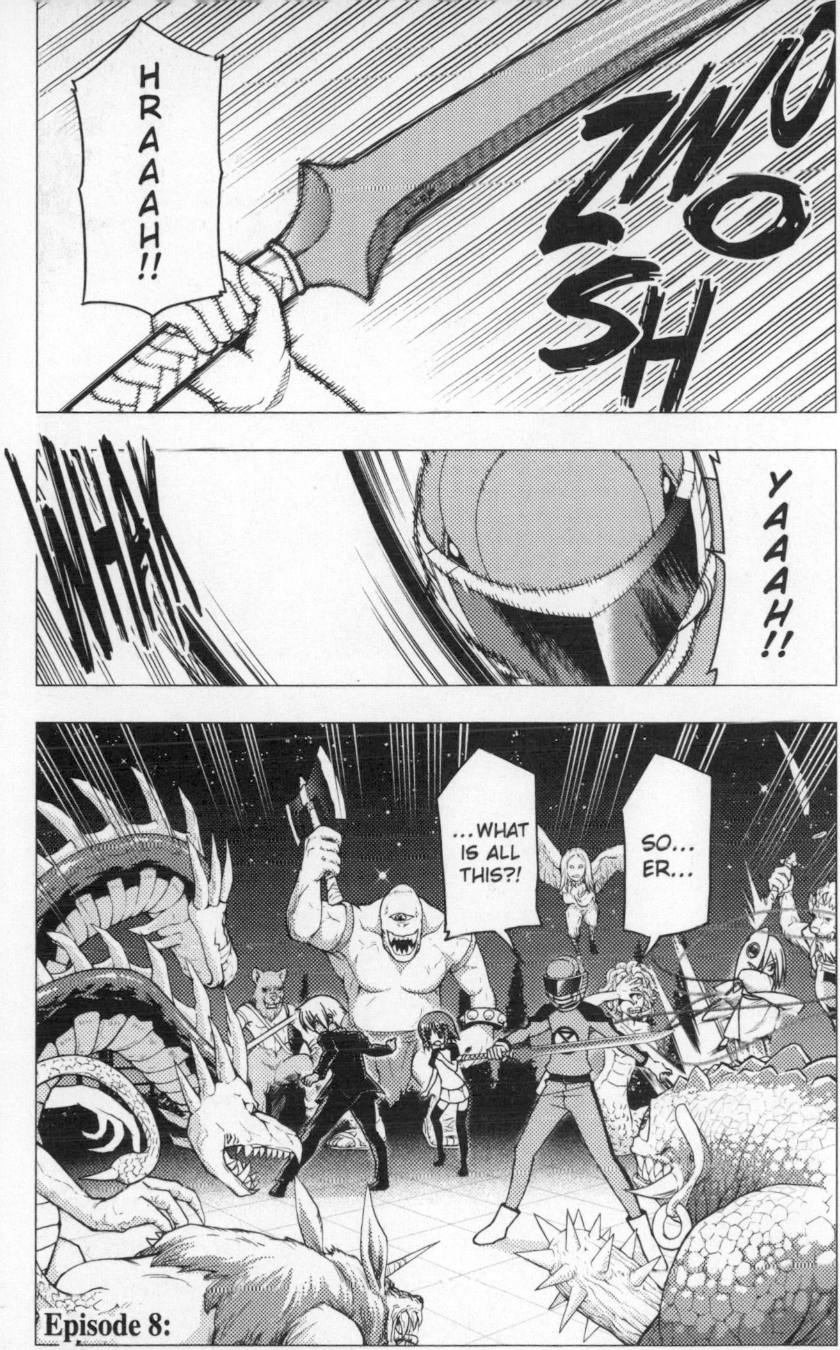
WHOOSH
HRAAAAH!!
YAAAAH!!
WHAK
SO... ER...
...WHAT IS ALL THIS?!

Episode 8:
"For Eternity, For You"

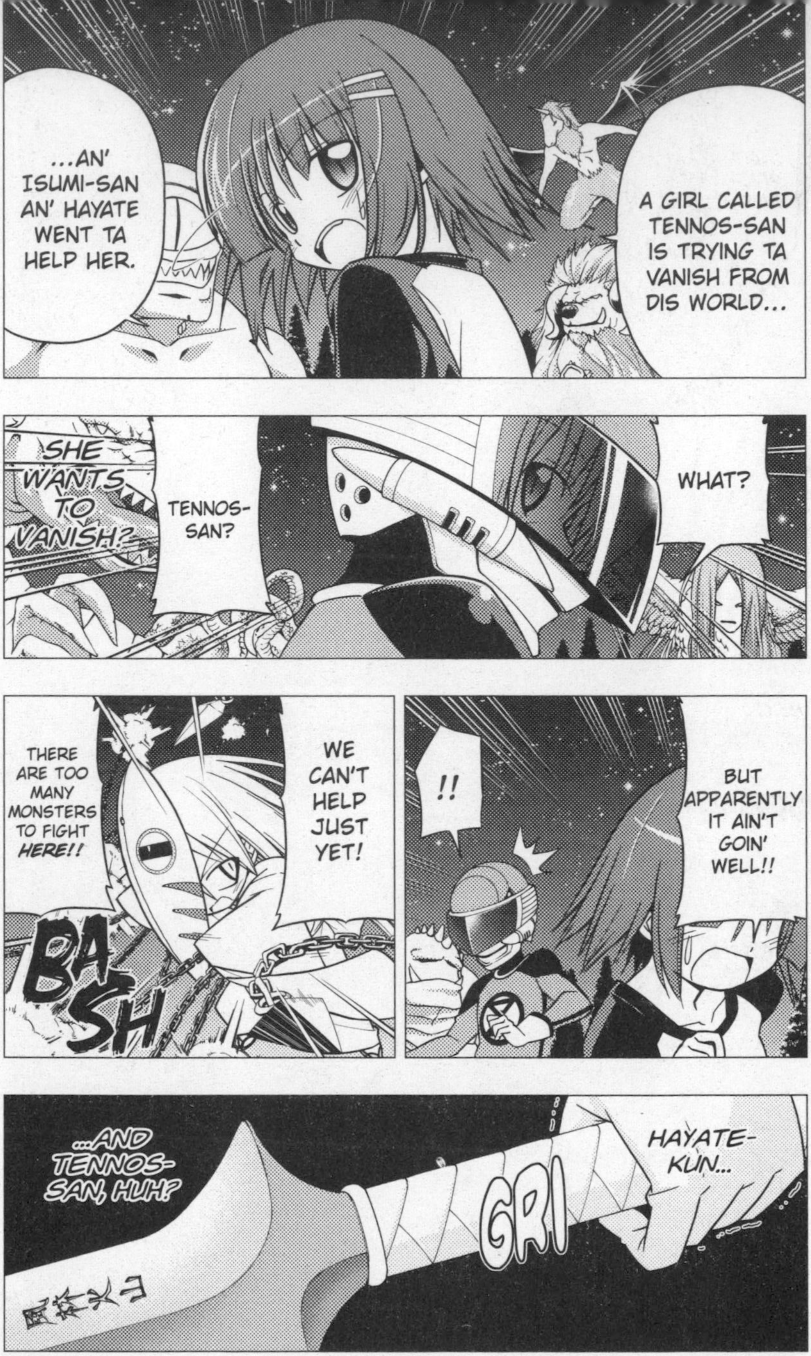
A GIRL CALLED TENNOS-SAN IS TRYING TA VANISH FROM DIS WORLD...
...AN' ISUMI-SAN AN' HAYATE WENT TA HELP HER.
WHAT?
TENNOS-SAN?
SHE WANTS TO VANISH?
BUT APPARENTLY IT AIN'T GOIN' WELL!!
!!
WE CAN'T HELP JUST YET!
THERE ARE TOO MANY MONSTERS TO FIGHT HERE!!
BASH
HAYATE-KUN...
GRI
...AND TENNOS-SAN, HUH?

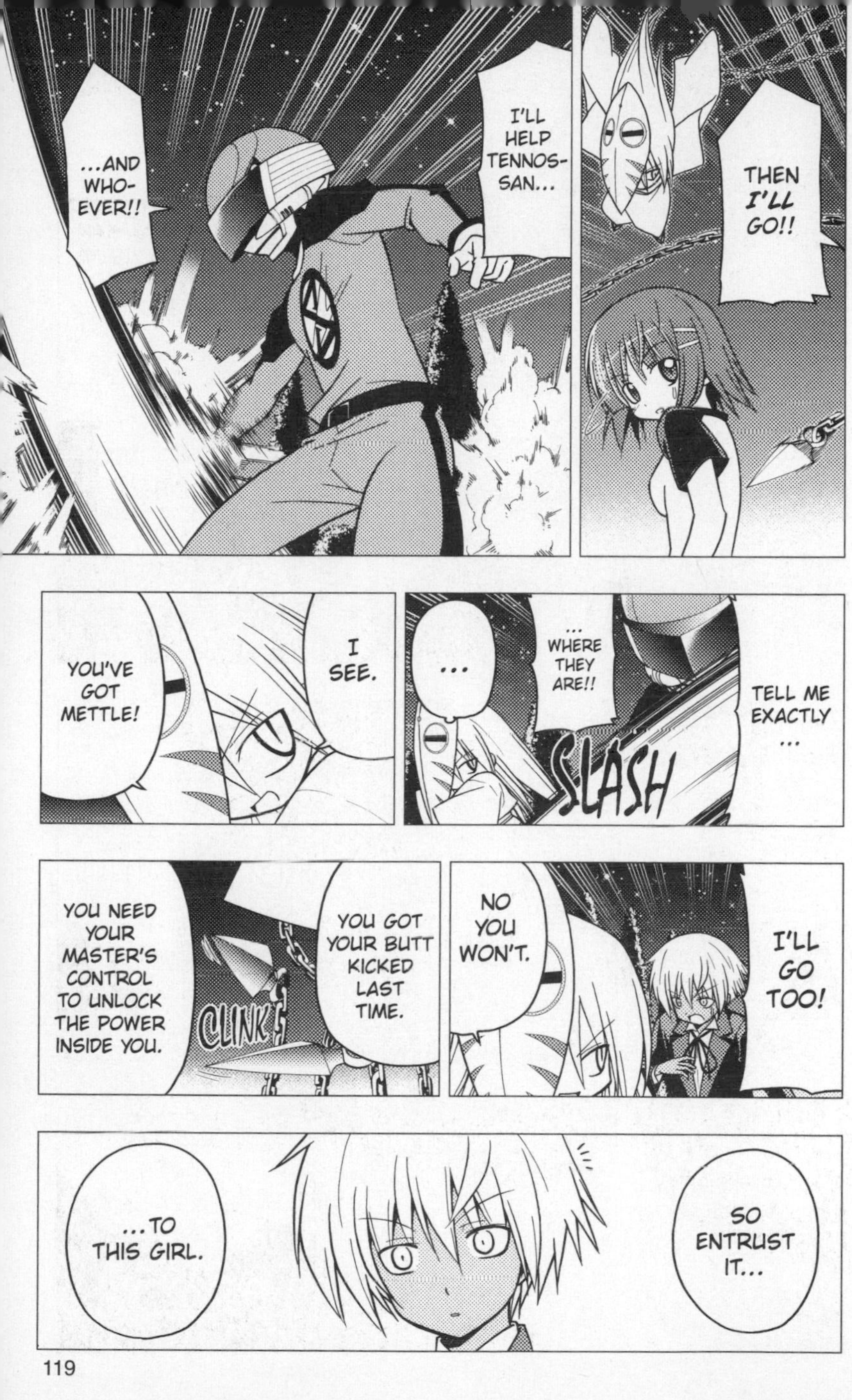
THEN I'LL GO!!
I'LL HELP TENNOS-SAN...
...AND WHO-EVER!!
TELL ME EXACTLY ...
...WHERE THEY ARE!!
SLASH
...
I SEE.
YOU'VE GOT METTLE!
I'LL GO TOO!
NO YOU WON'T.
YOU GOT YOUR BUTT KICKED LAST TIME.
CLINK
YOU NEED YOUR MASTER'S CONTROL TO UNLOCK THE POWER INSIDE YOU.
SO ENTRUST IT...
...TO THIS GIRL.

TAKE IT, GIRLIE !!!

HUH?

IT'S CALLED SHIRO-ZAKURA.

DON'T LET GO OF IT!!!

WHAT IS THIS?!

?!!

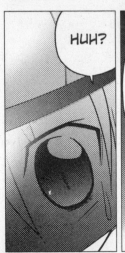

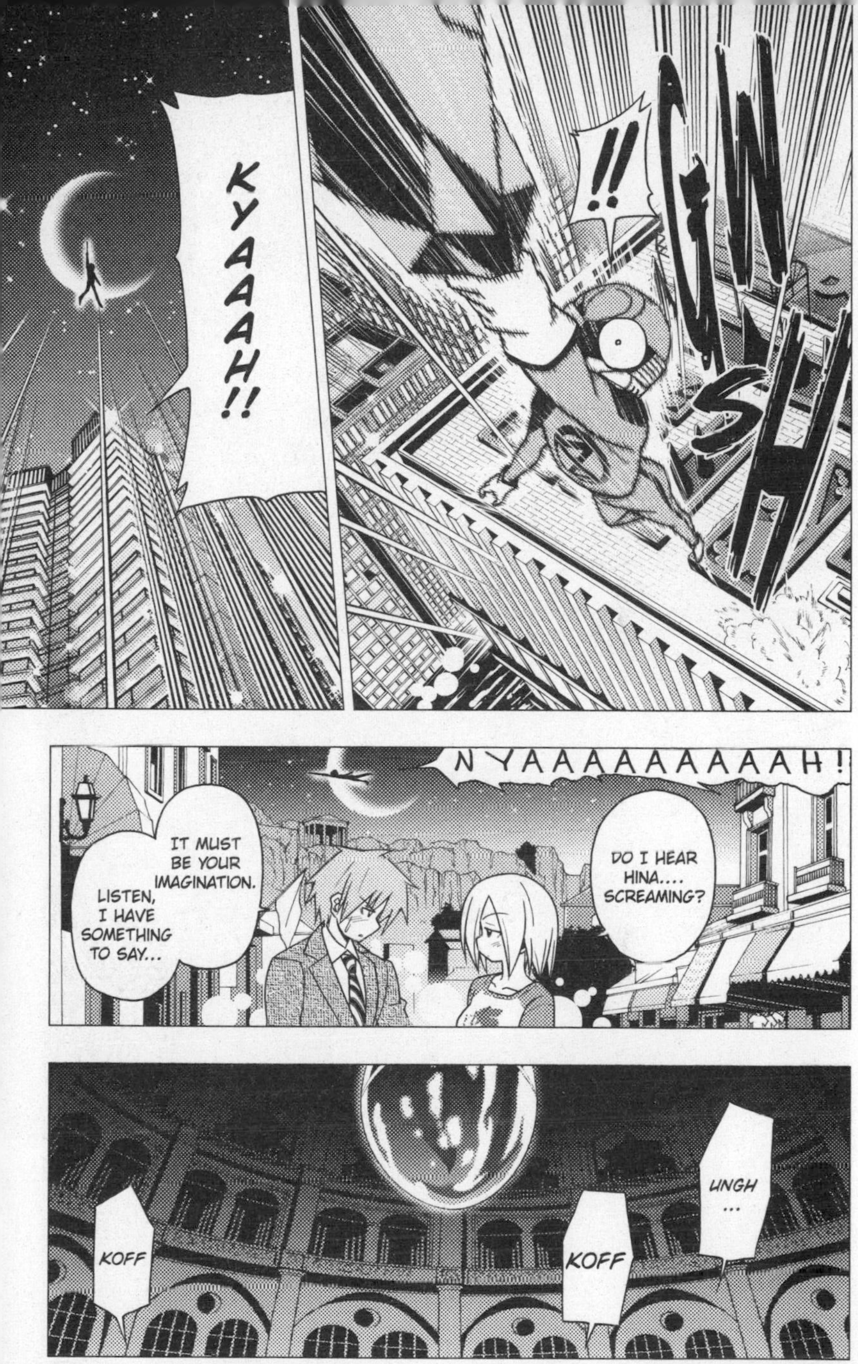
!!
CRASH
KYAAAAH!!
NYAAAAAAAAAAH!
DO I HEAR HINA.... SCREAMING?
IT MUST BE YOUR IMAGINATION.
LISTEN, I HAVE SOMETHING TO SAY...
UNGH...
KOFF
KOFF

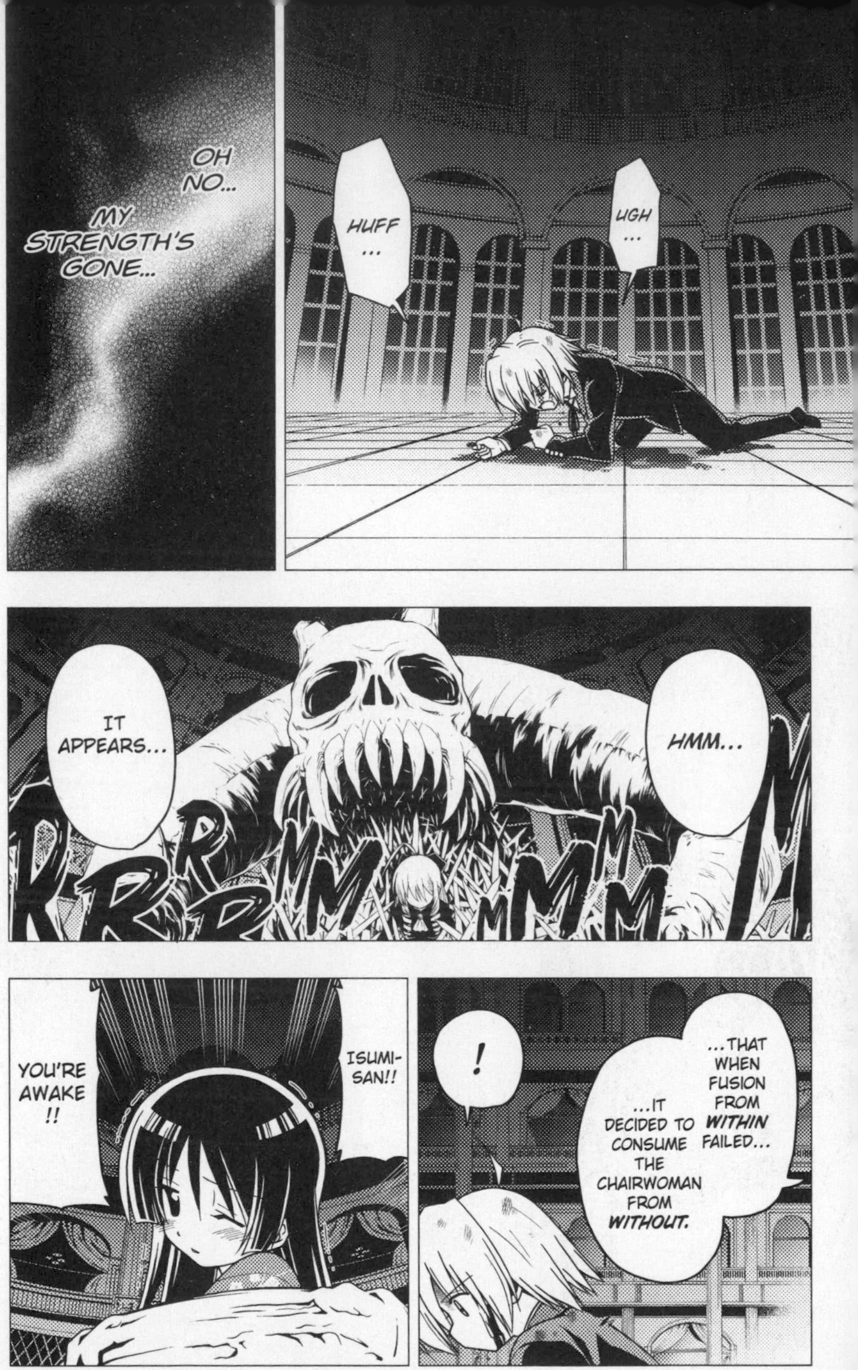
UGH ...
HUFF ...
OH NO... MY STRENGTH'S GONE...
HMM...
IT APPEARS...
KRRRMMMMMMMMM
...THAT WHEN FUSION FROM WITHIN FAILED...
...IT DECIDED TO CONSUME THE CHAIRWOMAN FROM WITHOUT.
!
ISUMI-SAN!!
YOU'RE AWAKE !!

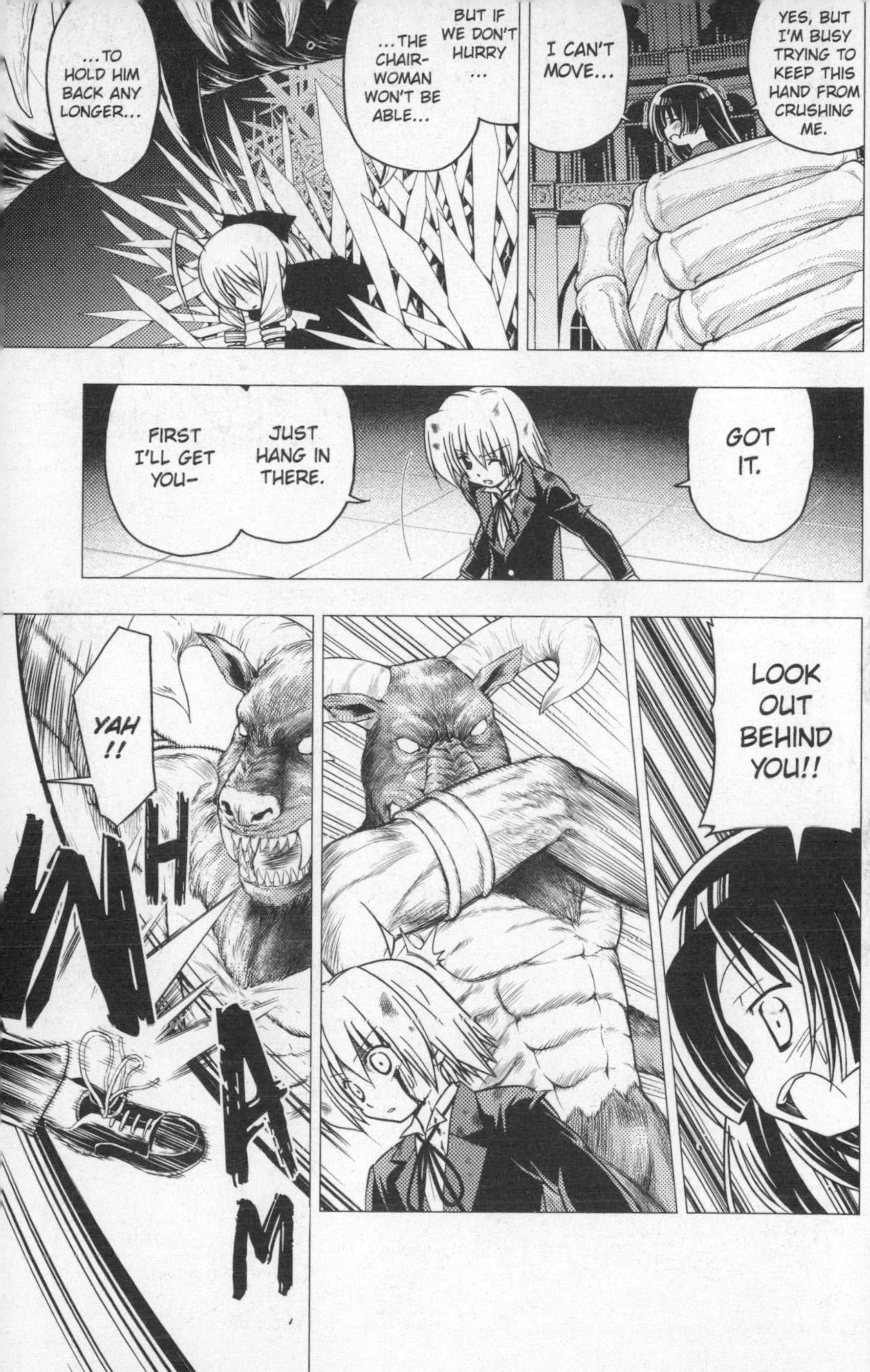
YES, BUT I'M BUSY TRYING TO KEEP THIS HAND FROM CRUSHING ME.
I CAN'T MOVE...
BUT IF WE DON'T HURRY...
...THE CHAIR-WOMAN WON'T BE ABLE...
...TO HOLD HIM BACK ANY LONGER...
GOT IT.
JUST HANG IN THERE.
FIRST I'LL GET YOU-
LOOK OUT BEHIND YOU!!
YAH!!
WHAM

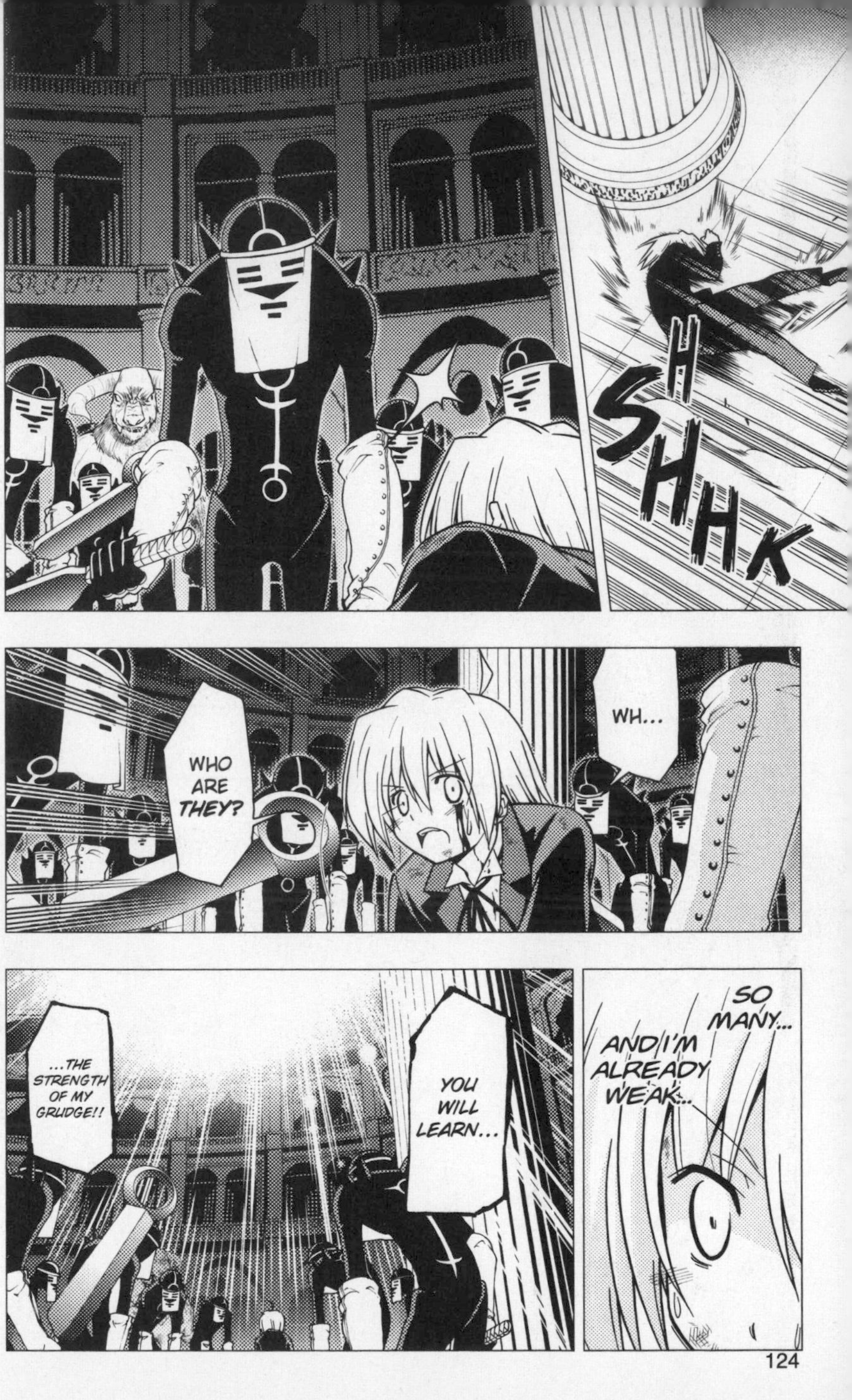
SHHHK
WH...
WHO ARE THEY?
SO MANY... AND I'M ALREADY WEAK...
YOU WILL LEARN...
...THE STRENGTH OF MY GRUDGE!!

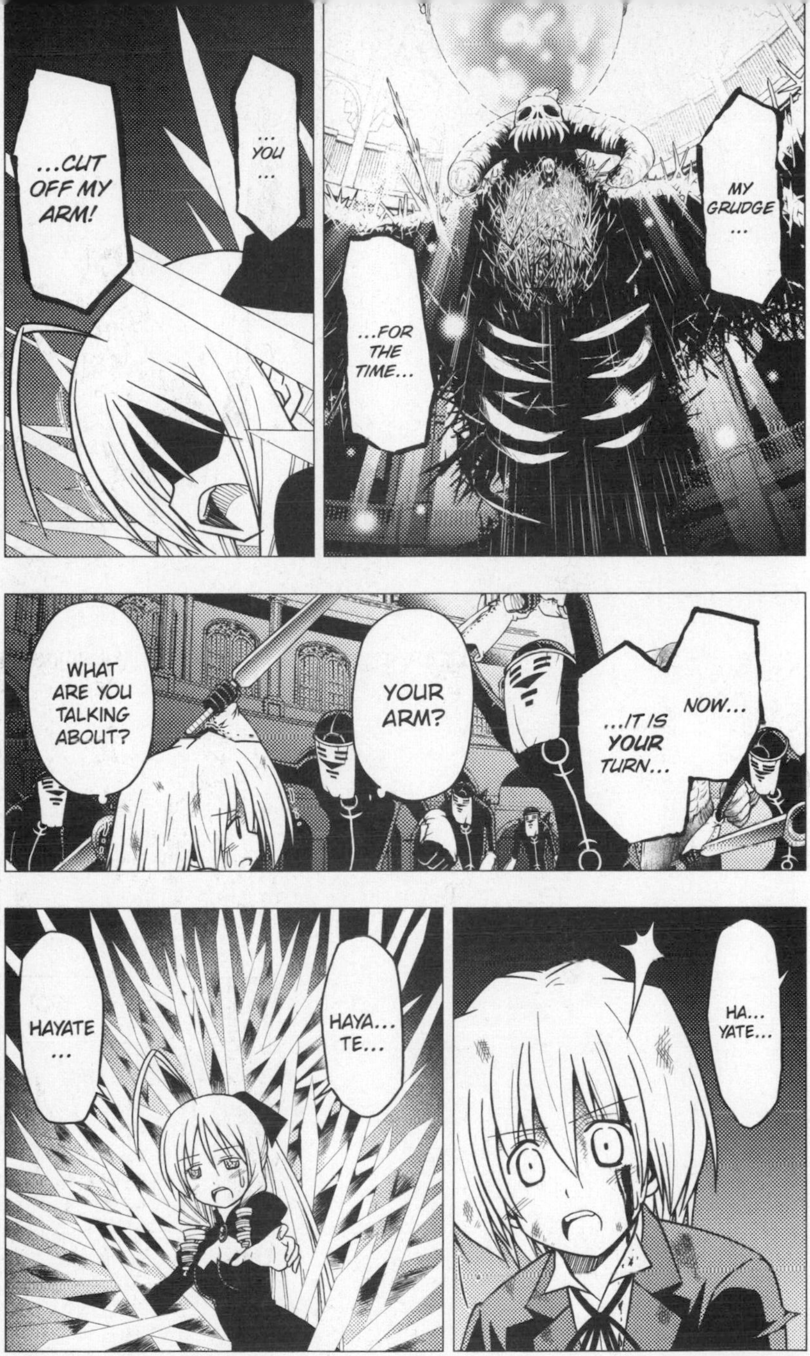
MY GRUDGE ...
...FOR THE TIME...
... YOU ...
...CUT OFF MY ARM!
NOW...
...IT IS YOUR TURN...
YOUR ARM?
WHAT ARE YOU TALKING ABOUT?
HA... YATE...
HAYA... TE...
HAYATE ...

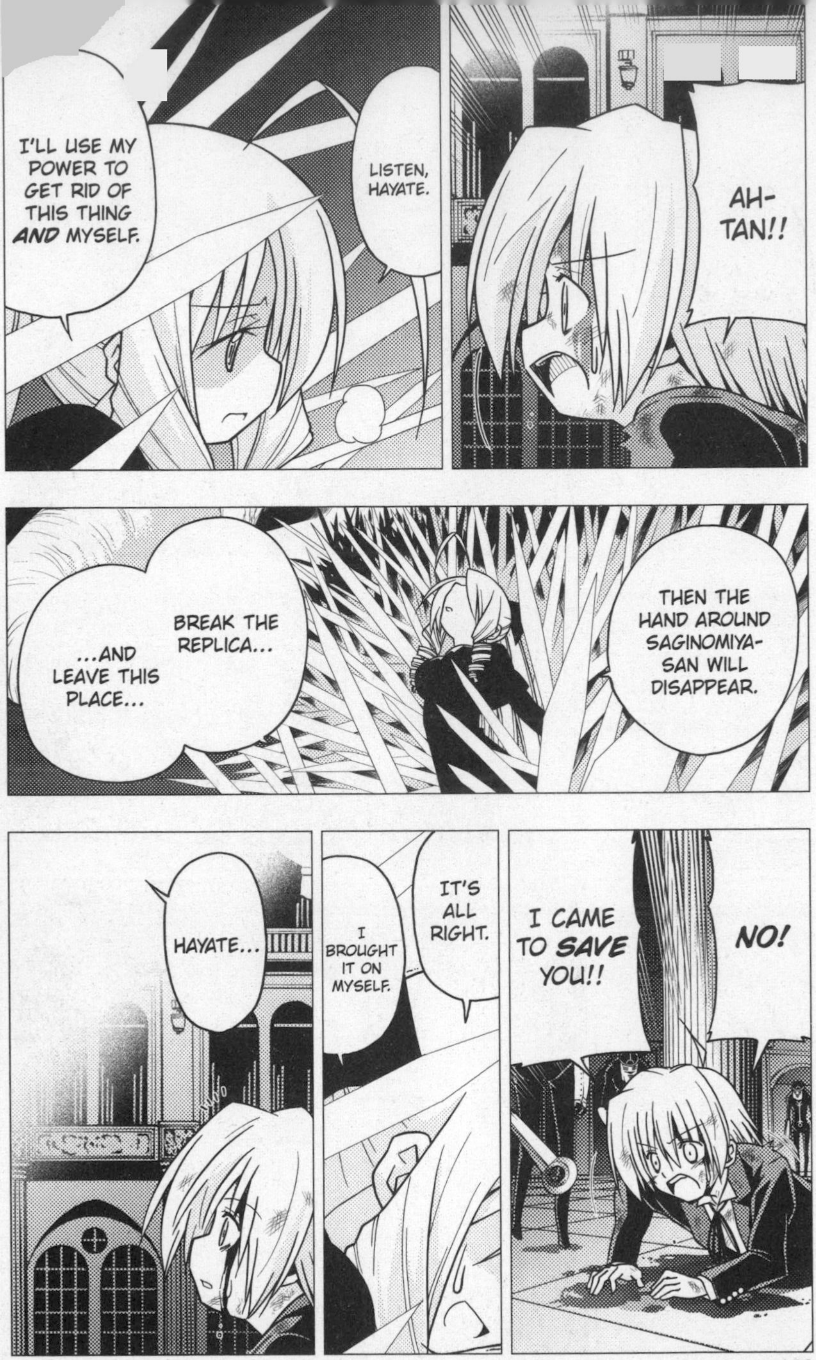
AH-TAN!!
LISTEN, HAYATE.
I'LL USE MY POWER TO GET RID OF THIS THING AND MYSELF.
THEN THE HAND AROUND SAGINOMIYA-SAN WILL DISAPPEAR.
BREAK THE REPLICA...
...AND LEAVE THIS PLACE...
NO!
I CAME TO SAVE YOU!!
IT'S ALL RIGHT.
I BROUGHT IT ON MYSELF.
HAYATE...

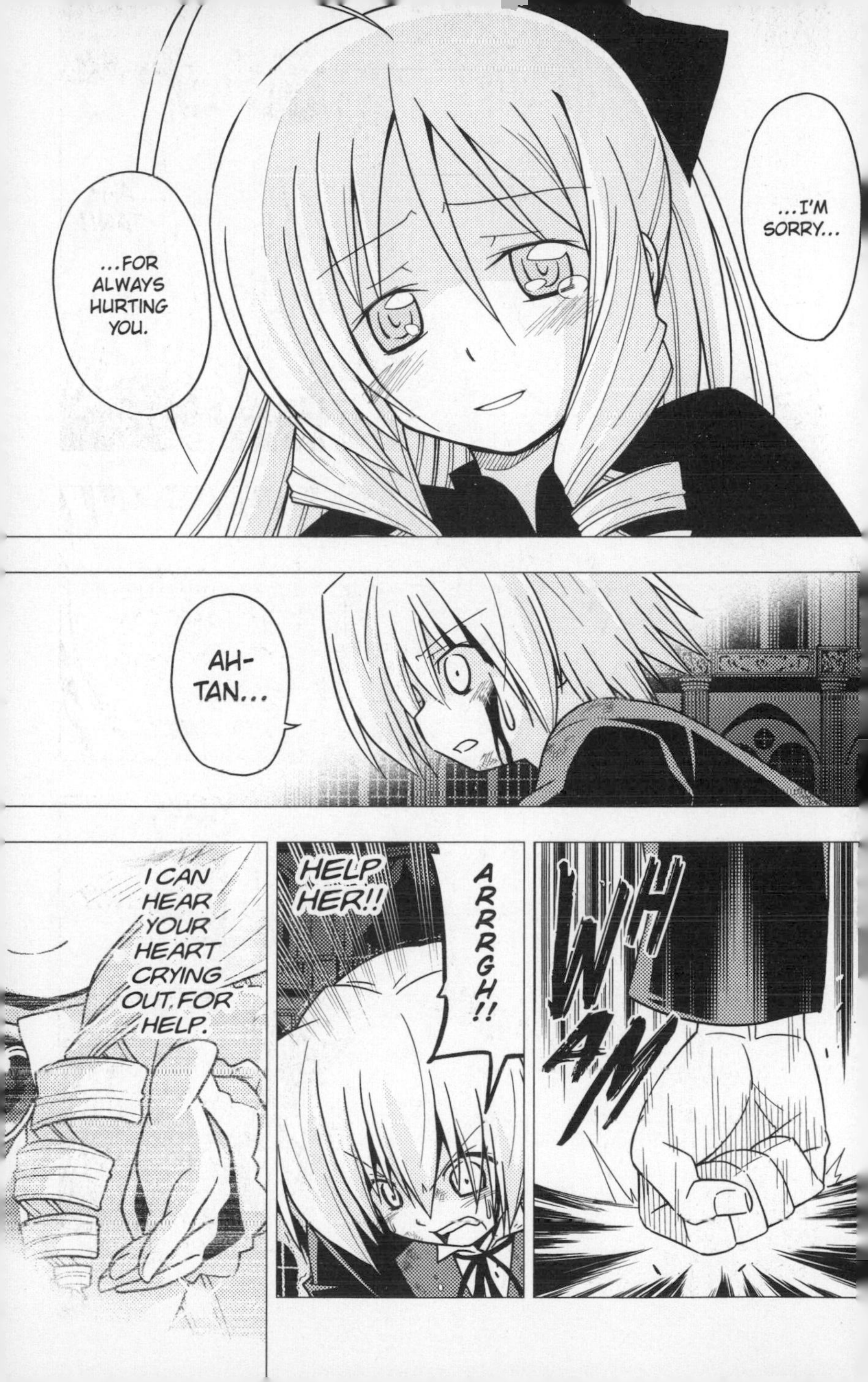
...I'M SORRY...
...FOR ALWAYS HURTING YOU.
AH-TAN...
WHAM
ARRRGH!!
HELP HER!!
I CAN HEAR YOUR HEART CRYING OUT FOR HELP.

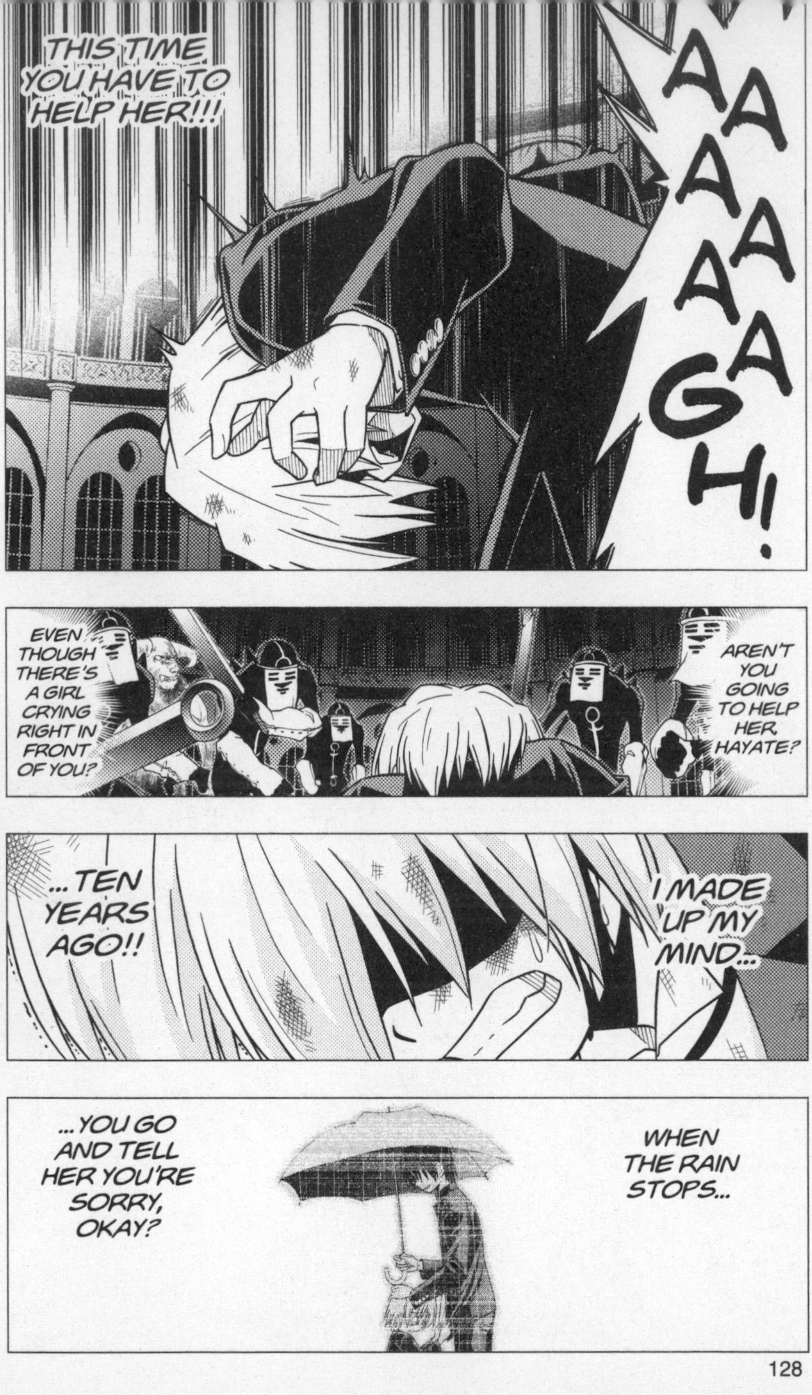
AAAAAAGH!
THIS TIME YOU HAVE TO HELP HER!!!
AREN'T YOU GOING TO HELP HER, HAYATE?
EVEN THOUGH THERE'S A GIRL CRYING RIGHT IN FRONT OF YOU?
I MADE UP MY MIND...
...TEN YEARS AGO!!
WHEN THE RAIN STOPS...
...YOU GO AND TELL HER YOU'RE SORRY, OKAY?

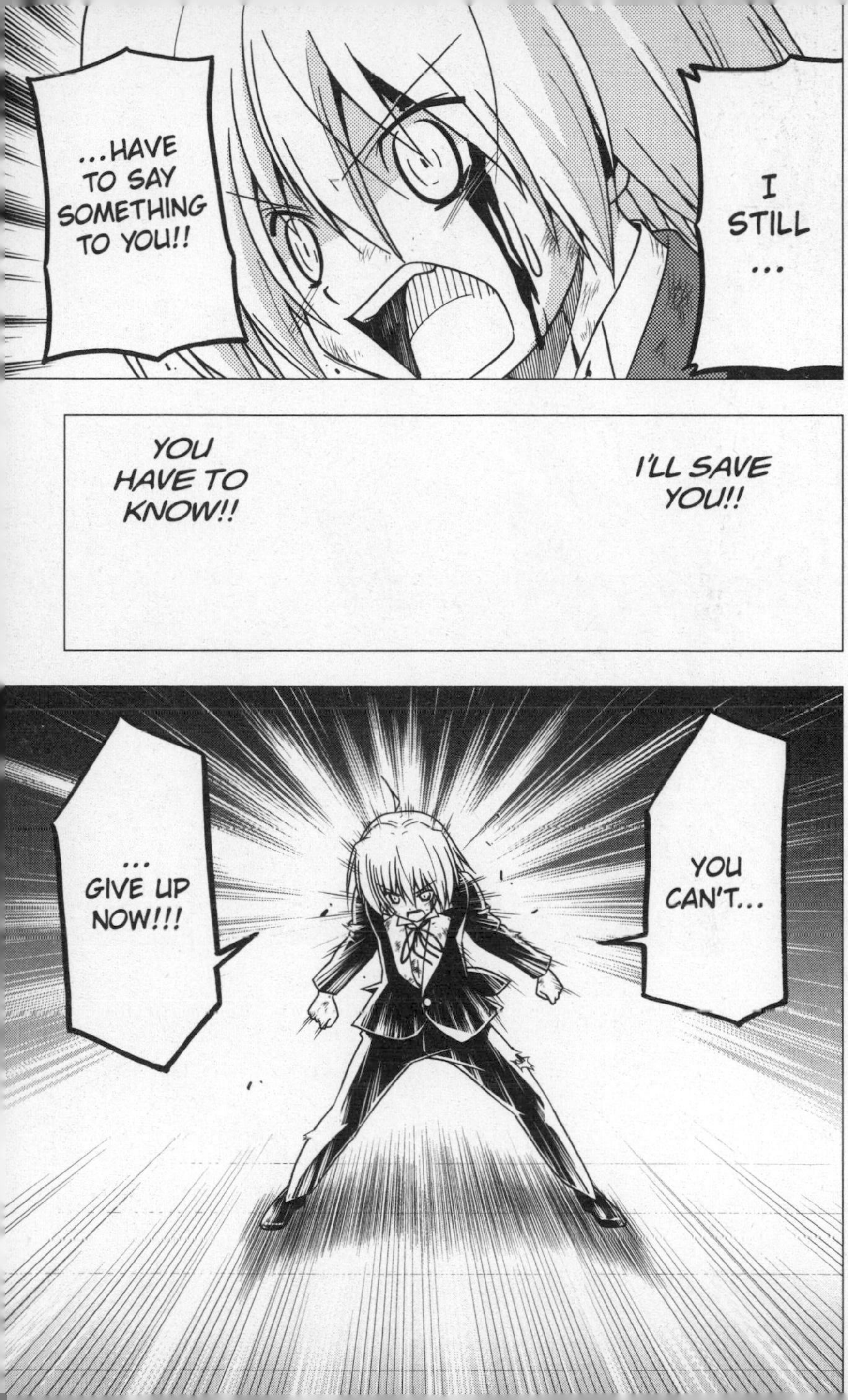
I STILL...
...HAVE TO SAY SOMETHING TO YOU!!
I'LL SAVE YOU!!
YOU HAVE TO KNOW!!
YOU CAN'T...
...GIVE UP NOW!!!

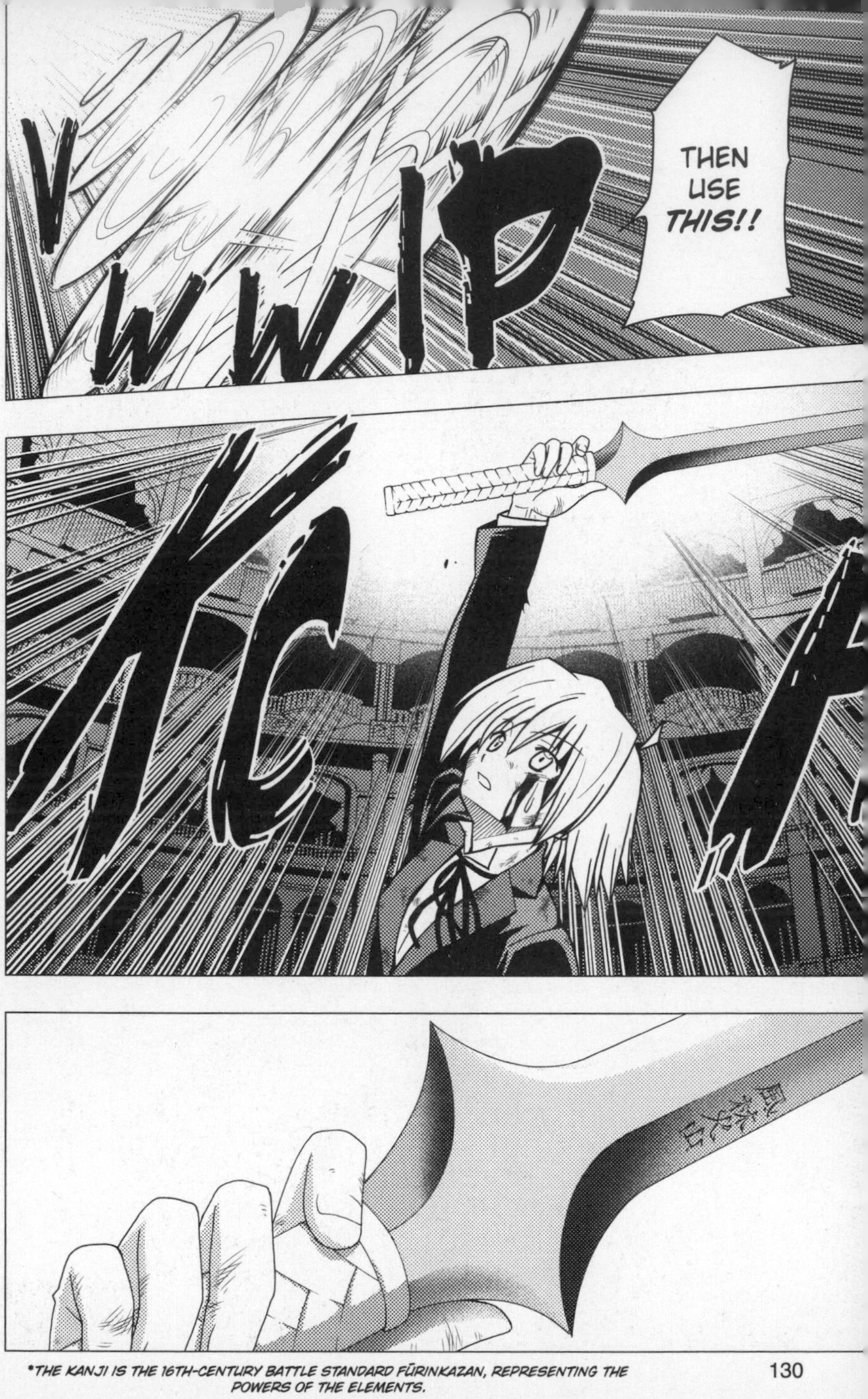
THEN USE THIS!!
VWWIP
風林火山

*THE KANJI IS THE 16TH-CENTURY BATTLE STANDARD FŪRINKAZAN, REPRESENTING THE POWERS OF THE ELEMENTS.

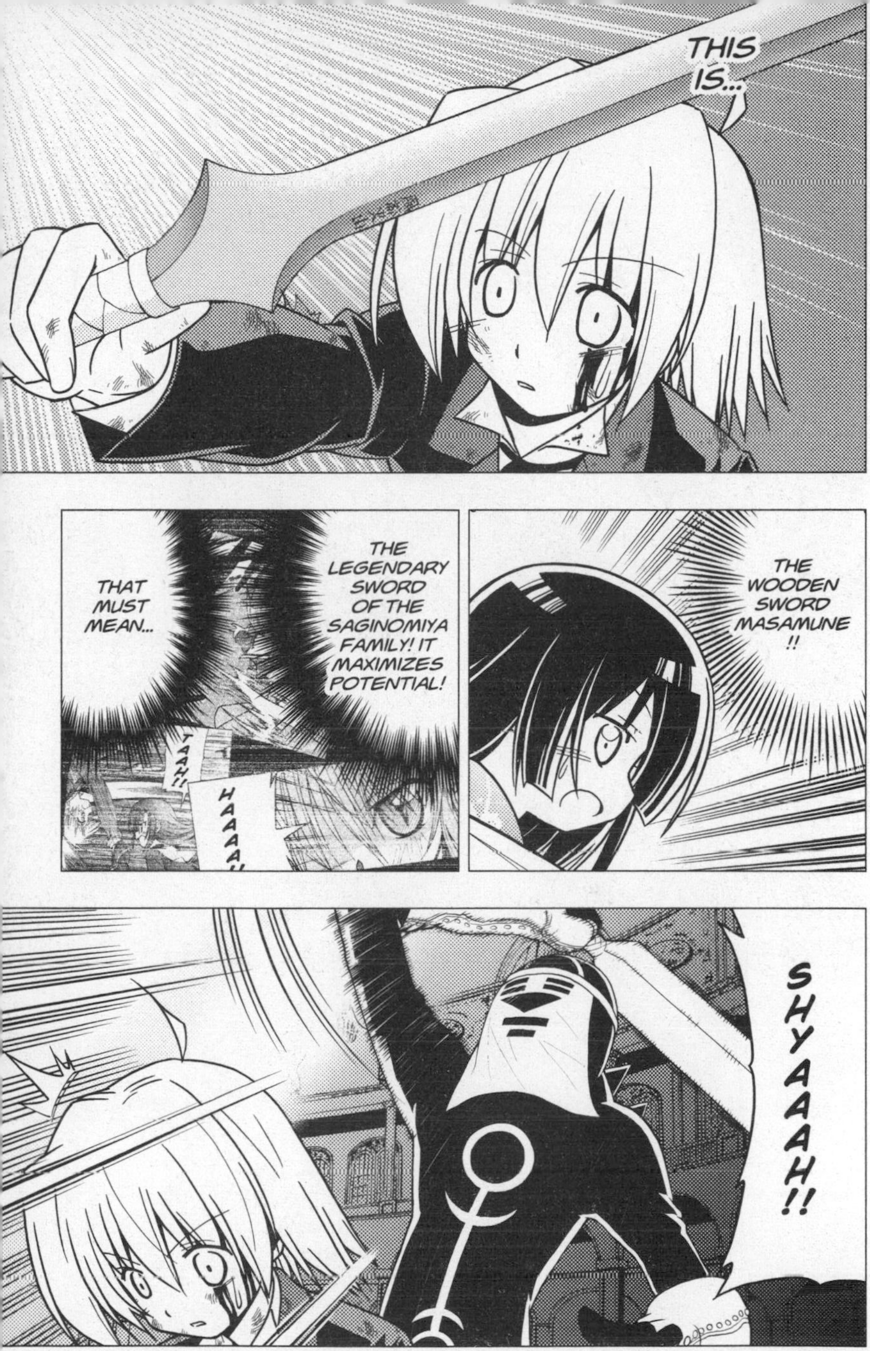
THIS IS...
THE WOODEN SWORD MASAMUNE!!
THE LEGENDARY SWORD OF THE SAGINOMIYA FAMILY! IT MAXIMIZES POTENTIAL!
THAT MUST MEAN...
HAAAA!!
TAAH!!
SHYAAAAH!!

I CAN MOVE!!

HEY!!

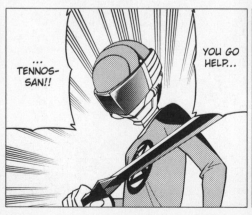

... TENNOS-SAN!!

YOU GO HELP...

I'LL HANDLE THESE SMALL FRIES!!

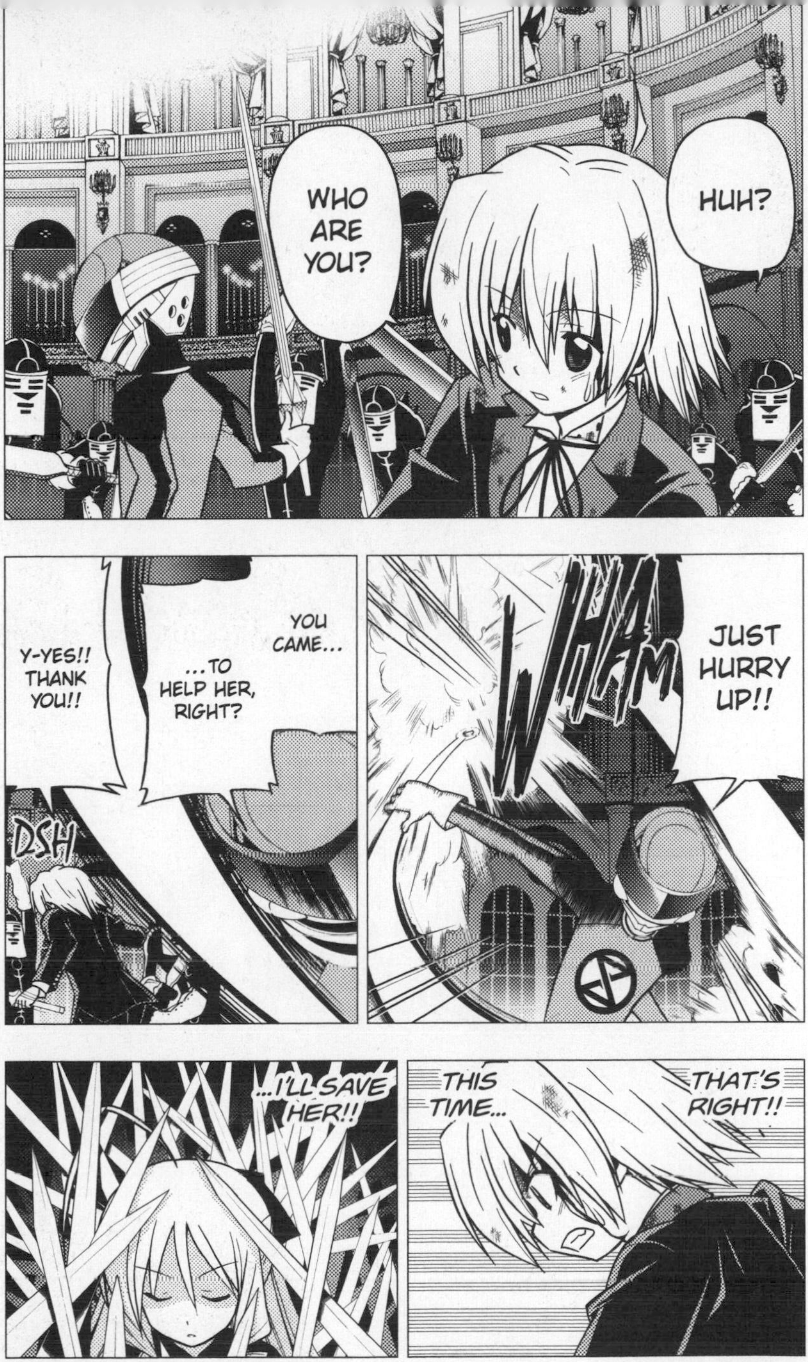
HUH?
WHO ARE YOU?
WHAM
JUST HURRY UP!!
YOU CAME...
...TO HELP HER, RIGHT?
Y-YES!! THANK YOU!!
DSH
THAT'S RIGHT!!
THIS TIME...
...I'LL SAVE HER!!

Episode 9: "~Fly High~"

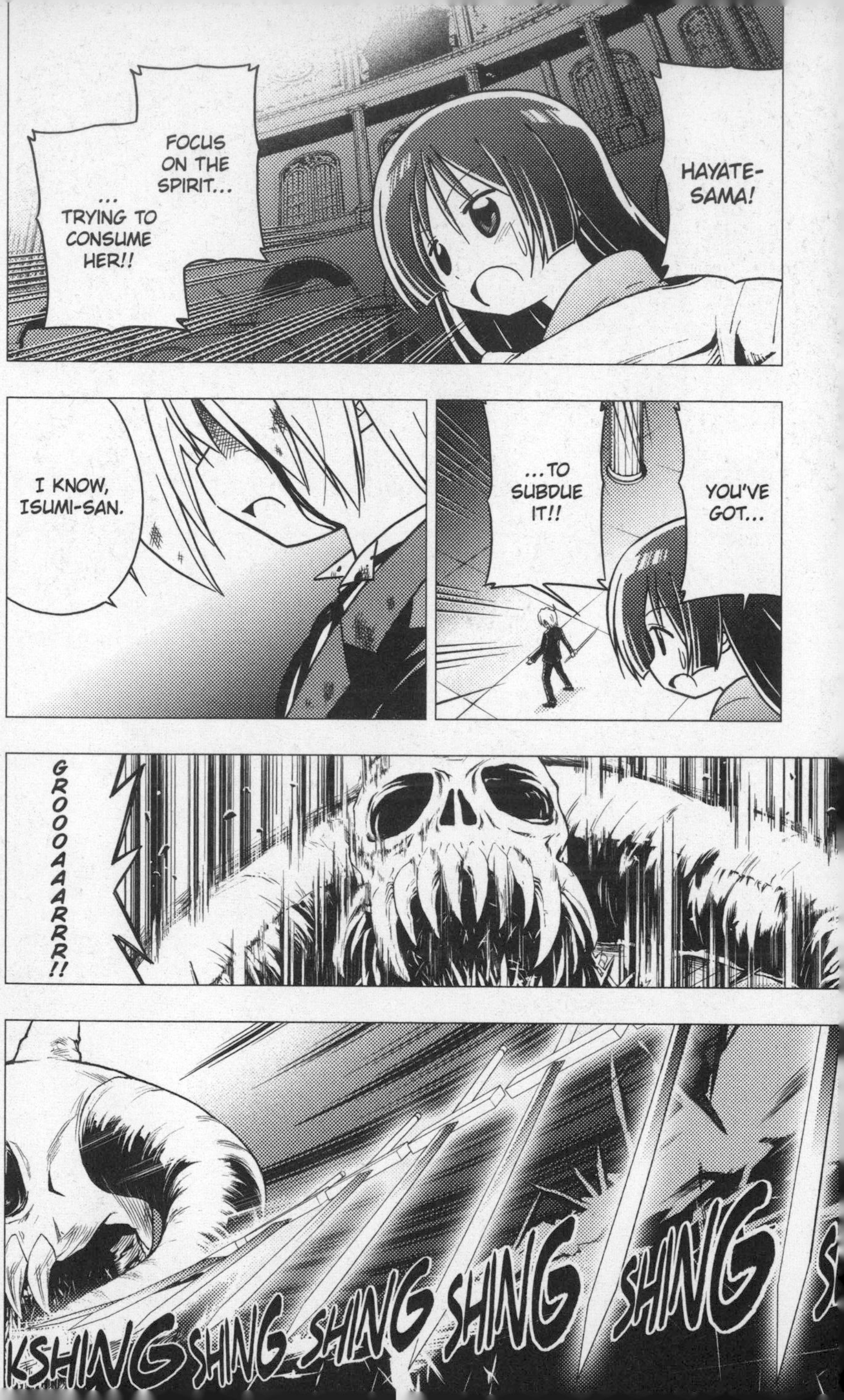
HAYATE-SAMA!
FOCUS ON THE SPIRIT...
...TRYING TO CONSUME HER!!
YOU'VE GOT...
...TO SUBDUE IT!!
I KNOW, ISUMI-SAN.
GROOOOAAAARRR!!
KSHING SHING SHING SHING

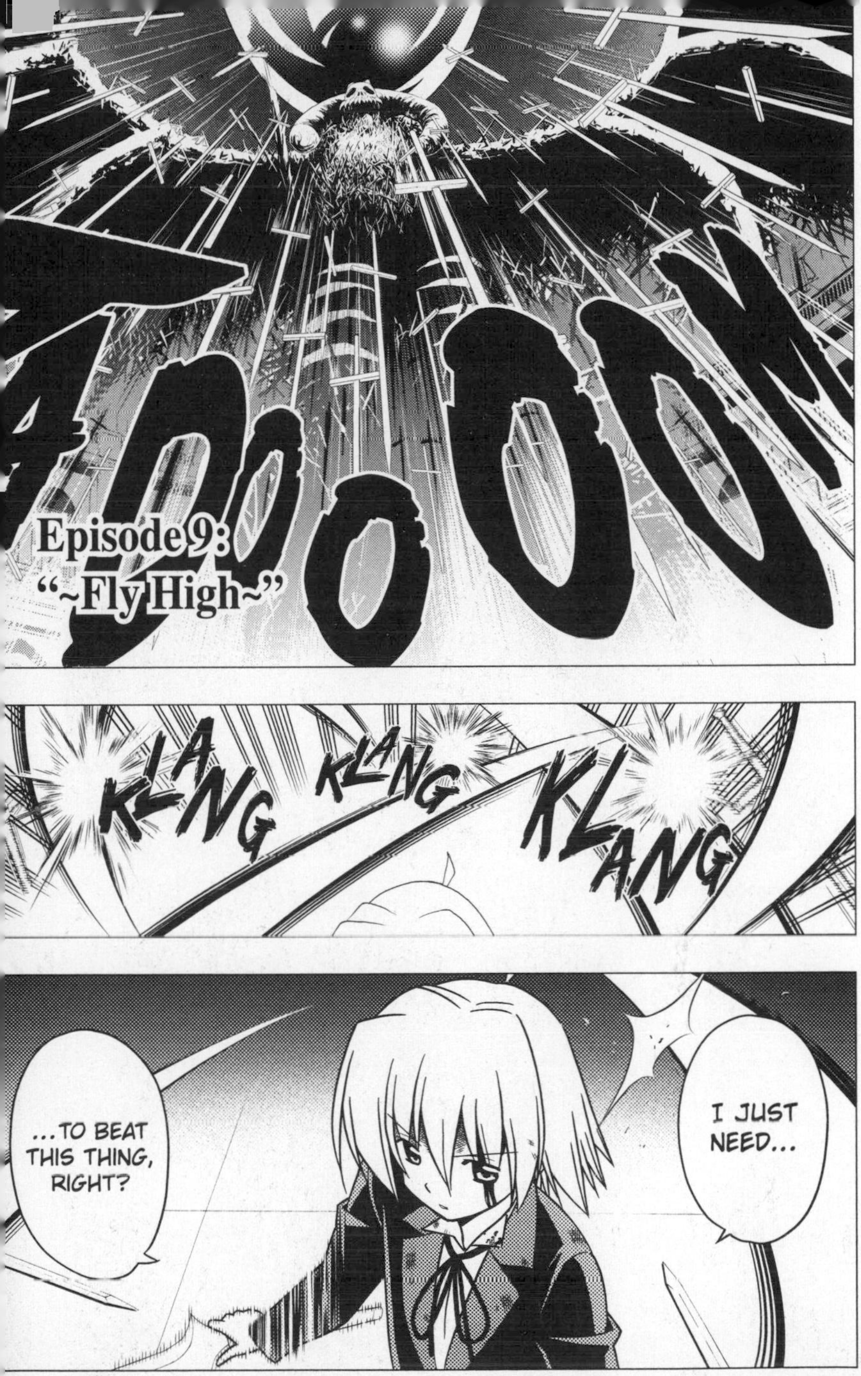
DOOOM
Episode 9:
"~Fly High~"
KLANG
KLANG
KLANG
I JUST NEED...
...TO BEAT THIS THING, RIGHT?

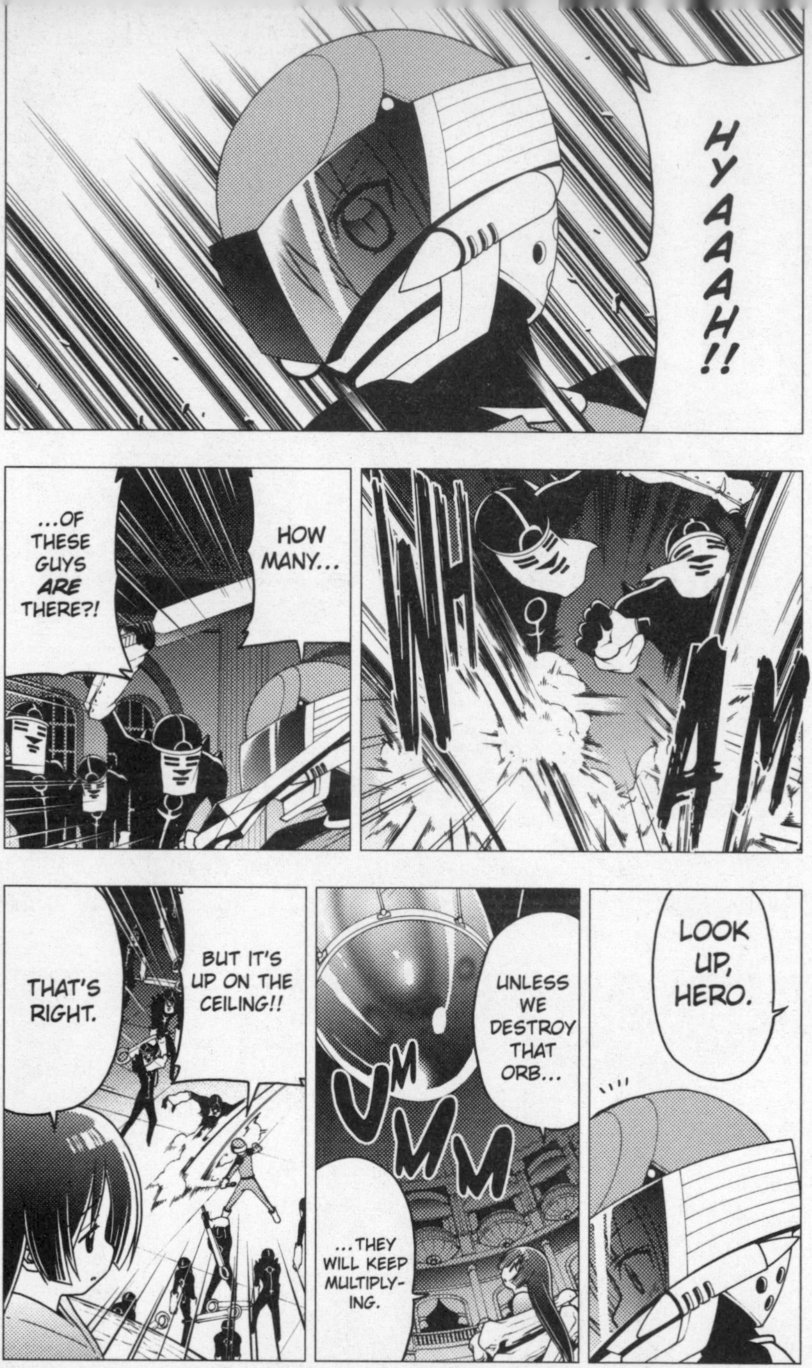
HYAAAAH!!
WHAM
HOW MANY...
...OF THESE GUYS *ARE* THERE?!
LOOK UP, HERO.
UNLESS WE DESTROY THAT ORB...
VMMM
...THEY WILL KEEP MULTIPLYING.
BUT IT'S UP ON THE CEILING!!
THAT'S RIGHT.

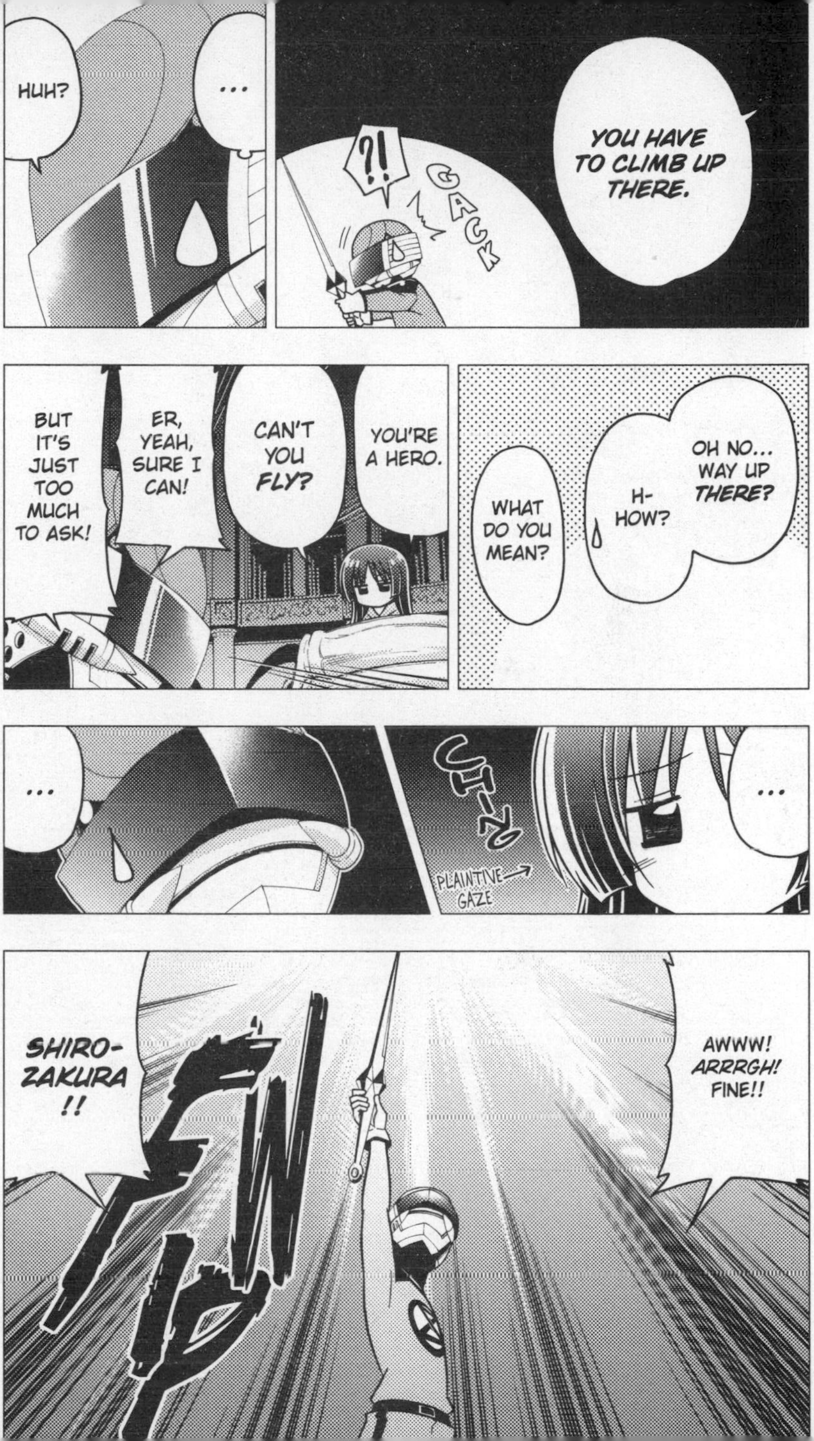
YOU HAVE TO CLIMB UP THERE.
?!
GACK
...
HUH?
OH NO... WAY UP THERE?
H- HOW?
WHAT DO YOU MEAN?
YOU'RE A HERO.
CAN'T YOU FLY?
ER, YEAH, SURE I CAN!
BUT IT'S JUST TOO MUCH TO ASK!
...
CHI-N
PLAINTIVE GAZE
...
AWWW! ARRRGH! FINE!!
SHIRO-ZAKURA!!

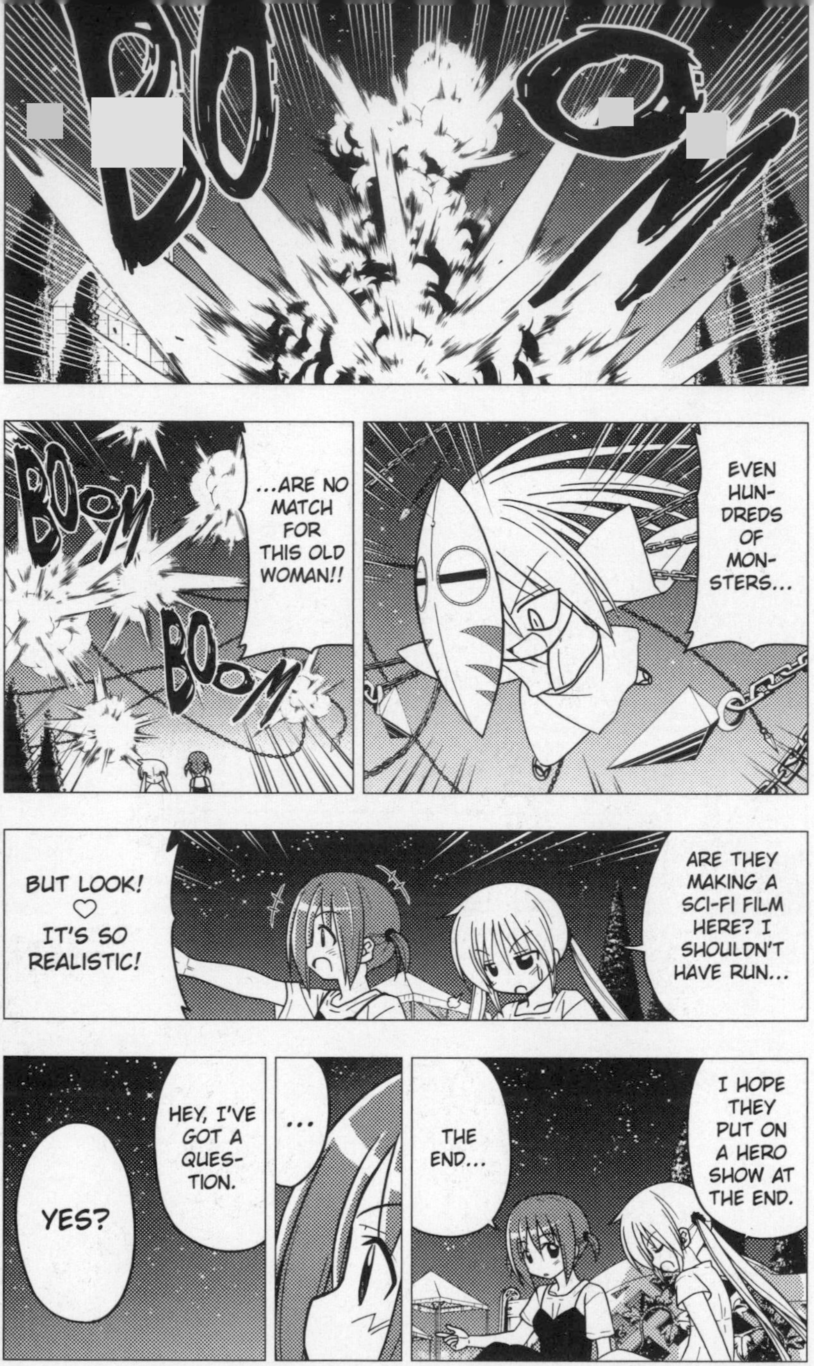
EVEN HUN-DREDS OF MON-STERS...
BOOM
BOOM
...ARE NO MATCH FOR THIS OLD WOMAN!!
ARE THEY MAKING A SCI-FI FILM HERE? I SHOULDN'T HAVE RUN...
BUT LOOK! ♡ IT'S SO REALISTIC!
I HOPE THEY PUT ON A HERO SHOW AT THE END.
THE END...
...
HEY, I'VE GOT A QUES-TION.
YES?

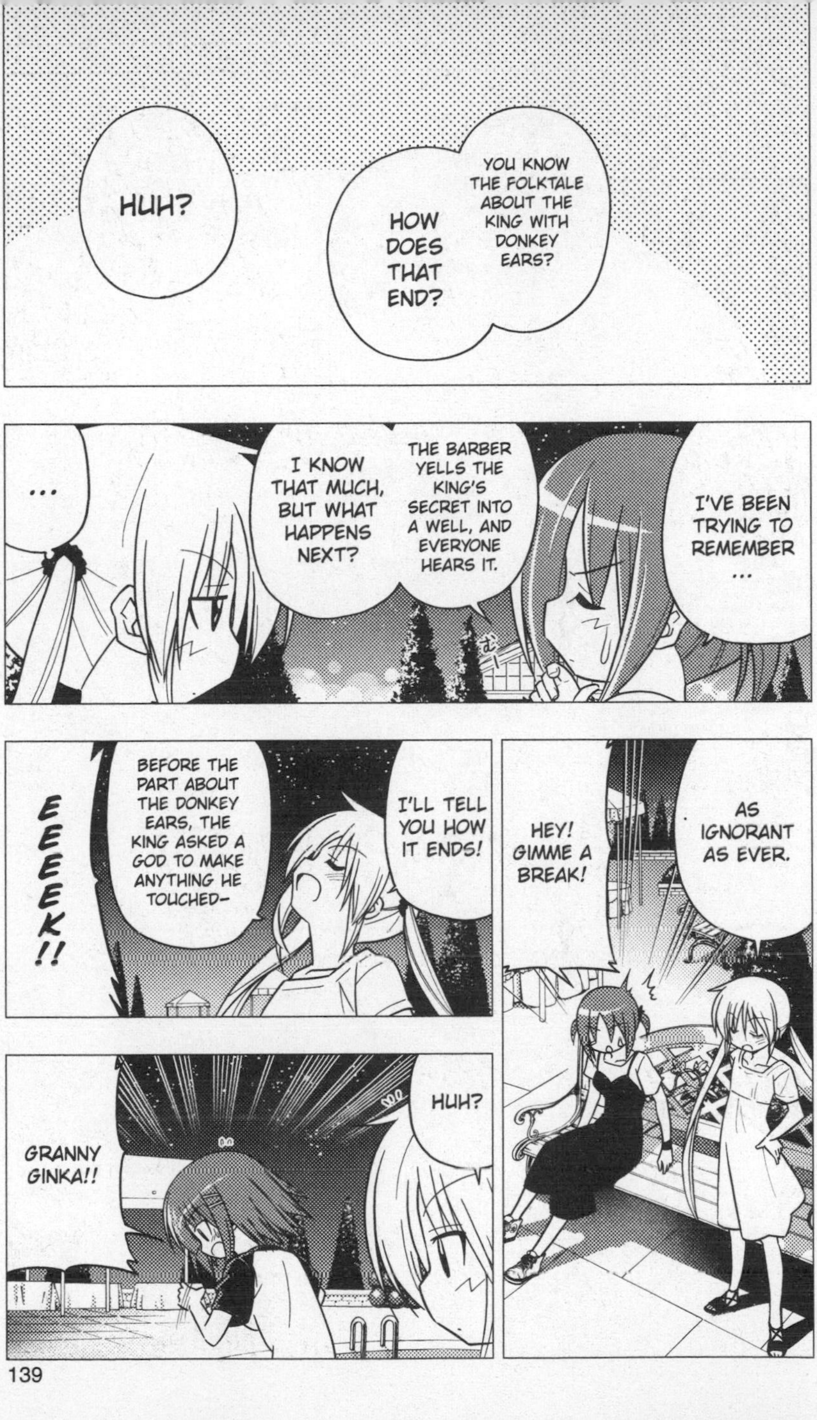
YOU KNOW THE FOLKTALE ABOUT THE KING WITH DONKEY EARS?
HOW DOES THAT END?
HUH?
I'VE BEEN TRYING TO REMEMBER ...
THE BARBER YELLS THE KING'S SECRET INTO A WELL, AND EVERYONE HEARS IT.
I KNOW THAT MUCH, BUT WHAT HAPPENS NEXT?
...
AS IGNORANT AS EVER.
HEY! GIMME A BREAK!
I'LL TELL YOU HOW IT ENDS!
BEFORE THE PART ABOUT THE DONKEY EARS, THE KING ASKED A GOD TO MAKE ANYTHING HE TOUCHED–
EEEEEK!!
HUH?
GRANNY GINKA!!

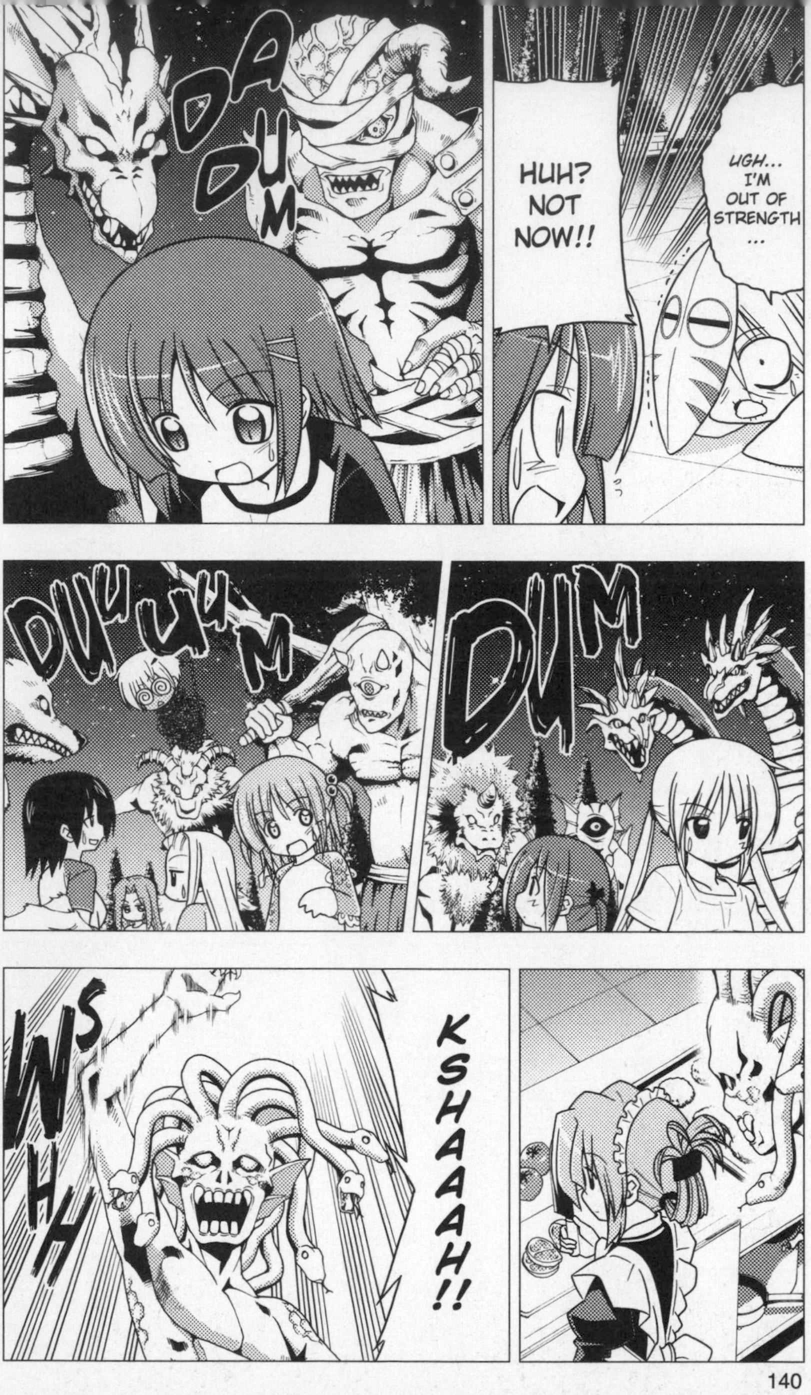
UGH... I'M OUT OF STRENGTH...
HUH? NOT NOW!!
DA DUM
DUM
DUUUUM
KSHAAAAH!!
WSHH

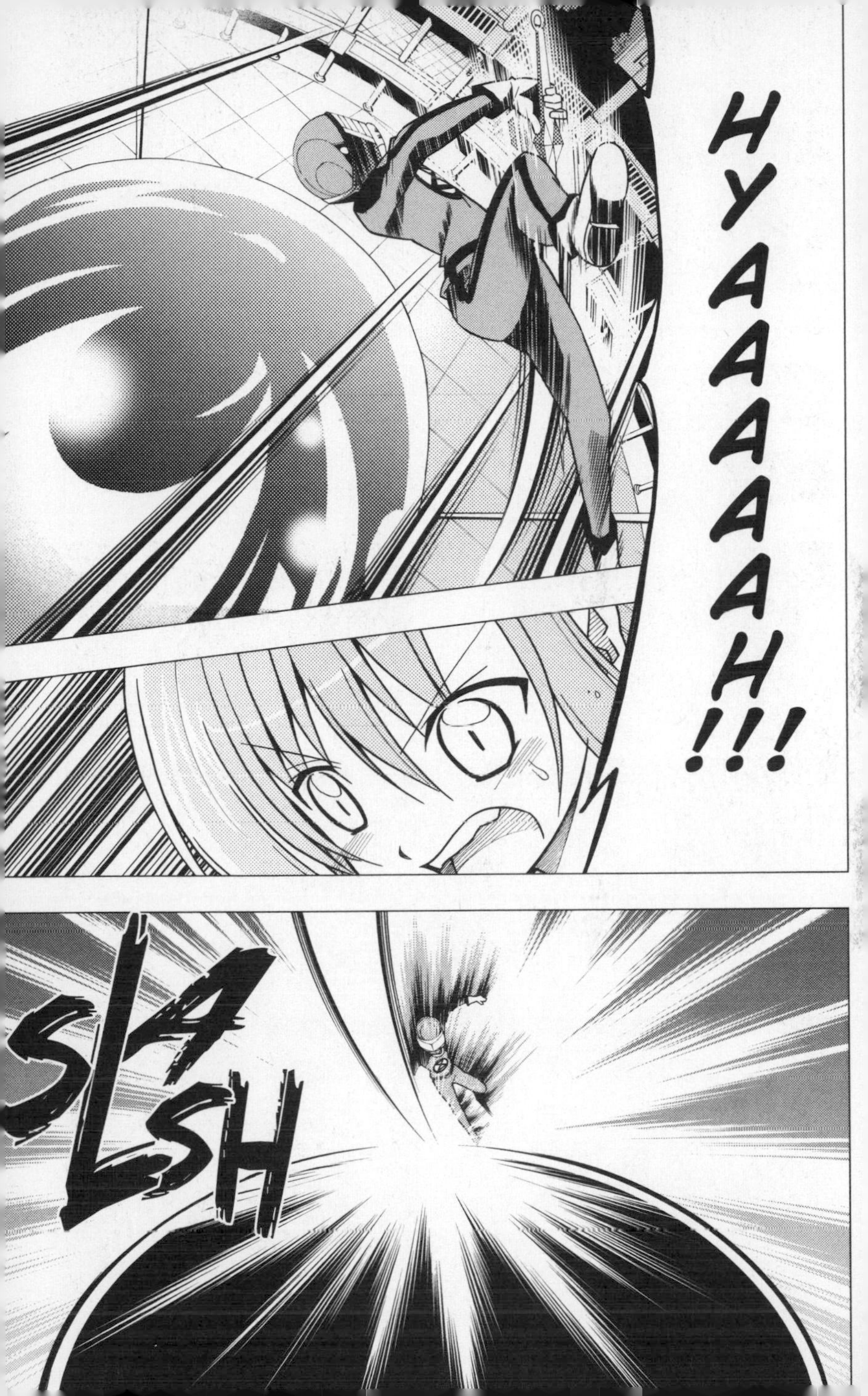
HYAAAAAAH!!!
SLASH

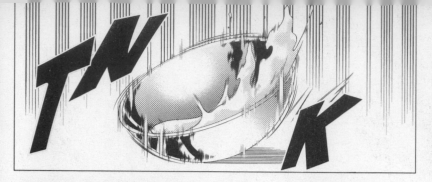

SLINKING OUT IN THE MIDDLE OF THE PREPARATIONS, EH? SHAME ON YOU!

HM?

KTNK KTNK

KRUMBL

KRUMBL

KRUMBL

I...HATE HEIGHTS...

UGH...

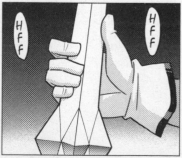

HFF

HFF

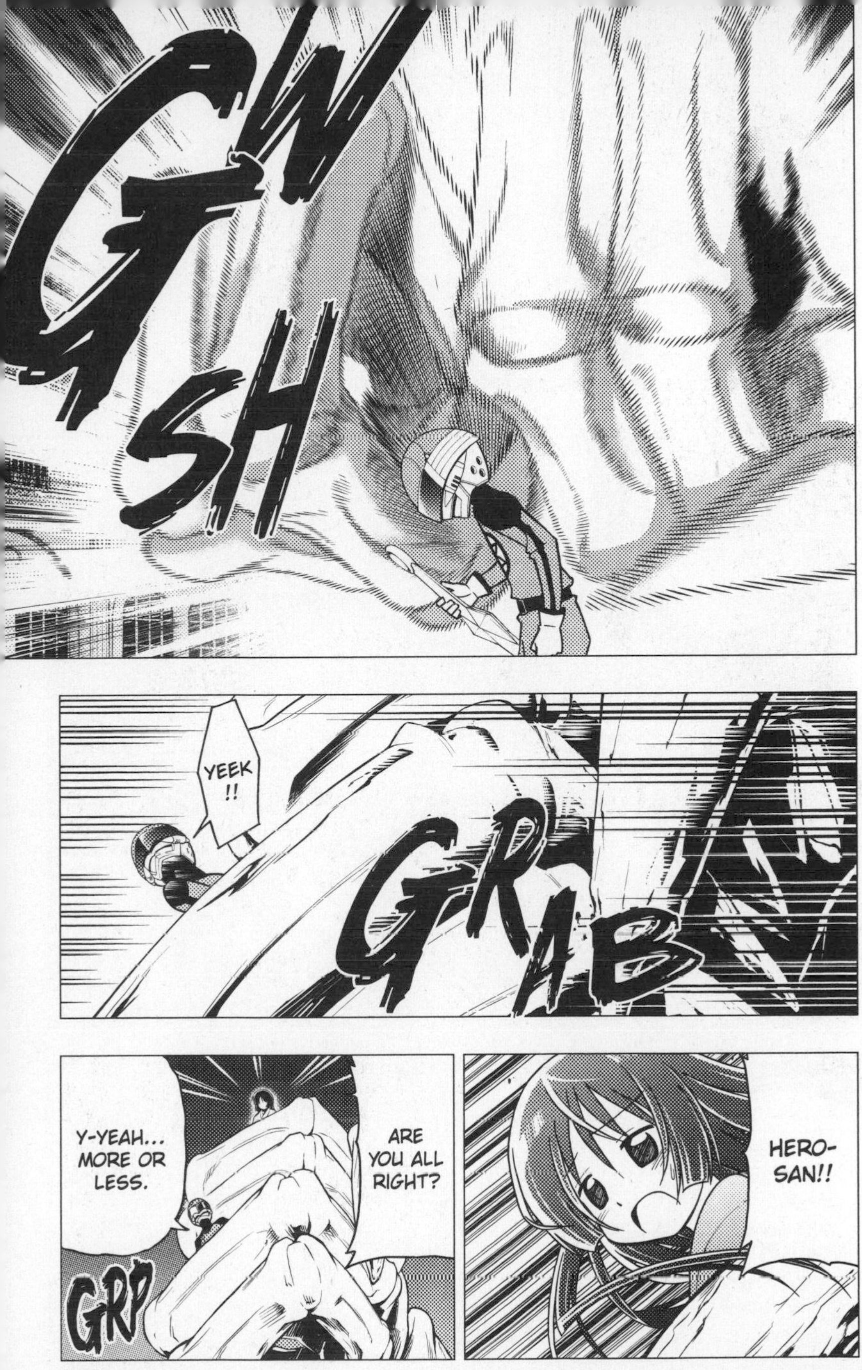
GWSH
GRAB
YEEK!!
HERO-SAN!!
ARE YOU ALL RIGHT?
Y-YEAH... MORE OR LESS.
GRP

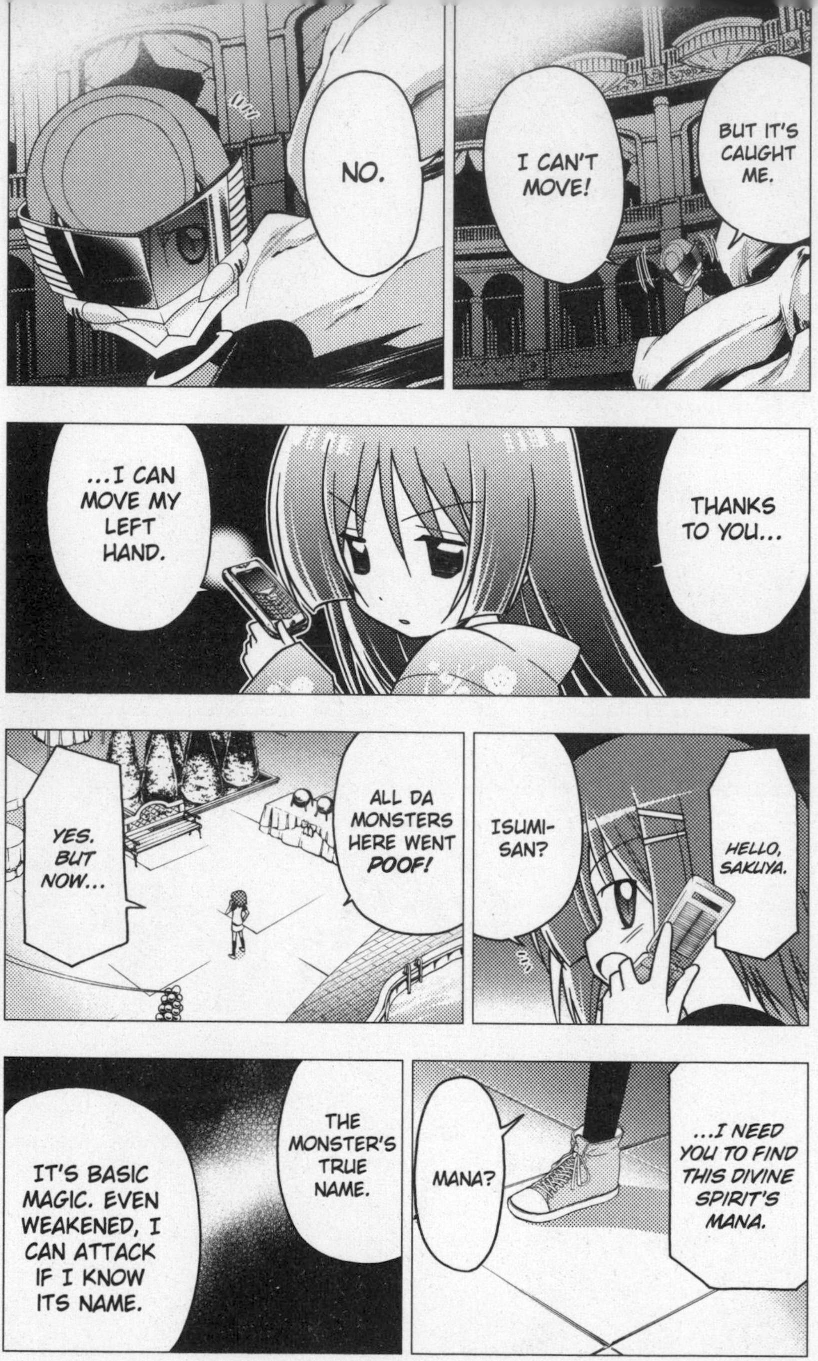
BUT IT'S CAUGHT ME.
I CAN'T MOVE!
NO.
THANKS TO YOU...
...I CAN MOVE MY LEFT HAND.
HELLO, SAKUYA.
ISUMI-SAN?
ALL DA MONSTERS HERE WENT POOF!
YES. BUT NOW...
...I NEED YOU TO FIND THIS DIVINE SPIRIT'S MANA.
MANA?
THE MONSTER'S TRUE NAME.
IT'S BASIC MAGIC. EVEN WEAKENED, I CAN ATTACK IF I KNOW ITS NAME.

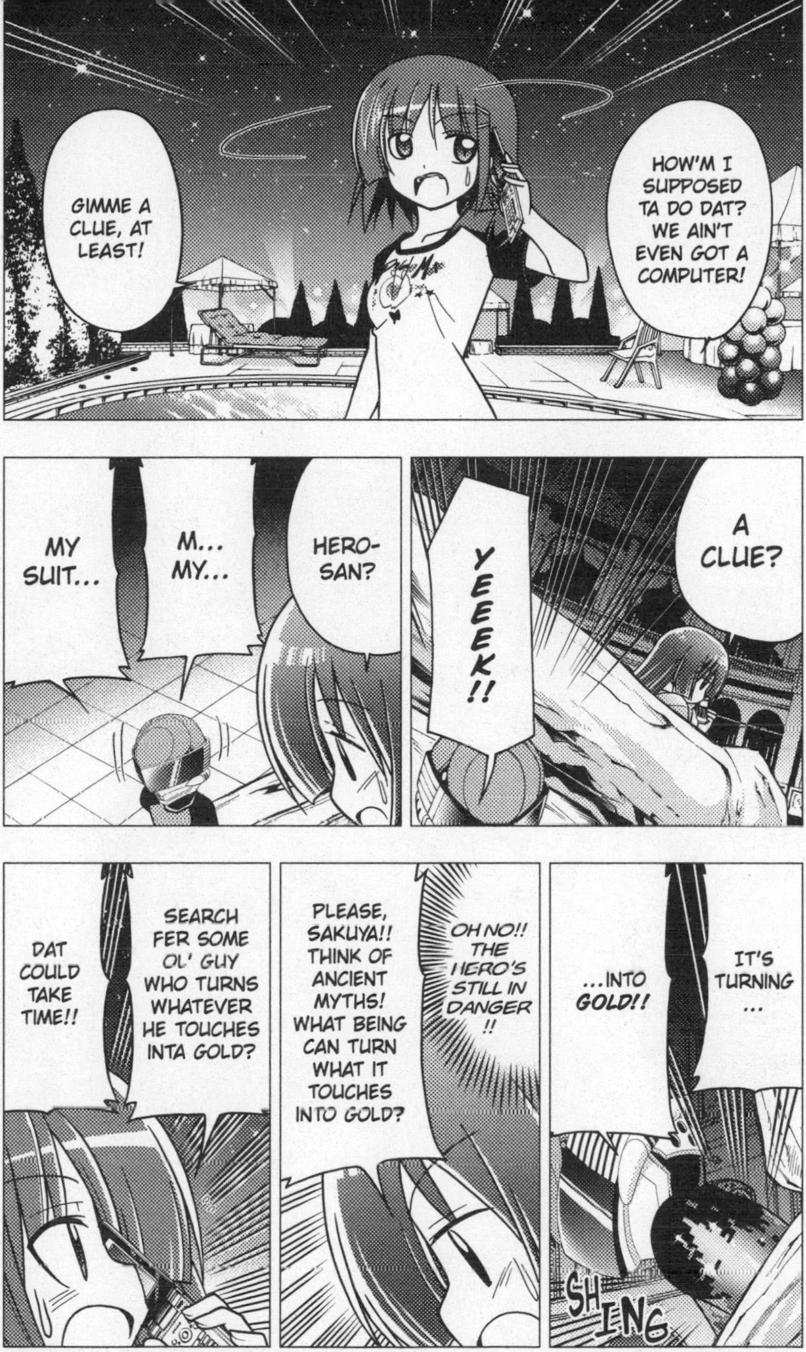
HOW'M I SUPPOSED TA DO DAT? WE AIN'T EVEN GOT A COMPUTER!
GIMME A CLUE, AT LEAST!
A CLUE?
YEEEK!!
HERO-SAN?
M... MY...
MY SUIT...
IT'S TURNING ...
...INTO GOLD!!
SHING
OH NO!! THE HERO'S STILL IN DANGER!!
PLEASE, SAKUYA!! THINK OF ANCIENT MYTHS! WHAT BEING CAN TURN WHAT IT TOUCHES INTO GOLD?
SEARCH FER SOME OL' GUY WHO TURNS WHATEVER HE TOUCHES INTA GOLD?
DAT COULD TAKE TIME!!

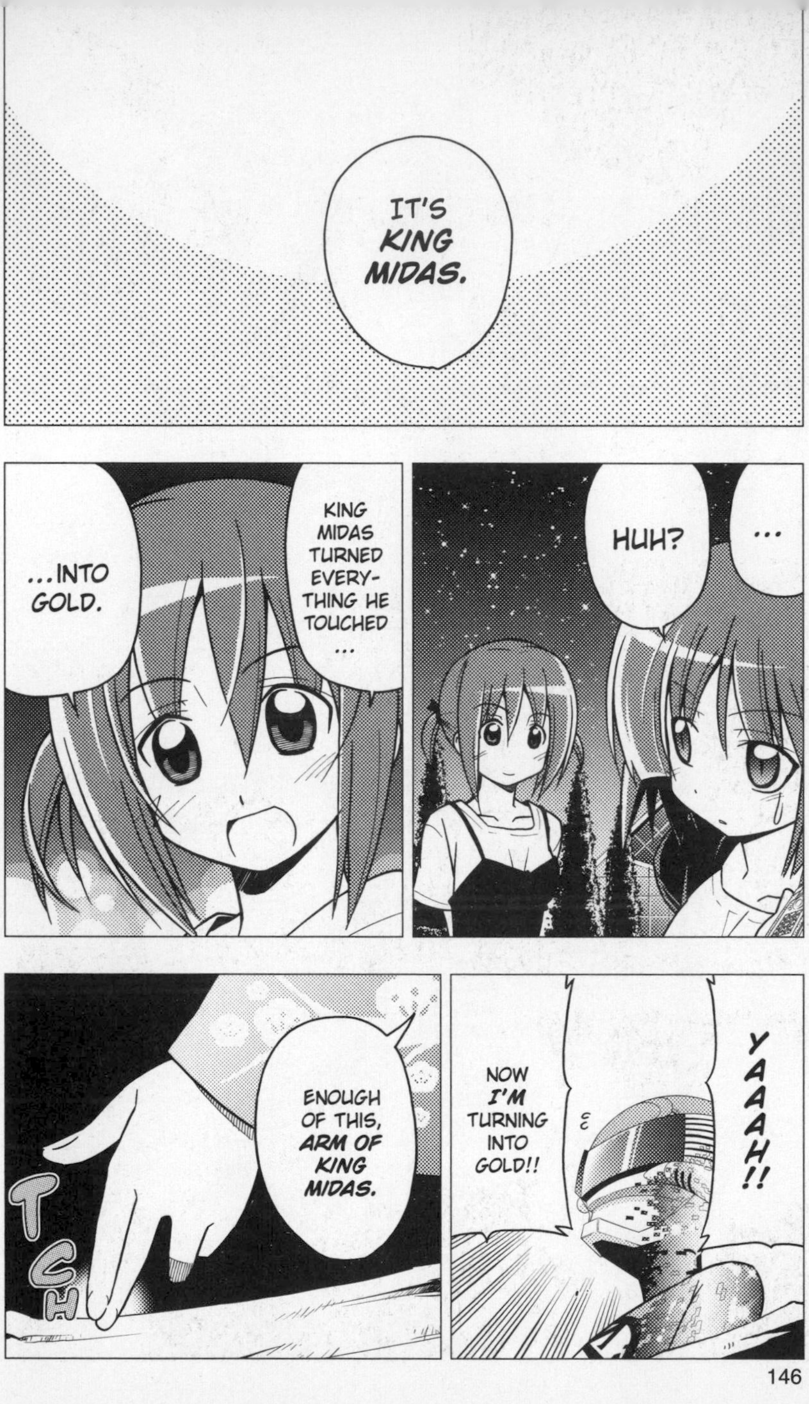
IT'S KING MIDAS.
...
HUH?
KING MIDAS TURNED EVERY-THING HE TOUCHED...
...INTO GOLD.
YAAAAH!!
NOW I'M TURNING INTO GOLD!!
ENOUGH OF THIS, ARM OF KING MIDAS.
TCH

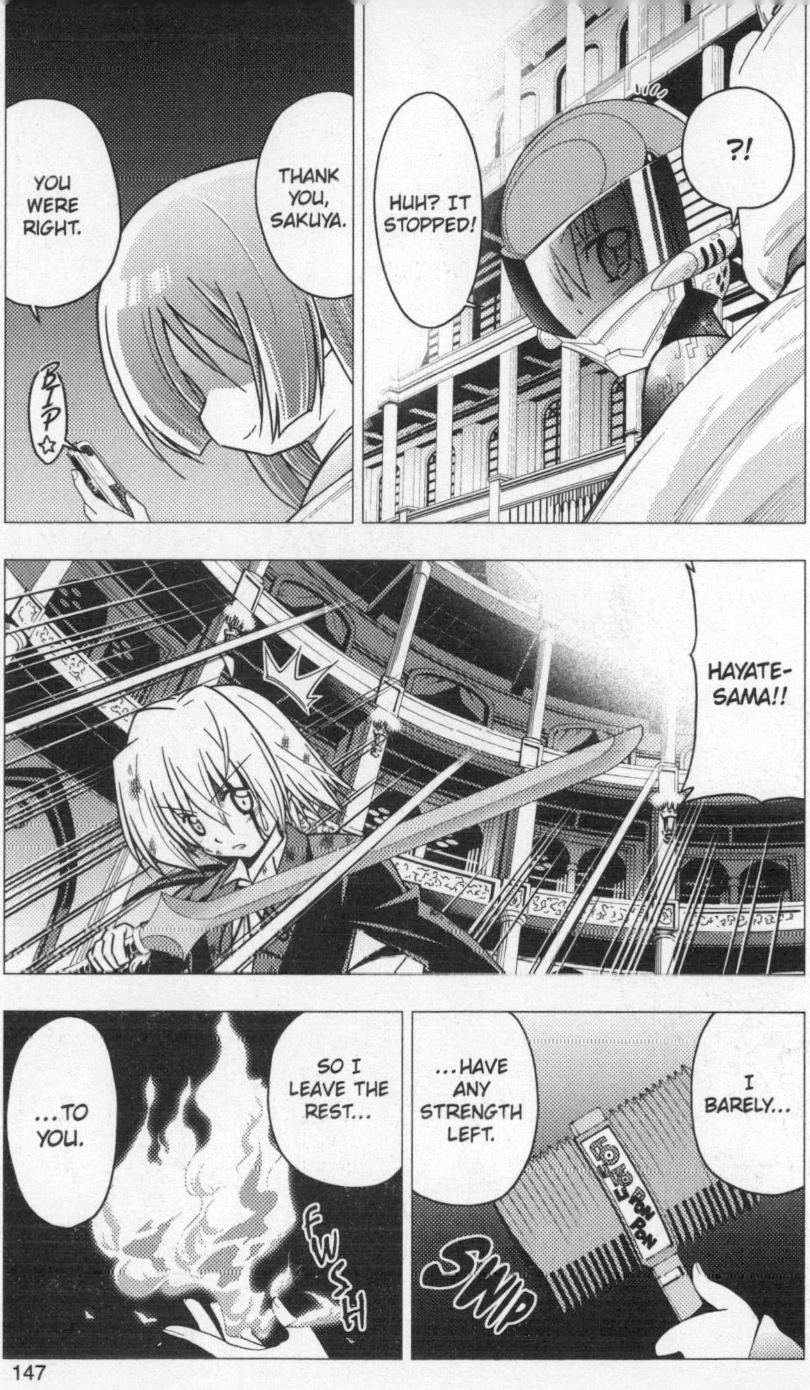
?!
HUH? IT STOPPED!
THANK YOU, SAKUYA.
YOU WERE RIGHT.
BIP☆
HAYATE-SAMA!!
I BARELY...
...HAVE ANY STRENGTH LEFT.
SNIP
SO I LEAVE THE REST...
...TO YOU.
FWSH

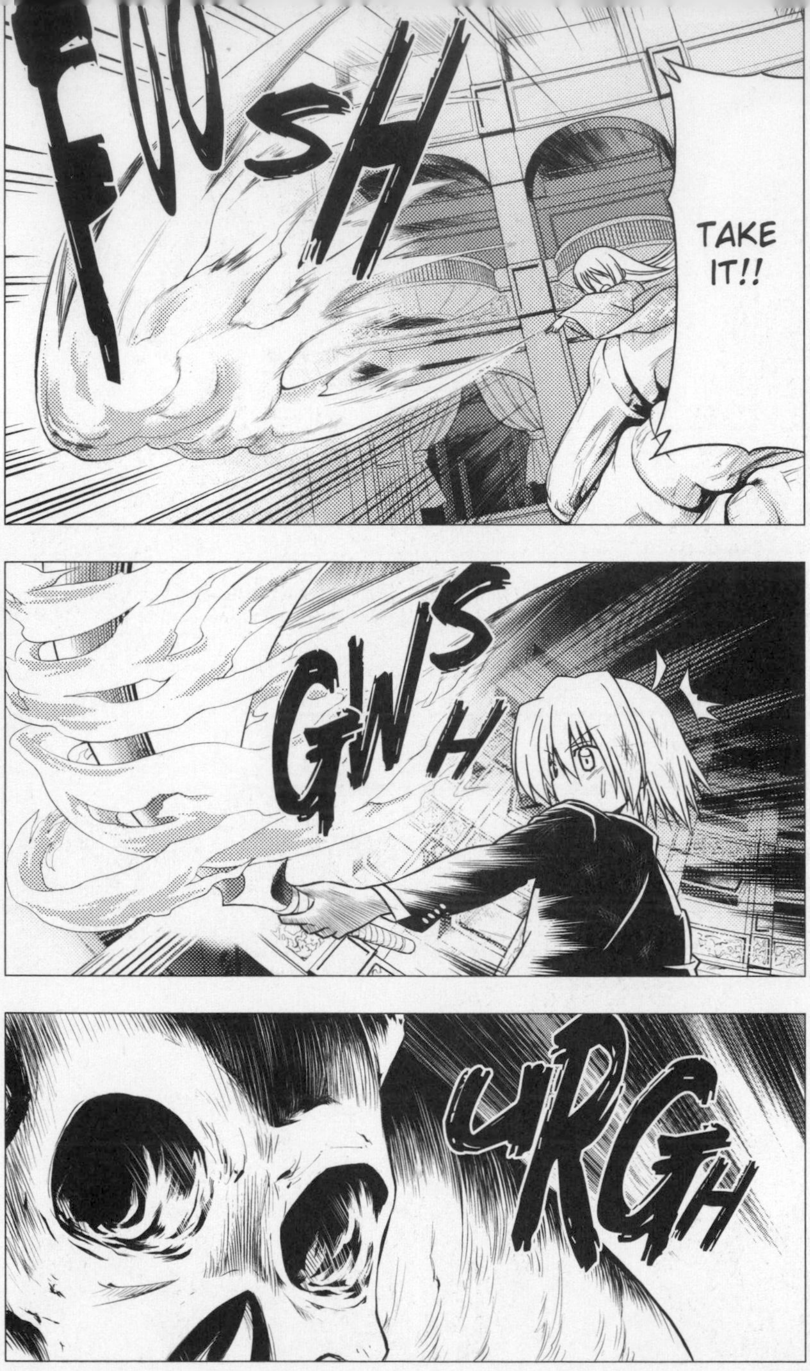

TAKE IT!!
FUUSH
GWSH
URGH

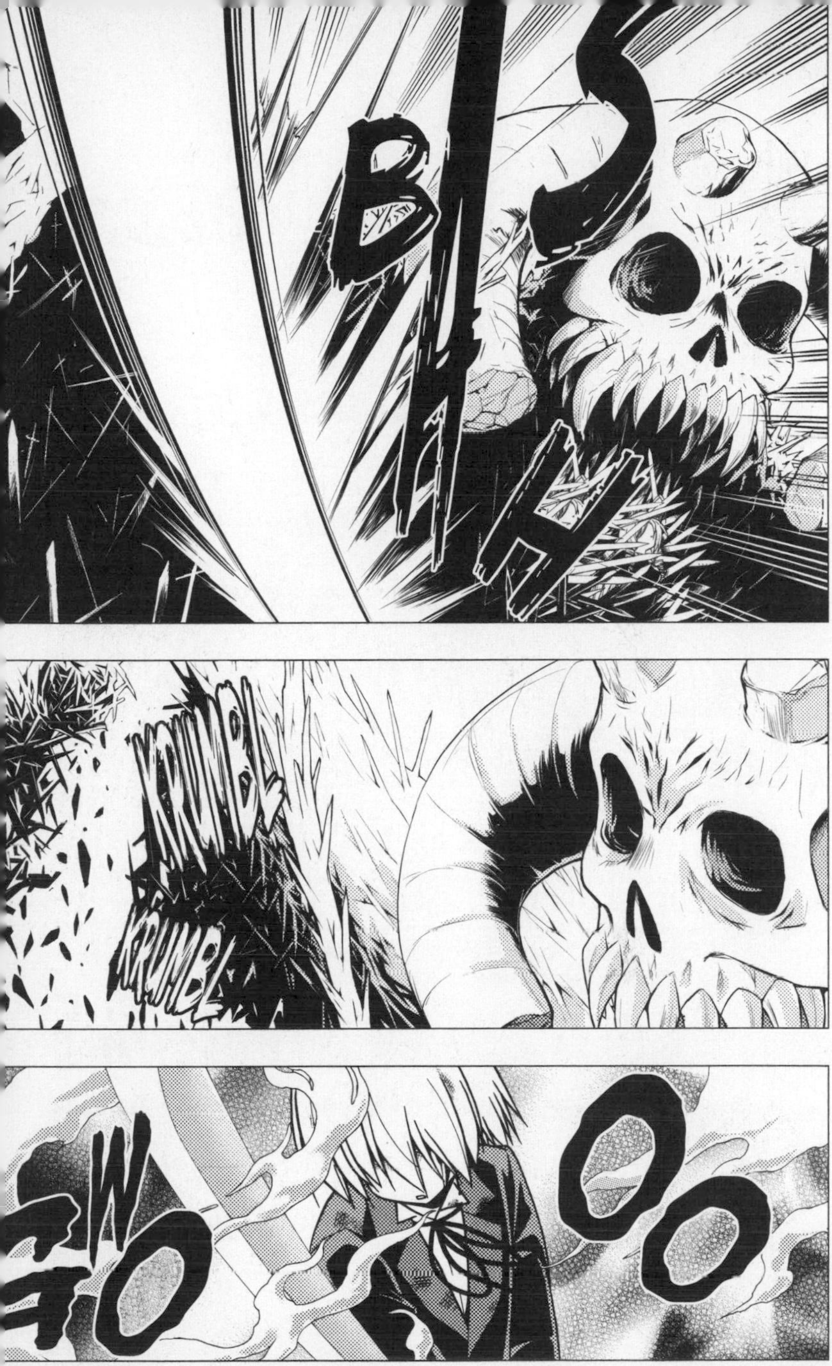
BISH
KRUMBL
KRUMBL
FWOOOO

Episode 10: "Eternal Wind"

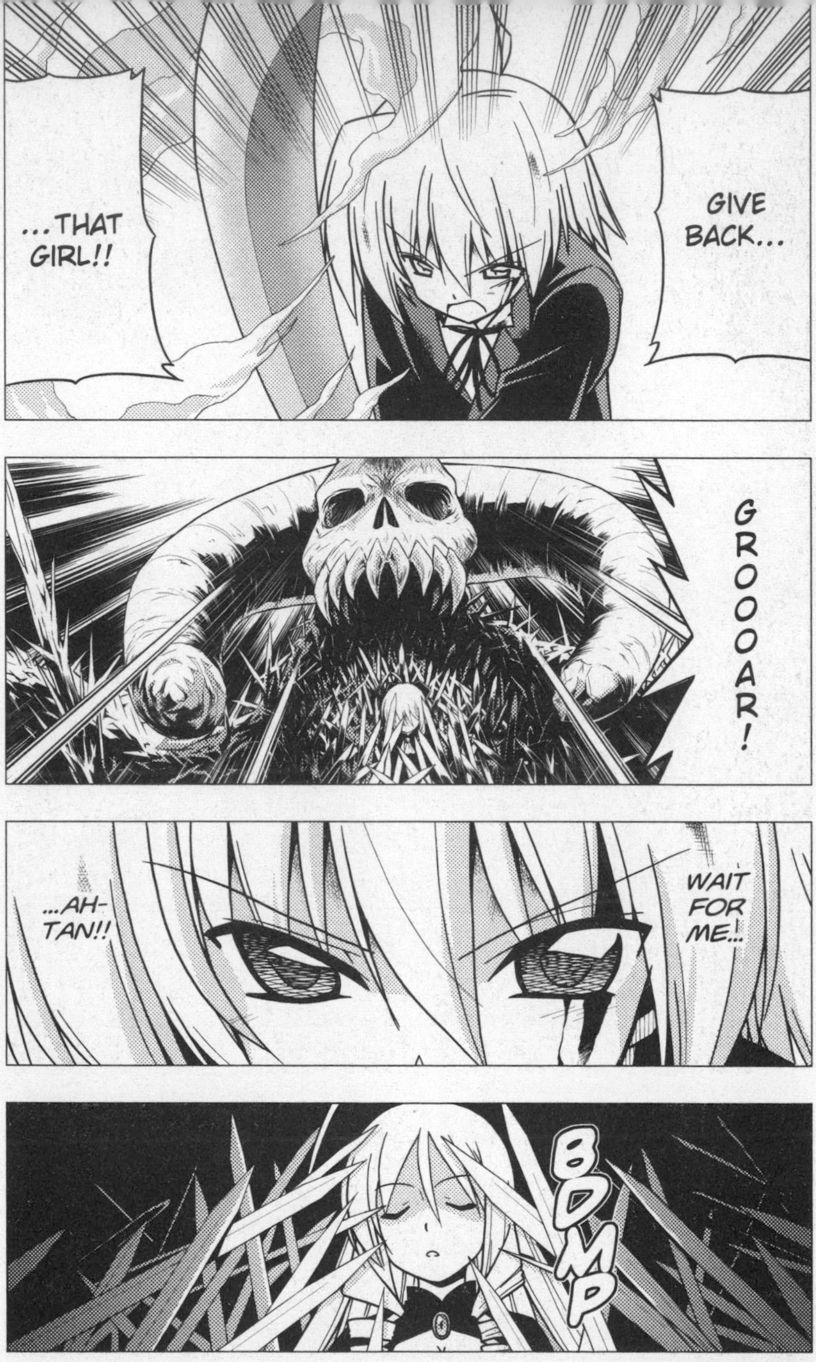
GIVE BACK...
...THAT GIRL!!
GROOOAR!
WAIT FOR ME!...
...AH-TAN!!
BDMP

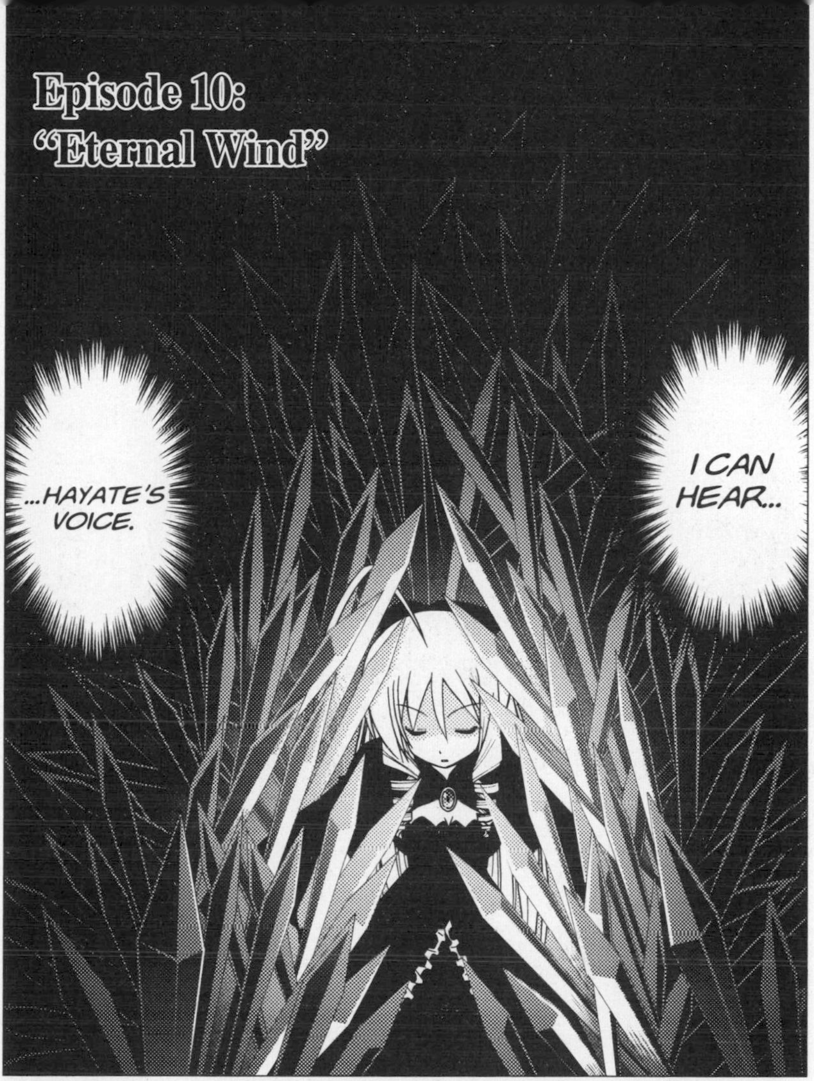
Episode 10:
"Eternal Wind"
I CAN HEAR...
...HAYATE'S VOICE.

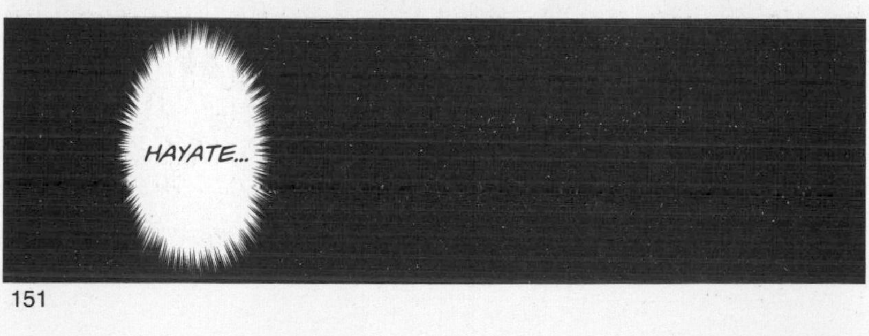
HAYATE...

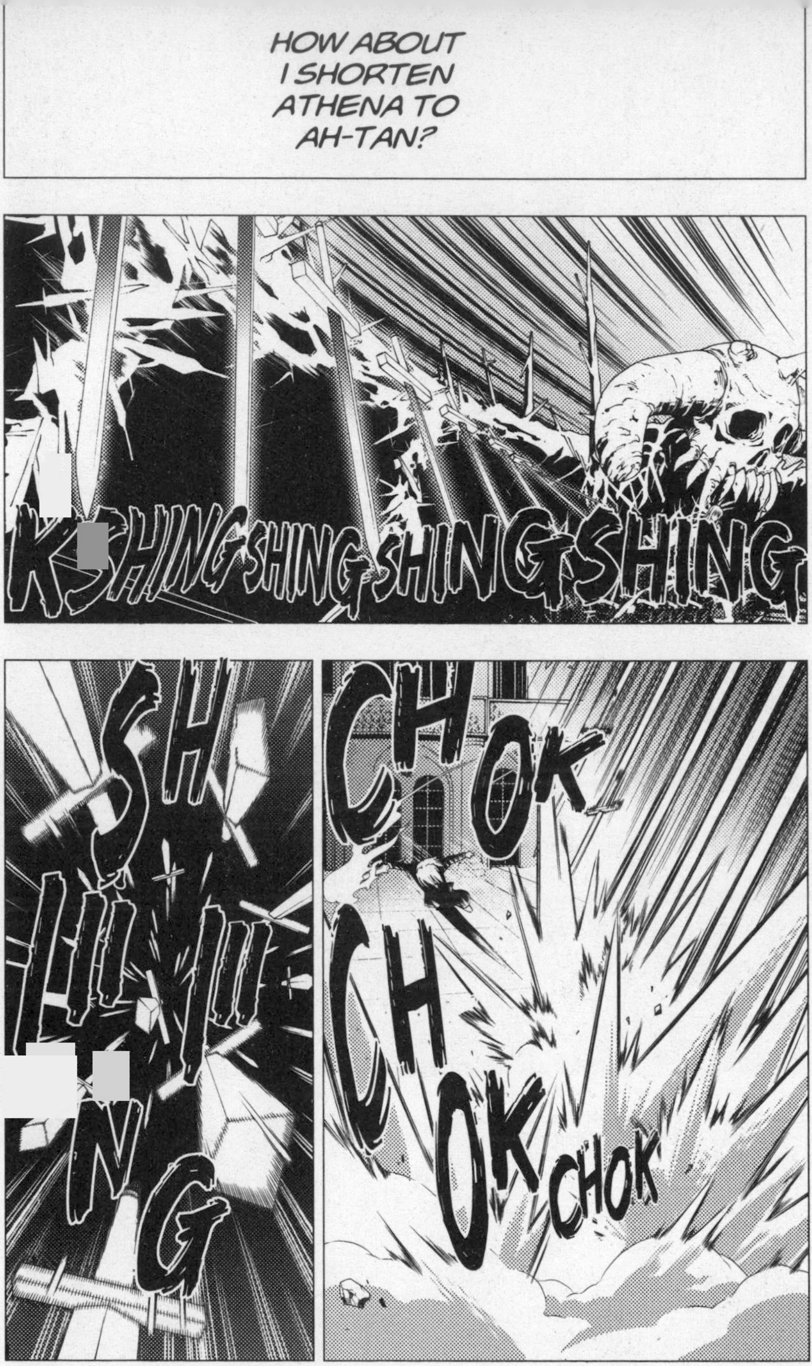
HOW ABOUT I SHORTEN ATHENA TO AH-TAN?
SHING SHING SHING
CHOK
CHOK
CHOK
SHIIIING

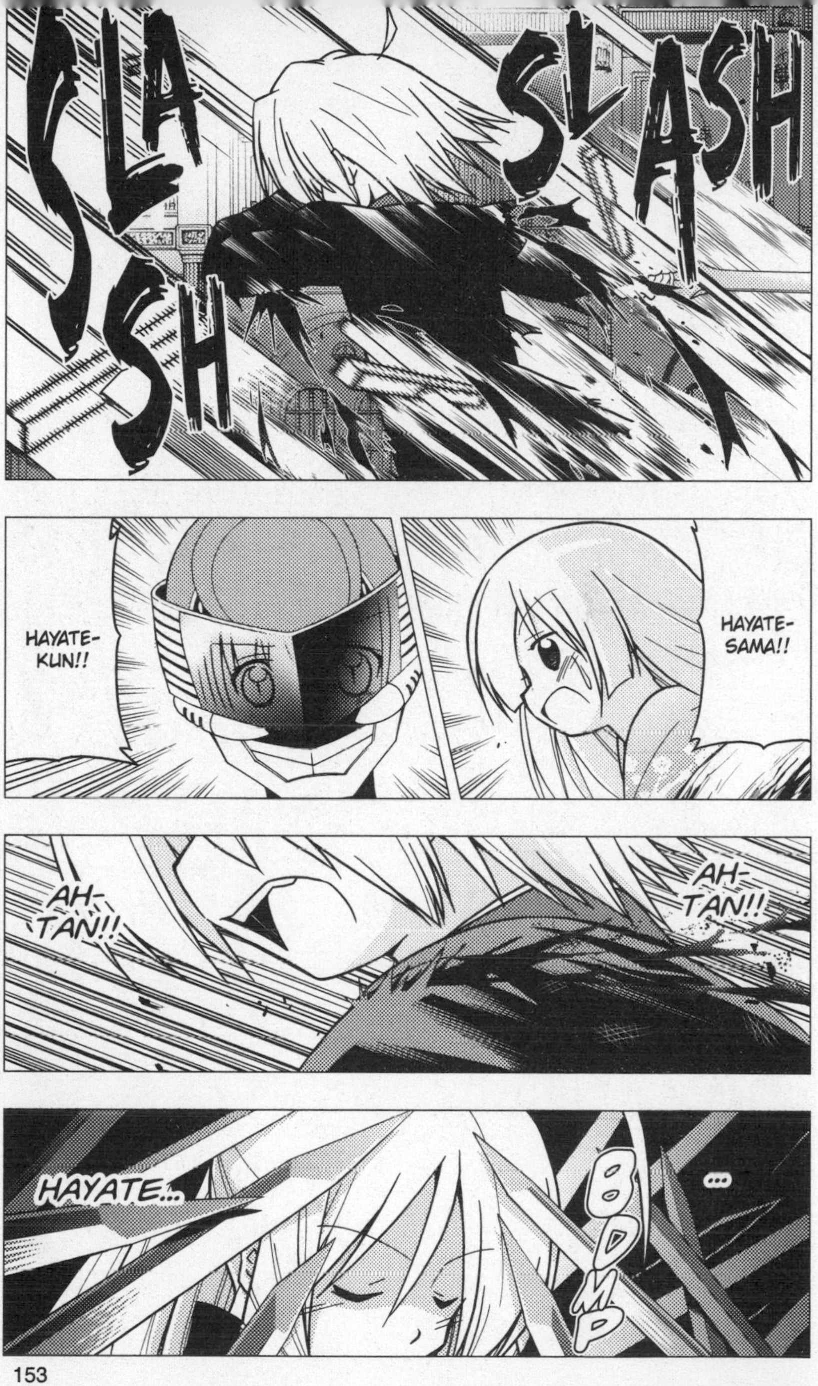
SLASH
SLASH
HAYATE-SAMA!!
HAYATE-KUN!!
AH-TAN!!
AH-TAN!!
...
BDMP
HAYATE...

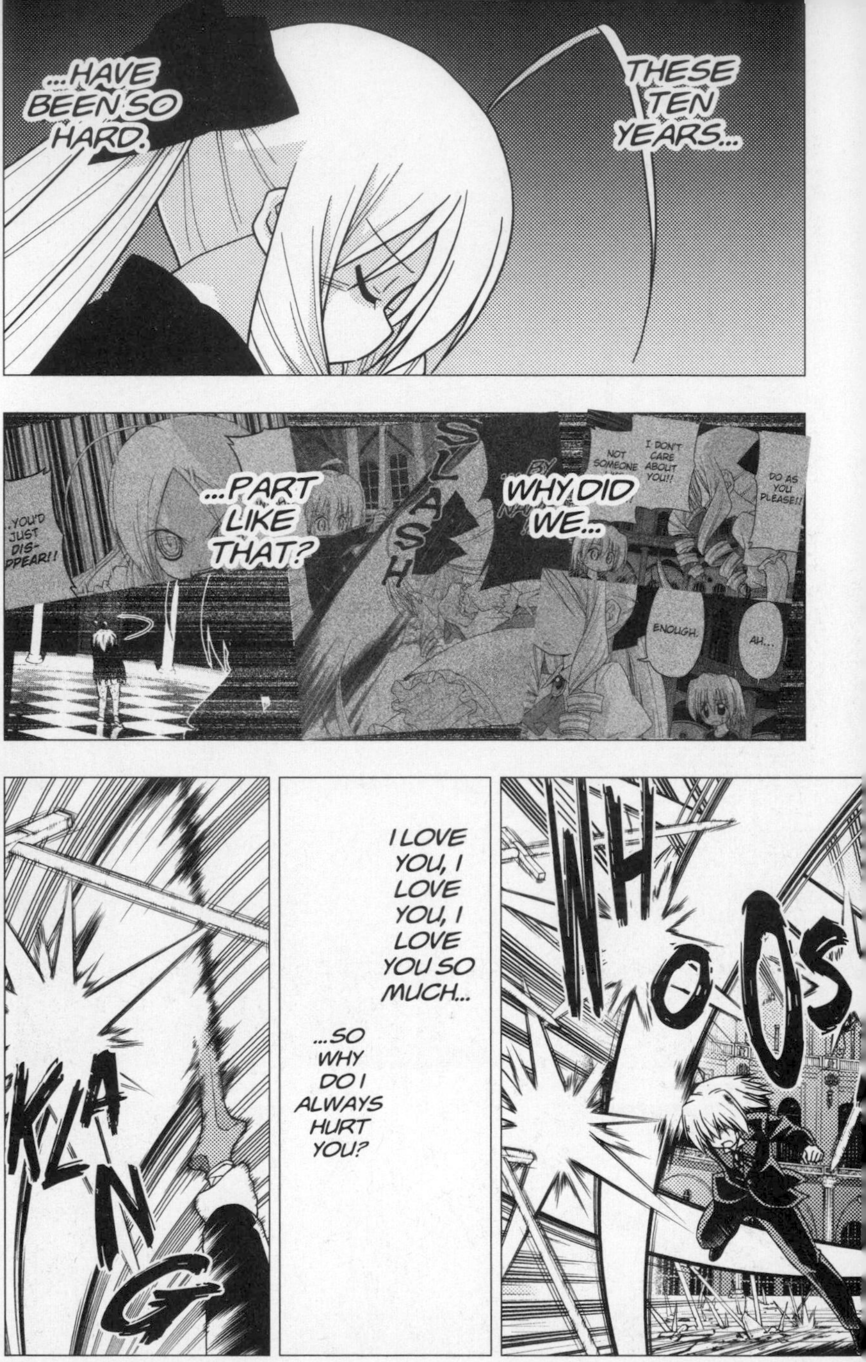
THESE TEN YEARS...
...HAVE BEEN SO HARD.
I DON'T CARE ABOUT YOU!!
NOT SOMEONE
DO AS YOU PLEASE!!
ENOUGH.
AH...
WHY DID WE...
SLASH
...PART LIKE THAT?
...YOU'D JUST DIS- PPEAR!!
WHOOS
I LOVE YOU, I LOVE YOU, I LOVE YOU SO MUCH...
...SO WHY DO I ALWAYS HURT YOU?
KLANG

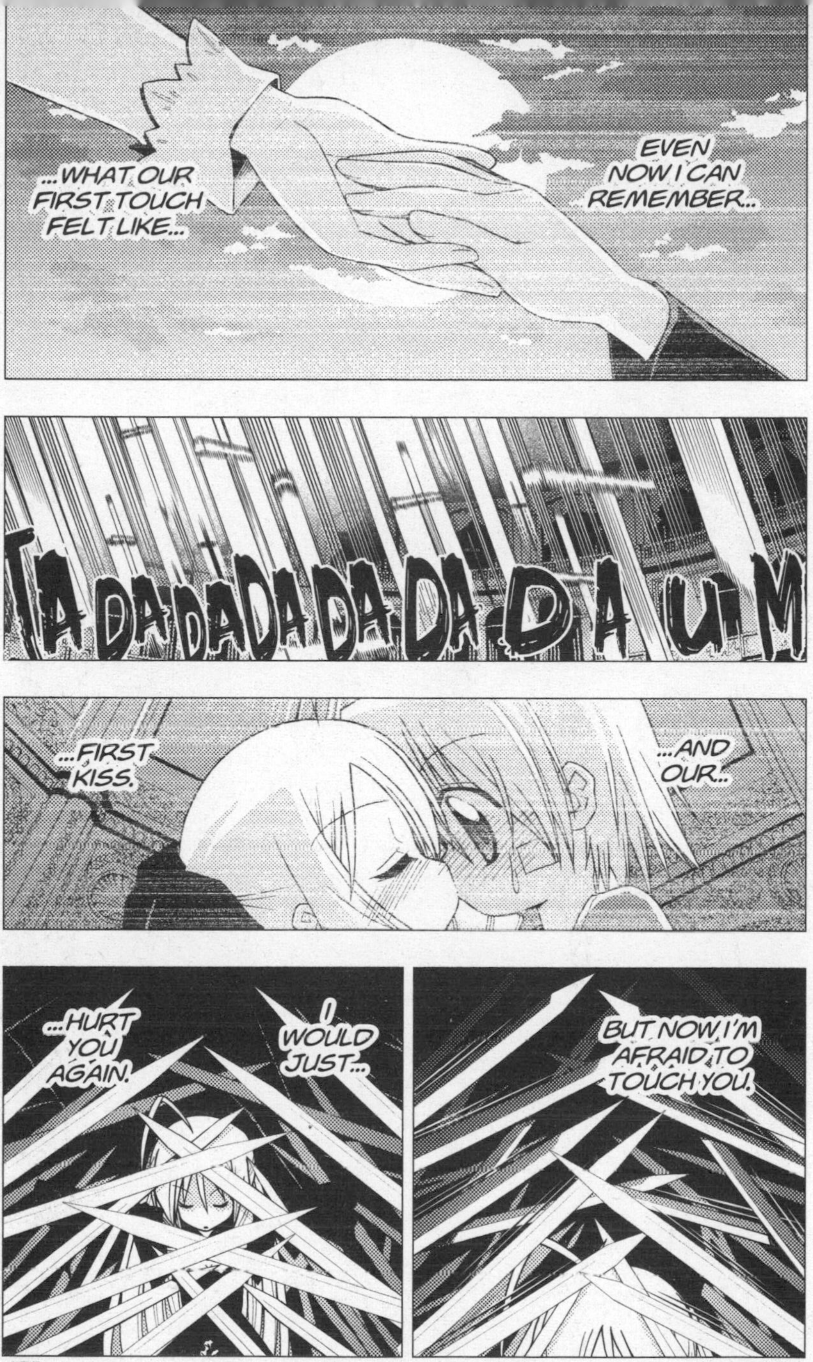
EVEN NOW I CAN REMEMBER...
...WHAT OUR FIRST TOUCH FELT LIKE...
TA DA DA DA DA DA DAUM
...AND OUR...
...FIRST KISS.
BUT NOW I'M AFRAID TO TOUCH YOU.
I WOULD JUST...
...HURT YOU AGAIN.

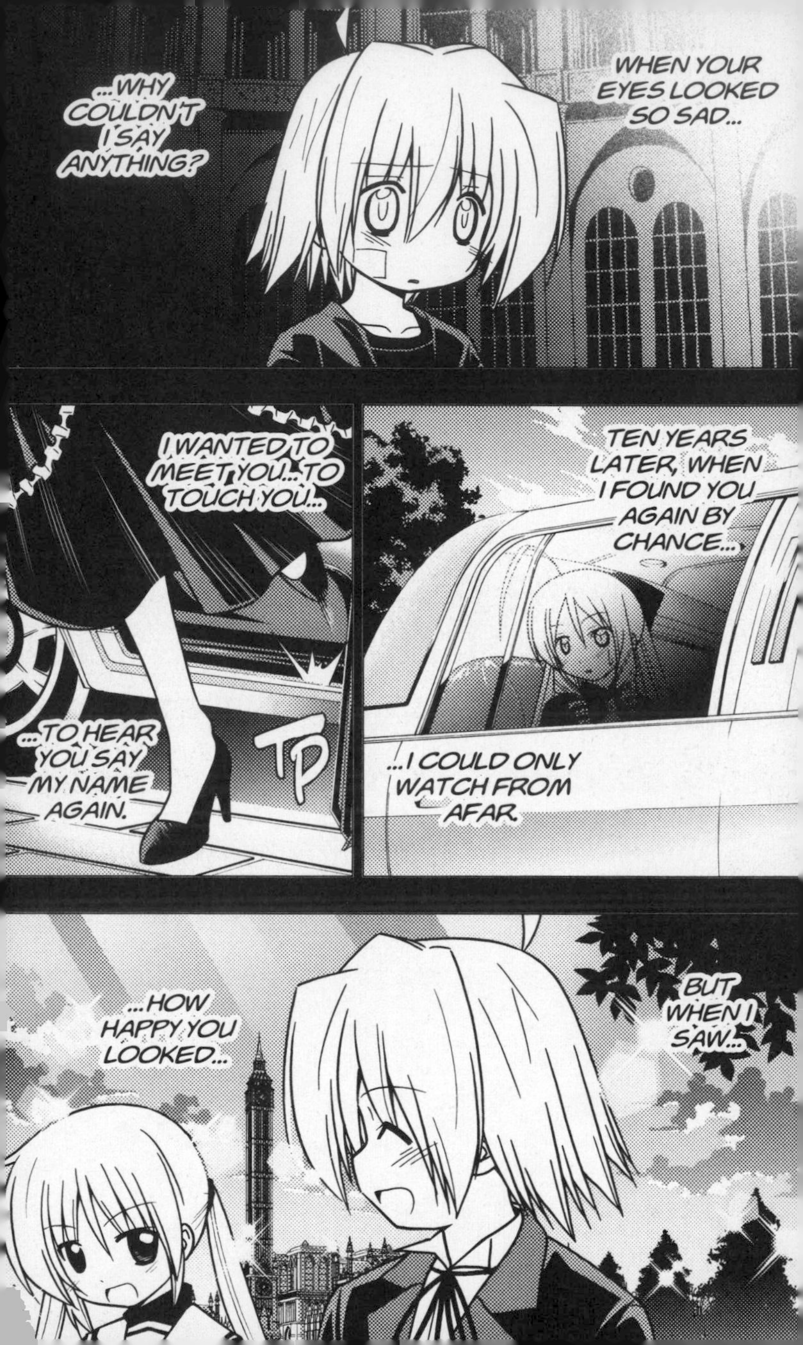
WHEN YOUR EYES LOOKED SO SAD...
...WHY COULDN'T I SAY ANYTHING?
TEN YEARS LATER, WHEN I FOUND YOU AGAIN BY CHANCE...
...I COULD ONLY WATCH FROM AFAR.
I WANTED TO MEET YOU... TO TOUCH YOU...
TP
...TO HEAR YOU SAY MY NAME AGAIN.
BUT WHEN I SAW...
...HOW HAPPY YOU LOOKED...

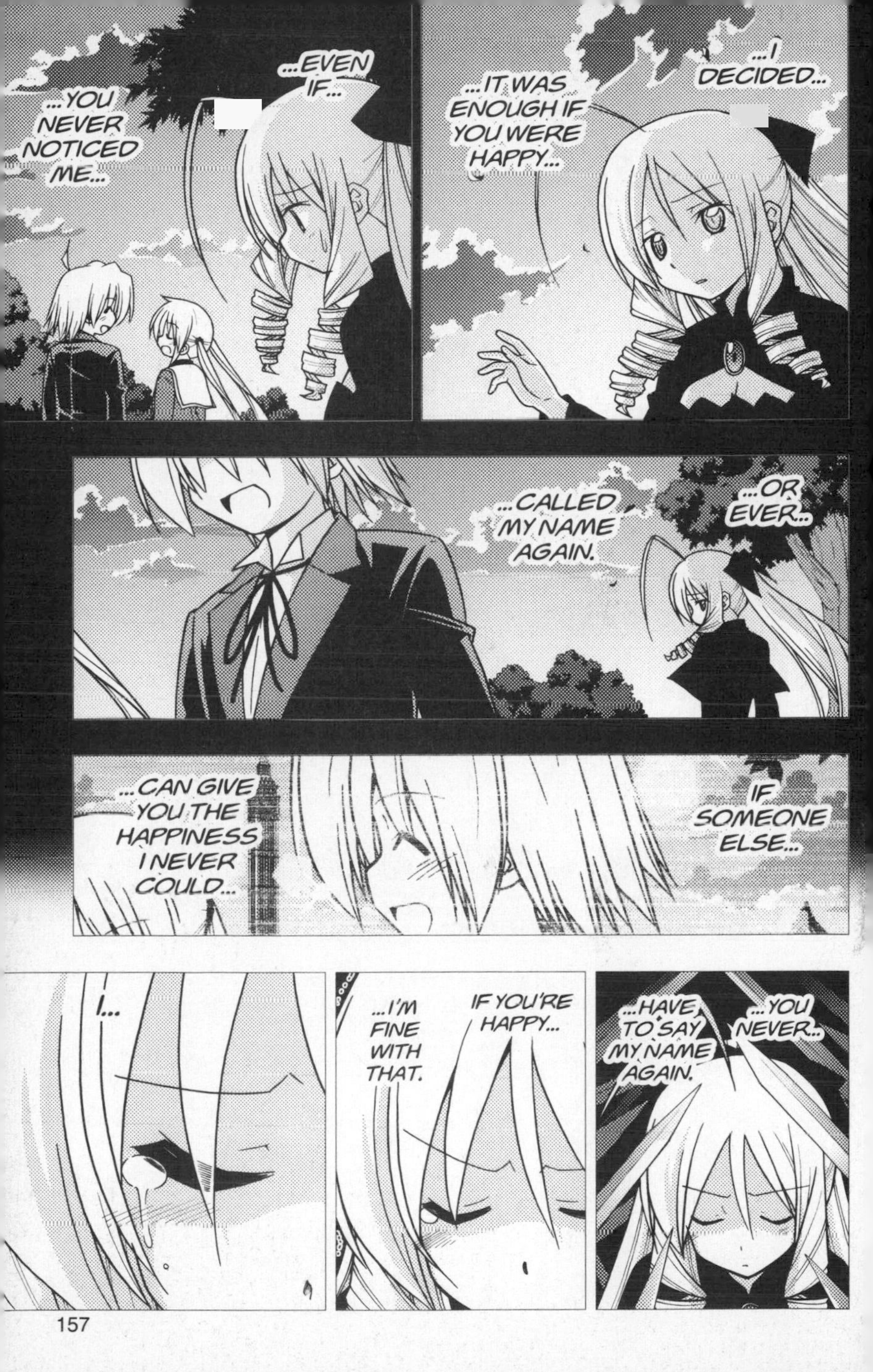
...I DECIDED...
...IT WAS ENOUGH IF YOU WERE HAPPY...
...EVEN IF...
...YOU NEVER NOTICED ME...
...OR EVER...
...CALLED MY NAME AGAIN.
IF SOMEONE ELSE...
...CAN GIVE YOU THE HAPPINESS I NEVER COULD...
...YOU NEVER...
...HAVE TO SAY MY NAME AGAIN.
IF YOU'RE HAPPY...
...I'M FINE WITH THAT.
I...

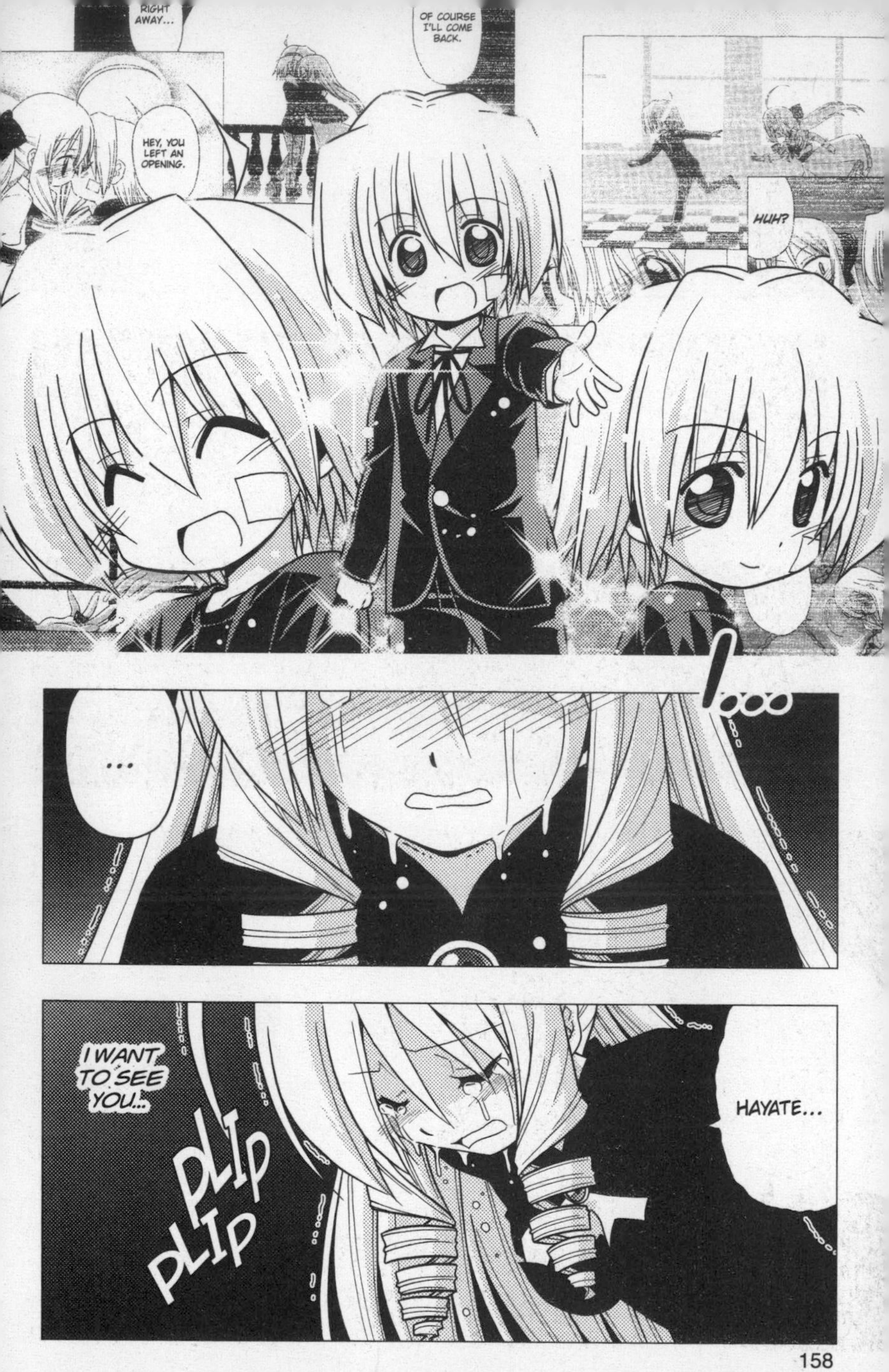
OF COURSE I'LL COME BACK.
RIGHT AWAY...
HUH?
HEY, YOU LEFT AN OPENING.
...
HAYATE...
I WANT TO SEE YOU...
PLIP PLIP

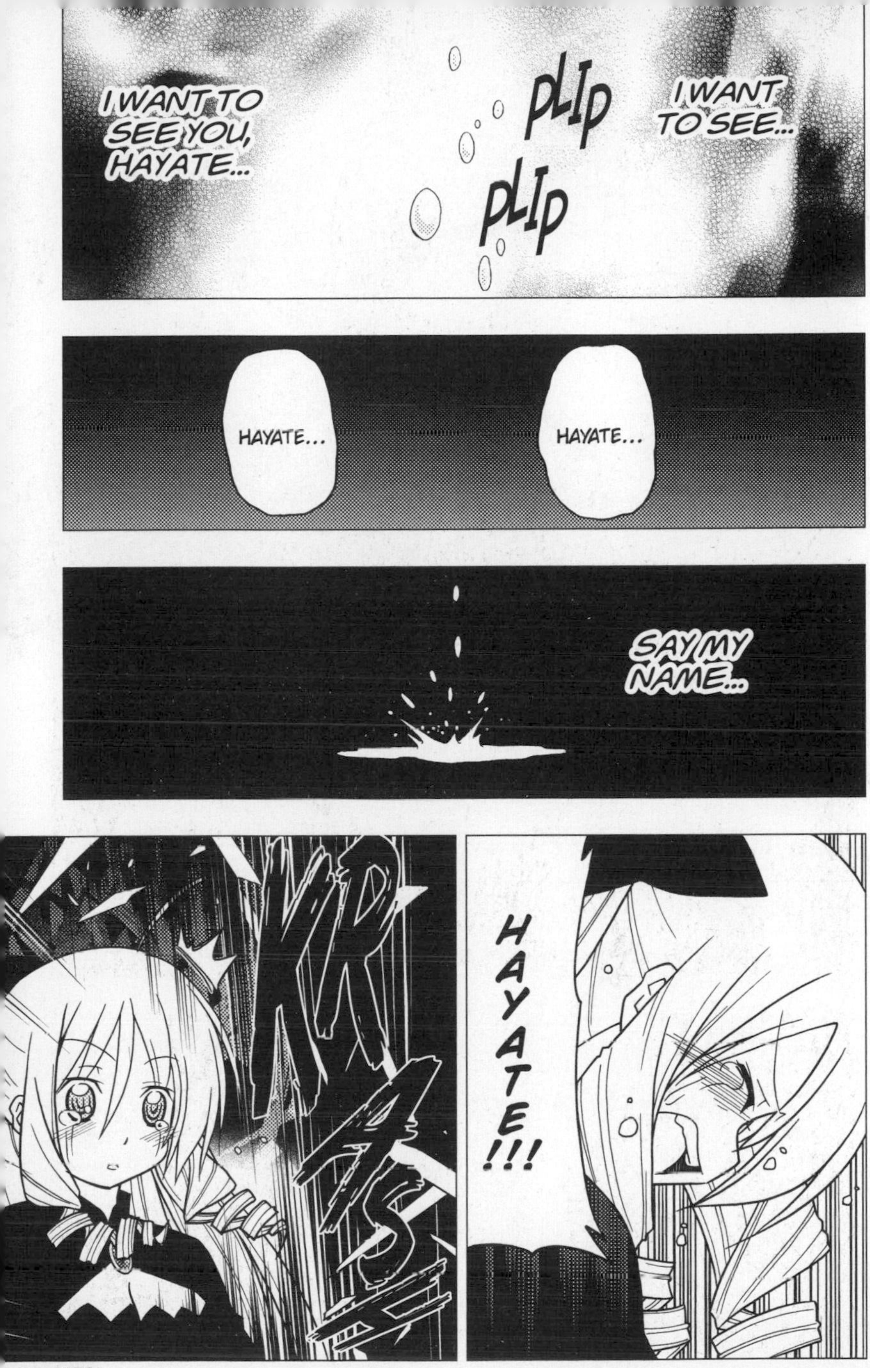
I WANT TO SEE...
PLIP
PLIP
I WANT TO SEE YOU, HAYATE...
HAYATE...
HAYATE...
SAY MY NAME...
HAYATE!!!

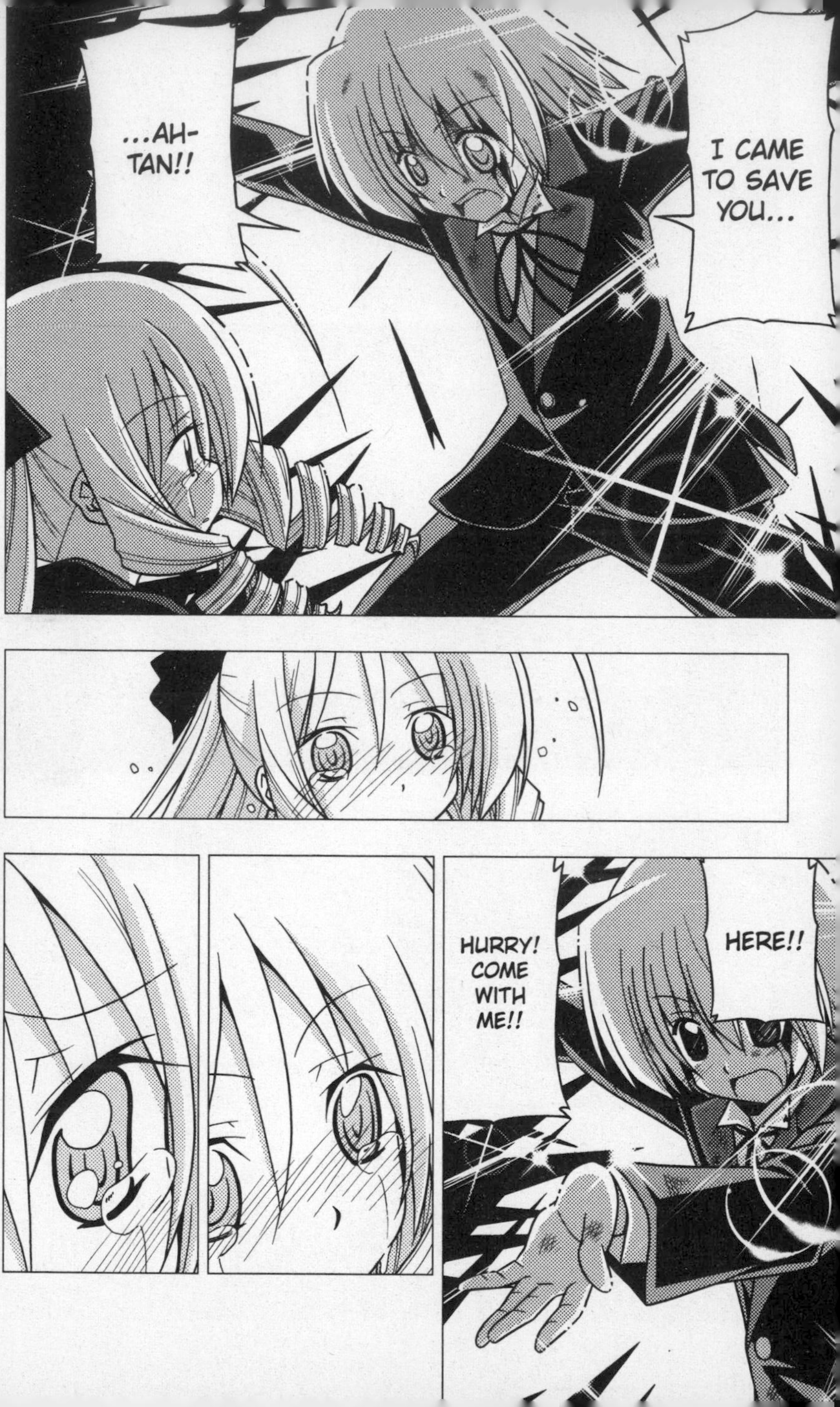
I CAME TO SAVE YOU...
...AH-TAN!!
HERE!!
HURRY! COME WITH ME!!

HAYATE...

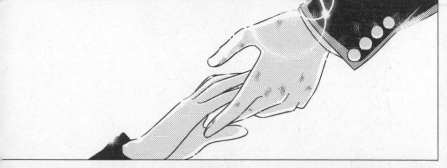

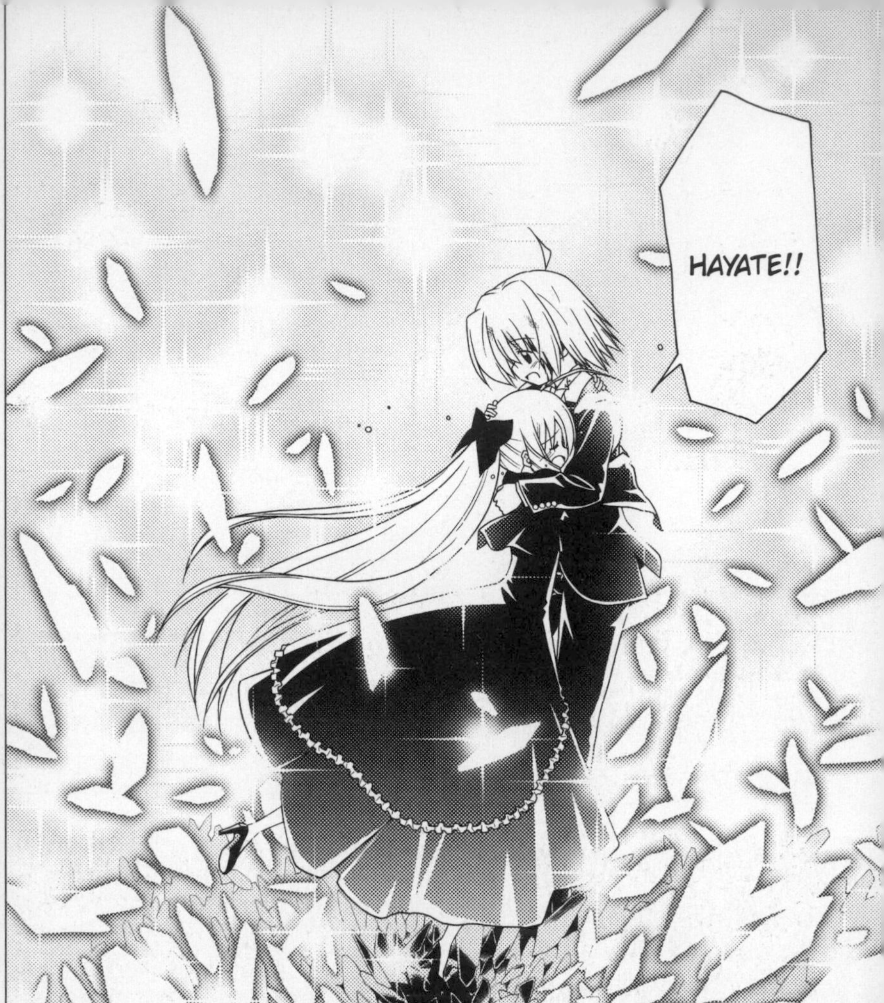
HAYATE!!

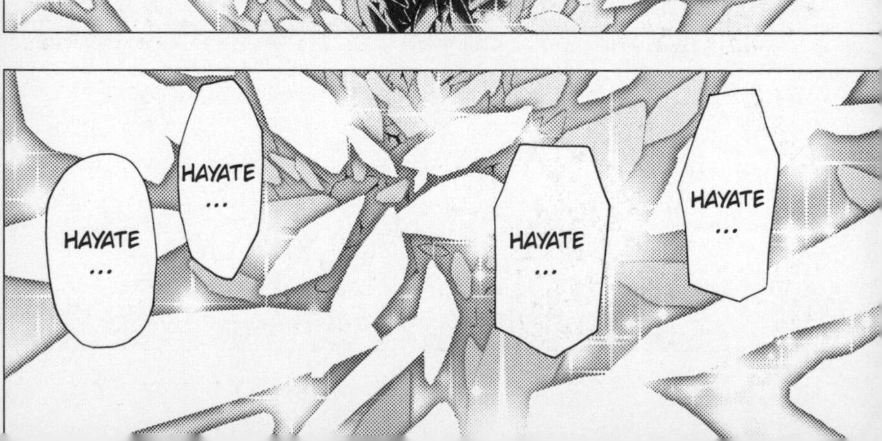
HAYATE
...
HAYATE
...
HAYATE
...
HAYATE
...

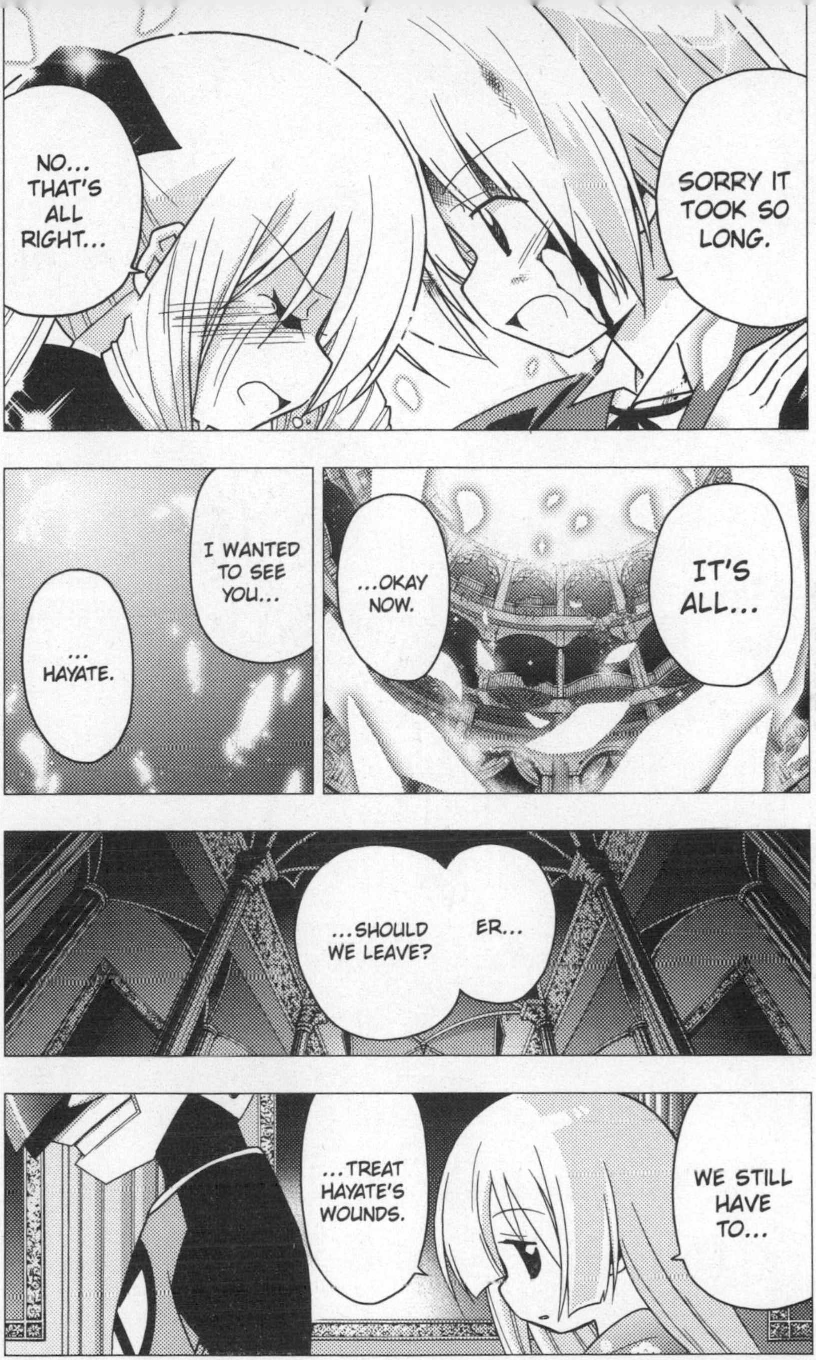
SORRY IT TOOK SO LONG.
NO... THAT'S ALL RIGHT...
IT'S ALL...
...OKAY NOW.
I WANTED TO SEE YOU...
... HAYATE.
ER...
...SHOULD WE LEAVE?
WE STILL HAVE TO...
...TREAT HAYATE'S WOUNDS.

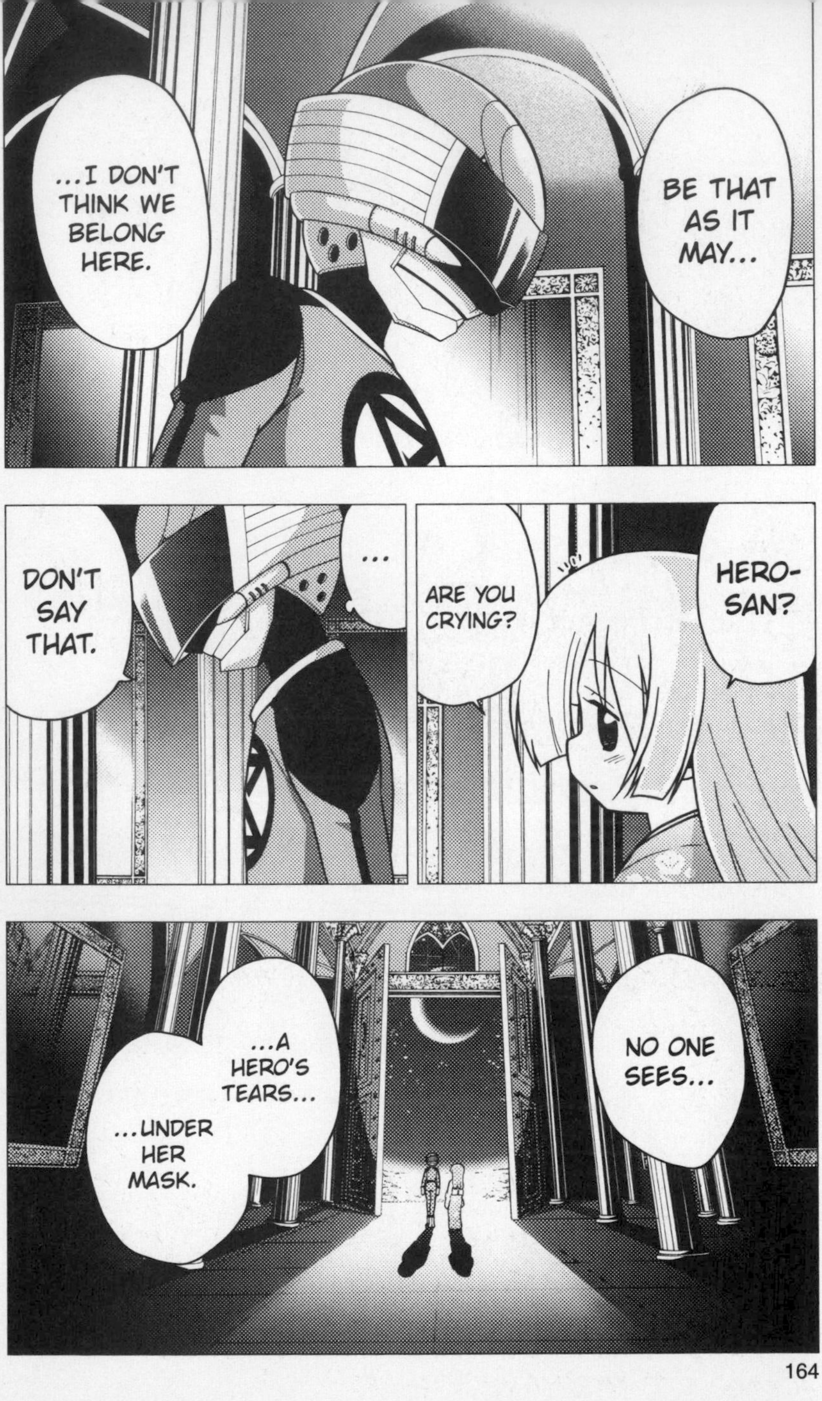
BE THAT AS IT MAY...
...I DON'T THINK WE BELONG HERE.
HERO-SAN?
ARE YOU CRYING?
...
DON'T SAY THAT.
NO ONE SEES...
...A HERO'S TEARS...
...UNDER HER MASK.

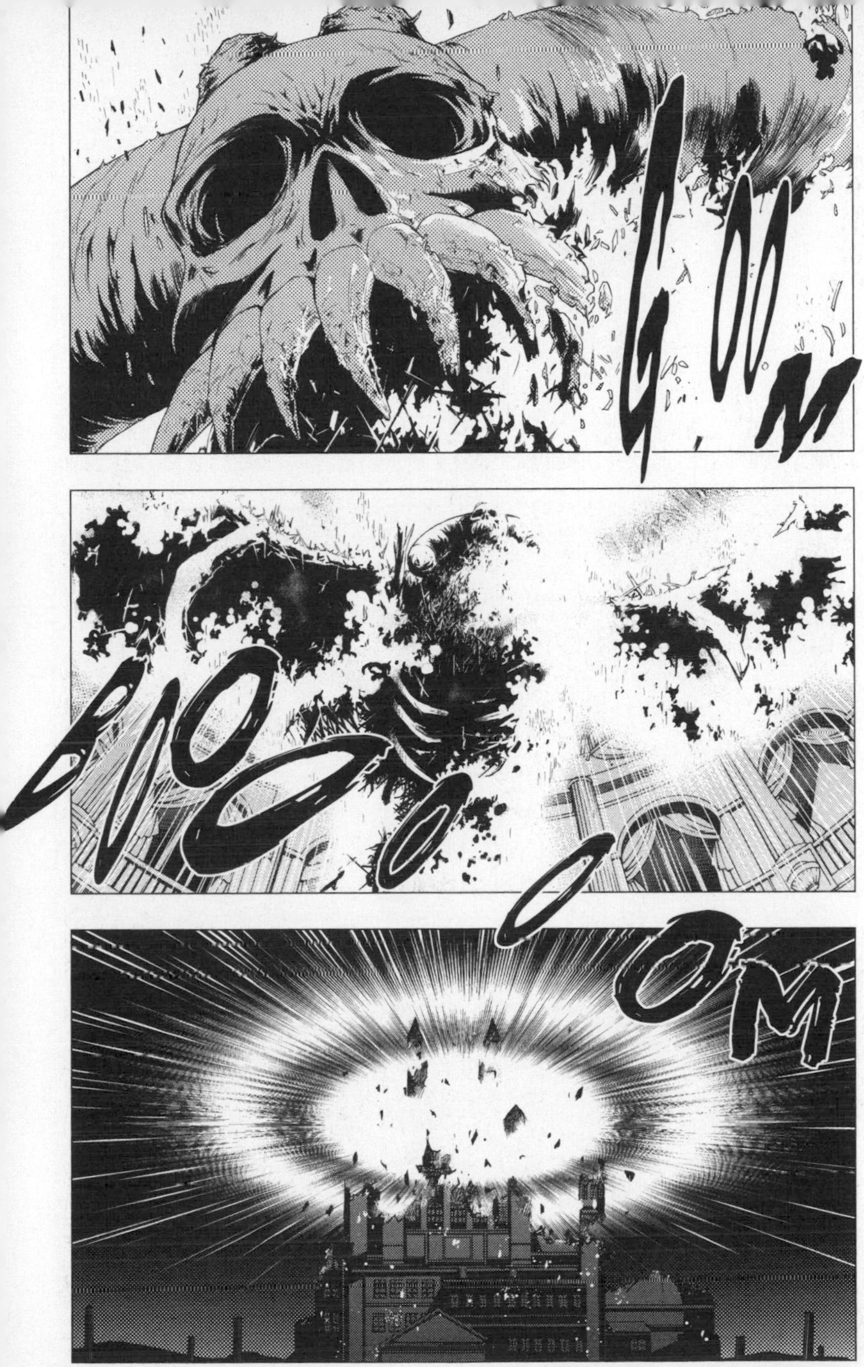
GOOM
BOOOOOM

Episode 11: "Snuggle Wuggle Snuggle Wuggle"

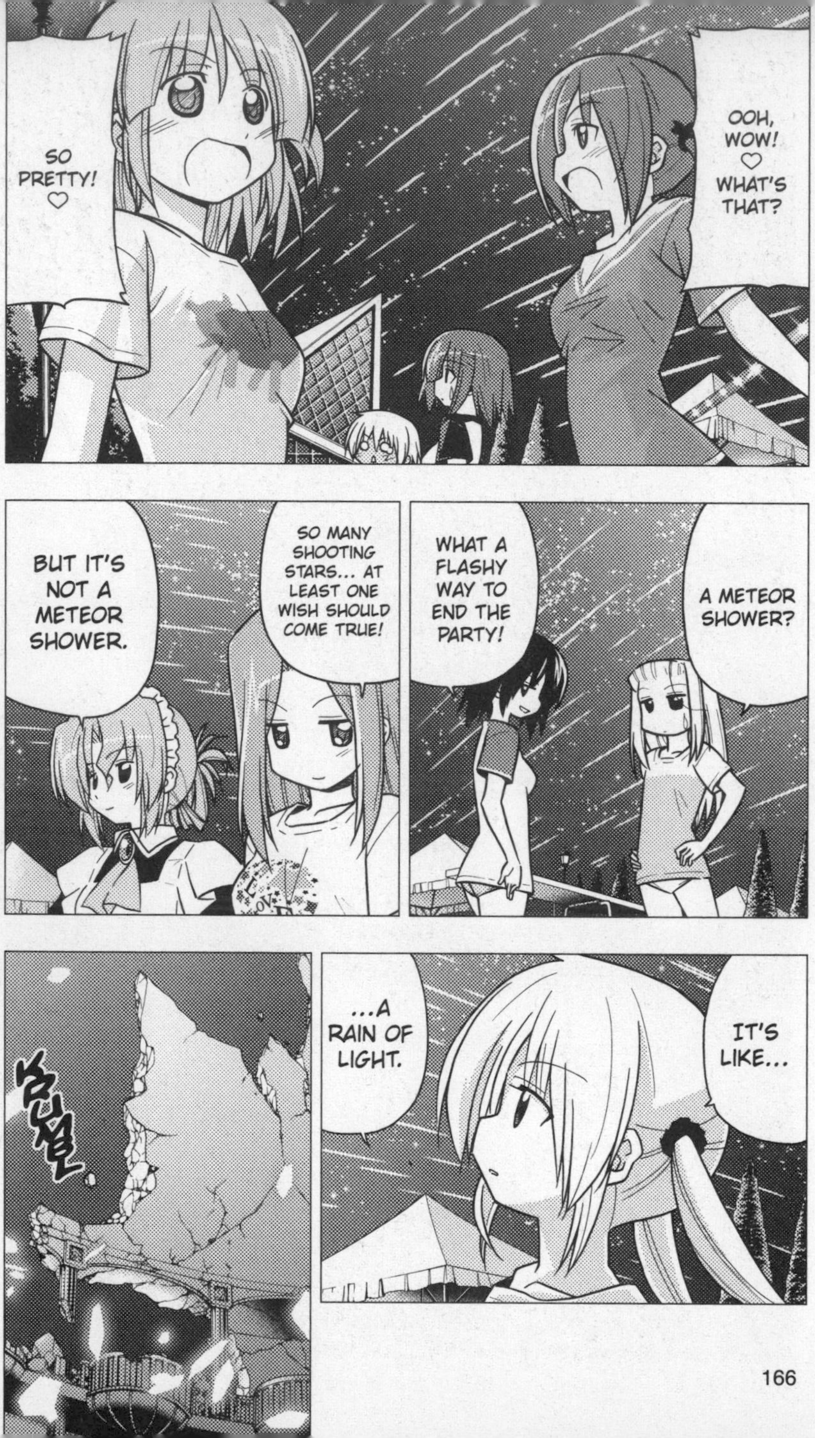
OOH, WOW! ♡ WHAT'S THAT?
SO PRETTY! ♡
A METEOR SHOWER?
WHAT A FLASHY WAY TO END THE PARTY!
SO MANY SHOOTING STARS... AT LEAST ONE WISH SHOULD COME TRUE!
BUT IT'S NOT A METEOR SHOWER.
IT'S LIKE...
...A RAIN OF LIGHT.

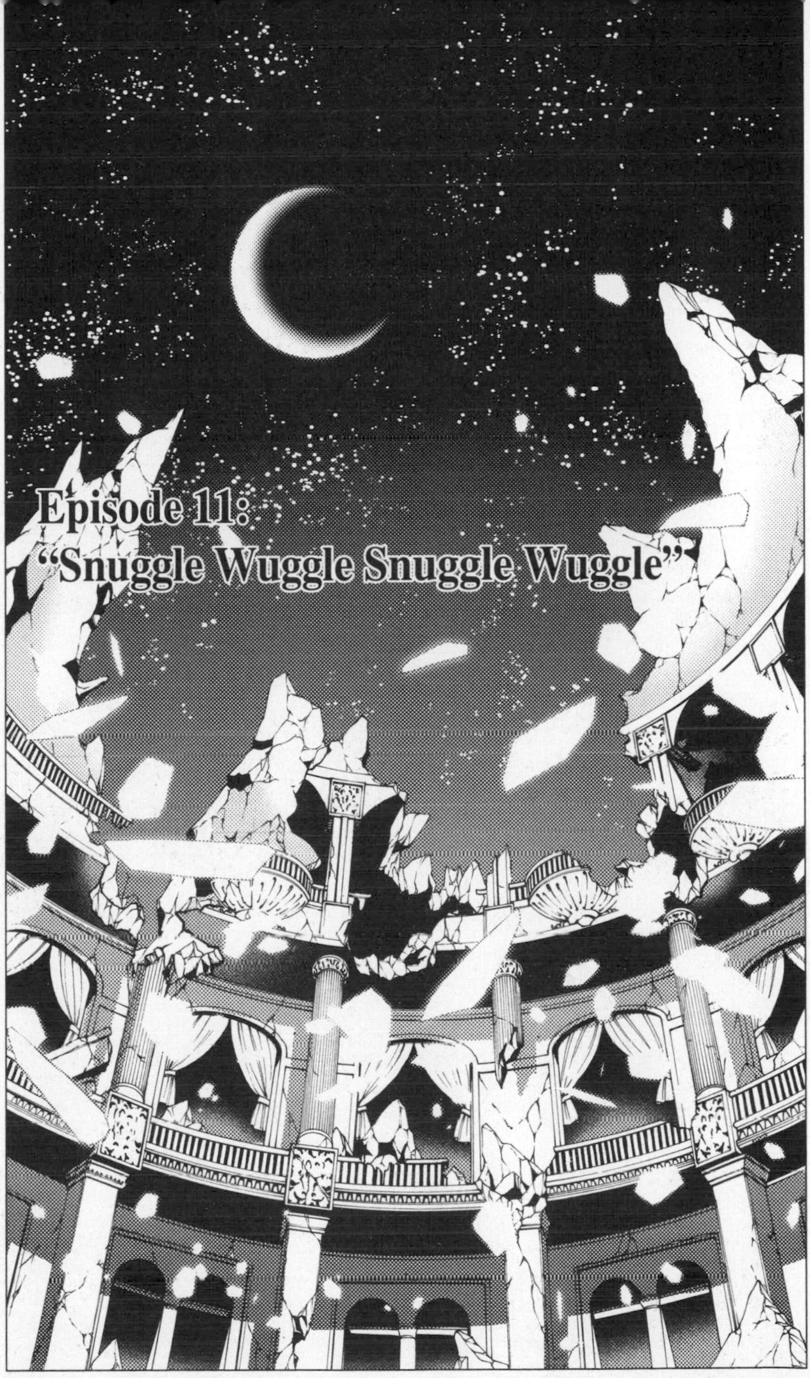
Episode 11:
"Snuggle Wuggle Snuggle Wuggle"

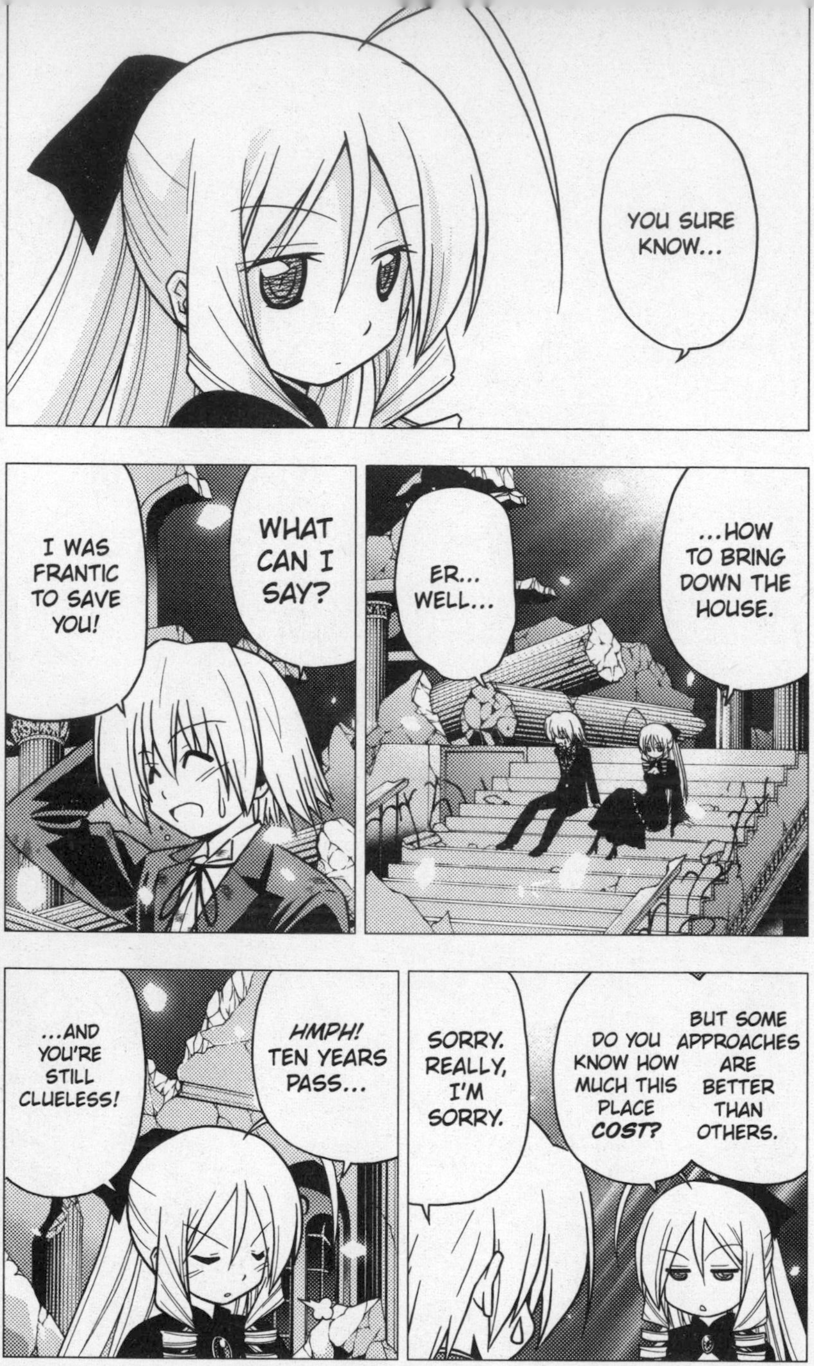
YOU SURE KNOW...
...HOW TO BRING DOWN THE HOUSE.
ER... WELL...
WHAT CAN I SAY?
I WAS FRANTIC TO SAVE YOU!
BUT SOME APPROACHES ARE BETTER THAN OTHERS.
DO YOU KNOW HOW MUCH THIS PLACE *COST?*
SORRY. REALLY, I'M SORRY.
HMPH! TEN YEARS PASS...
...AND YOU'RE STILL CLUELESS!

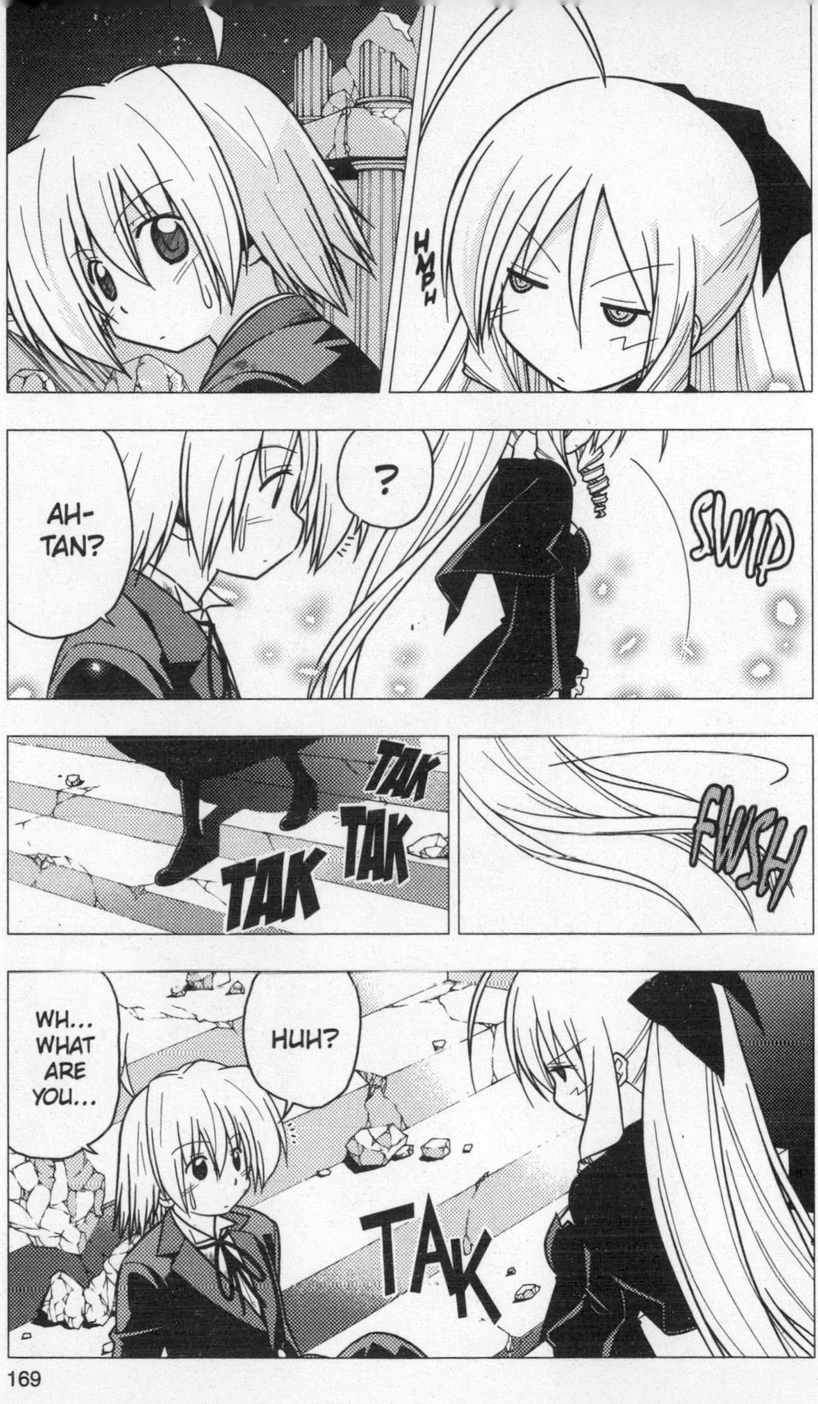
HMPH
?
AH-TAN?
SWIP
FWSH
TAK TAK TAK
HUH?
WH... WHAT ARE YOU...
TAK

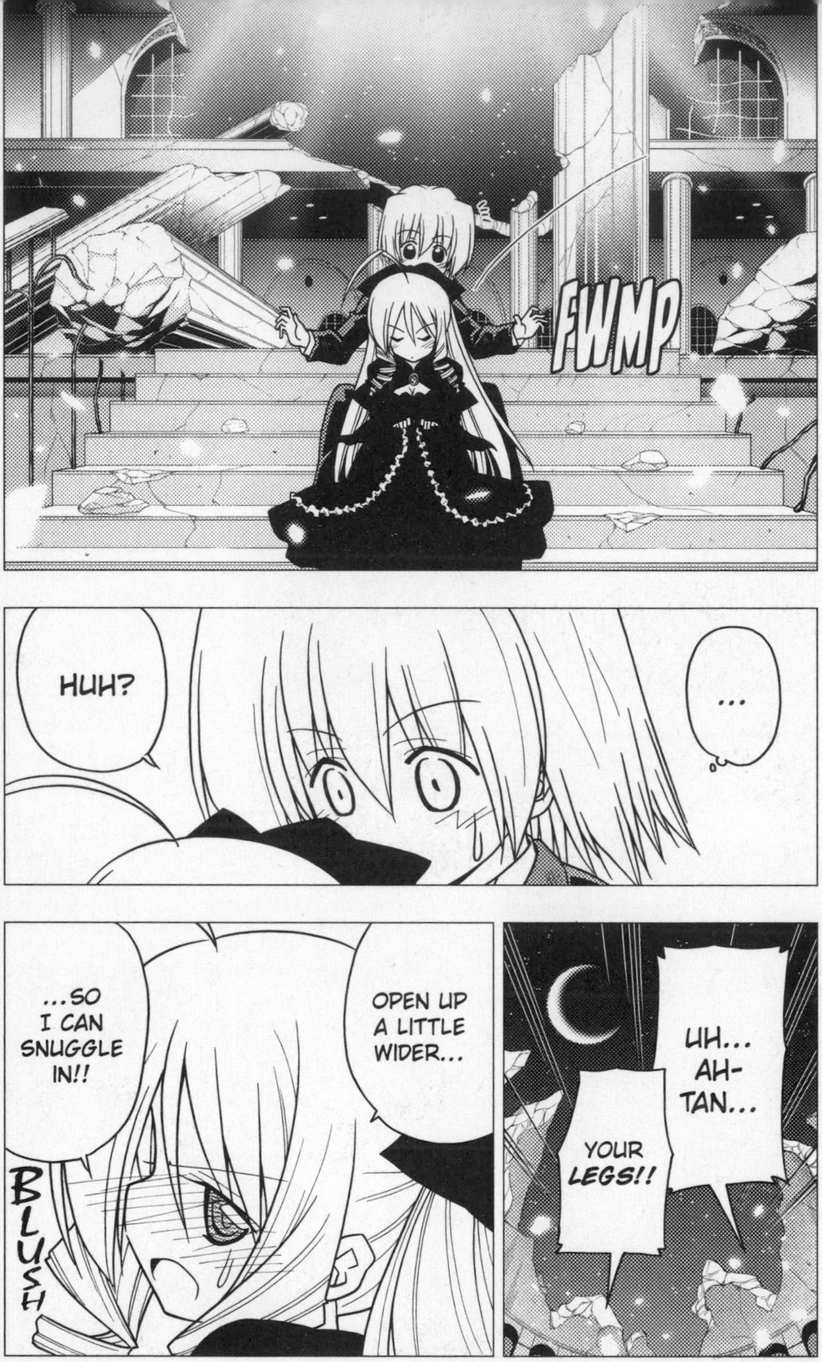
FWMP
...
HUH?
UH... AH-TAN...
YOUR LEGS!!
OPEN UP A LITTLE WIDER...
...SO I CAN SNUGGLE IN!!
BLUSH

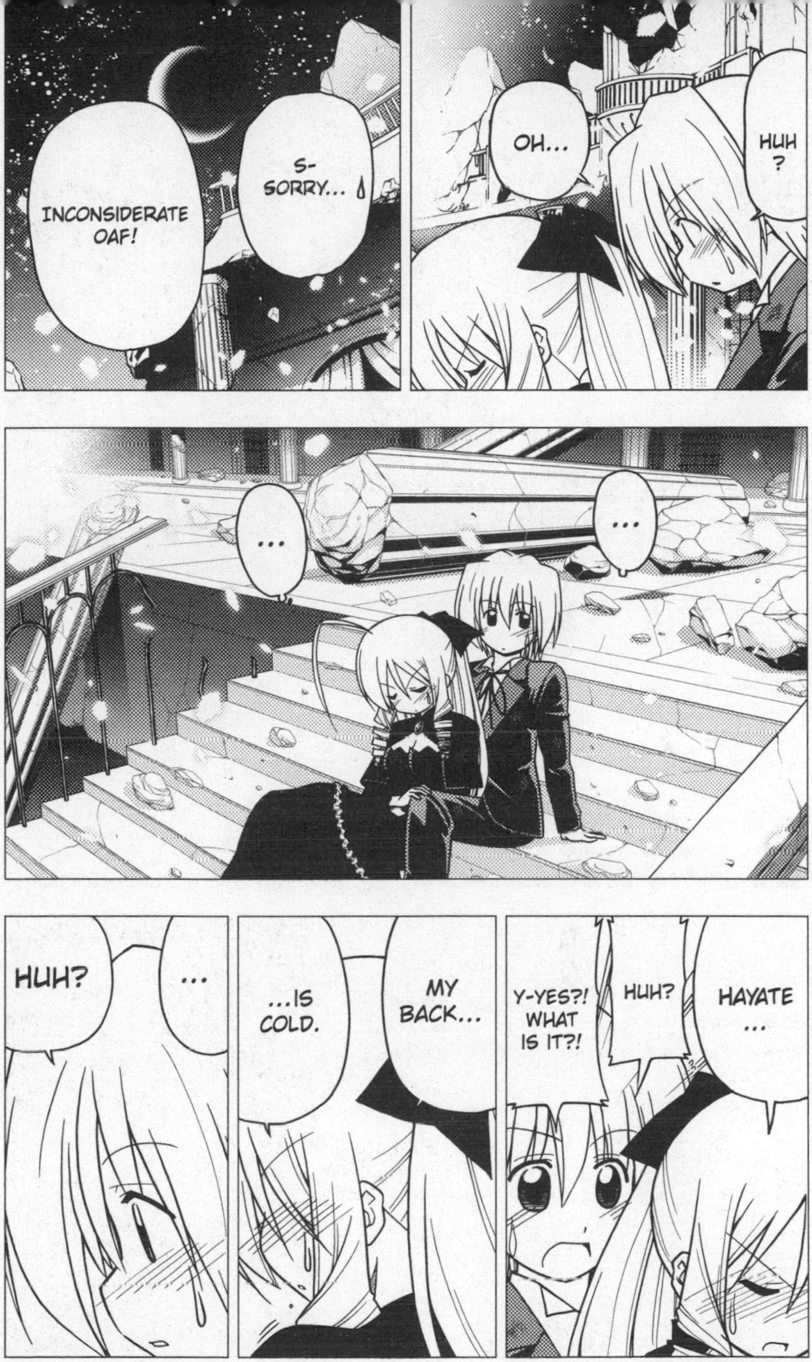
HUH?
OH...
S-SORRY...
INCONSIDERATE OAF!
...
...
HAYATE...
HUH?
Y-YES?! WHAT IS IT?!
MY BACK...
...IS COLD.
...
HUH?

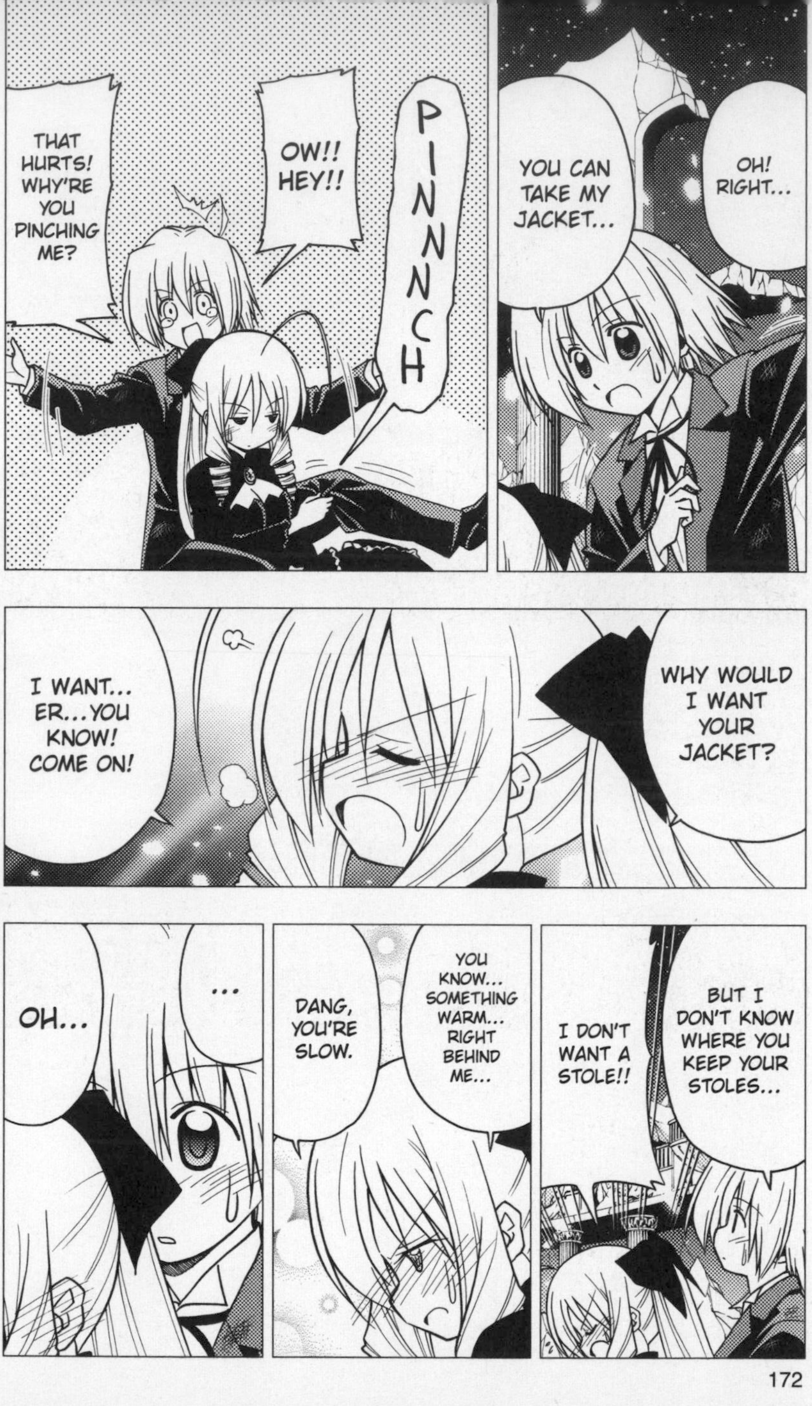
OH! RIGHT...
YOU CAN TAKE MY JACKET...
PINNNCH
OW!! HEY!!
THAT HURTS! WHY'RE YOU PINCHING ME?
WHY WOULD I WANT YOUR JACKET?
I WANT... ER...YOU KNOW! COME ON!
BUT I DON'T KNOW WHERE YOU KEEP YOUR STOLES...
I DON'T WANT A STOLE!!
YOU KNOW... SOMETHING WARM... RIGHT BEHIND ME...
DANG, YOU'RE SLOW.
...
OH...

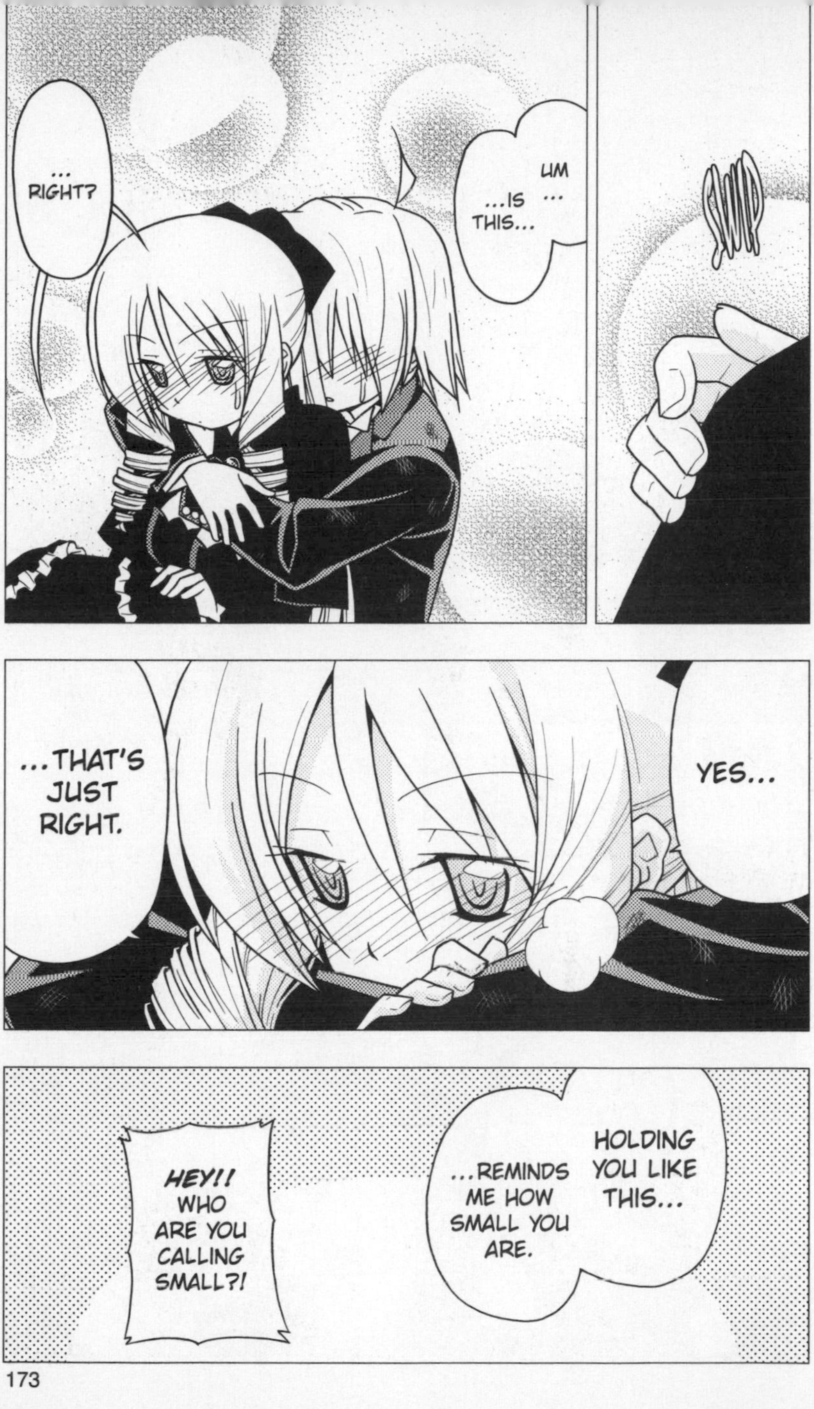
UM ... ...IS THIS...
... RIGHT?
YES...
...THAT'S JUST RIGHT.
HOLDING YOU LIKE THIS...
...REMINDS ME HOW SMALL YOU ARE.
HEY!! WHO ARE YOU CALLING SMALL?!

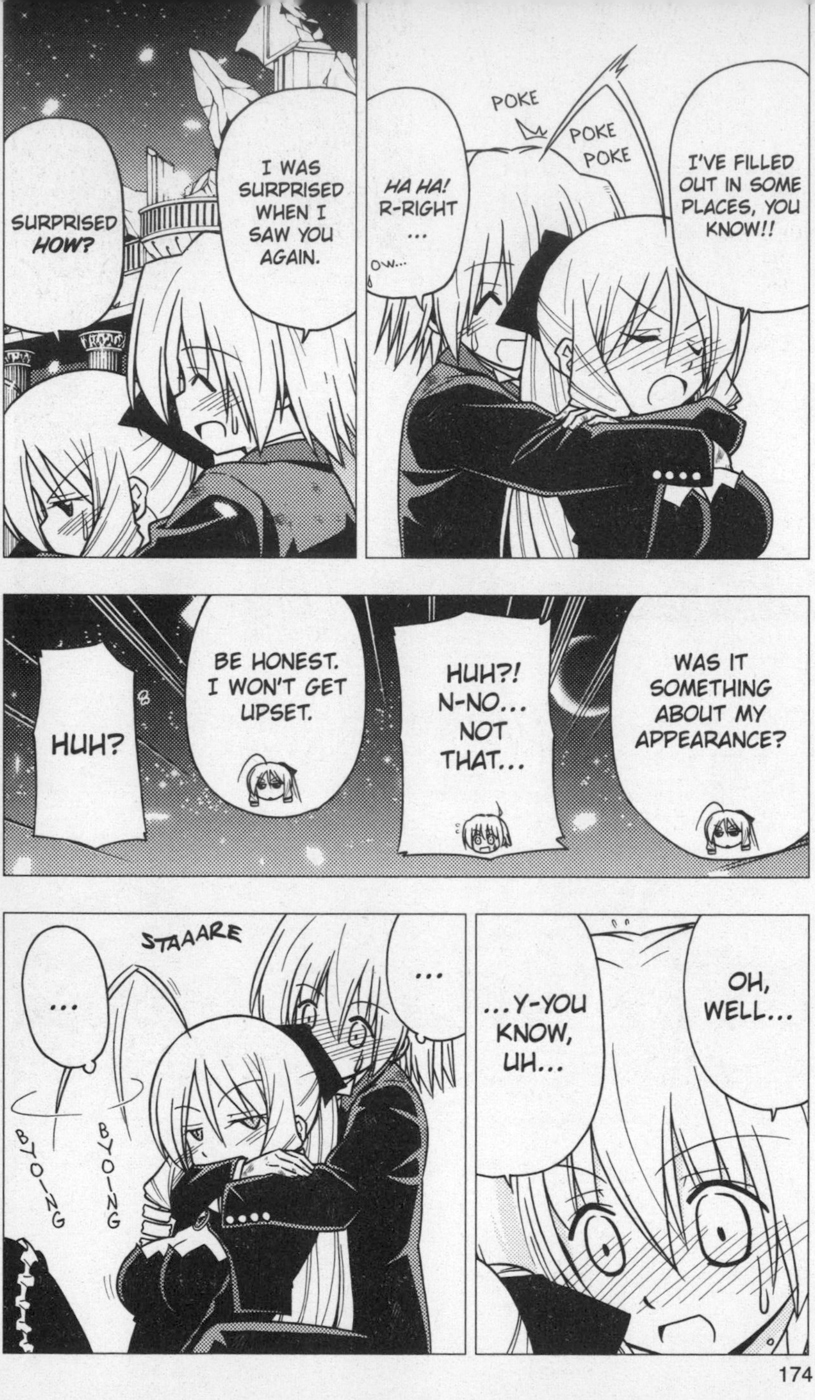
I'VE FILLED OUT IN SOME PLACES, YOU KNOW!!
POKE
POKE POKE
HA HA! R-RIGHT ...
OW...
I WAS SURPRISED WHEN I SAW YOU AGAIN.
SURPRISED HOW?
WAS IT SOMETHING ABOUT MY APPEARANCE?
HUH?! N-NO... NOT THAT...
BE HONEST. I WON'T GET UPSET.
HUH?
OH, WELL...
...Y-YOU KNOW, UH...
...
STAAARE
...
BYOING
BYOING

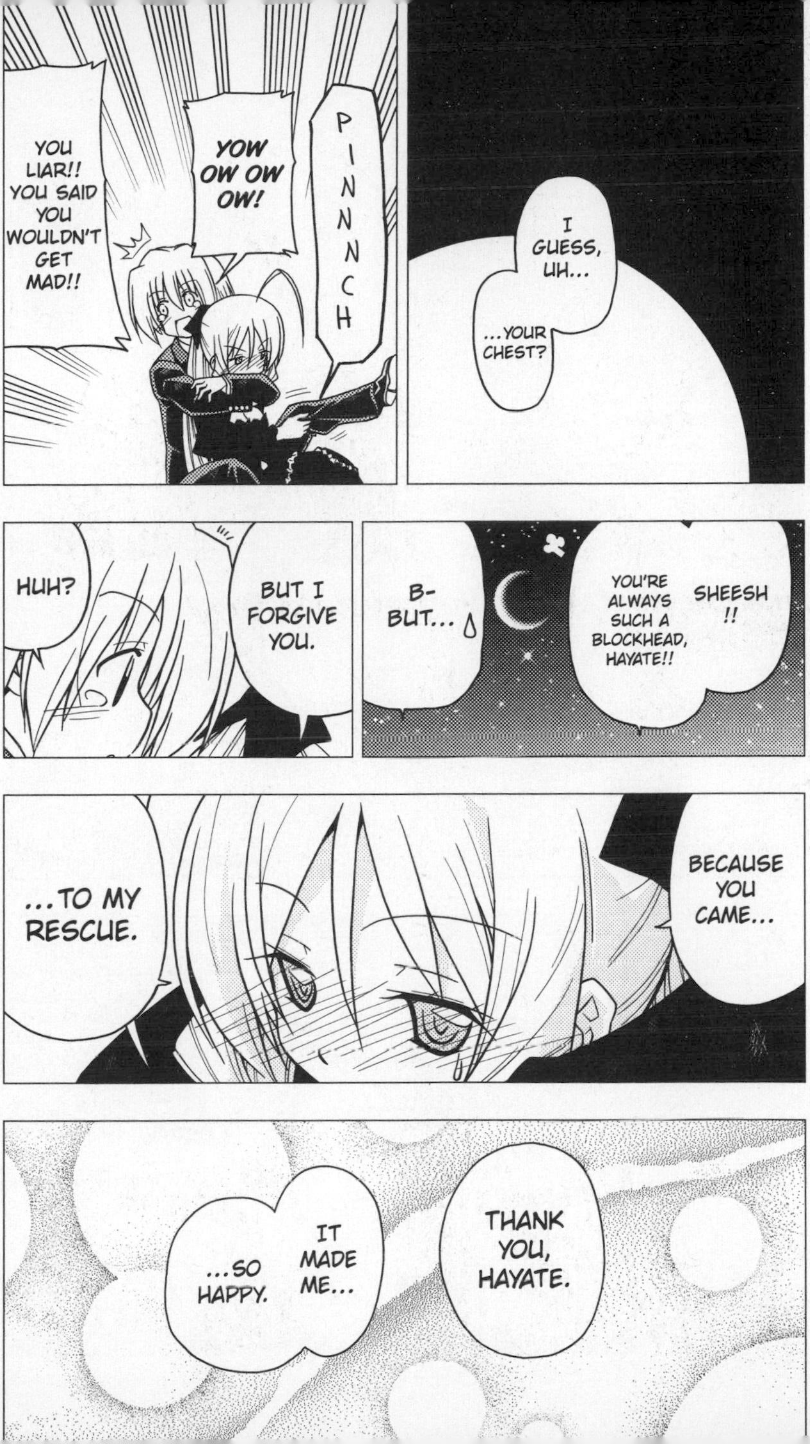
I GUESS, UH...
...YOUR CHEST?
PINNNCH
YOW OW OW OW!
YOU LIAR!! YOU SAID YOU WOULDN'T GET MAD!!
SHEESH!!
YOU'RE ALWAYS SUCH A BLOCKHEAD, HAYATE!!
B-BUT...
BUT I FORGIVE YOU.
HUH?
BECAUSE YOU CAME...
...TO MY RESCUE.
THANK YOU, HAYATE.
IT MADE ME...
...SO HAPPY.

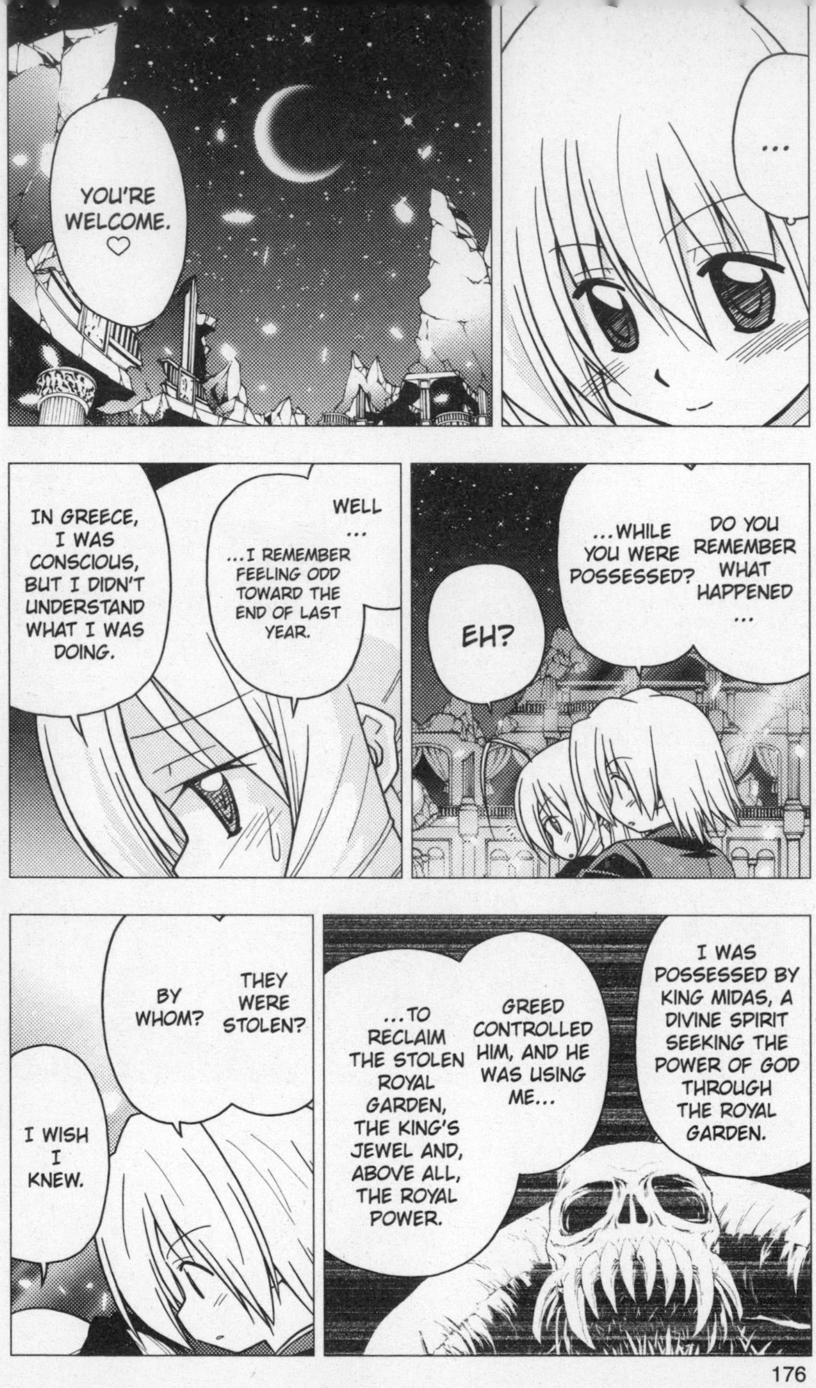
...
YOU'RE WELCOME. ♡
DO YOU REMEMBER WHAT HAPPENED ...
...WHILE YOU WERE POSSESSED?
EH?
WELL ...
...I REMEMBER FEELING ODD TOWARD THE END OF LAST YEAR.
IN GREECE, I WAS CONSCIOUS, BUT I DIDN'T UNDERSTAND WHAT I WAS DOING.
I WAS POSSESSED BY KING MIDAS, A DIVINE SPIRIT SEEKING THE POWER OF GOD THROUGH THE ROYAL GARDEN.
GREED CONTROLLED HIM, AND HE WAS USING ME...
...TO RECLAIM THE STOLEN ROYAL GARDEN, THE KING'S JEWEL AND, ABOVE ALL, THE ROYAL POWER.
THEY WERE STOLEN?
BY WHOM?
I WISH I KNEW.

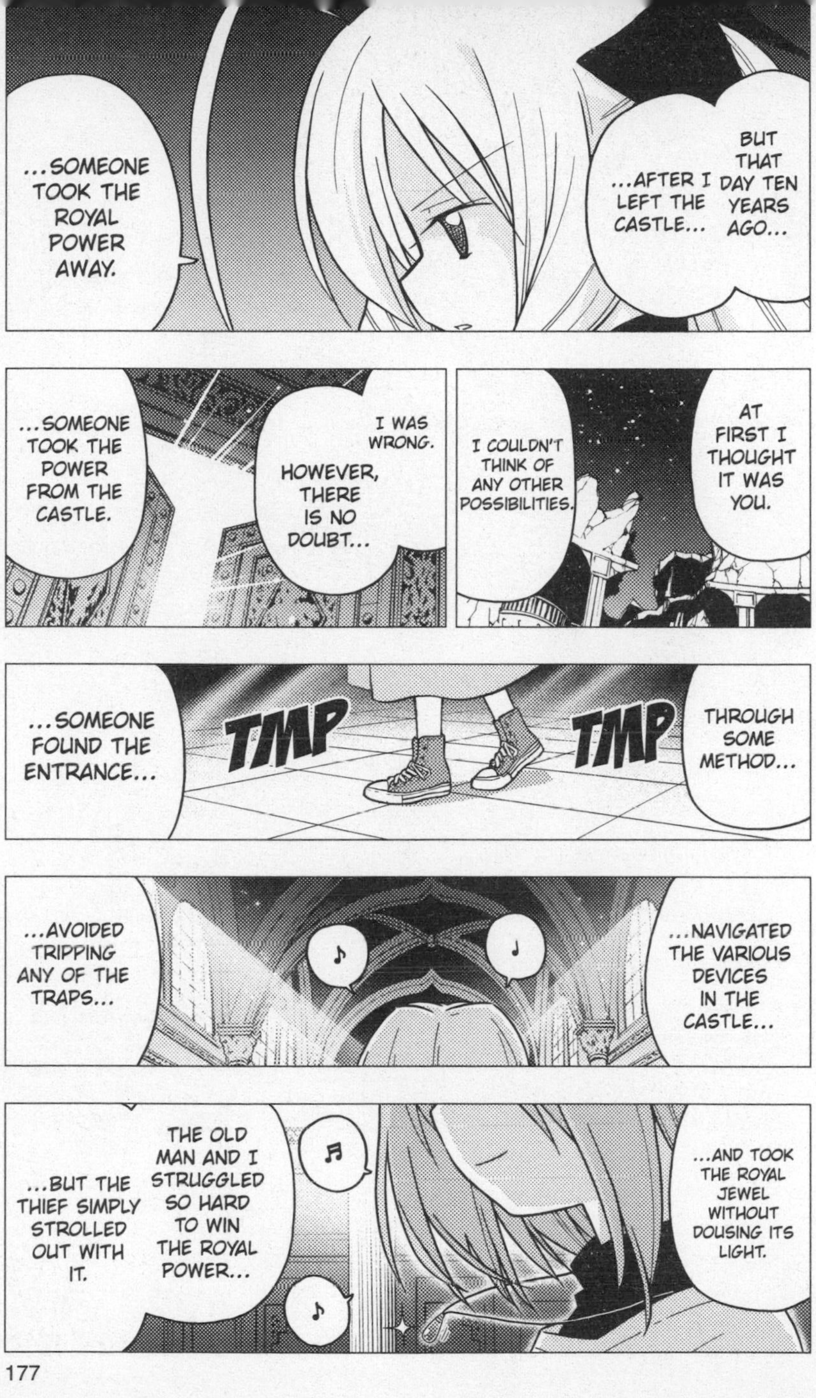
BUT THAT DAY TEN YEARS AGO...
...AFTER I LEFT THE CASTLE...
...SOMEONE TOOK THE ROYAL POWER AWAY.
AT FIRST I THOUGHT IT WAS YOU.
I COULDN'T THINK OF ANY OTHER POSSIBILITIES.
I WAS WRONG.
HOWEVER, THERE IS NO DOUBT...
...SOMEONE TOOK THE POWER FROM THE CASTLE.
THROUGH SOME METHOD...
TMP
TMP
...SOMEONE FOUND THE ENTRANCE...
...NAVIGATED THE VARIOUS DEVICES IN THE CASTLE...
♪
♩
...AVOIDED TRIPPING ANY OF THE TRAPS...
...AND TOOK THE ROYAL JEWEL WITHOUT DOUSING ITS LIGHT.
♬
♪
THE OLD MAN AND I STRUGGLED SO HARD TO WIN THE ROYAL POWER...
...BUT THE THIEF SIMPLY STROLLED OUT WITH IT.

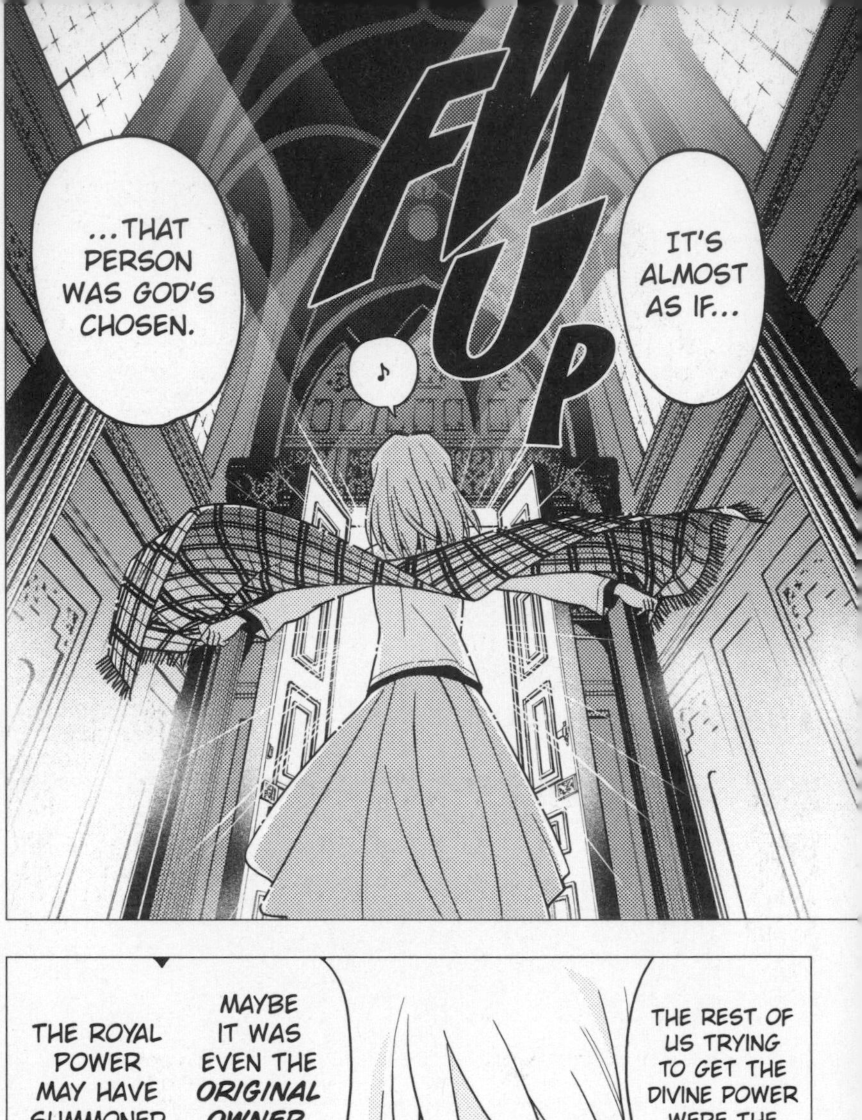
IT'S ALMOST AS IF...
FWUP
♪
...THAT PERSON WAS GOD'S CHOSEN.

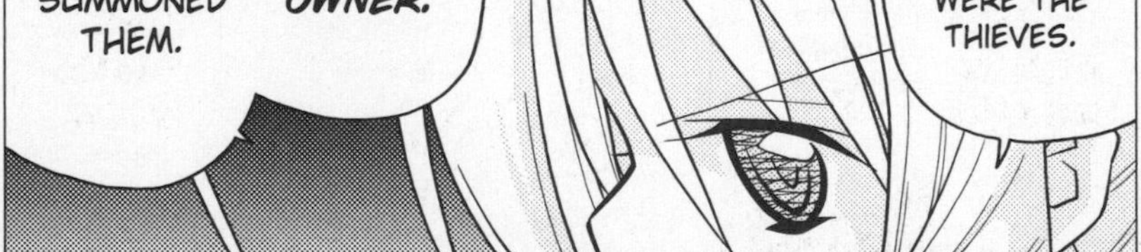
THE REST OF US TRYING TO GET THE DIVINE POWER WERE THE THIEVES.
MAYBE IT WAS EVEN THE *ORIGINAL OWNER.*
THE ROYAL POWER MAY HAVE SUMMONED THEM.

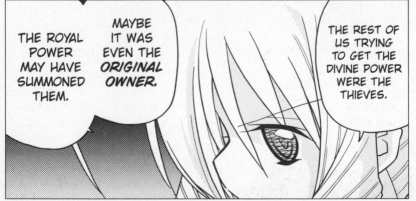

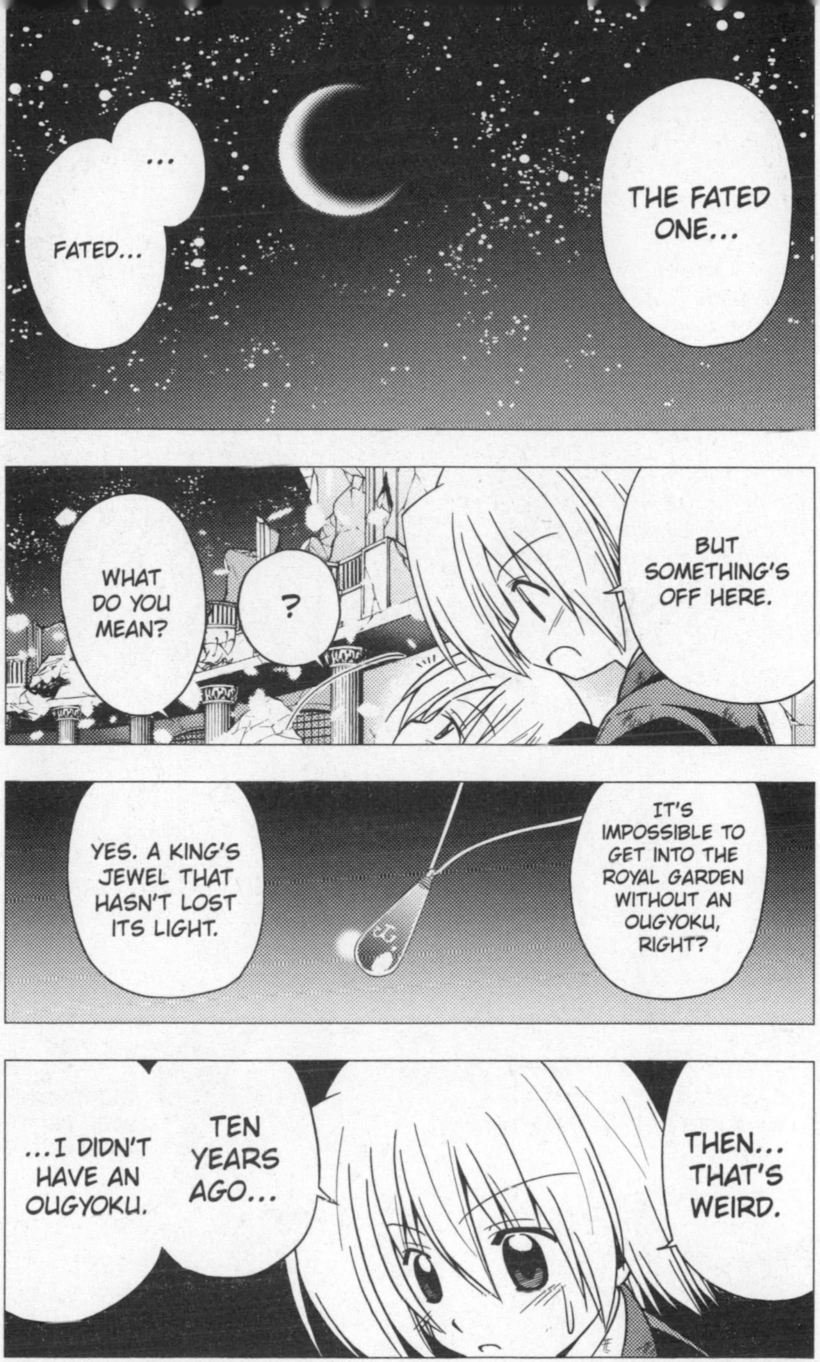
THE FATED ONE...
... FATED...
BUT SOMETHING'S OFF HERE.
?
WHAT DO YOU MEAN?
IT'S IMPOSSIBLE TO GET INTO THE ROYAL GARDEN WITHOUT AN OUGYOKU, RIGHT?
YES. A KING'S JEWEL THAT HASN'T LOST ITS LIGHT.
THEN... THAT'S WEIRD.
TEN YEARS AGO...
...I DIDN'T HAVE AN OUGYOKU.

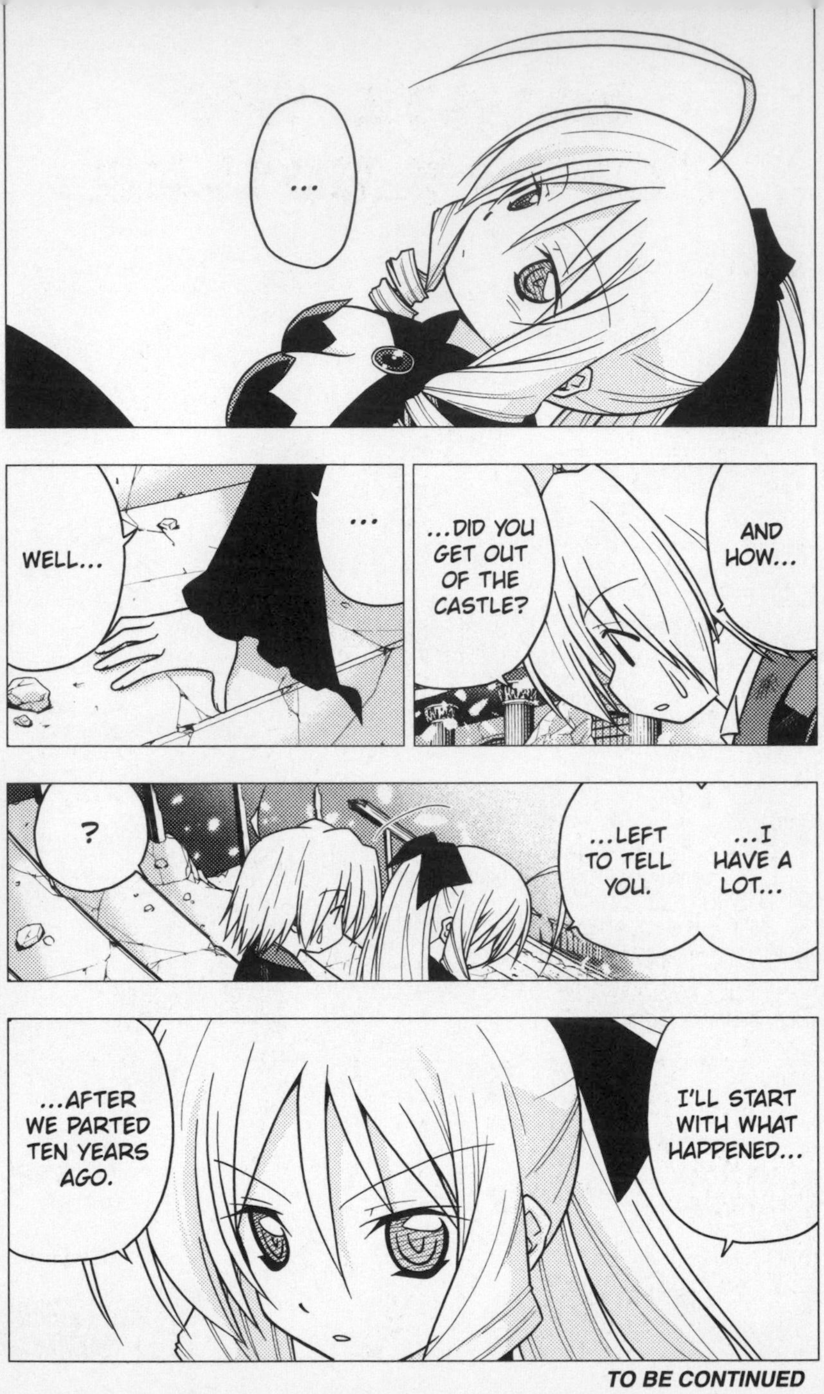
...
AND HOW...
...DID YOU GET OUT OF THE CASTLE?
...
WELL...
...I HAVE A LOT...
...LEFT TO TELL YOU.
?
I'LL START WITH WHAT HAPPENED...
...AFTER WE PARTED TEN YEARS AGO.

TO BE CONTINUED

HAYATE THE COMBAT BUTLER

BONUS SECTION

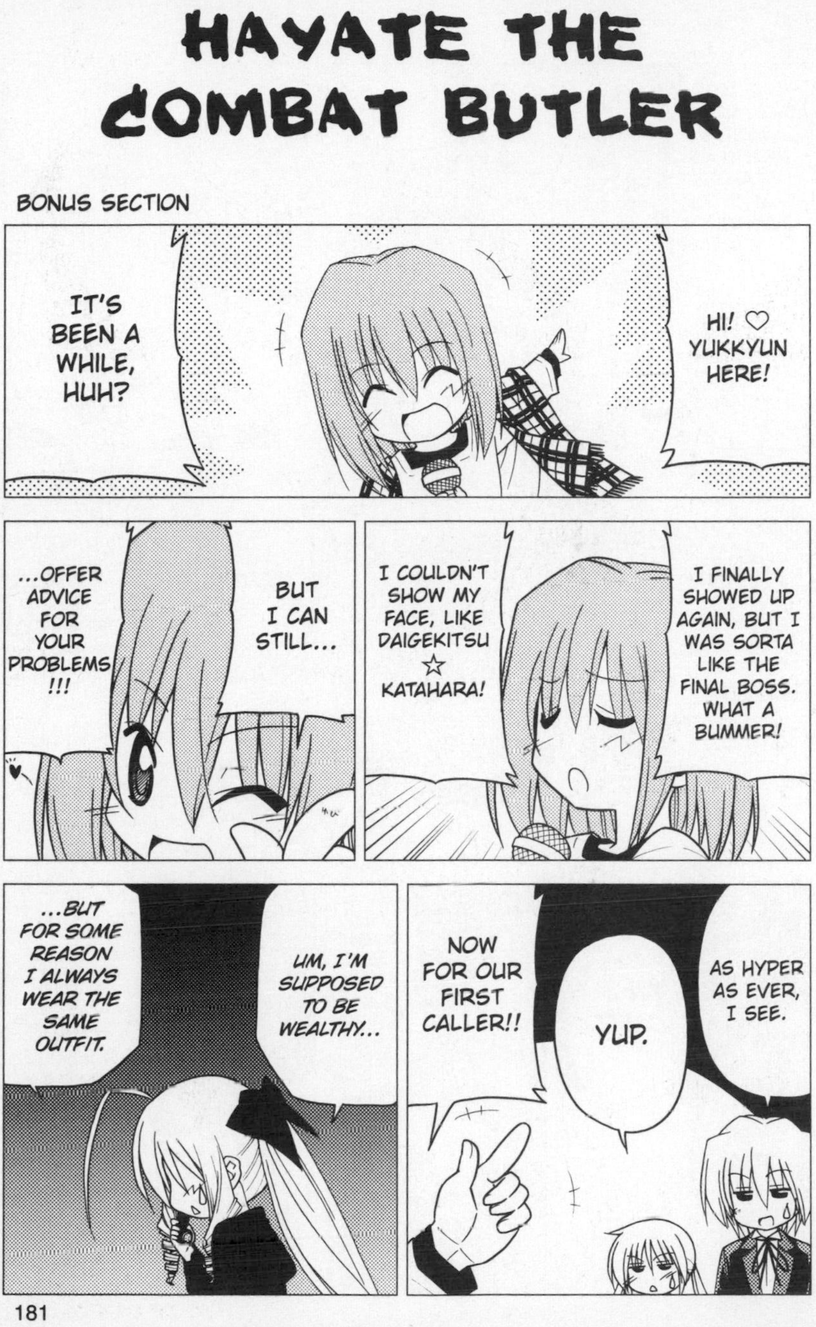
HI! ♡ YUKKYUN HERE!
IT'S BEEN A WHILE, HUH?
I FINALLY SHOWED UP AGAIN, BUT I WAS SORTA LIKE THE FINAL BOSS. WHAT A BUMMER!
I COULDN'T SHOW MY FACE, LIKE DAIGEKITSU ☆ KATAHARA!
BUT I CAN STILL...
...OFFER ADVICE FOR YOUR PROBLEMS!!!
AS HYPER AS EVER, I SEE.
YUP.
NOW FOR OUR FIRST CALLER!!
UM, I'M SUPPOSED TO BE WEALTHY...
...BUT FOR SOME REASON I ALWAYS WEAR THE SAME OUTFIT.

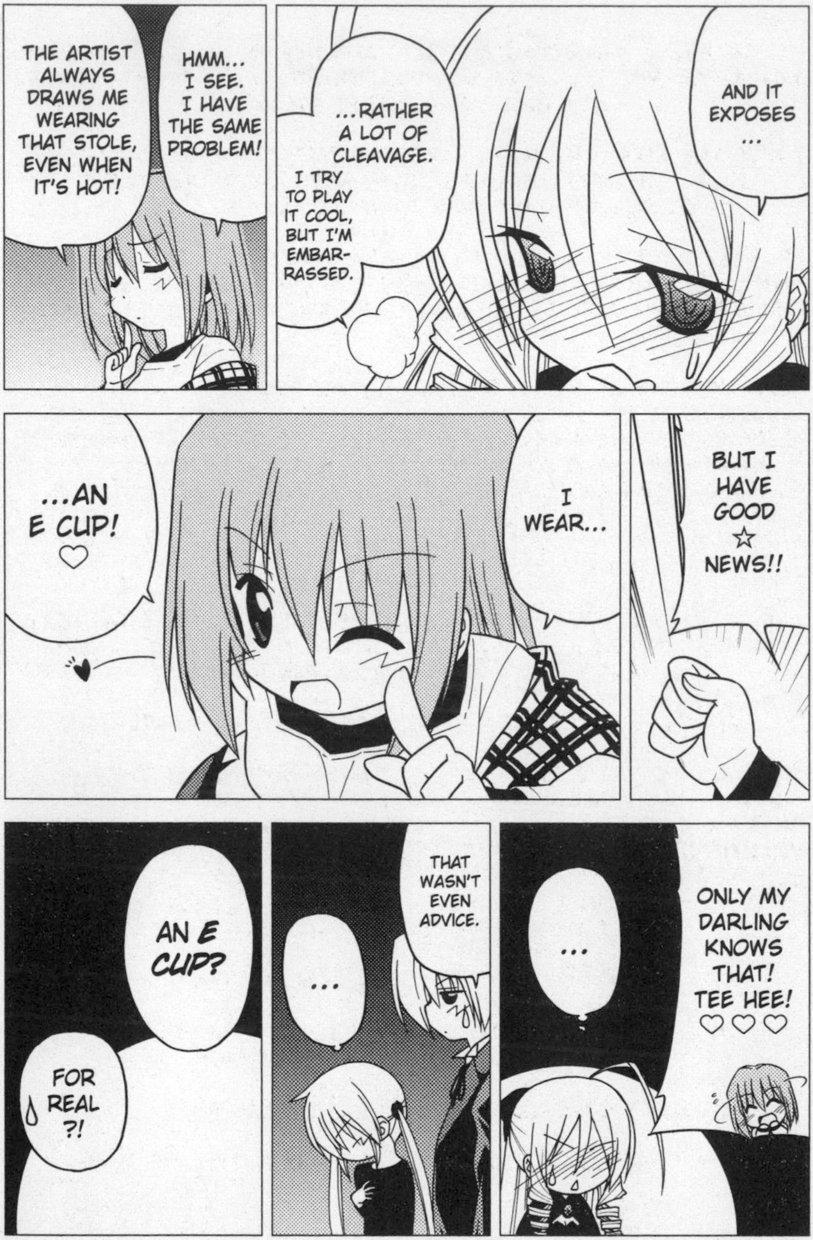
AND IT EXPOSES ...
...RATHER A LOT OF CLEAVAGE.
I TRY TO PLAY IT COOL, BUT I'M EMBAR-RASSED.
HMM... I SEE. I HAVE THE SAME PROBLEM!
THE ARTIST ALWAYS DRAWS ME WEARING THAT STOLE, EVEN WHEN IT'S HOT!
BUT I HAVE GOOD ☆ NEWS!!
I WEAR...
...AN E CUP! ♡
ONLY MY DARLING KNOWS THAT! TEE HEE! ♡♡♡
...
THAT WASN'T EVEN ADVICE.
...
AN E CUP?
FOR REAL ?!

IN THE WEEK THIS BOOK COMES OUT, THE ONGOING MANGA IN *WEEKLY SHONEN SUNDAY* WILL ENTER NEW POST-GOLDEN WEEK DEVELOPMENTS. HOW HAVE YOU BEEN? HI. I'M HATA.

I MISS THE DAYS WHEN MY EDITOR AND I USED TO SIT AROUND SAYING, "I HOPE WE CAN FINISH THE GOLDEN WEEK ARC IN ONE OR TWO VOLUMES." I DIDN'T THINK IT WOULD LAST SO LONG...

FROM MY POINT OF VIEW AS THE AUTHOR, IT WAS A LONG STORY AND I WANTED PEOPLE TO READ IT ALL AT ONCE, SO IN JAPAN THE PUBLISHER RELEASED VOLUMES 23 AND 24 SIMULTANEOUSLY. HOW DID YOU LIKE THEM?

NOW *HAYATE* IS ENTERING ITS SIXTH YEAR. I WROTE THE ATHENA ARC BECAUSE, AFTER GOING ON FOR SO LONG, I WAS HAVING TROUBLE TAKING THE MANGA AND MYSELF TO THE NEXT LEVEL. I'M WORRIED ABOUT HOW YOU READERS WILL LIKE IT, BUT I'LL BE HAPPY IF MY DESIRE TO TAKE ON SOMETHING NEW COMES ACROSS EVEN A LITTLE.

IF YOU HAVE FEEDBACK, SEND IT IN. EVEN A LITTLE POST TO MY TWITTER ACCOUNT BELOW WOULD BE FINE.

THIS STORY LINE HAS TAUGHT ME A LOT AS A MANGA ARTIST. THE NEXT VOLUME FEATURES A CONCLUSION OF SORTS, SO I WANT IT TO COME OUT SOON. I HOPE YOU'LL CHECK IT OUT.

ANYWAY, I'LL BE HAPPY IF YOU JUST ENJOYED THIS STORY.

AS FOR FUTURE DEVELOPMENTS, *HAYATE* WILL DEPART FROM THE PRETTY SERIOUS MOOD OF THE CURRENT STORY LINE AND SWITCH TO SOMETHING BRIGHTER. NEW CHARACTERS AND THE FOLKS WHO DIDN'T MAKE IT TO GREECE WILL BE JOSTLING FOR SPACE, SO STICK WITH ME!

OH, AND I INCLUDED THIS IN VOLUME 23 TOO, BUT HERE'S MY TWITTER ACCOUNT:

HTTP://TWITTER.COM/HATAKENJIRO

AND I CONTINUE TO DRAW COMIC STRIPS FOR *WEB SUNDAY* FROM TIME TO TIME, SO DON'T MISS 'EM!!

HTTP://WEBSUNDAY.NET/BACKSTAGE/HATA/

ALL RIGHT! SEE YOU IN VOLUME 25, OR THE MAGAZINE, OR ONLINE!!
BYE! ☆

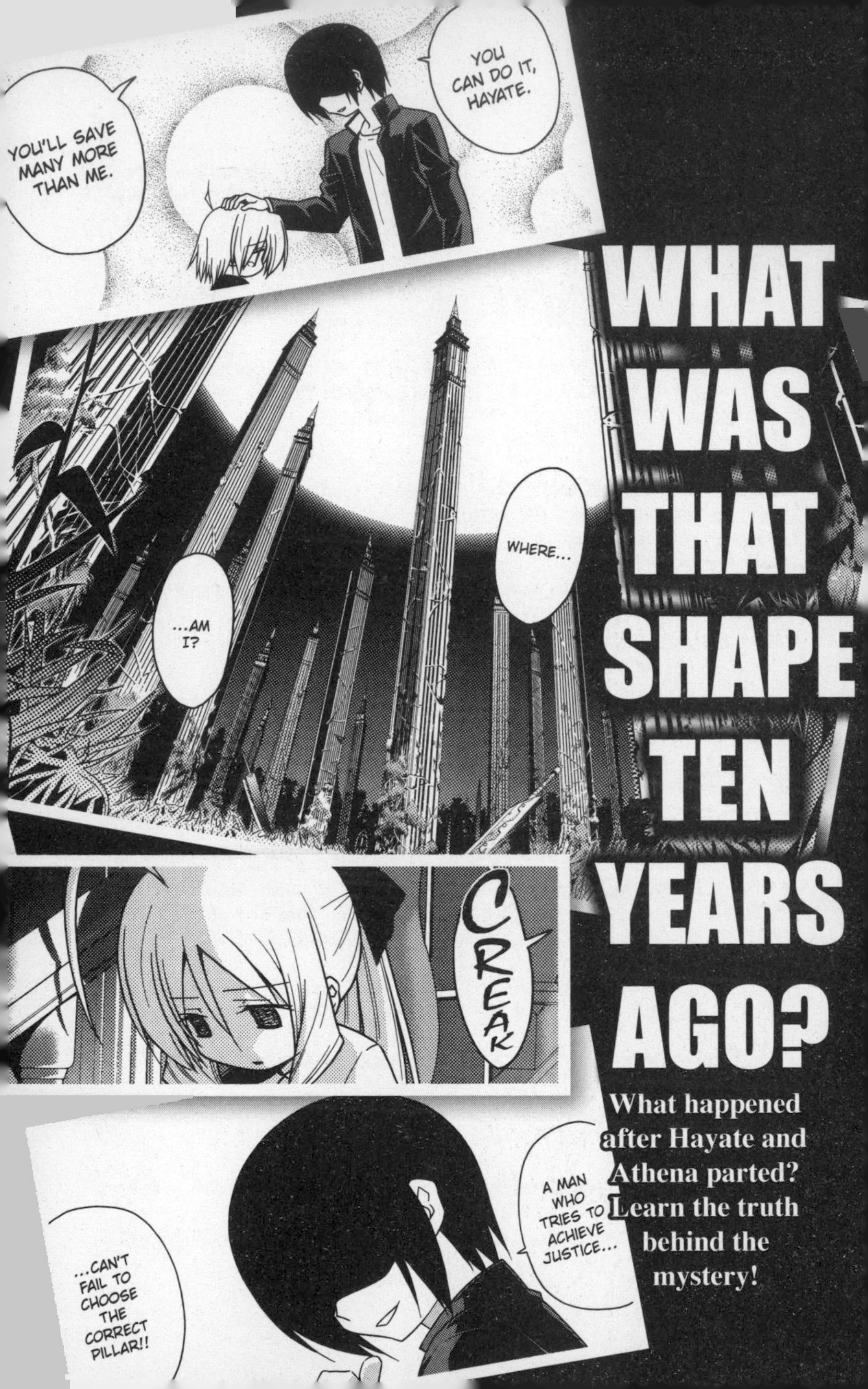
YOU CAN DO IT, HAYATE.
YOU'LL SAVE MANY MORE THAN ME.
WHERE...
...AM I?
CREAK
A MAN WHO TRIES TO ACHIEVE JUSTICE...
...CAN'T FAIL TO CHOOSE THE CORRECT PILLAR!!

WHAT WAS THAT SHAPE TEN YEARS AGO?

What happened after Hayate and Athena parted? Learn the truth behind the mystery!

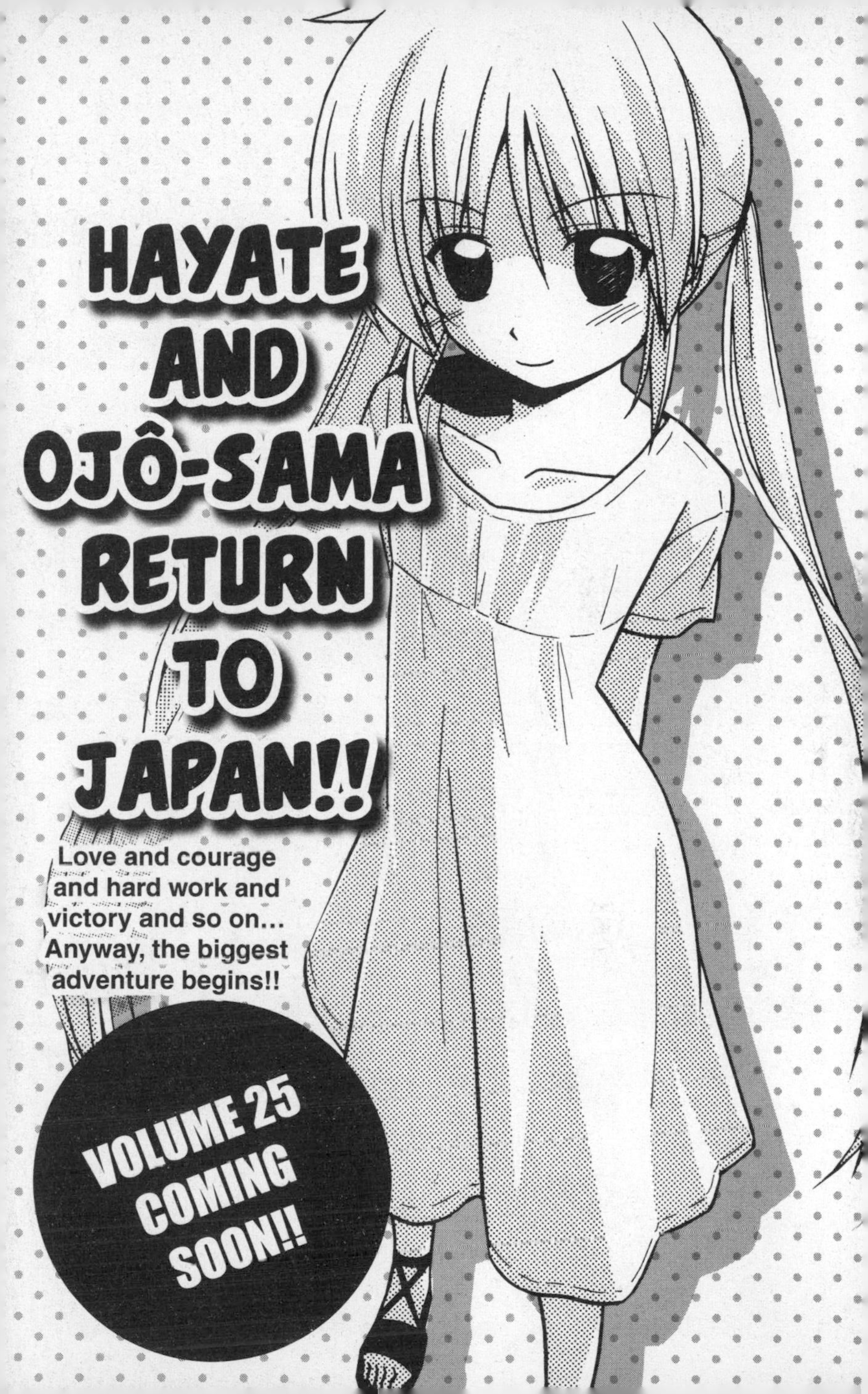

HAYATE AND OJÔ-SAMA RETURN TO JAPAN!!
Love and courage and hard work and victory and so on... Anyway, the biggest adventure begins!!
VOLUME 25 COMING SOON!!

An Interesting Companion

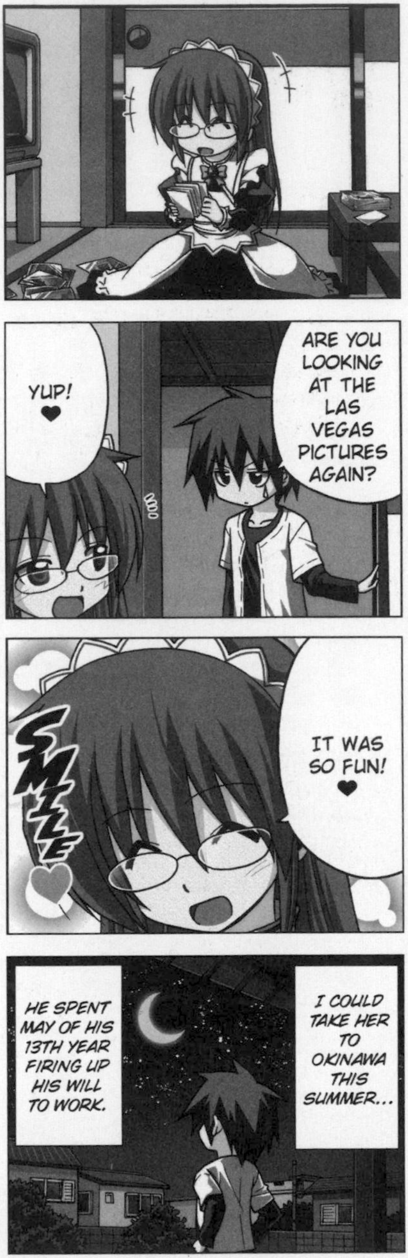

ARE YOU LOOKING AT THE LAS VEGAS PICTURES AGAIN?
YUP! ♥
IT WAS SO FUN! ♥
SMILE
I COULD TAKE HER TO OKINAWA THIS SUMMER...
HE SPENT MAY OF HIS 13TH YEAR FIRING UP HIS WILL TO WORK.

A Worthwhile Companion

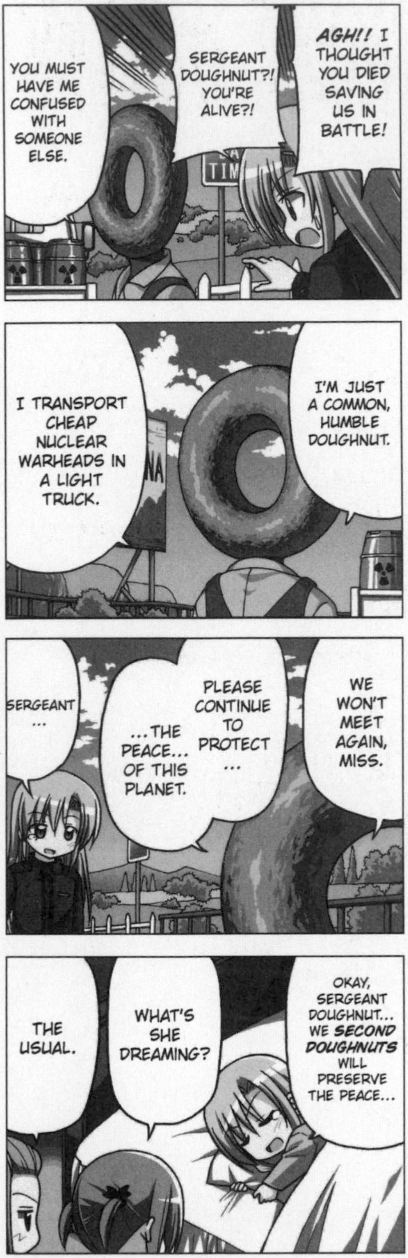

AGH!! I THOUGHT YOU DIED SAVING US IN BATTLE!
SERGEANT DOUGHNUT?! YOU'RE ALIVE?!
YOU MUST HAVE ME CONFUSED WITH SOMEONE ELSE.
I'M JUST A COMMON, HUMBLE DOUGHNUT.
I TRANSPORT CHEAP NUCLEAR WARHEADS IN A LIGHT TRUCK.
WE WON'T MEET AGAIN, MISS.
PLEASE CONTINUE TO PROTECT ...
...THE PEACE... OF THIS PLANET.
SERGEANT ...
OKAY, SERGEANT DOUGHNUT... WE **SECOND DOUGHNUTS** WILL PRESERVE THE PEACE...
WHAT'S SHE DREAMING?
THE USUAL.

HAYATE THE COMBAT BUTLER

(FINAL CHOICE)

FOR THE FINAL BATTLE, I'LL NEED...

- OJŌ-SAMA
BECAUSE SHE'S IMPORTANT.
- MARIA-SAN
SHE'S REASSURING.
- HINAGIKU-SAN
SHE'S RELIABLE IN A PINCH.
- NISHIZAWA-SAN
SHE'S CAPABLE OF MIRACLES.

↓

AND SO ON FOR EVERYONE...
THE TEAM I CHOOSE COULD HAVE A HUGE EFFECT
ON THE OUTCOME!!

UM...

MONITOR

COMPUTER

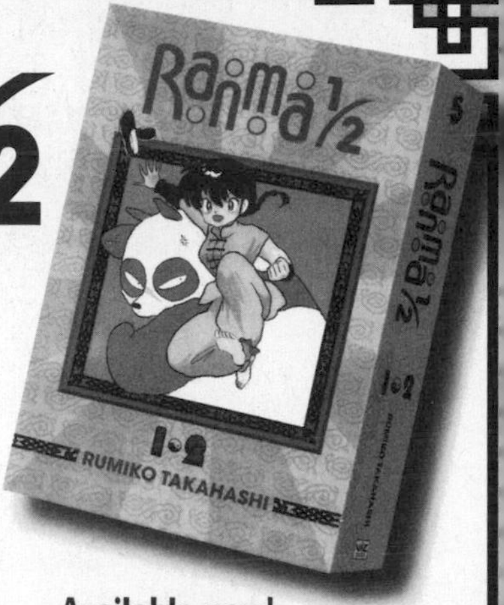
Ranma 1/2
1•2
RUMIKO TAKAHASHI

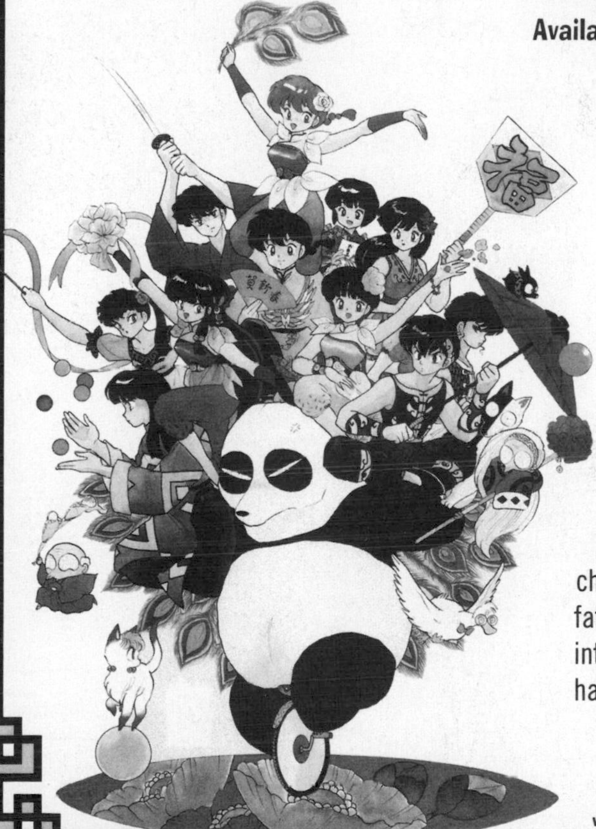